The Canadian Writer's Handbook

Cthe Canadian Writer's Handbook

William E. Messenger
Department of English
University of British Columbia

Jan de Bruyn
Department of English
University of British Columbia

Prentice-Hall of Canada, Ltd.
Scarborough, Ontario

For Ann and Betty—
without whom . . .

Canadian Cataloguing in Publication Data

Messenger, William E., 1931-
  The Canadian writer's handbook
Includes index.
ISBN 0-13-113340-3
1. English language - Composition and exercises.
2. English language - Grammar - 1950-
I. de Bruyn, Jan, 1918-   II. Title.

PEI408.M48   808'.042   C79-094788-9

Prentice-Hall, Inc., Englewood Cliffs, New Jersey
Prentice-Hall International, Inc., London
Prentice-Hall of Australia, Pty., Ltd., Sydney
Prentice-Hall of India Pvt., Ltd., New Delhi
Prentice-Hall of Japan, Inc., Tokyo
Prentice-Hall of Southeast Asia (Pte.) Ltd., Singapore

ISBN 0-13-113340-3

Cover design: Gail Ferreira
Production editors: Luba Zisser, Joerg Klauck
Typesetting: J & E Graphics Ltd.

1 2 3 4 5 AP 84 83 82 81 80

Contents

Preface: How to Use This Book

The Canadian Writer's Handbook is intended for people interested in improving their use of English, and especially in improving their writing. We have designed it primarily for students, but it should be just as useful to others who are interested in correct and effective writing. Although we have included a section on organization and have offered much advice on such things as clarity and emphasis, our principal aim has been to provide not a rhetoric but a handbook or reference book covering the important elements of correct writing: the conventions of grammar, punctuation, mechanics, spelling, and usage that prevail in Canada today.

The first thing to do with any book such as this is to familiarize yourself with its contents: what it has to offer, how it is arranged, what its table of contents and its index and its cross-referencing enable you to find. Some potentially useful advice buried in a given section will not help you if you never discover that it is there.

Writers who know themselves to be generally weak (or who are told as much by someone in a position to know) should begin at the beginning and proceed carefully and as slowly as necessary through the book. Many points in the later chapters will be clear only to someone with a fairly thorough grasp of the material in the early chapters. But if you understand basic grammar—the parts of speech and their functions, and the syntactic principles governing English sentences—then the first three chapters need not detain you long; except for points that you think require extra attention, a quick review may be sufficient. The obvious way to find out if you know the material is to test yourself on the exercises that appear with each section.

If you know—or find out—that you are weak on specific points, concentrate on them; do all the pertinent exercises and have them checked by an instructor or someone similarly knowledgeable. An instructor who considers a student weak in some particular way may assign the relevant section and its exercises for special study or review. Or an instructor may assign one or more sections to a whole class for study and discussion.

When you complete a piece of writing, check your work by going through the Omnibus Checklist (Chapter XII). If you come across something about which you feel less than confident, consult all the available cross-references for help.

When an essay is returned to you with marks and comments, first consult Chapter XI, "The Correction Symbols Explained." The information contained there may be enough to enable you to understand and correct your error. But if you need more than a reminder about a specific kind of error or weakness, if you are confused about the fundamental principles the error violates, simply follow the cross-references provided and study the sections where those principles are discussed and illustrated in greater detail. You should then be able to make the necessary corrections and revisions with understanding and confidence.

An important feature of this book is that the various kinds of error and weakness are discussed or illustrated, or both, in several places: in the main discussions themselves, in the exercises that accompany those discussions, in the review exercises at the ends of major chapters, in the sample essays, and in the chapter explaining the correction symbols. If one or another of these is not sufficient to clarify a point, remember that you have not yet exhausted the available resources: consult all the other relevant parts of the book as well.

The book is divided into sections and subsections that are numbered consecutively throughout, without regard to chapters. These numbers, which are printed in the margins and at the top of each page, enable one to refer—or be referred—to any particular item. Cross-references in the text are to these numbers or, occasionally, to chapter numbers (in Roman numerals). (In the index, the references are to page numbers.) Most instructors prefer to use the correction symbols to indicate errors, but some may wish to use these numbers instead. Or an instructor may use a correction symbol, such as p (for punctuation), and require a student to provide, as part of the correction, the precise number relevant to a particular error, such as *37a* (restrictive and nonrestrictive relative clauses).

The exercises are not numbered continuously but rather according to the sections or subsections they appear in. Thus Exercise 24 deals with dangling modifiers, the subject of section #24. Some sections do not include exercises. A particular exercise may be assigned for written submission, for discussion in conference with the instructor, or for oral presentation or group discussion in class.

The first time or two an important term is used, it appears in SMALL CAPITAL LETTERS, like that. Pay attention to these terms, for they make up the basic vocabulary necessary for the intelligent discussion of grammar and syntax.

Some final words of advice: Nobody is perfect. Though we have tried to offer a *de*scription of many conventions of good English, we have also offered many *pre*scriptions based on those and other descriptions; but an astute reader will surely find that we have more than once contravened our own advice. Our best advice, then, is that students (we are all students) should consult their own experience (common sense is a great provider), that they should think for themselves as much as possible, that they should consult reliable authorities, and that they should seek help wherever they can get it. It is our hope that this book will be a trustworthy and useful authority.

Acknowledgments: Over many years of teaching and being taught, one absorbs much from one's teachers, colleagues, books, and students. Further, a book such as this must by its nature owe much to its predecessors, each of which, like this one, builds upon the work of others. Such indebtedness is too broad and manifold to be detailed. We must however single out a few friends and colleagues for both their material and their spiritual contributions: Our thanks to Moira Farrow, Professor Raymond E. Parshall, Lilita Rodman, Professor Peter A. Taylor, and especially to Professors Ann P. Messenger and William H. New, who scrutinized the entire manuscript and made valuable suggestions for its improvement. We are also grateful to others who reviewed the manuscript and offered helpful suggestions and criticisms. Whatever faults remain in the book are of course our own doing. With the kind permission of the copyright holders, The Certified General Accountants' Association of British Columbia, we have incorporated into this book some material from *Writing Effective English* (1957) and *Effective Writing in Business* (1963), both by Jan de Bruyn. Throughout the project we have also benefited from the encouragement and editorial assistance of Frank Hintenberger and Marta Tomins of Prentice-Hall of Canada. And finally—reserving the position of emphasis and honour for them—we want to express our deep appreciation to all of our students over the years, and especially to those who have so kindly let us use their sentences and essays as illustrations and exercises in this book.

W. E. M.
J. de B.

PART ONE
Sentence Grammar and Punctuation

Introduction: **The Conventions of Language**

Words are the building-blocks with which we put together language structures that enable us to communicate with others. Combinations of words produce sentences; combinations of sentences produce paragraphs; combinations of paragraphs can form stories, detailed expositions, descriptions, arguments. In writing we represent speech sounds by symbols called letters which combine to form the units of sound called words. People who share familiarity with a language are able to communicate because each person knows the meaning of the sounds. If someone said "Look" when he meant to convey the meaning of "Listen," he would fail to communicate. The success of the process depends upon the universal acceptance of the convention. Dictionaries record in a precise and orderly way the meanings and sounds of the many words in our languages, so that one can always find out by consulting them what the standard contemporary usage is.

The combining of words into sentences is equally subject to conventions which help to ensure that the process of communication will be successful. Hence, words are arranged in certain orders, and certain ways of indicating relationships between words have become standard; in symbolizing speech in writing some visual conventions have been introduced that clarify meaning and facilitate unambiguous communication.

The conventions governing the arrangement of words and the relations between words constitute the GRAMMAR of a language. The visual non-verbal conventions necessitated by writing as opposed to speaking are called PUNCTUATION. In the next four chapters we will describe and illustrate these conventions and ways of avoiding common errors in their use. It is important not only that you familiarize yourself with the practical substance of these chapters, but also that you adopt and actively use the vocabulary involved so that the

3

subsequent discussions of language and its uses and conventions will be meaningful to you. We have for the most part retained the vocabulary of "traditional grammar," for it still has for many the virtue of simplicity and familiarity and, as well, of being the vocabulary most likely to be useful whenever you undertake to learn another language. It is also the vocabulary used by dictionaries in definitions and in discussing usage.

Chapter I **The Sentence:** A Brief Introduction

1 The terms and concepts that are briefly defined and illustrated here are dealt with in greater detail in Chapters II and III, but before you proceed to those chapters it may be helpful for you to review the basic elements that make up sentences.

1a Normally, a sentence consists of at least two parts, a SUBJECT and a PREDICATE. The subject is what is talked about, and the predicate is what is said about the subject.

Subject	Predicate
Grass	grows.
Money	talks.
Cats	scratch.

Obviously such a sentence must have a subject, something to be talked about or to perform an action: the subject, then, is the first essential element of a sentence. The other essential element, the VERB, is contained in the predicate part of the sentence; in the above examples, the words *grows, talks,* and *scratch* are the verbs. (The verb as a part of speech is discussed in Chapter II.) A subject and a verb, then, are the two essential elements for making a sentence; and usually they occur in tandem: every subject must have a verb, and every verb must have a subject.

Exercise 1a

In the following sentences, draw a vertical line between the subject and the predicate; then underline the single word that is the subject and circle the single word that is the verb.

1. Lightning flashed.
2. The sun shone through the window.

3. Everyone at the show applauded.
4. The lions roared loudly.
5. Jennifer's favourite cousin ate at our house last week.

1b Sentences seldom consist of only a one-word subject and a verb. A common way of building on such a basic sentence core is to add an OBJECT to the predicate part of the sentence:

Subject	Predicate	
	Verb	Direct Object
Cats	scratch	children.
Sandra	hates	books.
John	threw	stones.

In these sentences, *children, books,* and *stones* are words that are called DIRECT OBJECTS. The subject acts; the verb describes the action; the direct object is acted upon directly.

1c Sometimes a sentence with a direct object will also have an INDIRECT OBJECT: that is, the verb acting upon the direct object has a further—indirect—effect upon another object:

Subject	Predicate		
	Verb	Indirect Object	Direct Object
John	threw	me	the ball.
He	told	his friend	a story.
Sally	gave	Mary	a dollar.

1d Some verbs do not act upon an object in the way the verbs in the above sentences do. Instead, these verbs link the subject with something in the predicate part of the sentence, something which is necessary if the predicate and the sentence are to be complete:

Subject	Predicate	
	Linking Verb	Complement
Sally	is	rich.
John	is	an athlete.
He	feels	tired.

In these sentences *rich, athlete,* and *tired* are words that complete the predicates, and therefore the sentences, but clearly not in the same way that objects do; these words are called COMPLEMENTS—more precisely, SUBJECTIVE COMPLEMENTS, since they are linked by the verbs to the subjects of the sentences.

Exercise 1bcd

Label all the direct objects (do), indirect objects (io), and subjective complements (sc) in the following sentences.

1. Sam told me his address, but I still couldn't find his house.
2. Canada has a vast and undeveloped northern region.
3. Canada is a large country.
4. He struck the keys with great force.
5. Betty looked tired, so I gave her my recipe for a pick-me-up.
6. Calvin handed me the screwdriver and I attacked the packing case.
7. This is a brand which gives you good value for your money.
8. Nobody felt comfortable about the referee's decision, and the crowd booed loudly.
9. The judge threw the book at Mortimer.
10. Leonard cooked dinner, and Myrtle ate it.

1e Still, most sentences are richer than these simple examples. Much of the richness is contributed by MODIFIERS.

Subject	Predicate
The green grass	grows *profusely.*
Nervous cats	scratch *careless* children.
The bearded, dignified old sailor	*often* told *his eager* friends *fascinating* stories.
The aging champion	*now* feels *very* tired.

The italicized words in these sentences modify the subjects, verbs, objects, and complements of the sentences; that is, they change the reader's perception of those elements by describing or limiting them in various ways. These modifiers are all either adjectives or adverbs, so-called "parts of speech" which, along with verbs and others, are discussed in Chapter II.

Exercise 1e
In the following sentences, underline all the words that are modifiers.

1. The raucous noise almost deafened the audience.
2. Three garrulous old women dominated the tedious discussion.
3. The agile cat easily escaped the yapping puppy.
4. Succulent fiddleheads decorated our well-filled plates.
5. The flag, resplendently red and white, waved proudly.

1f All the above elements, then, make up the substance of sentences. In many sentences these elements occur with words like *and, but, for, of, under,* words which connect the elements in various ways and thus establish certain relations between them. Such words are called FUNCTION WORDS. They are often necessary but have no denotative meaning by themselves; they are drawn from two other classes of words, or parts of speech, conjunctions and prepositions (also discussed in Chapter II).

But before going on to the parts of speech and their grammatical functions, you should understand the difference between phrases and clauses.

1g A CLAUSE is a group of words which, like the sentences we have been discussing, contains a subject and a predicate. In fact, if it is what is called an INDEPENDENT CLAUSE, it can, as the term indicates, stand by itself; it can, if the writer so desires, be a sentence. For example:

Garbage smells.
Medicine is expensive.
Walter's opinions clearly revealed his middle-class values.
The middle class is always rising.
Then Jill closed the book and went quietly to sleep.
Nevertheless, one should avoid controversy if possible.

These are independent clauses and, as you see, are also complete sentences. An independent clause, however, can also be only a part of a sentence; for example, two independent clauses can be put together in such a way as to make up a single sentence:

Medicine is expensive; therefore one should try not to get sick.

If the semicolon were changed to a period, there would be two sentences:

Medicine is expensive. Therefore one should try not to get sick.

1h A SUBORDINATE (or dependent) clause, on the other hand, by definition cannot normally stand by itself, and therefore cannot be treated as a complete sentence. Even though, as a clause, it contains a subject and a predicate, it is nevertheless subordinate, dependent on another clause for its meaning. For example, the group of words

Because medicine is expensive

is obviously not independent; but if it is combined with an independent clause, it can function as a legitimate part of a larger sentence:

Because medicine is expensive, we should try not to get sick.

Similarly,

After Jill closed the book

is not complete. It must be made subordinate to an independent clause:

After Jill closed the book, she went quietly to sleep.

(Of course, such subordinate clauses *could* be used separately, for example as answers to questions, or in recorded conversation, where the context would be clearly understood:

When did Jill go to sleep? After she closed the book. Why should we try to stay healthy? Because medicine is expensive. Except in such special circumstances, a subordinate clause cannot stand by itself, cannot be punctuated as a complete sentence.) Each subordinate clause functions as a grammatical unit in its sentence.

1i A PHRASE is a group of words that does not contain both essential elements, a subject and a predicate, yet functions as a grammatical unit within a sentence. In order to understand how sentences work, one must be careful not to mistake phrases for clauses; the following groups of words, for example, are phrases, not clauses:

> the effects of rainfall on crop production (no verb)
> both teachers and students (no verb)
> went home (no subject)
> sat on the fence (no subject)
> driving a car (no subject, no verb)
> to fly a plane (no subject, no verb)
> at three o'clock (no subject, no verb)

Phrases are discussed in Chapter II, along with the various parts of speech, and in Chapter III, with sentence structure. No one is likely to mistake a phrase for a sentence (except, again, in such special circumstances as the answer to a question); what is important for understanding how sentences work is to be able to distinguish a phrase from a clause.

Exercise 1ghi
After each of the following groups of words, indicate whether it is an independent clause, a subordinate clause, or a phrase. Underline the subject and circle the verb of each clause.

1. not only Lily but Joan as well
2. never had he seen such a storm
3. for the first time in her life she was happy
4. since no one was looking
5. around the corner from our house

6. but the minister was not in his office
7. while she was on the telephone
8. the boat sank
9. after the ball was over
10. according to the elaborately printed instructions in the guidebook

Chapter II   Basic Grammar:
The Parts of Speech and Other Sentence Elements and How They Work

We begin this book—apart from the brief opening chapter on sentences—with a description of the PARTS OF SPEECH because we believe that an understanding of the way the language works must be founded upon an understanding of its words. An understanding of what one might call "word grammar," of the ways in which words combine to make phrases and clauses, helps one understand how sentences work. And only when one grasps the sentence—the basic element of meaningful communication—can one effectively communicate with others. But sentences are first of all made up of words.

The grammar of a language is based upon the nature and functions of the various kinds of words it contains and on the various ways in which the conventions of usage relate these words to one another. Words in the English language fall into eight categories called parts of speech. Some parts of speech are readily definable; others can best be recognized and understood by looking at some examples.

These eight parts of speech fall into two groups designated as UNINFLECTED and INFLECTED. This distinction recognizes the fact that some words never change their form. The word *in* is always *in*; the word *but* is always *but*. Such words are called uninflected. Other words require inflection, a change in form, when they are used in particular circumstances. If for example you want the word *boy* to denote more than one male youngster, you have to inflect it, give it the additional meaning of more than one, by adding an *s* to make it *boys*. If the verb *see* is used to denote the activity of seeing n past time, it must be changed to *saw*. To denote a number of people engaged in the activity of seeing, one uses the form *they see*; but to indicate that a particular person is seeing, one uses the form *he sees* or *she sees.*

As a result of various historical circumstances, the English language, compared to its early ancestor Anglo-Saxon or to Latin and the Romance languages which derive from Latin (French, Italian, Spanish), is relatively uninflected. Such inflections as remain are primarily those of the verb. A language like English, whose grammar is not predominantly expressed by inflection, is called analytic; a language like Latin or German, where inflection is the primary key to grammatical relationships, is called synthetic.

Five of the parts of speech are inflected in one or more ways:

Noun
Pronoun
Verb
Adjective
Adverb

The other three parts of speech are never inflected:

Preposition
Conjunction
Interjection

2 Nouns

A NOUN (from the Latin *nomen,* for *name)* is a word that names or stands for a thing, class, concept, quality, or action. PROPER NOUNS are names of particular persons, places, or things and begin with a capital letter: *Winnipeg, John, Ottawa River, Spring Garden Road, Mount Logan.* COMMON NOUNS are symbols that stand for ideas or things and are usually capitalized only if they begin a sentence: *boy, egg, liberty, vegetable, utensil, race, opinion, house.* One can also classify nouns as either CONCRETE, names of tangible objects (*boy, vegetable, utensil, house*), or ABSTRACT, names of intangible things or ideas (*liberty, honour, happiness*). And there are also what are called COLLECTIVE NOUNS (see #7f).

...flected for number and for possessive case. ...icates whether there is one or more than ... is, whether the noun is SINGULAR or PLURAL; for ...e, *boy, boys*: the addition of *s* or *es* is the usual inflec-...used to change the singular noun to the plural noun. ...ASE is a term used to designate the syntactical relation of a noun or pronoun to other words in a sentence. Although case is relatively unimportant in English, which depends more on word order than synthetic languages do, three cases are recognized: SUBJECTIVE (or nominative), OBJECTIVE, and POSSESSIVE. Nouns can be inflected for possessive case only; English makes no change in a noun to indicate that it is the object rather than the subject of a verb, but instead depends on word order and other sentence conventions:

> The *dog* chased the *cat*. (*Dog* is subject; *cat* is object.)
> The *cat* chased the *dog*. (*Dog* is object; *cat* is subject.)

Inflection for Number: For the formation of plurals of nouns, see #51t.

Inflection for Possessive Case: See #51w.

GRAMMATICAL FUNCTIONS: Nouns perform the following grammatical functions:

> Subject of a verb: The *show* was delightful.
> Object of a verb or preposition: He told *Nick* the *story* of the *tribe*. (*Nick*: indirect object; *story*: direct object; *tribe*: object of preposition)
> Complement of linking verb: Sarah is a *teacher*. (*teacher*: predicate noun; see #8d)
> An appositive to any of these: André, the *policeman,* saw Roger, the *thief*. (See #2a, immediately following.)

Nouns in the possessive case function like adjectives (see #9); they modify other nouns:

> *Maria's* coat (Which coat? Maria's.)
> a *month's* work (How much work? A month's.)

Words that are normally nouns can sometimes also function

as adjectives: The *school* paper, the *automobile* industry, the *dessert* course, *police* procedure (but see #59g).

2a An APPOSITIVE is a special kind of modifier consisting of a noun or a group of words functioning as a noun. It is placed immediately after another noun which it further defines or identifies. It has the same grammatical function as the noun it is in apposition with, or juxtaposed to. Some further examples:

> Heidi, *the girl who lives next door,* has invited me to a party.
> Dr. Davis, *our family physician,* advises us to get flu shots.
> Canada's youngest province, *Newfoundland,* joined Confederation in 1949.
> My uncle *Eugene* is an MLA.

Each italicized word or group of words is in apposition with the noun or noun phrase preceding it.

Exercise 2
On a separate sheet of paper, list (in a vertical column) each noun in the following sentences. After each noun, indicate whether it is a subject, a direct object, an indirect object, an object of a preposition, a complement (predicate noun), or an appositive.

1. Rudi, our gardener, insisted that we needed three sprinklers.
2. All twenty-one guns fired in succession, and the salute to the Queen was heard all over the city.
3. The mayor of Halifax gave the visiting dignitary the key to the city.
4. From Vancouver the group flew to Calgary, the next major city on their itinerary.
5. If you give Herbert an inch, he'll take a mile.
6. July was a month to remember: Marsha had never had such a holiday.
7. Shakespeare wrote many plays, but *Hamlet,* a tragedy, is his best-known work.
8. Any good scientist knows the binomial theorem by heart.

9. All work and no play makes Jack a dull boy.
10. The high cost of living proved a burden to all residents but the wealthy.

Now go back to the above sentences and underline all the proper nouns.

---

3 Pronouns

A PRONOUN, as its name indicates, is a word that stands for (*pro*) or in place of a noun, or at least functions like a noun in a sentence. A pronoun usually refers back to a noun that has appeared earlier, its ANTECEDENT. Pronouns are classified as *personal, interrogative, relative, demonstrative, indefinite, reflexive,* and *reciprocal.*

3a PERSONAL PRONOUNS are inflected for person (1st, 2nd, 3rd), number (singular or plural), case (subjective, objective, or possessive), and gender (masculine, feminine, or neuter):

		Subjective	Objective	Possessive
Singular	1st person (person speaking)	I	me	my, mine
	2nd person (person spoken to)	you	you	your, yours
	3rd person (person spoken about)	he (masc.)	him	his, his
		she (fem.)	her	her, hers
		it (neuter)	it	its
Plural	1st person	we	us	our, ours
	2nd person	you	you	your, yours
	3rd person	they	them	their, theirs

Like nouns in the possessive case, pronouns in the possessive case function as adjectives; the possessive pronouns *my, your, his,* etc. are thus sometimes called pronominal adjectives:

> *My* car is the red one, there at the end of the row.
> She gave *her* answer in a slow, deliberate way.

Caution: Never use apostrophes to indicate the possessive case of a personal pronoun. The most common error of this sort is to write *it's* (contraction of *it is*) when what is meant is *its* (possessive of *it*)—or vice versa. The word *it's* always and only means *it is*.

3b INTERROGATIVE PRONOUNS are not inflected for number, and only *who* and *which* are inflected for case:

Subjective	Objective	Possessive
who	whom	whose
which	which	whose
what	what	

Who refers to persons; *which* and *what* generally refer to things. *Which* can on occasion refer to persons (*Which of you is going?*). *Whoever, whomever, whichever,* and *whatever* are compounds that can also function interrogatively.

3c A RELATIVE PRONOUN introduces an adjective clause (see #17f) in which it functions as a subject, an object, or a complement, and relates to an antecedent in the same sentence, thus linking the subordinate clause to the rest of the sentence. Relative pronouns are inflected just as interrogative pronouns are:

Subjective	Objective	Possessive
who	whom	whose
which	which	whose
that	that	

Who refers only to persons, *which* can refer only to things, and *that* can refer to either things or persons. *What* and compounds with *ever* and *soever* (whoever, whosoever, whomever, whomsoever, whosesoever, whichever, whatever, whatsoever) can also function as relative pronouns.

3d Case

ca Only personal, relative, and interrogative pronouns can be inflected for SUBJECTIVE and OBJECTIVE CASE. Problems in choosing between the two arise in only a few kinds of sentences, and then largely only in formal writing. In speech we commonly say things like "Who are you lending the book to?" and "It's me" and "That's her," but in formal writing (and in strictly formal speech) you should abide by the rules of usage. The CASE of a pronoun is always determined by the grammatical function of the pronoun in its own clause (or sometimes in a prepositional phrase); it does not depend upon the case of its antecedent, for its grammatical function is independent of everything but its own immediate context.

1. A pronoun functioning as the subject of a verb must be in the subjective case:

> *Wrong:* Susan and me studied hard for the examination.
> *Right:* Susan and *I* studied hard for the examination.

2. A pronoun functioning as the object of a verb must be in the objective case:

> *Wrong:* They asked Ingrid and I to take part in the spring play.
> *Right:* They asked Ingrid and *me* to take part in the spring play.

The pronoun must be in the objective form, *me,* because it is part of the object of the verb *asked.*

Caution: Do not fall victim to what is called "hypercorrection." Since many people say incorrect things like "Jake and me went camping," where of course it should be "Jake and *I* went camping," others, lacking understanding of the grammar but wishing to seem correct, use the ". . . and I" form even when it is an object, as in example 2 above.

3. A pronoun functioning as the object of a preposition must be in the objective case:

> *Wrong:* The administration sometimes forgets about the needs of we students.
> *Right:* The administration sometimes forgets about the needs of *us* students.

Again, since to some the objective *us* sounds suspect

(because it is followed by *students,* as if at the beginning of a sentence that might read "We students demand that ....."), unthinking writers will overcorrect and use the subjective *we*; but the objective *us* is necessary, for it is the object of the preposition *of.*

4. A pronoun functioning as a subjective complement after any form of the verb *be* should be in the subjective case.

> It is *they* who must decide, not *we.*
> The girl who won the prize is *she,* over there by the pool.
> It is *I* who will carry the greater burden.
> It was *he* who climbed the flagpole.

If such usages sound impossibly stuffy and artificial to you—as they do to most—simply find another way to put it:

> We are not the ones who have to decide; they are.
> The girl over by the pool is the one who took first prize.
> I will be the one carrying the greater burden.
> He was the one who climbed the flagpole.

5. In formal usage, *as* and *than* are still considered conjunctions, not prepositions; pronouns following them in statements of comparison should therefore be in the subjective case even if their verbs are not expressed (the verbs are then said to be "understood"):

> Aaron is stronger than *I* (am).
> Roberta is brighter than *they* (are).
> Claude is as tall as *I* (am).
> Chris is not so tall as *he* (is).

Note: In formal writing, *so ... as* is often preferred to *as ... as* in negative comparisons, as in the last example. (See *so ... as* in #60.)

6. *Who* (subjective) and *whom* (objective):
   a. Use the subjective case for the subject of a main verb:

> *Who* is going?
> *Whoever* wishes can repeat the quiz next week.

b. Use the subjective case for the subject of a relative clause:

> Dickens was a novelist *who* entertained his readers in many ways.
>
> She is the one *who* most people think will win the Nobel Prize for chemistry.

In the last example, *who* is the subject of the verb *will win;* in such constructions, do not let an intervening parenthetical clause like "most people think" mislead you into thinking the objective *whom* is correct. Notice that you can remove the intervening clause without destroying the sense of the relative clause with *who* as its subject.

> The instructor intended to award a book-prize to *whoever* wrote the best essay.

Although many people would instinctively use the objective *whomever* here, *whoever* is correct because it is the subject of its clause, "whoever wrote the best essay," and it is the function of a pronoun in its clause that determines its case (a clause, so to speak, has the right-of-way over a phrase); the entire clause is the object of the preposition *to,* not just the relative pronoun that begins it.

c. Use the objective case for the object of a verb:

> She is the actress *whom* I admire the most.
>
> *Whomever* you choose, the committee is sure to raise an objection.

d. Use the objective case for the object of a preposition:

> *Whom* do you intend to award the book to?
>
> She is the minister for *whom* the members have the most respect.

Again, if these usages with *whom* sound unnatural and stuffy (even "To whom do you intend to award the book?"), rephrase the sentences.

See also #11a and #11e.
For the possessive case of pronouns, see #3a–c.
For the possessive case of nouns, see #51w.

Exercise 3d

In the following sentences, underline the correct pronoun in each of the pairs in parentheses.

1. There stood Eva, (who, whom) we had just said goodbye to.
2. He is a man (who, whom) will be long remembered.
3. Is she the person (who, whom) you think will do the best job?
4. Give it to (whoever, whomever) you please.
5. (Who, Whom) do you wish to see?
6. (She, Her) and (I, me) will try to find a solution by tomorrow.
7. The coach told (he, him) and (I, me) not to miss any more practice.
8. It was a case of (we, us) on one side and (they, them) on the other.
9. If it is (I, me) (who, whom) your remark is referring to, then it is scandalous.
10. He awarded the prize to (we, us) (who, whom) had persevered longest.

3e DEMONSTRATIVE PRONOUNS, which can be thought of as accompanied by a demonstrative gesture, namely pointing, are inflected for number only:

Singular:	this	that
Plural:	these	those

When followed by a noun, these words become demonstrative adjectives: *this* boy; *that* car; *these* buildings; *those* ideas.

3f INDEFINITE PRONOUNS do not refer to specific or definite things, and therefore have no antecedents. The principal indefinite pronouns are as follows:

any		none	some
anybody	everybody	nobody	somebody
anyone	everyone	no one	someone
anything	everything	nothing	something

few	all	one
many	both	other
more	each	another
most	either	several
much	neither	such

(*Anything, everything, nothing,* and *something* are sometimes considered nouns rather than pronouns.) Some indefinite pronouns can be inflected for possessive case; unlike personal pronouns, they take *'s* just as nouns do:

> anybody's, anyone's, everybody's, everyone's, nobody's, no one's, somebody's, someone's, one's, other's, another's

The rest must use *of* to show possession; for example:

> This was the belief *of many.*

Only *other* and *one* can be inflected for the plural: *others, ones* (the words *somebodies* and *nobodies* are nouns, not pronouns). In formal writing most of the indefinite pronouns should be considered always SINGULAR:

> another, anybody, anyone, anything, each, either, everybody, everyone, everything, much, neither, nobody, no one, nothing, one, other, somebody, someone, something

A few are obviously always PLURAL:

> both, few, many, several

The others can be either singular or plural, depending on meaning and context:

> all, any, more, most, none, some, such

This matter of NUMBER is very important for establishing grammatical agreement: see #4 and #7d.

Notes: Like demonstrative pronouns, when indefinite pronouns are used as modifiers they become adjectives:

> *any* boat, *some* people, *more* money, *each* day

Sometimes the cardinal and ordinal numerals (*one, two, three,* etc.; and *first, second, third,* etc.) are also classed as indefinite pronouns, for they often function similarly:

How many ducks are there? I see *several*. I see *many*. I see *seven*. I see *ten*.

3g REFLEXIVE or INTENSIVE PRONOUNS are formed by adding the suffix *self* (or plural *selves*) to the possessive case of personal pronouns (except for the irregular *itself* rather than *its self*, *himself* rather than *hisself*, and *themselves* rather than *theirselves*) and to the impersonal pronoun *one*: *myself, yourself, himself, herself, oneself, ourselves, yourselves, themselves*. They are used either to show that the object of a verb is the same as its subject, or to express emphasis:

Reflexive: He treated *himself* to a candy bar.
Intensive: Although he let the others choose their positions, Angelo *himself* is going to pitch.

3h RECIPROCAL PRONOUNS are always singular, but they can be possessive: *each other, one another, each other's, one another's*.

GRAMMATICAL FUNCTIONS: Pronouns function exactly as nouns do, and also in some of the special ways (linking, pointing, etc.) described above.

Exercise 3a–h
On a separate sheet of paper, list (in a vertical column) all the pronouns in the following sentences. After each pronoun, indicate whether it is personal, interrogative, relative, demonstrative, indefinite, reflexive, or reciprocal.

1. Who gave it to you?
2. He told himself that this would be his last chance.
3. He doesn't care whether one works at this desk or at that one.
4. Did she tell you who was going to get it?
5. One of these days you'll be able to get along with each other.

---

4 Agreement Between Pronouns and Their
agr Antecedents

4a A pronoun must agree with its antecedent in PERSON, NUMBER, and GENDER. An ANTECEDENT (literally "that which comes before") is the noun or pronoun to which a pronoun refers, for which it stands as a substitute.

> *Joanne* wants to go to university so that *she* will be trained to take *her* place in the world.

Here the proper noun *Joanne* is the antecedent of the pronouns *she* and *her*. Since *Joanne* is third person, singular, and feminine, the pronouns that refer back to it must also be third person, singular, and feminine: they then "agree" with their antecedent, as usage demands.

> *Wrong:* *One* must work hard if *you* are to earn a living.
> *Right:* *One* must work hard if *one* (or *he*) is to earn a living.

The antecedent, the pronoun *one,* is third person; in order to agree with it in person, the pronoun that refers back to it must also be third person: *you* is second person, and must be corrected to *one* or *he*, which are third person. (If you find the first *one* overly stiff and formal, change it to *a person* and use the pronoun *he*.)

> *Wrong:* If *someone* wants to buy fresh produce, *they* must go to the farmers' market early in the morning.
> *Right:* If *someone* wants to buy fresh produce, *he* must go to the farmers' market early in the morning.

The antecedent, *someone,* is singular; therefore, in order to agree with it in number, *they,* which is plural, must be changed to *he,* which is singular. (But see #4b below.)

> *Wrong:* *Either* of these women is likely to buy that sports car for *themselves*.
> *Right:* *Either* of these women is likely to buy that sports car for *herself*.

Since the indefinite pronoun *either* is the antecedent, *themselves* is wrong both in being plural (*either* is always singular) and in not being feminine (*either* here clearly stands for "one of these women"). The pronoun *herself* is therefore correct, for it agrees with the antecedent in both number and gender.

4b In formal writing, the indefinite pronouns *anybody, anyone, everyone, everybody, nobody,* and *no one* are considered singular. In order to agree in number, therefore, pronouns that refer to them should be singular:

> *Wrong:* *Everybody* must pay *their* taxes.
> *Right:* *Everybody* must pay *his* taxes.

Note: When the singular antecedent has no obvious gender, but can refer to either male or female, it is conventional to use the masculine pronoun. You can avoid using the masculine pronoun by making the subject of the verb plural and then using the plural pronoun, which has no gender: *All people must pay their taxes.* Do not, however, adopt the practice of using *they* and *their* after a singular subject. See also *he or she, his or her,* in #60.

Confusion about number sometimes arises with the indefinite pronoun *none.* Although *none* began by meaning *no one* or *not one,* it is now commonly found in a plural sense, meaning *not any:*

> *None* of the men removed *their* hats.

But if the intended meaning was *not one,* it would also be correct to treat *none* as singular:

> *None* of the men removed *his* hat.

Whenever you are not certain, use the singular; it is more formal and usually will be correct. See also #7d for the question of the number of some indefinite pronouns.

4c Demonstrative pronouns offer little or no trouble, but demonstrative adjectives may pose a problem, especially when followed by *kind* or *kinds.* Demonstrative adjectives must agree in number with the nouns they modify:

> *Wrong:* *These kind* of doctors work hard to maintain the humanitarian base of their profession.
> *Right:* *This kind* of doctor works hard ....
> *Right:* *These kinds* of doctors work hard ....

If "these kinds" sounds stuffy or awkward in a particular context (as it does here), take a moment to rephrase; for example: "Doctors like these work hard ...."

Exercise 4(1)

In the following sentences, underline the correct pronoun in each of the pairs in parentheses.

1. Everybody can express (his, their) opinion.
2. Una or Gwendolyn will lend you (her, their) textbook.
3. After studying his statements for over an hour, I still couldn't understand (it, them).
4. All the boys arrived on time, each with (his, their) books carried proudly in both hands.
5. None of the women agreed to those proposals which would limit (her, their) rights.

Exercise 4(2)

In the following sentences, correct any lack of agreement between pronouns and their antecedents.

1. Anyone who does not think for themselves can be deceived by advertising.
2. His arguments cannot alter my opinion, for it seems to me illogical.
3. It is usually a bad sign when a person stops caring about their appearance.
4. Everyone who plays will be given a pencil to write their name with.
5. In order to make sure that each sentence is correct, check them very carefully during revision and proofreading.

---

5 Reference of Pronouns

ref Since a pronoun refers back to an antecedent, that reference must be clear. If the antecedent is vague, remote, ambiguous,

or missing, the meaning of the pronoun itself and therefore the meaning of the statement it appears in will not be clear.

5a Remote Reference

Make sure the antecedent of a pronoun is close enough to the pronoun to be unmistakable, so that your reader will not have to pause and search for it. An antecedent should seldom be more than one sentence back.

> Anyone who expects to experience happiness in material things alone will probably discover that the life of the mind is more important than the life (if it can be called that) of the physical senses. Material prosperity may seem fine at a given moment, but in the long run its delights have a way of fading into inconsequential tedium and emptiness. *He* then realizes, too late, where true happiness lies.

The word *anyone,* which is rather vague to begin with, is too far back, too remote, to serve as a clear antecedent for the *He* which begins the last sentence. If the second sentence had begun with a *He,* it might have been all right. Or the third sentence might have used, instead of the weak pronoun, a more particularizing phrase, like "Such a person ...."

5b Ambiguous Reference

Make sure that a pronoun refers clearly to one antecedent only; if there is more than one possible antecedent for a given pronoun, revision will be necessary.

> *Ambiguous:*   When Donna's mother told her that *she* would have to have an operation, *she* was obviously upset.

Each of the *she*'s could refer either to Donna or to her mother. In revising such a sentence, do not try to clear it up by inserting explanatory parentheses; rather rephrase the sentence.

> *Weak:*   When Donna's mother told her that she (her mother) would have to have an operation, she (Donna) was obviously upset.
> *Clear:*   Donna was obviously upset when her mother told her, "I must have an operation."

Another example:

> *Ambiguous:* His second novel was far different from his first. *It* was an adventure story set in Australia.

A pronoun like *it* in this example tends to have as its antecedent the subject of a preceding independent clause, here "second novel"; but the *it* is also pulled toward the closest noun, here "first." The result is ambiguity.

> *Clear:* His second novel, an adventure story set in Australia, was far different from his first.
> *Clear:* His second novel was far different from his first, which was an adventure story set in Australia.

5c Vague Reference

Vague reference is particularly likely to occur with the demonstrative pronouns *this* and *that* and the relative pronoun *which*.

> *Vague:* There were three isolated people leaning against the wall, and it was very dark. *This* made Shelagh wary as she approached the bus stop.

(*This* could easily be changed to a relative *which,* which would be just as bad.) *This* (or *which*) seems to refer to the entire content of the preceding sentence, but it also seems to refer specifically to the fact that it was dark. Revision is necessary:

> *Clear:* The extreme darkness and the three isolated people leaning against the wall made Shelagh wary as she approached the bus stop.
> *Clear:* Three isolated people were leaning against the wall, and it was very dark. These circumstances [facts] made Shelagh wary as she approached the bus stop.
> *Clear:* Three isolated people leaned against the wall, and it was very dark, facts which taken together made Shelagh wary as she approached the bus stop.

A *this* (or *which*) could be adequate if the phrasing (and meaning) were appropriate—that is, if the reference of the pronoun was not ambiguous:

> *Clear:* Three separate people were leaning against the nearby building, but this did not worry Shelagh, for she was a

judo expert. But it was also getting very dark, which did make her a little wary as she approached the bus stop.

Here is another example:

> *Vague:*   Othello states many times that he loves Iago and that he thinks he is a very honest man; Iago uses *this* to his advantage.

The third *he* is possibly ambiguous, but more serious is the vague reference of *this*. Changing *this* to *this opinion, these feelings, this attitude, these mistakes, this blindness of Othello's* or even *Othello's blindness,* makes the reference clearer. Even the *his* is slightly ambiguous: "Iago takes advantage of" is better—or just omit the *his*.

In particular, avoid catching the "this" disease; sufferers from the "this" plague are driven to begin a large proportion of their sentences with *This*. Whenever you catch yourself beginning a sentence (or a clause) with *This*, look very carefully to see

1. if the reference to the preceding clause or sentence or paragraph is indeed as clear on paper as it may be in your mind;
2. if the *This* could be replaced by a specific noun or noun phrase, or otherwise avoided, for example by rephrasing or subordinating;
3. whether, if you finally decide to retain the *This*, it is a mere demonstrative pronoun; if it is, clarity can probably be improved by turning it into a demonstrative adjective, giving it a noun to modify—even if the noun is no more specific than something like "This *idea*," "This *fact*," or "This *argument*."

Also check to see if what your *This* is referring back to is truly singular, for it may be that *These* ideas, facts, or arguments would be more appropriate.

5d Missing Antecedent

Sometimes an antecedent may be indefinite or only implicit; the writer may have had an antecedent in mind but failed to write it down.

> *Vague:* In the early seventeenth century the Renaissance had concentrated mainly on the arts rather than on developing the scientific part of *their* minds.

The pronoun *their* has no antecedent; the writer was probably thinking of "the people of the Renaissance," but did not write it down. Simply changing *their* to *people's* would clear up the difficulty.

> *Vague:* After the senator's speech *he* agreed to answer questions from the audience.

The pronoun *he* has no real antecedent. The implied antecedent is of course *senator,* but it is not there, for *senator's* is in the possessive case and therefore functions as an adjective rather than as a noun. Several revisions are possible:

> *Clear:* When the senator finished his speech, he agreed to answer questions from the audience.
> *Clear:* At the end of the speech the senator agreed to answer questions from the audience.
> *Clear:* The senator agreed to answer questions after his speech.
> *Clear:* After his speech the senator agreed to answer questions from the audience.

Note that in this last version the pronoun *his* comes before its supposed "antecedent," *senator*. This is rare, but it is acceptable if the context is clear (e.g., if no other possible antecedent occurred in the preceding sentence) and when the two are close together, as they are here.

> *Vague:* Whenever a student assembly is called, *they* are required to attend.

Since *student* here is singular and functions as an adjective, it is necessary to replace *they* with *students*—and then probably one would want to omit the original *student*. Or one could refer to "an assembly of students" and then retain the *they*.

> *Vague:* Over half the cars were derailed, but *it* did not injure anyone seriously.

Again, no antecedent for the *it*. Change *it* to "the accident" or "the derailment," or use the passive voice: "but no one was seriously injured." (For the passive voice, see #6h.)

5e In formal writing, avoid the pronouns *you* and *they* when they are indefinite:

> *Informal:* In order to graduate, *you* must have at least sixty units of credit.
>
> *Formal:* In order to graduate, a student must have at least sixty units of credit.

(The impersonal pronoun *one* would be all right, but less good because less specific—and stuffier.)

> *Informal:* In some cities *they* do not have enough policemen.
>
> *Formal:* Some cities do not have enough policemen.
>
> *Formal:* Some city police forces are undermanned.

Although it is correct to use the expletive *it* (see #20) and say "*It* is raining," "*It* is difficult to get up in the morning," "*It* is seven o'clock," etc., one should avoid the indefinite use of *it* in such expressions as the following:

> *Informal:* *It* says in our textbook that we should be careful how we use the pronoun *it*.
>
> *Formal:* Our textbook says that we should be careful how we use the pronoun *it*.

Exercise 5

Correct any faulty pronoun reference in the following sentences.

1. Schools were of high quality—for those who could afford it.
2. If it rains on Maui it is soon evaporated into thin air.
3. In 1633 Charles I reissued the *Book of Sports* which he allowed to be indulged in on Sundays.
4. Many people believe that success is necessary for happiness, and they work hard to attain it.
5. You cannot suppress truth, for it is morally wrong.
6. Othello swore she was faithful and true and would have bet his life that she would not betray him, but he ends by taking her life for this very reason.
7. The deadline was a month away, but I failed to meet it, for something happened that prevented it.

8. The tone of the poem is such that it creates an atmosphere of romance.
9. In Shakespeare's Sonnet 65, it points out the differences between love and time.
10. Television usually shows regular commercial movies but this is sometimes supplanted by made-for-TV films.

---

6 Verbs

In the first chapter we discussed verbs as essential functional elements of sentences. Now we must consider the verb as a part of speech.

The verb is that part of speech which by its inflection indicates variation in time:

> Now I *see*; yesterday I *saw*; tomorrow I *will see*.

Verbs are the most highly inflected of our parts of speech. They are inflected for person and number, for action-character and tense, and for mood and voice.

6a Finite Verbs

FINITE VERBS are those verb forms that are restricted or determined by the person and number of a subject and by tense, mood, voice, and action-character. (See also #17b.)

Person and number:

Singular	1st person	I make	I see	I feel
	2nd person	you make	you see	you feel
	3rd person	he makes	he sees	he feels
		she makes	she sees	she feels
		it makes	it sees	it feels
Plural	1st person	we make	we see	we feel
	2nd person	you make	you see	you feel
	3rd person	they make	they see	they feel

Note that in the present tense there is inflection only in the third person singular (for the rule governing the spelling of these inflected forms, see #51u).

6b Every verb has three PRINCIPAL PARTS: its BASIC form (the form under which the dictionary lists it), its PAST TENSE form, and its PAST PARTICIPLE. It is from these three parts that all forms of a verb's tenses are made. For example, in the next illustration (#6c), *paint, painted,* and *painted* are the verb's principal parts. Verbs regularly form the past tense and past participle simply by adding *d* or *ed* to the basic form (*move, moved, moved; push, pushed, pushed; cook, cooked, cooked; agree, agreed, agreed*); for such regular verbs, your dictionary will usually give the basic form only.

Some English verbs, however, often very common ones, are IRREGULAR in the way they form their past tense and past participle (*make, made, made; see, saw, seen; read, read, read; lead, led, led; eat, ate, eaten;* etc.; see #6e); for all such irregular verbs, and even for regular verbs where there might be some uncertainty about spelling (e.g. *agreed*), your dictionary should list the principal parts (and the PRESENT PARTICIPLE as well). (For participles, see #11c.) If you are in doubt about the correct form or spelling of a verb's past tense or past or present participle, consult the dictionary.

Verbs that combine with main verbs to form different tenses are call AUXILIARY or helping verbs; in the following list, the auxiliaries are italicized: *am* going, *is* going, *were* going, *will* go, *might* go, *must* go, *can* go, *is able to* go, *would* go, *have* gone, *would have* gone, *should* go, *ought to* go, *should have* gone, *will be* going, *had to* go, *did* go, *does* go, *used to* go, *will have* gone, *should have been* going.

6c Action-character (sometimes called *aspect*) **and Tense**

t Action-character	Tense	Verb Form
Indefinite	Present	I paint
	Past	I painted
	Future	I will paint
Completed (formed by adding the *past participle* to the indefinite inflection of the verb "have")	Present Perfect	I have painted
	Past Perfect	I had painted
	Future Perfect	I will have painted

Progressive (formed by adding the *present participle* to the indefinite inflection of the verb "be")	Present Progressive	I am painting
	Past Progressive	I was painting
	Future Progressive	I will be painting

6d Tense and Sequence of Tenses

t Most people have little trouble with tense. But for some, especially those whose native language is not English, tense can sometimes cause problems. Here are some points to study and remember. Though they are sometimes oversimplifications of very complex matters, they may help you to keep in mind certain trouble spots.

The main tenses in English—present, past, and future—are normally simple and straightforward. They express the different *times* at which an action was, is, or will be taking place:

> present: Now I *hear* what you are saying.
> past: Yesterday I *heard* what you said.
> future: Tomorrow I *will hear* what you say.

But there are many exceptions, peculiarities, and variations in the use of English tenses that can be troublesome. Following are a few examples of the ways in which tenses are used for purposes that are not so simple and straightforward.

1. The present tense is often used to indicate a general or customary action or condition:

> She *spells* her name with an *e* at the end.
> The Grand Banks *are* a major fishing ground.
> Diamonds *are mined* in South Africa.
> I always *eat* breakfast before going to work.

2. Progressive tenses are frequently used for actions that began at some past time and continue, no time of completion being specified:

> I *am eating* my breakfast.
> He *was driving* very fast.
> She *had been training* for the high jump.

3. Sometimes the present and present progressive tenses can

be used to express future time:

> He *arrives* tomorrow.
> She *leaves* for Ottawa tomorrow afternoon .
> I *appear* in court next week.
> I *am going* to the bank first thing in the morning .

In these examples the underlined adverbial words and phrases specify future time; the verbs themselves remain in the present or present progressive tense.

4. The various past and perfect tenses indicate different kinds of past action:

> simple past: We *won* the game last night.
>
> present perfect: We *have beaten* them three times. (action completed in the past; time not specified)
>
> past perfect: Though I *had seen* the movie twice before, I went again last week. (action completed in the past prior to a specific past time)

5. Be particularly careful that combinations of tenses— especially past and perfect tenses, and especially in complex sentences—reflect sequences of time correctly:

> I *see* (present) in the paper that the premier *is* (present) in town today.
>
> I *saw* (past) in the paper last Friday that the premier *was* (past) then in town.
>
> I *see* (present) in the paper that the premier *is making* (present progressive, future sense) a speech tomorrow.
>
> I *see* (present) in the paper that the premier *will make* (future) a speech tomorrow.
>
> I *saw* (past) in the paper last Friday that the premier *was making* (past progressive) a speech the next day.
>
> I *see* (present) in the paper that the premier *has made* (present perfect) another speech.
>
> I *see* (present) in the paper that the premier *made* (past) a speech last night.
>
> I *saw* (past) in the paper last Friday that the premier *had made* (past perfect) a speech the night before.
>
> I *have seen* (present perfect) in the paper that the premier *makes* (present, generalizing) many speeches.
>
> I already *had seen* (past perfect) in the paper that the premier *had left* (past perfect) the capital.

6d t

Note: Normally past tense follows past tense:

> I *told* him that I *was* sorry.

But when the second verb states a universal or scientific fact or a general condition, it is usually in the present tense:

> She reminded me that London Bridge *is* now in Arizona.
> I had read somewhere that three-quarters of the earth's surface *is* covered by water.

Caution: Avoid constructions which force two or more tenses to overlap incongruously; instead, spell each of them out completely or rephrase the sentence:

> *Poor:*   The party has never and will never practise nepotism.
> *Better:*   The party has never practised and will never practise nepotism.
> *Better:*   The party has never practised nepotism and will never do so.

6. Normally, use the present tense of an infinitive (see #11a) after a verb in the past tense:

> I *was* pleased *to meet* you when you visited last week.
> It *was* a pleasure *to speak* to your brother yesterday.
> For a long time it *had been* difficult *to get* enough supplies through.

But occasionally the sense demands an infinitive in the present perfect tense:

> I *was* lucky *to have met* the manager before the interview.

7. When discussing or describing the events in a literary work, it is customary to use what is called the "historical present" tense:

> When Hamlet *returns* to Denmark he *meets* Horatio and they *observe* Ophelia's burial.

Other tenses can occur in such a context to indicate times before or after the "now" of the historical present being discussed:

> While he *was* away, Hamlet *had arranged* to have Rosencrantz and Guildenstern put to death. Now he *holds* Yorick's skull and

watches Ophelia *being buried*. And later he *will meet* his own death in the duel with Laertes. Clearly death *is* one of the principal themes with which Shakespeare *is* concerned in the play.

Note that it is customary to speak even of a long-dead author in the present tense when one is discussing a particular work. Here is another example of that:

In *Moby-Dick* Melville *tells* of mad Ahab's pursuit of the great white whale.

6e Be careful to use the correct forms of irregular verbs:

Wrong: He *sweared* that he had *took* all the necessary courses.
Right: He *swore* that he had *taken* all the necessary courses.

Whenever you are uncertain, consult your dictionary for the correct principal parts of irregular verbs. Here is a list to remind you of most of the common ones:

Present	*Past*	*Past Participle*
arise	arose	arisen
bear	bore	borne (passive *born* for "given birth to")*
beat	beat	beaten or beat
begin	began	begun
bet	bet	bet
bid (offer)	bid	bid
bid (order, invite)	bade	bidden
bind	bound	bound
bite	bit	bitten or bit
bleed	bled	bled
blow	blew	blown
break	broke	broken
breed	bred	bred
bring	brought	brought
burst	burst	burst
buy	bought	bought
cast	cast	cast
catch	caught	caught
choose	chose	chosen
cling	clung	clung

come	came	come
cost	cost	cost
creep	crept	crept
cut	cut	cut
deal	dealt	dealt
dig	dug	dug
dive	dived or dove	dived
do	did	done
draw	drew	drawn
dream	dreamed or dreamt	dreamed or dreamt
drink	drank	drunk
drive	drove	driven
eat	ate	eaten
fall	fell	fallen
feed	fed	fed
feel	felt	felt
fight	fought	fought
find	found	found
flee	fled	fled
fly	flew	flown
forbid	forbade or forbad	forbidden
forget	forgot	forgotten or forgot
forsake	forsook	forsaken
freeze	froze	frozen
get	got	got
give	gave	given
go	went	gone
grind	ground	ground
grow	grew	grown
hang	hung	hung
hang (execute)	hanged	hanged
have	had	had
hear	heard	heard
hide	hid	hidden or hid
hit	hit	hit
hold	held	held
hurt	hurt	hurt
keep	kept	kept
kneel	knelt or kneeled	knelt or kneeled
know	knew	known
lay	laid	laid

lead	led	led
leap	leaped or leapt	leaped or leapt
leave	left	left
lend	lent	lent
let	let	let
lie	lay	lain
light	lighted or lit	lighted or lit*
lose	lost	lost
make	made	made
mean	meant	meant
meet	met	met
mistake	mistook	mistaken
mow	mowed	mown
pay	paid	paid
put	put	put
read	read (changes pronunciation)	read (changes pronunciation)
ride	rode	ridden
ring	rang	rung
rise	rose	risen
run	ran	run
say	said	said
see	saw	seen
seek	sought	sought
sell	sold	sold
send	sent	sent
set	set	set
shake	shook	shaken
shed	shed	shed
shoot	shot	shot
shrink	shrank or shrunk	shrunk
shut	shut	shut
sing	sang	sung
sink	sank	sunk
sit	sat	sat
slay	slew	slain
sleep	slept	slept
slide	slid	slid
sling	slung	slung
slink	slunk	slunk
speak	spoke	spoken
speed	sped or speeded	sped or speeded
spend	spent	spent

spin	spun	spun
split	split	split
spread	spread	spread
spring	sprang or sprung	sprung
stand	stood	stood
steal	stole	stolen
stick	stuck	stuck
sting	stung	stung
stink	stank or stunk	stunk
strew	strewed	strewn
stride	strode	stridden
strike	struck	struck (or *stricken* for "ill" or "afflicted")*
string	strung	strung
strive	strove or strived	striven or strived
swear	swore	sworn
sweep	swept	swept
swell	swelled	swelled or swollen
swim	swam	swum
swing	swung	swung
take	took	taken
teach	taught	taught
tear	tore	torn
tell	told	told
think	thought	thought
thrive	throve or thrived	thrived or thriven
throw	threw	thrown
thrust	thrust	thrust
wear	wore	worn
weep	wept	wept
win	won	won
wind	wound	wound
write	wrote	written

6f Mood

English verbs are usually considered to have three moods: INDICATIVE, SUBJUNCTIVE, and IMPERATIVE.

---

*For verbs marked with an asterisk, check your dictionary for information about usages and definitions.

Indicative:	I *see*; I *saw*; I *will see*; etc.
Subjunctive:	If I *were* you (not "If I *was* you")
	I wish I *were* in Paris.
	It is necessary that we *be* there.
	Be that as it may; Long *live* the Queen; Heaven *forbid*; etc.
Imperative:	*Go* to the door. *Be* quiet. *Finish* your supper.

INDICATIVE is the normal mood of the verb, used as it is in direct statement; the SUBJUNCTIVE is used only in some conditional clauses and in a few standard expressions; and the IMPERATIVE is used for commands. The imperative frequently has no actual subject, since the *you* is usually "understood" rather than expressed, as in the examples above, though it could be expressed: "John, you carry the heavy end"; "You keep out of this!"

6g Voice

There are two voices, ACTIVE and PASSIVE. The active voice is direct statement: *I made this boat.* The passive voice inverts the normal pattern: *This boat was made by me.* Passive voice is easily recognized; the finite verb contains some form of the verb *be* followed by a past participle: *was made.* What in active voice would be a direct object, in passive voice becomes the subject of the verb (*boat*). (Usually, then, only transitive verbs can be put in the passive voice; see #8a.)

6h Although the passive voice has its uses, only in certain cir-
pas cumstances is it preferable to the active voice. Rhetorically, passive constructions are frequently weak because they are indirect and obscure; often the agent of the action or state they describe disappears from the scene. That is why politicians and civil servants are so fond of the passive voice: it enables one to make assertions which promise action without committing oneself to perform it, and makes possible the admission of error without anyone having to accept responsibility. For example:

Passive:	Be assured (by whom?) that action will be taken (by whom?).
Active:	I assure you that I will act.

> *Passive:* It is to be regretted (by whom?) that an error has been made (by whom?) in your account. The matter will be investigated (by whom?).
>
> *Active:* I am sorry we made an error in your account. I will look into the matter and correct it immediately.

The passive voice tends to be impersonal and lacks the vigour of directness. It often leads to fuzziness, wordiness, awkwardness, and even grammatical error. Therefore if you find yourself inclined to overuse the passive voice, foster a counter-tendency; make your assertions in the bolder and more lively active voice. Here are some examples from students' papers:

> *Passive:* All of this *is communicated* by Tolkien by means of a poem rather than prose. The poetry *is shown* as a tool which Tolkien employs in order to foreshadow events and establish ideas which otherwise *could* not *be* easily *communicated* to us.

The wordiness and general cotton-woolly consistency of this passage result largely from the passive voice. A change to active voice reduces the length, clarifies the sense, and produces a crisper, more vital style. Begin by making the agent of the action the subject of the finite verb; the rest then follows naturally and logically:

> *Active:* Tolkien *communicates* all this in poetry rather than prose because with poetry he can foreshadow events and establish ideas that would otherwise be difficult to convey.

Another example:

> *Passive:* And when I admired the small hills, rich grass, and tall poplars, as I had often done before, they *were* now *being compared* with the landscape at home.

The passive voice here serves only to confuse the reader. Clearly the *I* is the only possible agent:

> *Active:* And when I admired the small hills, rich grass, and tall poplars, as I had often done before, I was now comparing them with the landscape at home.

Another example:

> *Passive:* "Death by Water" is a very short section of the poem, but the religious theme *is carried on* in it.

One can avoid this awkwardness by keeping the subject (*"Death by Water," it*) clearly in the forefront. And while one is reworking the sentence, one can get rid of the *but*, for it points out no meaningful contrast; faulty co-ordination (see #28) has accompanied the passive voice in this weak sentence.

> *Active:* "Death by Water" is a very short section; it *continues* the religious theme.
>
> *Better:* "Death by Water," a very short section, continues the religious theme.

It should not have been a compound sentence in the first place; the emphasis is now clear. Here is one more example:

> *Passive:* By weeding out the errors in one's writing, good habits *are* also *learned*.

Here the passive voice has resulted not only in awkwardness and weakness, but also in a grammatical error: a dangling modifier (see #24). The frequency of this kind of error is in itself a sufficient reason to be careful with the passive voice. Change the passive to the active and the dangling modifier disappears.

> *Active:* By weeding out the errors in one's writing, one also *learns* good habits.

The passive voice should be used only when the active voice is impossible or unnecessarily awkward, or when the passive is for some other reason clearly preferable or demanded by the context. In the preceding sentence, for example, we began with a passive construction (*should be used*) in order to be able to begin the sentence emphatically with *The passive voice*; in addition, the agent in this instance—i.e. all writers—is less important than *The passive voice* itself, which we have emphasized by making it the subject of the sentence. Here are some good reasons for using the passive voice:

1. When the agent, or doer of the act, is indefinite or not known.

2. When the agent is not as important as the act itself.
3. When you want to emphasize either the agent or the act by putting it at the beginning or end of the sentence.

For example:

> It *was reported* that there were two survivors.

Here the writer does not know who did the reporting. To avoid the passive by saying "Someone reported that there were two survivors" would be to strain the point by seeming to emphasize the mysterious "someone." And the fact that someone did the reporting is, in this instance, less important than the content of the report.

> The accident *was witnessed* by more than thirty people.

Here the writer wishes to emphasize the large number of witnesses. One could say "More than thirty people witnessed the accident," but the emphasis is clearly greater at the end of the sentence than at the beginning. There will surely be other occasions when you will want to use the passive, but if you make it a habit never to use it unwittingly and uncritically, your writing will inevitably be better.

Remember, a verb in the passive voice consists of some form of the verb *be* followed by a past participle (*to be accompanied, was given, had been given, will be charged, is shown, are legalized, is being removed*). Whenever you find yourself forming such verbs in your writing, stop to consider whether an active structure might not be more effective.

Note: *Voice* has nothing to do with *tense*; do not confuse *passive* with *past*. Passive constructions can occur in any of the tenses.

GRAMMATICAL FUNCTION: Finite verbs are the most important single elements within the grammatical pattern of English expression. They function as the verbs in clauses; i.e., wherever there is a subject and a predicate, the predicate will include or consist of a finite verb.

Exercise 6h

Rewrite the following sentences, changing any verbs that are in the passive voice to the active voice if you think the change improves the sentence; leave in the passive voice any verb that you think should, or must, remain passive.

1. The house was broken into during the night, but only some loose change was taken.
2. The car was driven by Denise, while Anton acted as map-reader.
3. Some went swimming, some went on short hikes, some just lay around, and baseball was played by others.
4. The solution to the problem was worked out by our resident efficiency expert.
5. We were informed by our guide that the cathedral was built in the thirteenth century.

7 Agreement Between Subject and Verb

agr A finite verb should agree with its subject in NUMBER and PERSON. A finite verb is "limited" (made finite) in its form by the number and person of its subject; the subject governs the form of the inflected part of the verb. We say *I see,* not *I sees,* and *he sees,* not *he see.* Most English speakers automatically use the correct form of the verb to go with the PERSON of the subject, but they sometimes have trouble making verbs agree with their subjects in NUMBER. Here are the main points to watch out for.

7a Errors often occur when a singular subject is followed by a prepositional phrase in which the object of the preposition is plural. The verb must agree with the singular subject; do not let the intervening plural mislead you.

> *Wrong:* Far below, a *landscape* of rolling brown hills and small trees *lie* in disharmony with the grim structures of steel and cement. (*Lie* should be *lies.*)
> *Wrong:* *Each* of the poems *have* certain striking qualities. (*Have* should be *has.*)

> *Right:* *Neither* of these men *was* willing to volunteer.
> *Right:* *Either* of the women *is* likely to be elected to fill the vacant seat on the school board.

7b A compound subject made up of two or more singular nouns joined by *and* is always plural:

> *Right:* Careful thought and close attention to detail *are* essential for effective writing.
> *Right:* Coffee and tea *were* served on the balcony.

If you find yourself wanting to use a singular verb after a subject consisting of two singular nouns joined by *and,* look again: you may have joined two nouns that mean almost the same thing and are therefore redundant; for example:

> *Poor:* The *strength and power* of his argument *is* undeniable.

Get rid of one or the other, or find a single word to replace them both (*force?*)

7c When the parts of a compound subject are joined by the coordinating conjunction *or* (see #13a) or by the correlative conjunctions *either . . . or, neither . . . nor, not only . . . but also,* or *whether . . . or* (see #13c), the part of the subject nearest to the verb determines whether it is singular or plural:

> One or the other of you *has* the key. (both parts singular: verb singular)
> Neither the men nor the women *like* the proposal. (both parts plural: verb plural)
> Neither the mainland nor the islands *are* being served. (first part singular, second part plural: verb plural)
> Neither my parents nor I *was* to blame. (first part plural, second part singular: verb singular)
> Whether the captain or the crew *were* responsible for the wreck *has* not been determined. (first part singular, second part plural: verb plural)

Since the constructions used in the last two examples usually sound awkward, they should be avoided if possible; they can easily be rephrased; for example:

> Neither I nor my parents were to blame.
> My parents were not to blame, nor was I.

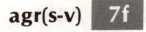

7d In formal usage, the indefinite pronouns *anybody, anyone, everybody, everyone, nobody,* and *no one* are always singular and take the singular form of the verb. *All, any, more, most, none, some,* and *such,* however, can be either singular or plural, depending on whether they refer to a single quantity or to a number of units within a group:

> *Some* of the money *is* missing. (a single sum)
> *Some* of the men *are* missing. (a number of men)
> *All* of this novel *is* good. (a whole novel)
> *All* of his novels *are* well written. (a number of novels)
> *Most* of the beef *is* grain fed. (a single mass)
> *Most* of the cattle *are* grain fed. (a number of individual animals)
> *None* of the runners *is* tired yet. (*not one*)
> *None* but the fainthearted *are* staying behind. (*only they*)

7e With expletive constructions (*here is, there is,* etc.), and at other times when the subject follows the verb, be sure that you make the verb agree with the real subject rather than some word that happens to precede it:

> *Wrong:*   There *is* also a number of different *ways* of approaching this problem.
> *Right:*   There *are* also a number of different *ways* of approaching this problem.
> *Wrong:*   Thirty days *have* September.
> *Right:*   Thirty days *has* September.
> *Wrong:*   Charging about all over the landscape *was* the group of scouts and their leader.
> *Right:*   Charging about all over the landscape *were* the group of scouts *and* their leader.

Caution: Do not let a predicate noun determine the number of the verb; the verb must agree with the subject of the sentence, not the complement:

> *Wrong:*   The last *word* in style that year *were* suede shoes and broad lapels.
> *Right:*   The last *word* in style that year *was* suede shoes and broad lapels.

7f Some nouns—called COLLECTIVE nouns—are names of groups and may be considered either singular or plural, depending on whether they refer to something as a whole, a unit, or to the individual persons or things that make up the whole:

> The faculty has made its decision regarding student representation. (singular)
> The faculty have not yet made up their minds about student representation. (plural)
> His family comes from Iceland. (singular)
> His family come from Jamaica, India, and southern Europe. (plural)
> The audience was composed and attentive. (singular)
> The audience were sneezing, coughing, blowing their noses, and chatting with each other. (plural)

Words like *number, half,* and *majority* can also be considered collective nouns and can be either singular or plural:

> A number of lumps of coal *are* missing.
> The number of people here *is* quite large.
> Half of the team *is* here. OR Half of the team *are* here.
> Half of the women *are* going.

(See also *amount, number* in #60.)

Other terms of quantity, like some of the indefinite pronouns (see #7d), can be either singular or plural:

> *Five pieces* of candy *is* quite enough for one day.
> *Five* of us *are* going to the play.
> *Eggs cost* too much.
> A *dozen* eggs *costs* too much.
> A *dozen* of them *need* not take the final examination.
> That *quartet plays* very well.
> The *quartet pick* up *their* instruments and the room grows quiet.

7g Some nouns, because of their meaning, cannot be inflected for number and will always be either singular or plural. For example:

> The *gold comes* from the Yukon. (always singular)
> *Oxygen is* essential to human life. (always singular)
> *Mathematics is* difficult for some people. (always singular)
> The *scissors are* in the kitchen. (always plural)

His *trousers are* soaking wet. (always plural)
Her *clothes are* very stylish. (always plural)

7h Whether a relative pronoun is singular or plural is determined by its antecedent; the verb in a relative clause must, then, agree with the number of that antecedent:

> *Wrong:* His success is due to his intelligence and perseverance, *which overcomes* all obstacles.
> *Right:* His success is due to his *intelligence and perseverance,* which *overcome* all obstacles.

Particularly troublesome is the *one of those who* construction:

> He is one of those people who *have* difficulty reading aloud.

The plural verb *have* is correct, since its subject is the relative pronoun *who,* and the antecedent of *who* is *people* (plural) not *one* (singular).

> He is the only one of those attending who *has* difficulty reading aloud.

Now the singular form *has* is correct, for its subject, *who,* has as antecedent the singular pronoun *one.* If you find such constructions annoying, try simplifying, for they are often wordy and unnecessarily cumbersome to begin with:

> He has difficulty reading aloud.
> Of those attending, he alone has difficulty reading aloud.

Exercise 7(1)

In the following sentences, underline whichever form of the two in parentheses is correct.

1. Both the chairman and the secretary (has, have) asked for volunteers, but neither Richard nor Lisette (is, are) likely to stand up.
2. The army (resent, resents) having to adopt a new style of uniform.
3. Linda and her sisters (is, are) going, but neither John nor his brothers (plan, plans) to attend.
4. The book as well as the magazines (contain, contains) useful information.

5. What data (is, are) available on this topic?
6. Each of the generals (want, wants) to take command of the operation.
7. There (is, are) only ten people present.
8. The number of pages assigned (was, were) reduced by half, but a large number of students (was, were) still unhappy.
9. Wood chips (makes, make) good ground cover.
10. She is the only one of those who (was, were) present who (think, thinks) that the bulk of our taxes (go, goes) for military spending.

Exercise 7(2)
In each of the following sentences, correct any lack of agreement between subject and verb.

1. Recent discoveries about the weather reveals that there are more than one kind of cycle.
2. Baroque sculpture in Germany and Austria were very imaginative.
3. There appears to be four different ways of approaching such a problem.
4. Day after day the media is feeding us advertisements.
5. Everything in this speech, the metre, the repetition of vowels and consonants, and the vibrant imagery, lead us to believe that this is the high point of Othello's love—and, as far as we know from this play, of his life.
6. Power and the desire for wealth is just as strong now as it was then.
7. Indeed, the exercise of careful thought and careful planning seem to be necessary for the successful completion of the project.
8. But scandal, unfair politics, and the "big business" of politics has led to the corruption of this system.
9. My faith and trust in him was complete.
10. The number of jobs available to students under sixteen are very few.

8 Transitive, Intransitive, and Linking (Copulative) Verbs

One further characteristic of verbs needs to be considered: whether or not a verb has a DIRECT OBJECT (see #1b). A verb that has a direct object is called a TRANSITIVE verb; a verb that does not have a direct object is called an INTRANSITIVE verb. *Transitive* means "effecting transition": a transitive verb makes a transition from its subject to an object; it is incomplete without an object. An intransitive verb is complete in itself; it needs no object. (Objects are always nouns or their grammatical equivalents.) See also #17c.

8a Some verbs are not normally used without an object and are considered transitive:

> He *stuffed* himself with pizza. (object: *himself)*
> She *has* good taste. (object: *taste*)
> He *introduced* his uncle. (object: *uncle*)
> She *expresses* her ideas eloquently. (object: *ideas*)
> He *neglected* his homework. (object: *homework*)

8b Some verbs, on the other hand, normally do not have objects and are considered intransitive:

> You should *lie* low for a while.
> He *lied* to his roommate.
> She *cringed*.
> The trophy *came* home.

8c Many verbs, however, can be either transitive or intransitive:

> I *ran* to the store. (no object: intransitive)
> I *ran* the business effectively. (object is *business*: transitive)
> He *paints* for a living. (no object: intransitive)
> He *paints* pictures for a living. (object is *pictures*: transitive)
> I can *see* well enough from here. (no object: intransitive)
> I can *see* the parade better from the balcony. (object is *parade*: transitive)
> She *wished* for good luck. (no object: intransitive)
> I *wish* that he were here now. (object is the noun clause *that he were here now*: transitive)

An object answers the question consisting of the verb and *what* or *whom*: Paints what? Pictures. See what? The parade.

In the second to last example, the prepositional phrase *for good luck* is not an object: prepositional phrases can normally act only as adjectives or adverbs (see #12).

In fact, very few verbs are exclusively either transitive or intransitive. Verbs felt to be clearly transitive, such as *remember,* can also be used intransitively:

> He leaned back in the chair and *remembered.*

Similarly, verbs felt to be clearly intransitive, such as *sleep,* can be used transitively, especially when the object is the noun form of the same word:

> She *slept* the *sleep* of the just.

If you are in doubt, your dictionary will be a useful guide. The important thing, in any event, is to be able to distinguish between transitive and intransitive function for a particular verb in a particular sentence.

8d Linking Verbs (Copulas)

One kind of verb that is always intransitive is the copula, or LINKING verb. The principal example is the verb *be* in its various forms. Some other common verbs in this class are *seem, appear, become, look, act,* and *remain.*

The distinguishing feature of linking verbs is that they do not take objects, but are yet incomplete, requiring a SUBJECTIVE COMPLEMENT. They are like equal signs in mathematical equations: something must come at the back (predicate) end to balance what is at the front (subject) end. The complement following a linking verb will be either a noun or an adjective; because complements occur in the predicate, after the linking verb, they are called PREDICATE NOUNS or PREDICATE ADJECTIVES (see also #17d).

> Angela *is* a lawyer. (*Lawyer* is a predicate *noun.*)
> Angela *is* tired. (*Tired* is a predicate *adjective.*)
> The opera *was* very artistic. (*Artistic* is a predicate *adjective.*)
> The opera *was* a true work of art. (*Work* is a predicate *noun.*)
> Irma *remains* a strong woman. (*Woman* is a predicate *noun.*)
> Irma *remains* strong. (*Strong* is a predicate *adjective.*)

A complement, like an object, answers the question consisting of the verb and *what* or *whom*: Is what? A lawyer. Is what? Tired.

A complement differs from an object in that it repeats the meaning of the subject or tells us something about the subject. With linking verbs other than *be,* however, the complement is usually an adjective:

> He looks *well.*
> She seems *stubborn.*
> The music sounds *loud.*
> He feels *fit.*
> The surface felt *sticky.*
> The steak tastes *good.*
> The garbage smells *terrible.*

Such verbs as *sound, taste, smell,* and *feel* can also of course be used as transitive verbs: *He sounded his horn. He smelled the hydrogen sulfide. I tasted the steak. He felt the bump on his head.* Similarly, verbs like *look, appear,* and *remain* can also function as simple intransitive verbs: *She looked at the cover of the book. He appeared before the magistrate. They remained in the room.*

Exercise 8(1)
Indicate whether each italicized verb in the following sentences is transitive, intransitive, or linking.

1. Virgil *left* his suitcase in the locker while he *went* into the restaurant for lunch.
2. He *offered* the committee a compromise that *provoked* much discussion.
3. Elizabeth *looked* around for the test-tube that *contained* the alcohol.
4. The doctor *questioned* her receptionist about the patient who *was* due at four.
5. Bruce *felt* pleased with himself at the way the experiment *ended.*

6. She *gave* me the answer I *needed*.
7. The thought *struck* Mahmoud that he *needed* more time to prepare.
8. *Ask* Yolanda about nutrition; she *is* the expert.
9. Everyone *expected* Irving by six, but he *arrived* much later.
10. He *served* us a dinner that *was* superb in every detail.

Now go back and label any direct objects, indirect objects, predicate adjectives, and predicate nouns.

Exercise 8(2)

After each transitive verb in the following, supply an object; after each intransitive verb, supply an adverb (or adverbial phrase) or a period. If a particular verb can be either transitive or intransitive, do both.

Examples: Donna *wants* money. (tr.)
Donna *waited*. (intr.) patiently. (intr.)
Donna *speaks* loudly. (intr.)
with authority (intr.)
her mind (tr.)

1. Lisa *drinks*
2. Eric *talks*
3. Suzie *expects*
4. The company *ordered*
5. William *learned*
6. Olivier *performed*
7. Monty *responded*
8. Sonya *planted*
9. Jane *bought*
10. Tony *washed*
11. Jennifer *knelt*
12. Yvonne *believed*
13. Jonathan *flew*
14. Pierre *repaired*
15. The council *vetoed*

16. Everybody *breathed*
17. Donald *opened*
18. They *liberated*
19. Claudia *relaxes*
20. Matilda *teaches*
21. Bianca *attempted*
22. Colin *sold*
23. Michael *selected*
24. Hilda *drove*
25. Horace *sang*

Exercise 8(3)
Underline the complement of each italicized linking verb in the following sentences and indicate whether it is a predicate adjective or a predicate noun.

1. She *was* sorry he *felt* so ill.
2. Since he *was* an experienced seaman, he *was* confident that he could handle the crisis.
3. The book *became* a best-seller even though it *was* critical of most people's beliefs.
4. Since the house *was* well insulated, it *stayed* warm throughout the severe winter.
5. Incredible as it *seems,* the mixture *tasted* as good as it *looked* odd.

Exercise 8(4)
After each linking verb, supply (a) a predicate noun, then (b) a predicate adjective.

Example: Kevin *was* (a) an engineer. (b) exhausted.

1. Erika *is*
2. Priscilla *became*
3. Luigi *remained*

4. They *were*
5. Lorne *had been*

---

9 Adjectives

An ADJECTIVE is a word that modifies a noun or pronoun. Normally an adjective precedes the word or words it modifies:

> The *angry* manager decided to discharge the *forgetful* clerk.
> *Happy* to get away, they all piled into the *ancient* car.

Here *happy,* though separated from its pronoun, still precedes it; actually, the whole phrase *happy to get away* modifies *they.* In some sentences, however, adjectives can follow the words they modify:

> Elfrida, *radiant* and *delighted,* left the room, *secure* in her victory.
> The storm, more *severe* than any other in this century, did extensive damage.

When an adjective is separated from its noun by a linking verb, it is called a predicate adjective (see the preceding section):

> This pensioner is very *poor.*
> Shortly after his operation he again became *sick.*

Inflection: Adjectives are regularly inflected for degree by adding *er* and *est* (as with verbs, your dictionary will list any irregular forms after the basic adjective):

Positive	Comparative	Superlative
high	higher	highest
rough	rougher	roughest
much	more	most
good	better	best
dirty	dirtier	dirtiest
funny	funnier	funniest

Most adjectives of more than one syllable, however, will require the addition of *more* and *most* to express degree:

| difficult | more difficult | most difficult |
| conscious | more conscious | most conscious |

Note: Some adjectives by their very nature cannot be compared. See *unique,* etc. in the Usage Checklist, #60.

GRAMMATICAL FUNCTION: Adjectives modify nouns and pronouns. See also #17g.

9a Articles

art ARTICLES—sometimes considered separately from parts of speech—are most conveniently thought of as kinds of adjectives. The definite article *the* and the indefinite article *a* (or *an*) are used idiomatically (see *Idiom,* #58). They are sometimes baffling to those whose native language is not English—and no wonder, for it is almost impossible to set down rules for their use. We nevertheless include here a few principles for your guidance. Most of these points arise from real difficulties experienced by real students.

1. The easiest thing to remember about articles is that the form *a* of the indefinite article is used before words beginning with a consonant (*a dog, a building, a wish, a yellow orchid*), including words beginning with *h* when the *h* is pronounced (*a horse, a historical event, a hotel, a hypothesis*) and words beginning with *u* or *o* whose initial sound is that of *y* or *w* (*a useful book, a one-sided contest*). The form *an* is used before words beginning with a vowel or a silent *h* (*an opinion, an underdog, an ugly duckling, an honour*). Similarly, the pronunciation of *the* changes from "thuh" to "thee" before a word beginning with a vowel sound.

2. Generally, the definite article designates a particular person or thing:

> *The* horse is in *the* barn.
> *The* building is on *the* corner.
> *The* teacher stands in front of *the* class.
> *The* town is near *the* city.

whereas the person or thing designated by the indefinite article generally is not specific:

> He wants to buy *a* horse.
> The company needs *a* new building.
> Each class has *a* teacher.
> She prefers living in *a* city to living in *a* small town.

The indefinite article should be considered as equivalent to *one*; it can be used only before singular nouns. Sometimes it is even used to mean *one*:

> I thought I would like the job, but I lasted only *a* week.
> This will take *an* hour or two.

Here are some further illustrations comparing *a* and *the*:

> He gave me *a* gift. (unspecified)
> He gave me *the* gift I had hoped for. (particularized)

> Give me *a* book. (any book that's handy)
> Give me *the* book. (a particular book, one already identified or otherwise clear from the context)

> Look up the word *schism* in *a* dictionary. (Any dictionary will do.)
> Look up the word *schism* in *the* dictionary. (This also means *any*, but considers all dictionaries as a class; or it implies "the particular dictionary you customarily use.")
> Look up the word *schism* in *your* dictionary. (the one you own)

3. Articles can also be used generically: *The horse is a beautiful animal*; this emphasizes the *class* "horse" (and is not, here, equivalent to *That horse, standing over there by the fence, is a beautiful animal*). *A horse is a beautiful animal*; this means the same thing, but using the indefinite article emphasizes an individual member of the class. If no article is used—*Horses are beautiful animals*—the plural *Horses* causes the emphasis to fall on all the individual horses.

4. The definite article is used with some proper nouns but not with others.

We say:	Canada	but:	the Dominion of Canada
	Russia		the Soviet Union, the USSR
	Great Britain		the United Kingdom
	America		the United States, the States
	Vancouver Island		the Leeward Islands
	Mount Garibaldi		the Rocky Mountains, the Rockies
	Great Slave Lake		the Great Lakes
	Hudson Bay		the Bay of Fundy
	Dalhousie University		the University of Manitoba

Notice that *the* is usually used with plurals, names containing *of* phrases, and names consisting of a modified common noun (the United *Kingdom*) as opposed to a modified proper noun (Great *Britain*).

5. The definite article can also be used to indicate exclusiveness; *the* is then equivalent to *the only* or *the best* (in both speech and writing, such a *the* is sometimes emphasized):

   He was *the* man for the job.

But if such exclusiveness is not intended, *the* should not be used:

   Wrong: He soon becomes *the* good friend of each of the main characters.

If *good* were changed to *best,* the definite article would be correct; otherwise, *a* is correct:

   He soon becomes *a* good friend of each of the main characters.

6. Mass nouns—i.e., nouns standing for something which cannot be counted, something which normally has no plural—and abstract nouns are not preceded by articles if the mass or abstract sense is the governing one:

Wrong: The poem is *a* direct, simple *praise* of God.

Here the *a* must be removed. But notice the difference if a concrete noun is inserted; then the article is correct:

The poem was *a* direct, simple *hymn* of praise.

If such a noun is used to specify a particular part of the totality, the definite article is used:

The praise she bestowed upon him made him blush.
Look at *the gold* that I panned.

Thus it is correct to say:

He lacks humility.
He lacks *the* humility necessary for that position.

Give me liberty, or give me death.
Give me *the* liberty to know, to utter, and to argue freely according to conscience, above all liberties.
The disclosure meant *the* death of his dreams.

Orange juice is good for you.
Drink *the* orange juice I gave you.

It sometimes helps to think of each *the* in such instances as similar to a demonstrative or possessive pronoun:

Her praise was generous.
Look at *my* gold.
Give me *that* liberty above all others.
Drink *your* orange juice.
Drink *that* orange juice sitting in front of you.

If an abstract noun is used in a concrete but not particularized sense, the indefinite article precedes it; if particularized, the definite article:

That horse is *a* beauty. He is *the* beauty I was telling you about.
This is *an* honour. He did me *the* honour of inviting me.
Hers is *a* very special honesty. She has *the* honesty of a saint.

7.   The definite article usually precedes an adjective used as a noun:

Only *the* strong will survive.
The poor will always be with us.
The French oppose independence for Brittany.
This is *the* most I can do.

But not always:

> More is sure to come.

Caution: A common error is to use *the* before *most* used adverbially:

> *Wrong:* What people want *the* most is security.
> *Wrong:* That is what they want *the* most of all.

8. Titles of artistic works are not usually preceded by articles, but, with the normal inconsistency characterizing the realities of usage, some titles can be and sometimes are preceded by the definite ariticle. It would never be correct to say this:

> Donne's poetic power is evident in *the* Sonnet X.

And one would not say "the *Alice in Wonderland*" or "the *Paradise Lost*." But one is more likely to say "in the *Areopagitica*" than "in *Areopagitica*," or "in the *Adventures of Huckleberry Finn*" than "in *Adventures of Huckleberry Finn*." (Of course if *A* or *The* is itself a part of a title, it must be included: *A Midsummer Night's Dream, The Portrait of a Lady*.) Yet if a possessive form of the author's name precedes, no article would be used: "in Milton's *Areopagitica*." One might well speak of one of Michelangelo's great sculptures as "the *David*" (but "In Florence we saw Michelangelo's *David*"), whereas one would never use the article before the title of Earle Birney's poem, *David*.

9. With the names of academic fields and courses, whether proper nouns or abstract common nouns, no article is used:

> She is majoring in Psychology.
> He reads books on psychology.
> He is enrolled in English.
> This is a program in English Language and Literature.

But if such terms are particularized common nouns or used adjectivally, the definite article is used:

> She studies *the* psychology of animal behaviour.
> You are learning more about *the* English language.

Yet it would be incorrect to speak of "*the* English literature."

10. The definite article is used before the names of ships:

    the *Golden Hind,* the *Titanic,* the *St. Roch*

    and trains:

    the *Super Chief,* the *Orient Express*

11. In some instances the indefinite article is used to identify something in a general sense; but once the context has been clearly established, the definite article takes over:

    Tonight I wish to discuss *a* problem that has arisen recently, for I think it is *an* important one. *The* problem to which I refer is that of ....

The idiomatic use of articles can be learned only through intimate familiarity with usage. When in doubt about a particular instance consult a good dictionary, which will outline briefly the various uses of articles. (See also *Idiom,* #58.)

GRAMMATICAL FUNCTION: Articles are said, like adjectives, to *modify* the nouns or their equivalents which they precede. They are also sometimes called *markers* or *determiners* in that an article always indicates that a noun is to follow (though of course other modifiers may intervene).

Exercise 9a

In each blank, place either *a, an,* or *the;* or put *0* if no article is needed. If an article could be used, but need not, place the article in parentheses, thus: (the) (an) (a). Some of the answers will be debatable, and we hope that you will debate them.

1. In ____ Canadian society, everyone is considered ____ equal.
2. After two years in ____ college, I decided to go to ____ business school.
3. My sister got ____ Honours degree for her work in ____ chemistry.

4. ____ weather report said we could expect ____ storms.
5. ____ hospital is prepared for ____ union walkout.
6. There was ____ uninterrupted movie on ____ television last night.
7. It was ____ lucky day when I bought ____ ticket in ____ lottery.
8. I think you should put ____ onion in ____ stew.
9. This is ____ picture of ____ amoeba, and notice that ____ picture is magnified ____ thousand times so that we can see ____ amoeba's structure.
10. If you belong to ____ union you must be prepared to honour ____ picket lines.

10 Adverbs

ADVERBS answer the questions *How? When? Where? Why? To what degree?* Many adverbs are formed by the addition of the suffix *ly* to an adjective:

high	highly
rough	roughly
happy	happily
capable	capably
fundamental	fundamentally

Here are some examples of adverbs in a variety of contexts:

Fully expecting to fail, he sat *down* and began the examination. (To what degree expecting? Fully. Sat where? Down.)

Under the new scheme profits increased *greatly.* (Increased to what degree? Greatly.)

Eventually they overcame the difficulty. (Overcame it when? Eventually.)

Badly constructed roads are *more* expensive *in the long run* than good roads. (Constructed how? Badly. To what degree expensive? More. Are expensive when? In the long run: the prepositional phrase functions as an adverb.)

The procedure you suggest is *very* irregular. (To what degree irregular? Very.)

The boxer jumped *quickly sideways.* (Jumped how? Quickly. Jumped where? Sideways.)

They lived *very happily together.* (Lived how? Happily and together. To what degree happily? Very.)

He succeeded *because he worked hard.* (Succeeded why? because he worked hard: the subordinate clause functions as an adverb.)

Fortunately, the cut was not deep.

In this last example, *fortunately* is what is called a SENTENCE MODIFIER; rather than modifying any single word or answering one of the specific questions, its meaning hovers over the whole sentence.

Note that adverbs are more flexible with regard to position than any other part of speech; often they can be moved almost anywhere in the sentence and still function clearly:

Quickly he jumped sideways.
He *quickly* jumped sideways.
He jumped *quickly* sideways.
He jumped sideways *quickly.*

Note that even in this simple example there are slight differences in meaning, depending on where the adverb is placed. It is therefore important that you know precisely what you want to say before you decide where an adverbial modifier should be placed. Do not just stick it in anywhere, under the assumption that it will do the job you want it to.

Inflection: Like adjectives, adverbs are inflected only for degree. And with most adverbs, such auxiliaries as *more* and *most* will be necessary (nearly all of the adverbs ending in *ly* will need them):

Positive	Comparative	Superlative
well	better	best
soon	sooner	soonest
much	more	most
little	less	least
often	more often	most often
highly	more highly	most highly
down	farther down	farthest down
happily	more happily	most happily

GRAMMATICAL FUNCTION: As you can see from the sentences above, adverbs can modify finite verbs (*sat* down, *increased* greatly) or verbals (see #11) (fully *expecting,* badly *con-*

structed) or adjectives (more *expensive*, very *irregular*) or other adverbs (very *happily*) or whole sentences (Fortunately, *the cut was not deep*). There are also a number of what are called conjunctive adverbs, such as *however, therefore, nevertheless*, which usually express some kind of logical relation and serve to modify entire clauses (see #33h).

Note: Though it is important to distinguish between adjectives and adverbs for correct usage, some words that were once adjectives only are becoming acceptable also as adverbs. For example: *close* can mean *closely*, and *strong* can mean *strongly*:

> Don't approach the edge too close, or you may fall over.
> He put his recommendation too strong for my taste.

But it is still preferable to use the *ly* forms of such words, especially in formal contexts; regardless of what the road signs may say, drive *slowly*, not just *slow*.

See also #17f.

Exercise 9–10
Underline all the adverbs and circle all the adjectives (including articles) in the following sentences.

1. The hot weather continued unabated; it was the fifth consecutive sweltering day.
2. Although he felt bad, he decided, reluctantly, to stay very quiet in his little corner.
3. The fireplace screen was too hot to touch.
4. When he was fully recovered, he returned eagerly to the scene of his grisly accident.
5. Surely we can find some way to leave this benighted area quietly.

---

11 Other Verb Forms: Verbals

Infinitives, participles, and gerunds are called VERBALS, words that function as non-finite verbs—that is, they are not restricted by person and number (see #6a). They function in sentences as other parts of speech, but at the same time retain some of the characteristics of verbs. That is, while functioning as nouns, adjectives, and adverbs, they can also be either present or past (tense); they can be either active or passive (voice); they can have subjects, objects, and complements; and they can be modified by adverbs. Verbals frequently introduce VERBAL PHRASES, which then function as other parts of speech.

11a Infinitives

When talking about verbs, people sometimes use a form called the INFINITIVE to identify particular verbs. They speak of "the verb *to be*" or "the verb *to dwell*." (In this book we use the simple dictionary form, *be, dwell.*) The infinitive form usually begins with the word *to* (often called "the sign of the infinitive"), which is followed by the first person singular of the present tense (the simple or basic form) of the verb. (A notable exception to this is the verb *be* itself. And the verb *can,* as in "I can read," has no infinitive form; one would have to say "to be able." Nor are there infinitive forms for the rest of the verbs known as MODALS or MODAL AUXILIARIES, verbs such as *may, might, could, would, will, shall, should, ought,* and *must.*)

Infinitives can function as nouns, adjectives, and adverbs:

> *To save* the horses was his primary intention.

Here the infinitive phrase *to save the horses* is the subject (noun function) of the verb *was;* the noun *horses* is the object of the infinitive *to save* (To save what? The horses.)

> The green coupons are the ones *to save.*

Here the infinitive *to save* modifies the pronoun *ones* (adjectival function).

> She was determined *to make* some changes.

Here the infinitive phrase *to make some changes* modifies the adjective *determined* (adverbial function, answering the question "How? In what way?"); the noun *changes* is the object of the infinitive *to make.*

> He begged me *to reconsider* my verdict.

Here the infinitive phrase *to reconsider my verdict,* along with the pronoun *me,* is the object (noun function) of the verb *begged;* the pronoun *me* is the subject of the infinitive *to reconsider,* and the noun *verdict* is its object.

Note: Whenever the subject of an infinitive is a pronoun, as in the preceding example, it must be in the objective case.

11b **Caution:** The reason it is usually considered wrong to SPLIT
split an INFINITIVE is that an infinitive is felt to be a unit; separating its parts can weaken it by destroying its integrity and almost always produces awkwardness.

> He wants *to* quickly *conclude* the business of the meeting.
> She claimed that it was too difficult *to* very accurately or confidently *solve* such a problem in the time allowed.

It is almost always possible to avoid such split infinitives by rearranging or rephrasing the sentence so that the adverbial modifiers do not interrupt the infinitive:

> He wants *to conclude* the business of the meeting quickly.
> She claimed that it was too difficult, in the time allowed, *to solve* such a problem with any degree of accuracy or confidence.

But opinion is divided. Some writers argue that there is nothing wrong with splitting an infinitive. Indeed, many would agree that it is better to split an infinitive than to sound awkward or over-refined:

> The yellow car swerved way over and contrived *to* narrowly *miss* the car that was near the edge of the track.

This is clearly better than *narrowly to miss,* and *narrowly* cannot comfortably go anywhere else in the sentence.

> It is impossible *to* more than *guess* at her intentions.

The *more than* cannot possibly be moved, though a conscientious writer might well insert *do* before *more* in order to avoid what many people frown on, whether justifiably or not. (A split infinitive is also an instance of a misplaced modifier; see #23.)

Note: After some verbs, the infinitive can occur without the customary *to:*

> Let sleeping dogs *lie.*
> We saw the man *jump.*
> He felt the house *shake.*

11c Participles

The perfect and progressive tenses of a finite verb include, respectively, the PAST PARTICIPLE and the PRESENT PARTICIPLE:

> I have painted.   (*Painted* is the past participle of *paint:* being formed regularly, it is of course identical to the simple past form.)
> I am painting.   (*Painting* is the present participle of *paint.*)

Present participles always end in *ing,* regular past participles in *ed*; irregular past participles end variously: *made, mown, slept, broken,* etc. Both present and past participles, however, can function independently of finite verbs. When they do, they not only act like the verb forms they are but also function as adjectives.

> *Painted* houses require more care than brick ones.

Here the past participle *painted* modifies the noun *houses.*

> Brightly *coloured* banners decorated the streets.

Here the past participle *coloured* modifies the noun *banners,* and it is itself, as a verbal, modified by the adverb *brightly.*

> The subject *discussed* most often was unemployment.

Here the past participle *discussed* introduces the participial phrase *discussed most often,* which modifies the noun *subject.* As a verbal, *discussed* is modified by the adverbial phrase *most often.*

> Suddenly *finding* himself alone, he became very *frightened.*

Here the present participle *finding* introduces the participial phrase *finding himself alone,* which modifies the pronoun *he*; *finding,* as a verbal, has as its object the pronoun *himself,* and is modified by the adverb *suddenly.* The past participle *frightened,* following the linking verb *became,* is the subjective complement; as a predicate adjective, it modifies the subject pronoun *he* and is modified by the adverb *very*.

> The team *having* the tallest players has a distinct advantage.

Here the present participle *having* introduces the participial phrase *having the tallest players,* which modifies the noun *team.* As a verbal, *having* has *players* as its object. When participles include an auxiliary verb such as *be* or *have,* the *ing* is attached to the auxiliary:

> The event *being celebrated* was forgotten by almost all present.
> *Having painted* himself into a corner, he climbed out the window.
> *Having been warned,* she knew better than to accept the offer.

In the first and third of these examples, the participles are in the passive voice.

11d Gerunds

GERUNDS, like present participles, are verbals ending in *ing.* But whereas present participles function as adjectives, gerunds always function as nouns. Present participles and gerunds look identical, but in order to analyze and understand the syntax of sentences, it is essential to distinguish between them:

> It was a very *moving* experience.

Here *moving* is a present participle, an adjective modifying the noun *experience:* What kind of experience? A *moving* experience.

> *Moving* furniture can be exhausting work.

In this sentence, *moving* is a gerund, a noun: it is the subject of the sentence and has as its complement the predicate noun *work*; it also, as a verbal, has *furniture* as an object: Moving what? Furniture.

> *Building* boats is his hobby.

Here the gerund *building* is the subject, and it has *hobby* as its predicate noun and *boats* as its object.

> Because he knew it was good exercise, Boris took up *swimming.*

Here the gerund *swimming* is the object of the verb *took up*.

His *driving* left much to be desired.

Here the gerund *driving* is the subject of the sentence; as a noun it is preceded by the possessive adjective *his*.

11e This last example raises another point: In formal usage, when a gerund is immediately preceded by a personal pronoun, the pronoun is usually in the possessive case. Here is another example, where the choice might not seem so obvious:

They were annoyed at *his* smoking his pipe in the office.

His is the correct form; the objective *him* would suggest that *smoking* was a participle, and the meaning would be slightly different (and a comma would probably be needed after *him*). This may seem odd, since the pronoun is in effect the subject of the gerund; however, since the gerund is functioning as a noun, it needs a possessive pronoun before it rather than a nominative or an objective pronoun. Just as one would not say *him car* but *his car,* so one should say *his smoking* rather than *him smoking*. Similarly, a proper noun immediately preceding a gerund is usually possessive:

She approved of *Bob's* cooking the dinner.

What she approved of was Bob's *cooking the dinner*; without the possessive, she would be approving of *Bob,* who happened to be cooking the dinner—and the expression would be a little awkward. If there is emphasis on the noun or pronoun preceding the gerund, however, the possessive case is usually not used:

She approved of *Bob* cooking the dinner rather than Jim.

As with many other points about style, the desired intonation should help you determine whether or not the possessive should be used. Further, if the gerund's subject is abstract, plural, multiple, or separated from the gerund by modifiers, the possessive case is usually not used:

He couldn't bear the thought of *disaster striking* again.
The possibility of the *thieves returning* to their hide-out was slim.

There is little likelihood of *Fortnum and Mason holding* a fire sale.

One might well wonder at a *man* with such a record *claiming* to be honest.

11f Infinitives and participles (but not gerunds) can function grammatically in ABSOLUTE constructions, phrases that are not grammatically connected with the rest of the sentence but that can be thought of as modifying it (see #17h):

To say the least, the day was not a success. (infinitive phrase as absolute)

The day *being* hot, she decided on a swim. (present participial phrase as absolute)

All things *considered,* the meeting was a success. (past participial phrase as absolute)

Exercise 11

Underline all the verbals in the following sentences and label each as an infinitive, a past or present participle, or a gerund. Indicate whether the infinitives are acting as nouns (n.), adjectives (adj.), or adverbs (adv.).

1. Coming as he did from the prairies, he found the coastal scenery to be stunning.
2. She wanted to fly, and learning was easier than she had expected.
3. My answering service had promised to buzz me if anything startling were to arise.
4. The celebrated performers got top billing for the first showing of the winning film.
5. Trying to study hard with a splitting headache is usually not very rewarding.
6. The party was certain to last until midnight, permitting everyone to eat and drink too much.
7. Turning table legs on a spinning lathe is one way to spend a pleasant and relaxed evening.
8. Sent as he had been from one office to another, Sherman was tired of running back and forth and up and down; he was now resolved to go straight to the top.
9. When doing one's daily exercising, one should be careful not to overstrain already taxed muscles.

10. The contrived plot of the currently running play is enough to make the audience get up and leave the theatre without worrying about the author's supposed talent or his past record of charming tired city-dwellers with rural high jinks.

---

12 Prepositions

A PREPOSITION is a function word that is part of a phrase—which it usually introduces—and that has an object dependent upon it. As its name indicates, a preposition usually *pre*cedes in *position* the rest of the phrase:

> He laid the book *on* the table.
> She sent a letter *to* her brother.

A question consisting of the preposition and the word *what* or *whom* will always produce as its answer the object of the preposition: On what? The table. To whom? Her brother. A prepositional phrase may consist of just two words: He gave the book *to me*. Or it may consist of more: *on the table*; *to her brother*; *around the next corner*; *in a large and dilapidated brick house*. When a preposition follows its object, as in a question, it usually comes at the end of the sentence:

> She is the *person* I am giving the book *to*.
> Which *house* do you want to look *at?*
> *Whom* are you buying the book *for?*

It is not inherently wrong to end a sentence with a preposition, even if it is not a question. The point is that one should not do so to excess or when it is unnecessarily awkward.

> That is the page the quotation came from.

is just as good as, though a little less formal than,

> That is the page from which the quotation came.

Here are some prepositions in common use: in, under, above, to, for, since, because of, on account of, out, of, up, into, from, concerning, with respect to, around, over, until, before, during, often, behind, and in front of. Note that some prepositions consist of more than one word. Note also that words that are usually considered to be prepositions can function as other parts of speech; they can do this, however, only when they do not have an object:

> He flew *over* the town. (preposition)
> At ten a.m. he flew *over*. (adverb)
> The game is finally *over*. (adjective)

GRAMMATICAL FUNCTION: A preposition introduces or is part of a PREPOSITIONAL PHRASE which in turn acts as either an adjective or an adverb. The preposition links its object, a noun or pronoun, with some other word in the sentence.

> He laid the book *on* the table.

In this sentence the preposition *on* links its object *table* with the word *book*; the prepositional phrase *on the table* functions as an *adverb* describing where the book was *laid*.

> He has a great fondness *for spaghetti*.

In this sentence the preposition *for* links its object *spaghetti* with the word *fondness*; the prepositional phrase *for spaghetti* functions as an adjective modifying the noun *fondness*. (Occasionally a prepositional phrase can function as a noun:

> *After class* is a good time to talk to the instructor.)

Exercise 12
Underline each prepositional phrase in the following sentences and label it as either adverbial (adv.) or adjectival (adj.).

1. He went into town to buy some bacon for his breakfast.
2. There stood a man of about forty, in the hot sunshine, wearing a heavy sweater with the collar turned up.
3. In the morning the president called his secretary on the telephone and told her to come to the office without delay.
4. The bulk of the material was sent ahead in trunks.
5. Louis looked under the table for the ball of yarn that had fallen from his lap.

---

13 Conjunctions

As its name indicates, a CONJUNCTION is a function word that "joins together." There are two kinds of conjunctions: co-ordinating conjunctions and subordinating conjunctions. There are only seven co-ordinating conjunctions; you should memorize them:

> and, but, or, nor, for, yet, so

(*So* as a co-ordinating conjunction is usually considered unsuitable for formal writing.) There are many subordinating conjunctions; here are some common ones:

> since, because, if, when, although, until, whereas, in order that

13a A CO-ORDINATING conjunction joins co-ordinate elements, that is, words, phrases, or clauses of equal importance and of similar or parallel grammatical function:

> I saw Jean *and* Ralph. (two objects of the verb *saw*)
> Jean *and* Ralph saw me. (two subjects of the verb *saw*)
> Jean saw me, *but* Ralph didn't. (two independent clauses)
> The men, who were quarrelsome *and* who were obviously preparing for a fight, were both the worse for drink. (two subordinate clauses—here relative clauses, i.e., adjectival)

Exercise 13a

Put an appropriate co-ordinating conjunction in each blank. If more than one is possible, say so.

1. Vernon got home late, ＿＿ he had a good excuse.
2. There is only one solution to this problem, ＿＿ I know what it is.
3. You can sign up for the club today, ＿＿ you can wait until next week.
4. No one likes pollution, ＿＿ some people insist that we have to live with it.
5. I cannot give you an answer tonight, ＿＿ should you expect me to give one tomorrow.
6. It was an extremely well-written novel, ＿＿ I enjoyed it very much.
7. Ernest decided not to skip class, ＿＿ there was to be a quiz that day.

8. My mother arrives tomorrow morning, ____ she expects to be met at the airport.
9. The fishing season is postponed two weeks this year, ____ Arthur is somehow controlling his impatience.
10. Keep a bandage on that cut, ____ it will take weeks to heal.

13b A SUBORDINATING conjunction joins a subordinate (dependent) clause to the independent (main, principal) clause to which it is grammatically related:

> I will not attend class, *because* I have a severe headache.
> (*Because* introduces the adverbial clause and links it to the independent clause.)

Note that a subordinating conjunction can also introduce a subordinate clause that comes first in the sentence:

> *Because* I have a severe headache, I will not attend class.

Even though *because* does not occur between the two unequal clauses, it still grammatically links them.

> *That* she will win the prize is a foregone conclusion.

Here *that* introduces a subordinate clause, in this case a noun clause that functions as the subject of the sentence. Note that whereas a co-ordinating conjunction is a separate unit, like a spot of glue connecting two independent things without being a part of either one, a subordinating conjunction is a part of the clause it introduces.

13c There are also what are called CORRELATIVE conjunctions, conjunctions that correlate ("relate together") two parallel parts of a sentence; these conjunctions always come in pairs.

> *Either* Rodney *or* Elliott is going to drive. (Note that the verb remains *singular*.)
> She accepted *neither* the first *nor* the second offer.
> *Both* the members *and* the visitors applauded the announcement.
> *Whether* it was good *or* bad remained unclear.
> *Not only* does she play well, *but* she *also* sings well.

Conjunctions   75

Caution: In the kind of sentence represented by the last example, the *also* (or some equivalent) should be explicit. A careful writer would not permit an incomplete construction to stand uncorrected.

> *Wrong:* He was *not only* tired, *but* hungry.
> *Right:* He was *not only* tired, *but also* hungry.
> *Right:* He was *not only* tired, *but* hungry *as well.*

This is a simple example. The longer and more complicated a sentence is, the easier it is to be careless and omit the *also*. If the second part doesn't add to or complete the first part, however, but merely intensifies it, the *also* is not included:

> As predicted, the day was not only hot, but downright stifling.

See also #7c.

GRAMMATICAL FUNCTION: A conjunction links words, phrases, or clauses.

14 Interjections

An INTERJECTION is a word interjected into (i.e., "thrown into") a sentence, usually in order to express strong feeling:

> But—*good heavens!*—what did you expect?
> *Oh,* what fun!
> *Well,* aren't you the sly one!
> *My goodness,* it's been a long day.

An interjection may also be relatively mild:

> It was, *well,* a bit of a disappointment.

An exclamatory interjection may in effect be a sentence by itself:

> *Ouch!* That hurt!

GRAMMATICAL FUNCTION: Since interjections are simply thrust into sentences and play no part in their syntax, they cannot be said to have a grammatical function—unless one wishes to think of them as in some way modifying whole sentences.

List all the words in the following sentences in a column and beside each word write its part of speech and its grammatical function.

1. The skyline of modern Toronto provides a striking example of what modern architecture can do.
2. Well, to tell the truth, I just did not have the necessary patience.
3. Forestry is one of the principal industries of British Columbia.
4. Pamela, please put back the chocolate cake.
5. In a few seconds, the computer told us more than we needed to know.

Chapter III

Sentences and Their Syntax:
Principles, Kinds, Structure, Analysis; Common Errors and Weaknesses

In order to arrange words into meaningful and acceptable patterns of expression, one must be familiar with the underlying grammar of English speech. The sentence is the initial pattern that must be mastered; it is the most important single unit in writing. The basic elements of the sentence are outlined in Chapters I and II. This chapter examines the grammatical arrangement of words, phrases, and clauses in sentences — that is, sentence structure or SYNTAX—and the various kinds of errors caused by insufficient understanding of how sentences work.

The sentence has been variously defined, but most definitions are unsatisfactory and unrealistic. For example, one definition asserts that a sentence is a group of words containing a subject and a finite verb, which is not necessarily true. Here are some sentences which have neither subject nor verb:

Yes. No. Now or never. Oh my goodness! Wow!

Here are some with a "subject," or a noun or pronoun that could serve as a subject, but no verb:

Who, me? Well, I never! John. Spaghetti.

Here are some with finite verbs but no subjects:

Come here. Never mind. Call me Ishmael. Sink or swim.

Out of context, these sentences do not tell us very much, but no one will dispute the fact that they are acceptable units.

Moreover, there are groups of words which do contain subjects and finite verbs and yet are not sentences. Starting a subordinate clause with a capital letter and ending it with a period does not make it an acceptable sentence:

> I decided to make a list. Before I went shopping.
> He bought me the bicycle. That I had stared at in the store the week before.

The second clause in each of these examples remains a *fragment*. (See # 16.)

Another common definition claims that a sentence is a complete thought. But there is nothing complete about *Yes* unless we know what precedes it. The same is true of *Oh my goodness! Spaghetti, Never mind,* and the other examples. Moreover, there is nothing necessarily *incomplete* about the thoughts expressed by such symbols as these: *dog, hand, chair, liberty, love;* yet these words are not normally thought of as sentences.

Remember that language is speech sound, and you will find that a more realistic definition of a sentence is the following: *A sentence is a satisfyingly complete pattern of intonation or expression*: i.e., a complete utterance. Your voice and natural tone should soon tell you whether or not a certain group of words is a sentence. Get into the habit of reading your written work aloud whenever possible, or at least sound it over in your mind's ear. This practice will help you to avoid serious errors.

Sentences (i.e., acceptable patterns of expression) are of two kinds, which we call MAJOR and MINOR. Though most of what this and similar books have to say about sentences pertains to major sentences, and though you are not likely to have much use for the minor sentence in formal writing, it is as well to understand it, if only so that you can occasionally use it effectively for emphasis or perhaps in a piece of dialogue. It is also important that you be able to distinguish between the minor sentence, which is acceptable, and the fragmentary expression, which is not.

15 A MINOR SENTENCE is an acceptable pattern of expression which nevertheless lacks either a subject or a finite verb, or both. There is no difficulty, however, in supplying the missing element or elements from context. The minor sentence (like the major) is grammatically independent.

An expression which we call a minor sentence is usually one of four kinds:

1. Exclamations: Oh! Well, I never! Heavens!
2. Responses to questions: Yes. No. Perhaps. Please. Who is the best-looking boy in the room? John. What is your favourite food? Spaghetti.
3. Imperatives (commands or requests) when the subject is not stated: Come here. Never mind. Please do not smoke. Bring it with you.
4. Proverbial expressions or aphorisms which are so much a part of the language as to be universally understood: Easy come, easy go. Now or never. In a pig's eye!

Such sentences may sometimes be rhetorically effective, though generally they are of little practical value in expository writing.

16 Fragments

Frag Be careful to distinguish between acceptable minor sentences and unacceptable FRAGMENTS:

> frag: I did not attend the meeting. Because I felt that it would be a waste of time.

The "because" clause is a fragment; the period after *meeting* should be changed to a comma so that the subordinate clause can take its rightful place in the sentence. (Note, however, that "Because I felt that it would be a waste of time," like many other fragments, would be acceptable in a different context, for example if it were the answer to an immediately preceding question: Why didn't I go to the meeting? Because I felt that it would be a waste of time.)

> frag: It was a terrible scene. One that I will never forget.

The clause beginning with *one* should be linked to the preceding independent clause with a comma, not separated from it by a period; it can then take its rightful place as a noun clause in apposition to *scene.*

> frag: She gave me back the ring. Being of a forgiving nature.

The participial phrase beginning with *being* is not a separate sentence but an adjective modifying *She*: it should be introduced by a comma, or even moved to the beginning of the sentence:

> Being of a forgiving nature, she gave me back the ring.

The fragments in these examples (which tend to come after the independent clauses with which they should be joined) are not satisfyingly complete patterns of intonation, and therefore should not be treated as minor sentences.

Exercise 15–16

Indicate whether the second group of words in each of the following pairs of groups is a minor sentence or a fragment.

1. He stayed in the parking place. Until the time on the meter had run out.
2. Just look at the way she's dressed. Good heavens!
3. You say you've never seen this man? Never?
4. He decided to stay in bed until eleven. It being a Sunday, after all.
5. How much wood can a woodchuck chuck? Plenty.

---

17 A MAJOR SENTENCE is grammatically independent and contains at least two essential structural elements: a subject and a finite verb (see #1a).

17a The SUBJECT is (as the word suggests) that which is talked about. More precisely, it is the source of the action or the possessor of the state of being indicated by the finite verb.

> *Rosa* saw the car. (*Rosa* is the source of the action of seeing.)
> *We* were resting halfway up the mountain. (*We* indicates those in possession of the state of rest.)

> *Dick and Jane* are skiing. (*Dick and Jane* indicates those involved in the activity of skiing.)

If in doubt, ask the question *Who?* or *What?* followed by the finite verb; the answer will be the subject of the sentence:

> Who saw? *Rosa* saw. Who was resting? *We* were resting. Who was skiing? *Dick and Jane* were skiing.

The subject of a sentence will normally be one of the following: noun, pronoun, noun clause, gerund, or infinitive (see Chapter II if you do not understand these terms):

> The *cow* chewed slowly. (noun)
> *He* likes to discuss politics. (pronoun)
> *That the firm is solvent* is obvious from these records. (noun clause)
> *Swimming* is an excellent exercise. (gerund)
> *To study* a text closely is the only way to appreciate it fully. (infinitive)

17b The FINITE VERB is the focal point of the sentence. It is that form of the verb which is "limited" by the NUMBER and PERSON of its subject and by the MOOD and TENSE desired by the speaker or writer; hence its name, FINITE. (See also #6a.)

> The teacher *described* the examination.
> We *rested* halfway up the mountain.

The verb answers the question formed by the subject followed by *What?* or *Did what?*

> The teacher did what? The teacher *described*. We did what? We *rested*.

17c In a sentence whose main verb is TRANSITIVE, a DIRECT OBJECT is required to complete the pattern. In such sentences, therefore, three sentence elements, not just two, are essential. (For discussion of transitive verbs, see #8a. See also #1b.) The direct object answers the question formed by the finite verb followed by *What?*

> Described what? Described the *examination*.

Like the subject, the object may be a noun, pronoun, clause, gerund, or infinitive:

He likes *flowers.* (noun)
The dog accepted *him* as master. (pronoun)
The supervisor knew *that she was a good worker.* (noun clause)
He enjoys *playing* golf. (gerund)
They decided *to go.* (infinitive)

17d Similarly, after a LINKING verb a third element, a COMPLE-MENT, is also essential to complete the pattern. (See #1d and #8d.) This complement will be a predicate noun or a predicate adjective:

She is a *doctor.* (predicate noun)
He became a *lawyer.* (predicate noun)
He remained a *student* for three more years. (predicate noun)
She is very *intelligent.* (predicate adjective)
He became *impatient.* (predicate adjective)
He remained *unconvinced.* (predicate adjective)

These three elements—subject, finite verb, and object or complement—are the bare bones of the structure of the major sentence. They are closely tied in the ways discussed above, with the finite verb as the focal and uniting element.

Exercise 17abcd
In each of the following sentences, label the essential elements: subjects (s.), finite verbs (v.), direct objects (d.o.), and complements (c.).

1. 1979 was a federal election year.
2. Hubert ate five hot-dogs, and soon felt sick.
3. The east and the west must cooperate on this project.
4. Only those in good condition can survive such a gruelling test.
5. The provincial premiers are holding a meeting this summer.
6. Appearance on the best-seller list is no guarantee of quality.
7. It rained cats and dogs.
8. Student government is not a suitable activity for the timid.
9. Geologists collect rocks, frequently braving hazardous conditions to do so.

10. Does the honours program in your department require a graduating essay?

17e Other grammatical elements put flesh on the bones. Such elements are called MODIFIERS, because they limit or describe each of the modified elements so as to modify—that is, change—the listener's or reader's idea of them (see also #1e). The bare bones of a thought can be conveyed in such a sentence as the following:

> The house was sturdy. (subject, finite verb, complement)

By adding modifiers, a writer can enlarge the reader's knowledge of the material being presented and give precision and clarity to the sentence, as well as improving its style and varying its pattern of intonation:

> The large house which the Smiths built on the brow of Murphy's Bluff was so sturdy that even the icy blasts of the continual north wind in December and January made no impression on it.

Breaking this sentence up, we can see how its various elements work:

> The (definite article, specifying a particular house)
> large (adjective describing the house)
> house (noun as essential element: subject)
> which the Smiths built on the brow of Murphy's Bluff (adjectival clause further modifying *house*)
> was (linking verb as essential element)
> so (adverb modifying the adjective *sturdy*)
> sturdy (predicate adjective modifying *house*; essential element—complement—after linking verb)
> that even the icy blasts of the continual north wind in December and January made no impression on it. (adverbial clause further modifying *sturdy*)

Note that the adjectival clause itself contains two prepositional phrases (*on the brow,* adverbial prepositional phrase modifying the verb *built* and answering the question Where? and *of Murphy's Bluff,* adjectival prepositional phrase modifying the noun *brow* and answering the question Which? or

What?); and that the adverbial clause similarly contains three more prepositional phrases (*of the continual north wind*: adjectival; *in December and January*: adverbial; *on it*: adverbial). As this sentence illustrates, modifiers are of two kinds: *adverbial* and *adjectival*.

17f ADVERBIAL modifiers commonly answer the questions How? When? Where? Why? To what degree?

> He moved very slowly because the fog was exceedingly thick.

Moved how? *Slowly.* To what degree slowly? *Very* slowly. Why slowly? *Because the fog was exceedingly thick.* To what degree thick? *Exceedingly* thick.

> He soon moved to the suburbs.

Moved when? *Soon.* Moved where? *To the suburbs.*

Adverbial modifiers, as these examples illustrate, may be single words, phrases, or clauses:

> words: very, slowly, exceedingly, soon
> phrases (prepositional): to the suburbs
> clauses: because the fog was exceedingly thick

See also #10.

17g ADJECTIVAL modifiers commonly answer the questions Which one? What kind? How many?

> Thinking back, I remembered that the man who spoke to us last night said that lazy people will never attempt to plod through five years of night school to obtain certificates of professional standing.

Which man? *The man who spoke to us last night.* Which night? *Last* night. What kind of people? *Lazy* people. How many years? *Five* years. What kind of school? *Night* school. What kind of certificate? Certificate *of professional standing.* What kind of standing? *Professional* standing. The phrase *thinking back* is also an adjectival modifier describing the subject, *I.*

Adjectival modifiers, like adverbial modifiers, may be single words, phrases, or clauses:

single words: last, lazy, five, night, professional

phrases:

   prepositional: of professional standing

   participial: thinking back

clauses (relative):   who spoke to us last night

Exercise 17efg

Indicate whether each of the italicized elements in the following sentences is adjectival or adverbial.

1. Everyone *who saw the program* agreed that it was *good*.
2. The main point *of the speech* was lost *in all the verbiage*.
3. *Before you hand in an assignment,* be sure to proofread it *very carefully*.
4. *In the afternoon* I find a cup of tea *refreshing*.
5. *Thinking the game was over,* he threw down his racquet.

See also #9.

17h There is also what is called an ABSOLUTE CONSTRUCTION, a kind of modifying phrase that is grammatically independent of the rest of the sentence, but yet a part of its thought. Although absolute constructions are strictly speaking neither adjectival nor adverbial, they function much as a sentence adverb does, modifying the rest of the sentence by hovering over it like an umbrella. The most common kind of absolute construction consists of a noun followed by a participle:

> *All things considered,* it was not a successful experiment.
> Jeffy, *his face and hands washed and his hair combed,* sat down with the adults.
> Janet insisted on checking the figures yet again, *she being a perfectionist.*

Often a participial form of the verb *be* is omitted before a complement in an absolute phrase:

> *The table* (being) *set,* the guests were called in to dinner.
> *His hair* (being) *unkempt and his arm* (being) *in a sling,* the colonel directed the rescue party.

Some absolute phrases begin with infinitives:

To tell the truth, I was inadequately prepared.

See also #11f.

18 Kinds of Sentences

Sentences are usually classified as simple, compound, complex, and compound-complex.

18a SIMPLE sentences have one subject and one finite verb, and therefore contain only one clause, an independent clause:

Denis works.

The boat leaks.

The dilapidated old building collapsed during the night.

The subject or the verb, or both, can be compound—that is, consist of more than one part—but the sentence containing them will still be simple:

Jules and Kim left early. (compound subject)
He *watched and waited.* (compound verb)
The *sergeant and his men moved* down the hill *and crossed* the river. (compound subject, compound verb)

18b COMPOUND sentences in effect consist of two or more simple sentences—that is, independent clauses—linked together by co-ordinating conjunctions, by punctuation, or by both:

The starter's flag fell and the race began.

The clouds massed thickly against the hills; soon the rain fell in torrents.

He wanted to go by plane, but she insisted on taking a ship.

Gabriel's patience and persistence worked: he not only won the prize but also earned his competitors' respect. (compound subject in the first clause, compound verb in the second)

The day was warm, the breeze was mild, and everyone had a a good time.

18c COMPLEX sentences consist of one independent clause and one or more subordinate clauses; in the following examples, the subordinate clauses are italicized:

> He claimed *that he was innocent*. (noun clause as direct object)
> She left *before the party was over*. (adverbial clause modifying *left*)
> Ivan is the one *who is most likely to win*. (adjectival clause modifying *one*)
> Anita, *who is the most intelligent*, scored highest. (adjectival clause modifying *Anita*)
> *When the time came*, he put his belongings in the suitcase *which he was carrying*. (adverbial clause modifying *put*; adjectival clause modifying *suitcase*)
> *Although it was late*, they decided to start anyway. (adverbial clause of concession, in effect modifying the whole sentence)

Note that subordinate clauses are most often introduced by some subordinating word, such as a relative pronoun (*who, which*) or a subordinating conjunction (*before, when, although*). But note that, when the meaning is clear, such particles as the *that* introducing the noun clause, or the relative pronouns *that* or *which*, can be omitted:

> He claimed *he was innocent*.
> . . . the suitcase *he was carrying*.

The clauses in question nevertheless remain subordinate.

18d COMPOUND-COMPLEX sentences consist of two or more independent clauses and one or more subordinate clauses:

> Because he knew that the job was important, he began very carefully, but as time passed he grew impatient and therefore he failed to obtain the results he had hoped for.

Analyzing this example:

> Because he knew (adverbial clause)
> that the job was important (noun clause)
> he began very carefully (independent clause)
> but (co-ordinating conjunction)
> as time passed (adverbial clause)
> he grew impatient (independent clause)

and (co-ordinating conjunction)
therefore (conjunctive adverb)
he failed to obtain the results (independent clause)
[that] he had hoped for (adjective clause)

Exercise 18
Label each of the following sentences as simple, compound, complex, or compound-complex.

1. Although Canada has a vast territory, its population is relatively small.
2. Nobody is going to give you something for nothing.
3. The man who fixed my car yesterday is the same one I took it to last year.
4. It never rains but it pours.
5. Few things are more pleasant than a lovingly prepared and carefully served elegant meal consisting of several courses, consumed in good company, with soft background music, and accompanied by noble wines.
6. He saw the book he wanted on the top shelf, but he couldn't reach it.
7. Josephine decided against going for a ride in his flying machine.
8. A Philosophy major may learn to think clearly and may even acquire a sense of cultural history, but when he graduates he will probably have difficulty finding a job that makes use of his training.
9. Whether violence on television is responsible for violent behaviour in children, or even in adults, is debatable.
10. Northern oil and gas deposits have created a mixture of benefits and problems for Canadians and Americans alike.

---

19 Sentence Structure and Analysis

One of the best ways to acquire greater confidence and facility in writing effectively—as well as to increase your ability both to avoid committing errors and to catch those committed inadvertently—is to analyze your own and others' sentences as often as you can. The more thoroughly you understand how sentences work—sentences of whatever kind—the better able you will be to write sentences that are both effective and correct. The principal aim of our discussions and examples has been to foster such an understanding—and of course a working grammatical vocabulary has been and will continue to be essential.

A good test of a sentence is a grammatical analysis of its structure. It should be easy to see at a glance the grammatical links that tie together all the parts of a sentence (words, phrases, clauses) into a coherent and unified pattern. Analysis will enable you to account for *each word*: no essential element should be missing, nothing should be left over, and the grammatical relations among all the parts should be clear. If these conditions are not met, then the sentence in question is almost sure to be incorrect—or at least in some way inadequate or unsatisfactory.

The first step in the process of analysis is to establish the elemental structure, that is, the SUBJECT, the FINITE VERB, and the OBJECT or COMPLEMENT, if any. (If the sentence is not a simple sentence, of course, there will be more than one set of these essential parts.) Then you can proceed to the modifiers of these elements, and next, to modifiers of modifiers. Finally, if any of the modifiers are themselves phrases or clauses, these too should be broken down. The following examples show one kind of convenient arrangement for examining the structure of a sentence.

19a   **The angry coach severely punished the wayward goalie.**

Subject	Finite Verb	Object or Complement	Adjectival Modifier	Adverbial Modifier
coach	punished	goalie (direct object of verb *punished*)	The (modifies *coach*) angry (modifies *coach*) the (modifies *goalie*) wayward (modifies *goalie*)	severely (modifies verb *punished:* "how?")

This most beautiful summer is now almost gone.

Subject	Finite Verb	Object or Complement	Adjectival Modifier	Adverbial Modifier
summer	is (linking verb)	gone (predicate adjective as complement)	This (demonstrative adj. modifies *summer*) beautiful (adj. modifies *summer*)	most (modifies adj. *beautiful*: "to what degree?") now (modifies verb *is:* "when?") almost (modifies adj. *gone:* "to what degree?")

The very befuddled Roger realized that driving a car was not easy.

Subject	Finite Verb	Object or Complement	Adjectival Modifier	Adverbial Modifier	Other
Roger	realized	that ... easy (noun clause as direct obj.)	The (modifies *Roger*) befuddled (modifies *Roger*)	very (modifies adj. *befuddled*)	
driving (gerund)	was (linking verb)	easy (predicate adj. as complement)		not (modifies adj. *easy*)	that (in the noun clause, a subordinating conjunction)

In the last example, the items below the dotted line belong to the subordinate clause in this complex sentence.

19b For more complicated sentences, you may find that a different scheme of analysis is more convenient, one such as the following, for example, where the sentence is written out vertically:

When the canoe trip ended, Philip finally realized that the end of his happy summer was almost upon him.

complex sentence	Ind. cl.	Sub. cl. (adv.)	When — conj.	Subordinating / Intro. sub. cl.
			the — art.	mod. *trip*
			canoe — adj.	mod. *trip*
			trip — noun	subj. of *ended*
			ended — verb	finite v. of cl. / Intrans.
			Philip — noun (proper)	subj. of ind. cl.
			finally — adv.	mod. *realized*
			realized — verb	finite v. of cl. / trans.
		Sub. cl. (n.) dir. obj. of verb	that — conj.	subordinating / intro. noun cl.
			the — art.	mod. *end*
			end — noun	subj. of *was*
			of — prep.	prep. phrase, adj., mod. *end*
			his — adj. (pron.)	mod. *summer*
			happy — adj.	mod. *summer*
			summer — noun	obj. of prep.
			was — verb (linking)	finite v. of clause
			almost — adv.	mod. adj. phr. *upon him*
			upon — prep.	Prep. phr. / adj. compl. after linking verb
			him — pron.	obj. of prep.

As you can see, this method virtually forces you to account for the grammatical function of every word in the sentence.

19c Another way to analyze sentences is to use the old but still serviceable diagramming method. This method does have its drawbacks: there is no way to distinguish between adjective and adverb, for example, unless you label each one; and it also requires learning a separate and sometimes complicated system. Nevertheless, it can be usefully graphic in revealing the workings of a sentence. Here are sample diagrams of the most common kinds of sentences:

1. Simple Sentences

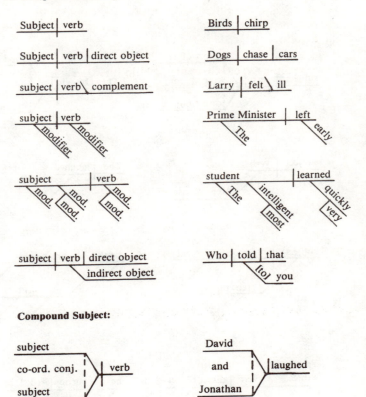

Compound Subject:

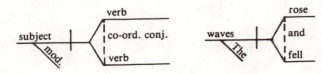

Compound Verb:

Compound Object:

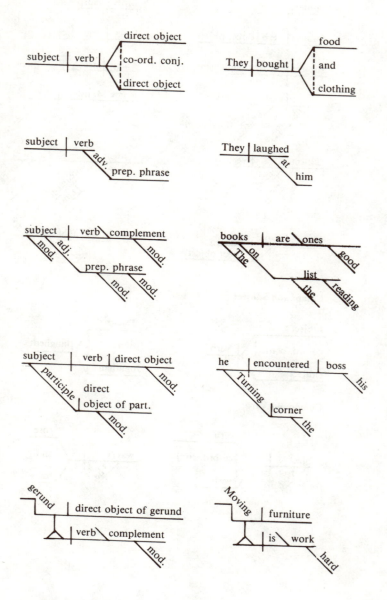

Infinitive Phrase as Noun:

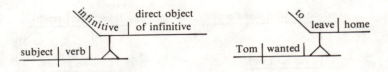

Infinitive Phrase as Adjective:

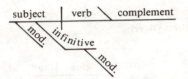 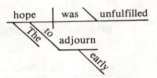

Infinitive Phrase as Adverb:

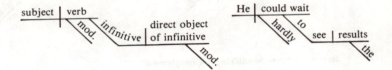

2. Complex Sentences

Noun Clause as Direct Object:

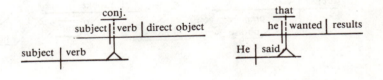

Noun Clause as Object of Preposition:

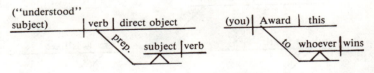

Relative Clause Modifying the Subject:

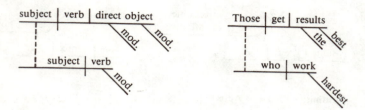

Relative Clause Modifying a Direct Object:

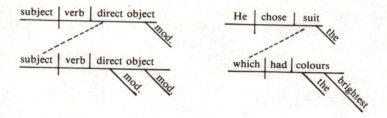

Relative Clause Modifying a Complement:

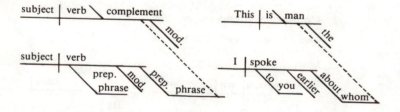

Adverbial Clause:

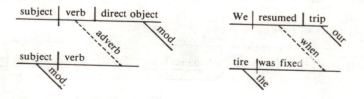

3. Compound Sentences

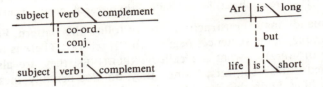

4. The various kinds of compound-complex sentences are diagrammed following similar patterns.

Grammatical analysis, by whatever method, is not an end in itself. Its purpose is to give you insight into the accepted structures of the basic unit of communication, the sentence, and to enable you to construct sound sentences and to discover and eliminate errors in your writing. As you become more familiar with the analytic process and with the demands of correct sentence structure, you will find the process becoming automatic and the elimination of errors immediate.

Exercise 19
Analyze the following sentences by each of the three methods suggested. This should give you a clearer sense of the advantages and disadvantages of each method; then you can decide which one you prefer.

1. Police rushed to the scene of the accident.
2. A chinook is a warm wind blowing eastward off the Rocky Mountains.
3. Many potentially good films are spoiled by sensationalism.
4. Both the beaver and the maple leaf are Canadian emblems.
5. Although he was discouraged, Joel persevered, and after a few more tries he succeeded in clearing the two-metre bar.

---

20 Order of the Essential Elements

Subject, finite verb, and object or complement appear in that order in most sentences. This order has proved itself to be the most direct and forceful pattern of expression.

I (subject) read (finite verb) the report (object).
Mr. Stevens (subject) is (finite verb) an architect (complement).
That tree (subject) looks (finite verb) diseased (complement).

Some idiomatic constructions do not follow this pattern. For example, some sentences begin with "It is" or "There is (or *are* or *were*)"—what are called EXPLETIVES: they are also called "false subjects," since they do not actually mean anything, but rather provide a way to invert the normal structure of sentences:

It is said that life begins at forty.
It is difficult to succeed.
There is no plumbing in the cabin.
There were twenty-five students in the class.

In expletive constructions with *there,* the number of the verb is determined by the real subject, which follows the verb (see also #7e); the real subject can be found by converting the sentences to the normal pattern:

No *plumbing* is in the cabin.
Twenty-five *students* were in the class.

Note: Such expletive constructions are often unnecessarily wordy; use them only when they are clearly preferable to the alternatives. (See #59.)

Other exceptions to the common patterns of subject-verb-object or -complement can be used to create special stylistic effects, to achieve special emphasis, and to introduce occasional pleasing variations. Any pattern that departs from the usual one almost inevitably calls attention to itself; for that reason such variations are only rarely appropriate in normal prose, though in poetry, for example, they can sometimes be very effective:

Discouraged (complement) he (subject) may have been (verb), but he pressed on with the job.
Happy (complement) was (verb) the day (subject) when she received her diploma.
"Such thoughts (direct object) to Lucy I (subject) will give (verb) ...." (—Wordsworth)
"No motion (object) has (verb) she (subject) now ...." (—Wordsworth)
Thirty days (object) hath (verb) September (subject) ....

21 Order of Modifiers

21a Adjectival Modifiers

Analysis shows that in normal expression single-word or compound adjectives usually precede the nouns they modify:

> The *weather* map shows a *cold* front moving into the *northern* prairies.

One would never say "the map weather" or "a front cold" or "the prairies northern." Certain deviations from this standard pattern are possible, but should not be used very often; for example:

> He had faith *extraordinary.*
> His friend, *faithful and true,* came at once to his aid.

(And note such phrases as *Governor General, court-martial.*) Other kinds of adjectival modifiers reverse the adjective-noun order.

Adjectival (relative) clause:

> He is an inspector *who believes in being very thorough.* (modifies *inspector*)

Adjectival prepositional phrase:

> The president *of the company* will address the employees at ten o'clock. (modifies *president*)

Infinitive:

> The time *to build* is now! (modifies *time*)

In normal usage, the only adjectival modifier not restricted in its position relative to the noun it modifies is the participial phrase:

> *Having had abundant experience,* Kenneth applied for the job.
> Kenneth, *having had abundant experience,* applied for the job.
> Kenneth applied for the job, *having had abundant experience.*

Such a variety of possible positions enables you to choose, and your choice will be guided by your taste and by stylistic appropriateness. This movability of the participial phrase makes it a popular device for introducing variety into one's writing, but it is not without its dangers for the writer: see #24a.

21b Adverbial Modifiers

Adverbial modifiers are almost always movable:

> *Because she likes drama,* Sue often goes to the theatre.
> Sue, *because she likes drama,* often goes to the theatre.
> Sue often goes to the theatre, *because she likes drama.*

Common Sentence Errors and Weaknesses

22
frag
cs
run-on
The three most serious sentence errors are the *fragment,* the *comma splice,* and the *run-on* sentence. The members of this unholy trinity are usually felt to be signs of illiteracy, and therefore they must be assiduously avoided by those who care about the quality of their writing. The *fragment* has already been discussed, along with the minor sentence, which it resembles: see #15 and #16. The *comma splice* and the *run-on,* though they are actually errors caused by a failure to understand *sentences,* are nevertheless discussed under *punctuation,* since they require attention to punctuation marks: see #33e and #33j. See also Chapter XI.

Other sentence errors, less serious but nevertheless to be avoided, are analyzed and illustrated in the sections that follow.

23 Misplaced Modifiers
mm

23a As already noted, there is some flexibility in the possible arrangement of the parts of a sentence; adverbial modifiers especially can often move about. Because of this flexibility, a modifier—whether a word, a phrase, or a clause—is sometimes placed where it conveys a meaning not intended by the writer or where it is linked to a word it cannot logically modify. Note the changes in meaning that result from the different placement of the word *only* in the following sentences:

> Only his son works in Halifax. (No other members of his family work there.)
> His only son works in Halifax. (He has no other sons.)
> His son only works in Halifax. (He does not live in Halifax, but commutes.)
> His son works only in Halifax. (He works in no other place.)

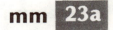

One therefore must consider carefully the placing of such modifiers—especially adverbs—in order to say precisely what one intends. The following sentence demonstrates how misplacement can result in absurdity:

> mm: He watched the sun set at the beach.

Obviously the sun does not set at the beach. The adverbial phrase *at the beach* can logically modify the finite verb *watched* but not the finite verb *set*. The error can be corrected by changing the clause *the sun set* to a noun—*the sunset*—or by moving the phrase *at the beach* to the beginning of the sentence, nearer the verb it modifies and away from the verb it cannot logically modify:

> *Clear:*   He watched the sunset at the beach.
> *Clear:*   At the beach he watched the sun set.

Here is another example; the writer found himself in a tangle of modifiers, and placed an adverbial modifier in a position that resulted in ambiguity and confusion:

> mm: A man soon learns not to scatter his clothes about after he is married in the bathroom.

The distortion in meaning here is obvious: the adverbial prepositional phrase *in the bathroom* has been so placed that it seems to modify the finite verb *is married* instead of the infinitive *to scatter*. Revising the sentence makes the intended meaning come through clearly:

> *Clear:*   After he is married, a man soon learns not to scatter his clothes about in the bathroom.

It is best to keep modifiers and the words they modify as close together as possible. Note that in this example the adverbial clause *after he is married* could also be placed—between commas—following *learns,* still leaving the adverbial phrase and the infinitive it modifies next to each other. Here is yet another example of carelessly placed adverbial modifiers causing ambiguity and conveying an unintended meaning:

> mm: We visited the cottage *in Stratford* where Will Shakespeare courted Anne Hathaway *last summer.*

Does the writer mean to convey that Will courted Anne last year? Obviously not—yet that is what the sentence says. Further, are we meant to think of Stratford or of the cottage as the place where the courtship took place? As the sentence stands the point is ambiguous. Revised, the sentence states precisely what the writer intended:

> *Clear:* Last summer in Stratford we visited the cottage where Will Shakespeare courted Anne Hathaway.

Here is an example of an adjective awkwardly out of place:

> *mm:* Love is a *difficult* emotion to express in words.
> *Clear:* Love is an emotion (that is) difficult to express.

And an example of a misplaced relative clause:

> *mm:* In 1683, the first St. Cecilia's Day festival was held in London, which is a festival of the performing arts.

London is a festival? Perhaps—especially to those trying to lure tourists. But what the writer of this sentence meant was something else:

> *Clear:* In 1683, the first St. Cecilia's Day festival, (which is) a festival of the performing arts, was held in London.

23b Be particularly careful with such adverbs as *only, almost, merely,* and *even.* Colloquially we toss these around like tiddlywinks, but in formal writing we should put them where they clearly mean what we want them to:

> *mm:* Hardy *only* wrote novels as a sideline; his main interest was poetry.
> *Clear:* Hardy wrote novels *only* as a sideline; his main interest was poetry.
> *mm:* The students *almost* washed thirty cars last Saturday.
> *Clear:* The students washed *almost* thirty cars last Saturday.

23c One particular kind of misplaced modifier is what is called a SQUINTING modifier. This error occurs when a word or phrase occupies a position between two elements, either of which it could modify—but the reader cannot be sure which one was intended. That is, a modifier "squints" so that one cannot tell which way it is looking, resulting in awkward ambiguity.

Squinting: It was so hot *for a week* we did hardly any work at all.

Which clause does the adverbial phrase modify? Although the meaning would be about the same either way, no reader should be subjected to such ambiguity. Sometimes one is tempted to mend the flaw by putting a comma before or after the squinting modifier, but that is like putting a band-aid on a serious wound: very seldom can a comma be effective; in fact, it usually makes the problem worse because it makes the sentence sound awkward. It is much better to revise somehow. Here, simply inserting a *that* removes the ambiguity at once:

Clear: It was so hot that for a week we did hardly any work at all.

Clear: It was so hot for a week that we did hardly any work at all.

Another example:

Squinting: My father advised me *now and then* to invest in stocks.

With this kind of squinting modifier, rearrangement is necessary:

Clear: My father now and then advised me to invest in stocks.

Clear: My father advised me to invest now and then in stocks.

Even a modifier at the end of a sentence can in effect "squint," be ambiguous. When rearrangement does not work, substantial revision will be necessary:

Ambiguous: He was upset when she left for more reasons than one.

Clear: He was upset for more reasons than one when she left.

Clear: He had more than one reason to be upset when she left.

Clear: He was upset because she had more than one reason for leaving.

Note: An awkwardly split infinitive is also caused by a kind of misplaced modifier; see #11b.

Exercise 23

Revise the following sentences to eliminate awkwardness resulting from misplaced modifiers.

1. His outbursts were only viewed as signs of bad temper.
2. I vowed to never discriminate against children when I became an adult.
3. He decided that on this day he would skip dinner entirely in the morning.
4. I could see my grandfather coming through the window.
5. He was naturally upset by her remark.
6. They discussed rebuilding the hotel for three days but decided against it.
7. Another reason why David lives a barren emotional and social life more pertinent to the theme of this essay is his thwarted love for Judith.
8. A piano stands in the centre of the stage with its outline only visible to the audience in the darkness.
9. Farmer Jones only plowed three acres yesterday.
10. It merely seemed a few days before they were back again.

24 Dangling Modifiers

dm A dangling modifier is one that has no actual word in the rest of the sentence to hook on to, but only an implied or obviously incorrect one (it is similar to a pronoun without an antecedent); it is therefore said to "dangle," to be left hanging there, grammatically unattached. Most dangling modifiers are verbal phrases; be particularly careful with them when you write.

24a Dangling participial phrases:

> dm: *Striding* aggressively into the room, my eyes fell upon the figure cowering in the corner.

The participial phrase *striding aggressively into the room* is adjectival, and therefore it wants a noun to modify; it usually picks the subject of the adjacent clause, here *eyes*. One's eyes may be said, figuratively, to "fall" on something, but they

can scarcely be said to "stride." If one were to say, "Striding aggressively into the room, my eyes tripped over the edge of the carpet," the absurdity would be immediately obvious. To avoid the unintentionally humorous dangler, simply change the participial phrase to a subordinate clause:

> *As I strode aggressively into the room,* my eyes fell upon the figure cowering in the corner.

Or, if you wish to keep the effect of the opening participial phrase, merely rephrase the following clause so that its subject is the logical word to be modified:

> *Striding* aggressively into the room, *I* at once directed my gaze toward the figure cowering in the corner.

Here is another example:

> dm: *Living* in a small town, there wasn't much to do for entertainment.

The participle *living,* along with the rest of its phrase, is left dangling because it has no noun to modify; "there" is an expletive, not a real subject. Something must be provided for the participle and its phrase to modify, in a logical way, or the sentence must be revised in some other way.

> Correct: *Living* in a small town, *we* had little to do for entertainment.
> Correct: Since we lived in a small town, there wasn't much to do for entertainment.

The first correction provides a true subject, *we,* for the participle to modify. The second correction changes the participial phrase to a subordinate clause with its own subject. Another example; the passive voice got this writer into trouble (see #6h):

> dm: *Looking* up to the open sky, not a cloud could be seen.
> Correct: *Looking* up to the open sky, *I* could not see a cloud.
> Correct: There was not a cloud to be seen in the open sky.

24b Dangling gerund phrases:

> dm: After *being* informed of the correct procedure, our attention was directed to the next steps.

The verbal phrase has no proper subject to modify, since obviously it is not "our attention" that was "informed." Again the lapse into the passive voice is at least partly to blame.

> *Correct:* After *being* informed of the correct procedure, *we* were directed to attend to the next steps.

But this is still passive and awkward. Such a sentence can be better revised another way:

> *Correct:* After informing us of the correct procedure, the instructor directed our attention to the next steps.

24c Dangling infinitive phrases:

> dm: *To follow* Freud's procedure, the speaker's thoughts must be fully known.

Passive voice is again the culprit, depriving the infinitive of a logical word to modify.

> *Correct:* *To follow* Freud's procedure, *one* must know the speaker's thoughts fully.

Another example:

> dm: *To make* the mayor's plan work, it requires the people's cooperation.

The error in this example is more complicated, since the pronoun *it,* to which the infinitive phrase seems to be attached, has no antecedent (see #4). The infinitive phrase can be treated as a noun phrase, or the sentence can be revised in some other way:

> *Correct:* To make the mayor's plan work will require the people's cooperation.
> *Correct:* If the mayor's plan is to work, the people will have to cooperate.

24d Dangling elliptical clauses:

An elliptical clause is an adverbial clause that has been abridged so that its subject and verb are only "understood" or implied rather than stated; the subject of the independent clause then automatically serves also as the subject of the subordinate clause. If the implied subject is different from the

subject of the independent clause, the subordinate element will dangle, sometimes ludicrously:

> dm: Once in the army, a person's life is totally regimented.

It is not *a person's life* that is in the army, but a person himself. One can correct such a sentence by supplying a subject for the elliptical clause and making the subject of the independent clause agree logically with it:

> *Correct:*   Once *one* is in the army, *one* finds that his life is totally regimented.
> *Correct:*   Once a *person* is in the army, *his life* is totally regimented.

or by retaining the elliptical clause and making the subject of the independent clause conform to it:

> *Correct:*   Once in the army, a *person* finds that his life is totally regimented.

Another example:

> dm: When well oiled, put the parts of the rifle back together.

Here the understood subject is *the parts,* but the understood subject of the independent clause of this imperative sentence is *you.* Supply a subject for the elliptical clause and it will no longer dangle:

> *Correct:*   When the parts of the rifle are well oiled, put them back together.

24e Dangling prepositional phrases and appositives:
Prepositional phrases and appositives can also dangle. For example:

> dm: Like a child in a toy-shop, *it* is all she can bear not to touch everything.
> *Correct:*   Like a child in a toy-shop, she can hardly bear not to touch everything.

The dangerous indefinite *it* (see #5e) is again the troublemaker.

dm: A superb racing car, the engine of a Ferrari is a masterpiece of engineering.

"A superb racing car" seems to be in apposition with "engine"; but since it is illogical to equate an engine with an entire car, revision is necessary:

Correct: A superb racing car, a Ferrari has an engine that is a masterpiece of engineering.

(Note that one could not say "a Ferrari's engine," since the possessive form is adjectival and cannot serve as a noun to be modified (see # 2 and # 3a.)

Exercise 24

Revise the following sentences to eliminate dangling modifiers.

1. Feeling carefree and nonchalant, all my problems were forgotten.
2. In order to ski one must be outdoors, thereby being good for physical and mental health.
3. Réaumur introduced the idea of testing small sample rods and then studying their structure when fractured.
4. When not going to school or working, my hobbies range from athletics to automobiles.
5. The colonel began to send groups of reinforcements to the weakened position only to be ambushed along the jungle trails.

---

25 Mixed Constructions

mix A writer may occasionally begin a sentence with one construction and then absent-mindedly shift to a different construction. It is at least as awkward as changing horses in midstream. Such a lapse can easily occur in the heat of composition and rapid thought—though even then it argues a weak sentence sense and a failure to think clearly. If you find yourself apt to commit mixed constructions, some practice with sentence analysis may help (see #19).

> mix: Physical education can be enjoyable for both the non-competitive student as well as the competitive one.

In the latter part of this sentence the writer set up a *both ...
and* pattern, but then shifted to *as well as* instead of following
through with the *and*. Remedy: change *as well as* to *and,* or
omit the *both*.

> mix: Since Spain was a devout Catholic country, therefore most of its art was on religious themes.

This writer began with a subordinating *since,* but then used
therefore to introduce the second clause, which would be correct only if the first clause had been independent. Remedy:
drop either the *since* or the *therefore* (if *since,* the comma
must become a semicolon; See #33e).

Exercise 25
Revise the following sentences to eliminate mixed constructions.

1. Piranesi worked on a colossal scale, putting more emphasis on density and texture rather than on outline.
2. The reason for the drop in production was due to labour
   troubles.
3. It wasn't until five years later before he returned to the
   place again.
4. I found that the introductory part of the book to be very
   helpful.
5. The new styles were popular with both men and women
   alike.

---

26 Point of View—Shift in Perspective

pv Be consistent in your point of view within a sentence—and
shift usually from one sentence to the next, as well. Avoid
awkward or illogical shifts in the tense, mood, or voice of
verbs, and in the person and number of pronouns.

26a Shift in tense:

> pv: The professor *told* us what he expected of us and then he
> *leans* against the desk and *smirks*.

Change *leans* to *leaned,* and *smirks* to *smirked,* past tense like *told.*

26b Shift in mood:

> pv: If it *were* Sunday and I *was* through with my homework, I would go skiing with you.

The awkward shift from subjunctive to indicative can be corrected by changing *was* to *were.*

> pv: First *put* tab A in slot B; next *you will put* tab C in slot D.

Omit the *you will* to correct the shift from imperative to indicative.

26c Shift in voice:

> pv: The reader should not have to read a second time before some sense can be made of the passage.
> pv: We drove thirty miles to the end of the road, after which five more miles were covered on foot.

Such awkward shifts from active to passive could also be marked *pas* (see #6h). (Note that such shifts also cause an awkward shift of subject from one clause to the next.) These wobbly sentences can easily be restored to health and vigour by retaining the active voice:

> The reader should not have to read a passage a second time before he can make sense of it.
> We drove thirty miles to the end of the road and then covered another five miles on foot.

26d Shift in person of pronoun:

> pv: If *one* wants to learn about trees, *you* should study Forestry.

The shift from third to second person can be corrected by changing *you* to *one* or *he.* (This and the following pronoun errors could also be marked *agr*: see #4a).

26e Shift in number of pronoun:

> pv: If the committee wants *its* recommendations followed, *they* should have written *their* report more carefully.

The committee changed from a collective unit (*it*) to a collection of individuals (*they, their*); the committee should have been either singular or plural throughout.

> pv: If a job candidate dresses reasonably neatly and behaves with reasonable politeness, *their* chances of having a good interview are improved.

The singular *candidate* suddenly became a plural *their*; change it to *his*.

See also collective nouns, #7f.
See also #27a.

27 Faulty Parallelism

fp, //

27a Co-ordinate elements in a sentence should have the same grammatical form. If they differ from each other grammatically, the sentence will lack parallelism and therefore be awkward at best.

> fp: Mario is wealthy, handsome, and a bachelor.

Here the three elements following the copula *is* are co-ordinate in that they constitute a series of complements. But the first two are predicate adjectives (*wealthy, handsome*) and the third a predicate noun (*bachelor*). Here revision is easy: simply change the noun to an equivalent adjective:

> Mario is wealthy, handsome, and unmarried.

Sometimes the problem is more complicated:

> fp: Trolls were very large, ugly, hoarded treasure, killed for pleasure, and ate raw flesh.

Again a series of attributes follows a copulative verb, *were*. But after the first two, which are adjectives (*large, ugly*), the writer switched to verb phrases (*hoarded . . . killed . . . ate*). One cannot logically say "Trolls were hoarded treasure" or "Trolls were ate raw flesh," and note that "Trolls were killed for pleasure" completely changes the meaning. The writer no doubt intended to co-ordinate the verbs *hoarded, killed,* and *ate* with the verb *were,* but the placing of the second adjective, *ugly,* by itself, between commas, before those verbs, leads to a breakdown of parallel structure and creates confusion. Here is a possible correction:

> Trolls were large and ugly; they hoarded treasure, killed for pleasure, and ate raw flesh.

The co-ordinate parts of compound subjects, verbs, objects, and modifiers—whether or not these parts are joined by co-ordinating conjunctions—should also be parallel in form.

> fp: Eating huge meals, too many sweets, and snacking between meals can lead to obesity.

This sentence can be corrected either by making all three parts of the subject into gerunds:

> Eating large meals, eating too many sweets, and snacking between meals can lead to obesity.

or by using only the first gerund and following it with three parallel objects:

> Eating large meals, too many sweets, and between-meal snacks can lead to obesity.

Here is another example:

> fp: He described the computer in terms suggesting a deep affection for it and that also demonstrated a thorough-going knowledge of it.

Here the compound adjectival modifier has a participial phrase (*suggesting* . . .) for its first part and relative clause (*that demonstrated* . . .) for its second part. The best way to revise it would be to change the first part to a relative clause (*that suggested* . . .) to match the second part.

It is particularly easy for a careless writer to omit a second *that:*

> fp: Rachel of course has to tell Nick *that* her mother will be worrying about her and therefore she should get home as soon as possible.

Another *that* is needed before *therefore.* Here is another example:

> fp: Marvin was convinced *that* the argument was unsound and he could profitably spend some time analyzing it.

A second *that,* before *he,* corrects the error. In effect this error is not only a breakdown in parallelism but also an implied shift in point of view (see the preceding section); it could be marked *pv* as well as *fp;* it could also be marked *ambig.* In the second sentence, for example, the lack of a second *that* invites or at least allows the reader to take "he could profitably spend some time analyzing it" as an independent clause—expressing the writer's own opinion about what Marvin should do—rather than what the writer intended, a second subordinate clause expressing a part of Marvin's opinion. The same point applies to the sentence about Rachel.

27b One must be especially careful when using correlative conjunctions (see #13c):

> fp: Whether for teaching a child the alphabet or in educating an adult about the latest political development, television is the best device we have.

The constructions following the *whether* and the *or* should be parallel; change the *in* to *for.*

The correlative pair *not only . . . but also* can be particularly troublesome:

> fp: She not only corrected my grammar but also my spelling.

Such an error can be corrected either by repeating the verb *corrected* (or by adding some other appropriate verb, such as *criticized* or *repaired*) after *but also*:

> She not only corrected my grammar but also corrected my spelling.

or by moving *corrected* so that it occurs before *not only* rather than after it:

> She corrected not only my grammar but also my spelling.

Either method makes what follows the *not only* parallel in form to what follows the *but also.* Obviously the second version is more economical.

27c In any series of three or more parallel elements, make sure that little beginning words like prepositions, pronouns, and signs of the infinitive (*to*) precede either the first element alone, or each of the elements, and that necessary articles aren't omitted:

> fp: The car was equipped with a CB radio, stereo tape deck, an AM-FM radio, and a miniature television receiver.

The missing *a* before the second item breaks the parallelism.

> fp: He exhorted his followers to obey the rules, to think positively, and ignore criticism.

Since the *to* occurs in the first two phrases, it must either lead off *"to* ignore criticism" as well or be omitted from the second phrase.

Exercise 27

Correct any faulty parallelism in the following sentences.

1. Disagreements were not only apparent between clergymen and scientists, but between various elements of the church as well.
2. It is necessary that we tighten our belts and to try to control our spending.
3. We are told that we should eat more protein, less fat, and exercise regularly.
4. About 1750, it became clear to the French that the arrival of the few American traders was only the beginning and soon masses of settlers would follow and destroy the French empire in North America.
5. When she grows up she wants to be a teacher, a home-owner, and travel.

Co-ordination and Subordination: Logic, Emphasis, and Unity

28 Faulty Co-ordination

fc If unrelated or unequal elements—usually clauses—are presented as co-ordinate, the result is faulty co-ordination. Similarly, if two elements are joined by an inappropriate co-ordinating conjunction, the result is again faulty co-ordination—sometimes referred to as "loose" co-ordination. Here is an example of the first kind:

> fc: Watches are usually water-resistant *and* some models have the ability to glow in the dark.

There is no logical connection between the two clauses—other than that they both say something about watches. The ideas would be better expressed in two separate sentences. Note also that co-ordinating two such clauses produces a sentence **u** with little or no UNITY. Here is another example of faulty co-ordination—from a description of a particular jar—in which the resultant lack of unity is even more glaring:

> fc: One might find this kind of jar in a small junk shop *and* it can be used for anything from cotton balls to rings and things, or just to stand as a decoration.

Since there is no logical connection between the jar's location and its possible uses, the suggestion about the junk shop clearly belongs in another sentence.

The second kind of faulty co-ordination is a more common weakness:

> fc: Nationalism can affect the relations between nations by creating a distrustful atmosphere *and* an ambassador's innocent remark can be turned into an insult by a suspicious listener.

The *and* joining these two clauses misrepresents the relation between them; the second clause is not an additional fact, as the *and* implies, but rather an example or result of the fact stated in the first clause. Simply joining the two clauses with a semicolon would be preferable. Note that this compound sentence could also be changed to a complex one by changing **sub** the first independent clause to a subordinate clause:

> Because nationalism can affect the relations between nations by creating a distrustful atmosphere, an ambassador's innocent remark can be turned into an insult by a suspicious listener.

emph Such a version, however, probably does not reflect the EMPHASIS the writer intended; if anything, the first clause appears more important than the second. Here is a clearer example, from a student's description of how a particular scene in *Hamlet* should be staged:

> fc: In this scene Rosencrantz is the main speaker of the two courtiers; therefore he should stand close to Hamlet.

sub This sentence could be marked *sub* or *emph* as well as *fc,* in-
emph dicating that its logical emphasis would be more accurately expressed by subordinating one of the independent clauses. Since the positioning of the characters is clearly the main point, that idea should be expressed in an independent clause, the rest in a subordinate clause:

> Because in this scene Rosencrantz is the main speaker of the two courtiers, he should stand closer to Hamlet.

Granted that the *therefore* in the original sentence does express this relation, the sentence was nonetheless a compound one, tacitly equating the two clauses. Emphasis and clarity are much better served by acknowledging, by means of the syntax, the logically subordinate nature of the first clause. The original sentence, then, could also have been marked *log,* for LOGIC, though that would not have been a very precise indication of its weakness. Sometimes, however, *fc* and *log* are about equally applicable to an offending sentence. Consider this example:

log   fc, log: Alliteration is a very effective poetic device when used sparingly but appropriately.

The meaning expressed by the conjunction *but* in this sentence is entirely illogical, for it implies an opposition; it "says" that if one uses alliteration sparingly, one is then very likely to use it inappropriately—but just the opposite is more likely true: a poet who uses it sparingly will also probably be careful to use it appropriately. In this instance the writer should have used a simple and neutral *and* for a co-ordinating conjunction.

Another kind of faulty co-ordination is that which links several short independent clauses with co-ordinating conjunctions, mostly *and*'s; the result is a loose string of seemingly unrelated parts. Such sentences tend to ramble on and on:

Rambling: The ferry rates were increased and the bigger commercial vehicles had to pay more to use the ferry service and so the cost of transporting goods rose and the consumers who bought those goods had to pay more for them but they had to pay higher fares on the ferries as well and naturally most people were unhappy about it.

The data needed to make the point are here, but the ineffective syntax of the sentence leaves the poor reader floundering, trying to decipher the connections. The *but* seems to be used less for logic than for variety, and the vague *it* at the end effectively dissipates any emphasis the sentence might have had. A little judicious tinkering sorts out and rearranges the facts, shortens the sentence by half, reduces the five co-ordinating conjunctions to a pair of correlative conjunctions, reduces the six independent clauses to two independent and one subordinate, and achieves at least some emphasis at the end:

The increased ferry rates not only cost travellers more, but, since the commercial vehicles also had to pay more, the cost of transported goods rose as well, affecting all consumers.

Exercise 28(1)

Convert each of the following pairs of sentences into one sentence, subordinating one or the other with an appropriate subordinating conjunction. When possible, subordinate each part of a pair in turn.

1. The book was very well written. I did not find it rewarding.
2. The wind was very cold. He wore a heavy sweater.
3. It stopped snowing. He shovelled the driveway.
4. She read a good book. He played solitaire.
5. The meeting was contentious. A consensus was reached.

Exercise 28(2)

Revise the following sentences to eliminate faulty or loose co-ordination; keep in mind good subordination, unity, emphasis, and logic.

1. There are no windows in the room, and all lighting is from fluorescent fixtures.
2. Rachel is afraid of God and when Calla takes her to the Tabernacle service she goes crazy.
3. We want more than our neighbours and then buy the most ridiculous things.
4. Her experiments with chimpanzees were unusual but they were interesting.
5. The city's streets are well paved and some of them badly need repair.
6. He is a genius; some people claim that he is an impostor.
7. Texans are noted for their chauvinism and they often brag unreasonably about their state's virtues.
8. She prepared diligently for the examination and failed it the first two times, and then passed it with flying colours the third time.
9. Unemployment is unusually high and one should not expect to be hired at the first place one tries.
10. A sports car is one with unusual styling or high power or one with an unusually high price.

---

29 Logic

log   Clear and logical thinking is essential to clear and effective writing. For example, writers must be careful not to make sweeping statements unsupported by specific evidence: overgeneralization is one of the most common weaknesses in student writing. Writers must also make sure that the evidence they use is sound and that the authorities they cite are reliable. Such matters are particularly important in writing arguments (and in a sense all writing is argument, for every essay tries to convince a reader of something—if only the accuracy of the point of view being expressed). A writer must also avoid bad reasoning; such logical missteps as begging the question,

reasoning in a circle, jumping to conclusions, and leaning on false analogies can mar the effectiveness of an essay.

There are many ways in which logic is important even in something so small as a sentence. The problems discussed in the preceding sections, from Misplaced Modifiers on, have in part been problems in logic, as we have noted. (We discuss one other category in the next section, *Alignment*.) Here are some examples of other ways in which sentences can be illogical. (Some of these are discussed and illustrated elsewhere in the book as well, as noted below.)

Unsound reasoning leads to sentences like this:

> log: James's father was proud of him, for he had the boy's picture on his desk.

The conclusion may at first seem reasonable, but it would at least have to be qualified with a *probably,* or more evidence would have to be provided, for there are other possible reasons for the picture's being on the desk. James's mother could have put it there, for example, and the father just not bothered to remove it; perhaps he lacks the courage to do so. Or he could feel love for a lazy son, and therefore display the picture, without feeling pride. Or he could use it to feign love and pride, knowing inside that he does not feel those emotions.

> log: Wordsworth is *perhaps* the first English Romantic poet, *for* his major themes—man, nature, human life—are characteristic of the Romantic style of poetry.

To begin with, the word *perhaps* is pointless, for either the writer is making a point of Wordsworth's primacy and there is no "perhaps" about it, or there is no point to be made and the whole clause is superfluous. Even more important is the inadequate evidence given to substantiate the statement. If Wordsworth's use of themes common to Romanticism makes him first, then all Romantic poets are first. The writer probably meant something like this:

> Wordsworth is the first English Romantic poet to develop the major themes of the Romantic movement: man, nature, human life.

In the preceding example, muddy thinking was reflected by muddy writing. But even if a writer knows what he wants to say, he must be careful that the words he chooses and the ways he uses them actually communicate what he intended. For example:

> log: The town is surrounded on one side by the ocean.

Of course *surrounded* is illogical here; if the place were indeed surrounded, it would be an island. The correct word here is *bounded*. This error might equally well be designated an error in diction: see *ww* (Wrong Word) in Chapter XI.

> log: Having a car with bad spark plugs or points or a dirty carburetor causes it to run poorly and to use too much gas.

Here the sentence structure wins, the writer loses. The intention is clear enough, but the verb, *causes*, has as its subject the gerund *having*; consequently the sentence implies that mere possession of the car is what causes it to run poorly—as if one could borrow someone else's similar car and it would run well. The plugs and points and carburetor—clearly the real cause—are mere objects of the preposition *with,* and are therefore unable to do the syntactic job expected of them. A logical revision:

> Bad spark plugs or bad points or a dirty carburetor cause a car to run poorly and to use too much gas.

The parallelism was also faulty, for *points* alone would not have caused trouble (see #27).

> log: Throughout history man has been discussing and proposing theories about his purpose on earth, and thus far they can be divided into three general camps.

Here the pronoun *they,* being plural, has only one possible antecedent, *theories*. But one divides not theories, but men, into *camps*. To correct this, either change *camps* to *groups, classes,* or *categories,* or change *man* to *men* or *people*.

> log: The mood and theme play a very significant part in this poem.

This might be called an empty sentence; it would be illogical for the very *theme* of a poem to play other than a significant part in it.

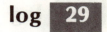

> log: For the next five years my memory is quite vague.

This sentence, taken from a student's autobiographical narrative, should have been caught during revision or proofreading. Obviously what was intended was this:

> My memory of the next five years is quite vague.

Sometimes a careless writer will let an extra word creep in that ruins an otherwise logical sentence:

> log: Alexander Graham Bell is known as the modern inventor of the telephone.

The writer was probably—perhaps subconsciously—thinking of the telephone as a *modern* invention, and the word just popped into the sentence. If we took the statement at face value, it would have to mean that there was also another, earlier, perhaps ancient, inventor of the telephone. The word *modern* must go.

> log: Captain Beard appears as more heroic, while MacWhirr is more stupid, but both would face anything just for duty's sake. *So* as skippers both are respected highly by their crews.

In this passage comparing the captains in two of Joseph Conrad's sea stories ("Youth" and "Typhoon"), the second sentence is a *non sequitur* (Latin for "it does not follow"), for the word *so*—an informal equivalent of *therefore*—tells us that MacWhirr's crew respect him because he is *more stupid,* which is unlikely. The writer clearly intended the *so* to hinge on the two captains' adherence to *duty,* which is reasonable; for that meaning to prevail, the first clause should have been subordinated:

> Although Captain Beard is heroic and MacWhirr stupid, they both would face anything for duty's sake; therefore they are highly respected by their crews.

Now the emphasis is clear and the logic no longer faulty. Nevertheless, you will notice that we have changed the first part of the sentence in another way: the comparisons using *more* were removed because they were illogical and incomplete. *Heroic* and *stupid* are not logical opposites; in fact, some heroes are heroic simply because they are stupid. But the original statements were also examples of incomplete comparison (see *comp* in Chapter XI). That is, to be logically complete, one would have to say that Beard is more heroic *than MacWhirr,* and MacWhirr more stupid *than Beard.* (Even if one reads between the lines and assumes that the two skippers are being compared, the implied contrast breaks down on the logical grounds already mentioned.) Here is an example of another kind of incomplete comparison that causes problems:

> log: French painting did not follow the wild and exciting forms of Baroque art as closely as most European countries.

Again the meaning is apparent but the syntax faulty. A reader should not have to read between the lines—or the words—in order to understand a sentence clearly. As stated, the sentence says either that "European countries followed the wild and exciting forms of Baroque art" to some degree or that "French painting followed most European countries more closely than they followed the wild and exciting forms of Baroque art," neither of which makes logical sense. The necessary completion of the comparison straightens out the syntax and permits the intended meaning to come through unambiguously:

> French painting did not follow the wild and exciting forms of Baroque art as closely as *did that of* most European countries.

Another kind of ambiguity appears in this sentence:

> log: Numerous scientific societies were founded in every developed country.

Once again the intended meaning is fairly clear, but the sentence could mean that each developed country had "numerous scientific societies," when the more probable and logical meaning is that "Numerous scientific societies were founded, at least one in every developed country." See *ambig* (Ambiguous) and *cl* (Clarity) in Chapter XI.

Be sure that your words and sentences say what you want them to say. Here is one more example of a failure to do that:

> log: They were a strong and hearty race, physically developed to withstand attacks from Indians.

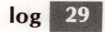

Nonsense. No amount of "physical development" will enable one to stop an arrow with safety. What the writer probably meant was something like this:

> They were a strong and hearty race, so physically developed as to be capable of successfully resisting Indian attack.

(*Hearty*, however, unless it means something rather different and irrelevant to this sentence, looks suspiciously redundant; the words *and hearty* could be dropped.)

> log: His lack of knowledge of the subject was visible on every page.

This example illustrates another way in which a sentence can be illogical. Once more the meaning is clear, but it is odd to think of a *lack* being *visible*. It would be preferable to say something like this:

> Every page revealed his ignorance of the subject.

Finally, make sure that nouns are inflected to agree logically with the context:

> log: All the students suffered mental stiffness as a result of the unusual exercise involved in using their brain.

Brain obviously must be changed to *brains* in order to conform logically to the sense.

Exercise 29

Analyze the errors in logic in the following sentences, then eliminate them by revising the sentences.

1. As he approached the shore, he felt a challenge between himself and the sea.
2. Milton's influence on other subsequent poets was very great.
3. Some auto accidents are unavoidable, but can be prevented by proper maintenance.
4. Shakespeare fashioned *A Midsummer Night's Dream* around the theme of love and created the characters and situations to illustrate it in the best possible way. Thus he freely used a variety of comic devices in developing the theme.

5. By the use of imagery, diction, symbolizing, and sound, we may also see the structure of the plot.

6. It employed the technique of using projected images on a screen and a corresponding taped conversation which visually enforced the lesson.

7. Its shape is a rectangle about three times as long as it is wide or high.

8. Through the use of too much abstract language, jargon, and clichés the clarity and effectiveness of this article have been destroyed.

9. As I think back to the days when we were in our early teens, we had a lot of fun together.

10. After his wife died, his paintings of excited forms changed to quiet ones.

---

30 Alignment

al Another kind of illogical sentence results when a writer tries to make words do work that their meanings will not permit. We call this error ALIGNMENT, meaning that two or more elements of a sentence are illogically or incongruously aligned with each other. Such errors often take the form of a verb saying something illogical about its subject. This is sometimes called faulty PREDICATION; that is, what is predicated about the subject is an impossibility. For example:

> al: Many new inventions and techniques occurred during this period.

An invention could, with some strain, be said to *occur*, but *techniques* do not *occur*. The sentence needs to be revised; one way is to use the passive voice:

> revised: During this period there were many new inventions, and many new techniques were developed [or *discovered*].

Another example:

> al: The setting of the play takes place in Denmark.
> revised: The play takes place in Denmark.
> better: The play is set in Denmark.

Usually errors in predication involve a form of the verb *be:*

> al: The amount of gear to take along is the first step to con-
> sider when planning a long hike.

But an *amount* cannot be a *step;* again, drastic revision is
needed:

> revised: The first step in planning a hike is to decide how
> much gear to take along.

Note that this also removes the other illogicality: one does not
consider a *step*; rather the considering, or deciding, *is* the
step.

> al: The value of good literature is priceless.

It is not the *value* that is priceless, but the *literature* itself.

> al: The cost of my used car was relatively inexpensive.
> revised: The cost of my used car was relatively low.
> revised: My used car was relatively inexpensive.

Other errors in alignment are not errors in predication, but
are similar:

> al: In narrative, the author describes the occurrences, environ-
> ment, and thoughts of the characters.

It is logical to speak of characters having thoughts and an
environment, but not *occurrences*; substitute the word
experiences.

> al: Its fine texture was as smooth and hard as a waterworn
> rock.

This, which illogically equates *texture* and *rock,* is also one
form of incomplete comparison (see *comp* in Chapter XI);
insert *that of* after *hard as*.

> al: Physical Education is one of the many things students can
> do to keep healthy.

But one does not *do* Physical Education; *take part in* or
engage in would suffice, though the sentence could be revised
in other ways as well.

> al: Beliefs such as being a Christian or a Jew or a Moslem or
> even an atheist should not cause anyone to be denied a job.

But *being* a Christian, etc., is not a *belief*. One could begin the sentence with *Being,* or one could recast it completely:

> revised: People should not be denied jobs because of their religious beliefs, be they Christian . . . or anything else.

Exercise 30

Revise the following sentences to remove illogical or incongruous alignments.

1. I decided not to buy it, for the price was too expensive.
2. Even religious principles were being enlightened, giving man the freedom he should have.
3. It is clear that this general conception of his ability is greatly underestimated.
4. The only source of light in the house came through the windows.
5. By taking Physical Education, students can learn what activities they can do in their leisure time.
6. The poem expresses the meaningless and useless achievements of war.
7. The character of the speaker in the poem seems weary and tired.
8. The need for such great effort on the part of the reader represents serious weakness in the writing.
9. Life and death was a constant idea in the back of the pioneers' minds.
10. He started university at a very young age.

---

31 Sentence Coherence

coh Although the word *coherence* is usually used to refer to the connection between sentences and between paragraphs, the parts of a sentence must also cohere, stick together. Each sentence fault discussed in the preceding sections is capable of making a sentence incoherent (the dictionary meanings *disjointed, illogical, confused, loose, inconsistent, disorganized*, and so forth, all apply). If a sentence lacks coherence, the fault probably lies in one or more of the following: faulty arrangement (word order, misplaced modifier), unclear or missing or illogical connections and relations between parts (faulty reference, lack of agreement, dangling modifier, faulty co-ordination, faulty logic, incongruous alignment), syntactic shift from one part to another (mixed construction, shift in point of view, faulty parallelism); or the weakness may be due to something that can only be labelled *awkward* or *unclear* (see *awk* and *cl* in Chapter XI). Consult these specific sections, as necessary, to ensure that your sentences are coherent within themselves.

Review Exercise: Chapters II and III

Revise the following sentences to eliminate the various errors and weaknesses they contain. Note that a sentence may have more than one thing wrong with it.

1. Our coach is overweight, Hungarian, overpaid, and over forty.
2. Borelli supposed that there was a tendency for celestial bodies to attract each other but a fluid pressure prevented this.
3. Shakespeare's *Othello* is a brilliant but tragic story of the betrayal of the Moor of Venice by his most trusted friend, Iago.
4. He has on an old worn coat which is far too big for him, but alterations are something he has neither money for nor feels the need to get done.
5. Age had not weakened or worn them out, but instead, it seemed to have given them a kind of strength.
6. The beginning of the eighteenth century was a period when the church had lost much of its power, and science and philosophy based upon science gained strength.
7. At the beginning, he played things very cautious.
8. The poet suggests that our lives are but a speck in time and there is nothing we can do about it.
9. Her success is credited to her slyness and wit which always prevails over her daughter's weaknesses.
10. Many people think of themselves as a well-educated person when they really are not.

11. He had been given instructions on how to repair the engine, but it did not do much good.
12. Vico's theories omitted many countries because they did not have the highly evolved pattern of civilization as Greece and Rome did.
13. It was not Shakespeare's intention to separate the world of reverie from the world of reality, but rather his desire to intermingle them.
14. Good nutrition need not be expensive, for junk food often costs more.
15. Always look both to the left and the right before you cross a busy street.

Chapter IV **Punctuation**

p There are two common misconceptions about punctuation: one is that punctuation is of little consequence, that it has little to do with the effectiveness of written English; the other is that good punctuation is somehow arcane, a mystery whose secrets are available only to those with a special, instinctive gift. Those who labour under one or both of these delusions usually approach the task of punctuating with a combination of fear and abandon: some omit necessary punctuation for fear of making mistakes; others strain so hard to find the right mark that they make mistakes; still others punctuate with slapdash unconcern, as if they were playing Pin the Tail on the Donkey, sticking in various punctuation marks here and there in the hope that somehow it will come out all right.

The first assumption could not be further from the truth: good punctuation is essential to clear and effective writing. It helps a writer to clarify meaning and establish tone, and consequently it helps a reader to understand what the writer wishes to communicate. In addition, punctuation in itself can have meaning. Like words, some punctuation marks are symbols: they enable a writer to indicate meaning that would, in spoken language, be indicated by pauses and by pitch and tone and stress. In effect, correct punctuation enables a reader to hear a sentence the way the writer intended. Marks like the comma, the semicolon, and the colon also help to clarify the internal structure of sentences; often the very meaning of a sentence depends on how it is punctuated. The word *punctuation* is related to the word *pointing*; when you are *punctuating* you are in a sense *pointing to* meaning and tone and emphasis, *pointing out* just what it is you want a reader to understand. Punctuation marks are like signposts to help guide the reader through your sentences. Even someone who is poor at punctuating must depend on punctuation in order to understand what he reads; such a person needs to raise his unconscious habits to a conscious level so that he can control punctuation and use it effectively.

As for the second misconception, the principles of good punctuation are not mysterious or remote; a command of them should not be difficult to attain. And here yet another common misconception should be corrected at once: what are often called the "rules" of punctuation are not really rules but conventions. For example, English-speaking people have agreed upon the convention that the word for a feline animal, especially the small domestic feline, is *cat*: if you wish to write something about this animal, you will almost surely use that word to identify it. If you spelled it *kat* you would probably be understood, though readers would wonder why you had strayed from the conventional spelling—and to that extent you would have lost touch with them, disturbed the quality of their understanding of the meaning you intended. However, if you chose to call the small domestic feline you were writing about a *zyb,* you would not just have strayed slightly from the convention; you would have completely departed from it. And you would have lost your readers entirely, for they could have no idea of what you meant. The "rule" that *cat* is spelled c-a-t is of course not a moral or legal restraint on behaviour; no one is going to sue you or put you in jail if you choose to spell it z-y-b. But you will have exercised that degree of your freedom of choice at the cost of defeating your purpose: clear and effective communication.

The conventions of punctuation are similar: they have come to be agreed upon by writers and readers of English for the purposes of clear and effective communication. To be sure, good writers will often stray from the conventions of punctuation, but they usually do so not out of ignorance but rather because they have a sufficient command of the convention to break the "rule" in order to achieve a desired effect. One of the best ways to improve your own punctuation is to become more aware of other people's punctuation. Look not only for good things but for bad things as well, for weaknesses as well as strengths. If you do this consciously and conscientiously as you read, you will soon acquire a better sense of what punctuation does and how it does it—a sense which you can then apply to your own writing, a process which will soon become instinctive.

The following explanations of the conventions are intended for your guidance. They cover the most common circumstances, and even some relatively uncommon ones; if you understand them, they will help you to punctuate your writing correctly and effectively. Note that a clear understanding of many of these principles depends on a clear understanding of the syntax of the sentence in question; if you are unable to grasp the principles clearly, review the sections on grammar and sentence sense. Note also that, far from being like straitjackets, repressing and limiting your individuality and freedom, many of the principles that follow not only allow but actually invite you to exercise a considerable amount of choice.

Internal Punctuation

32 The Marks Defined

32a The Comma
The COMMA is a light separator, the most neutral, the least obtrusive; it is the most frequently used punctuation mark. It is used to separate words, phrases, and clauses from each other when no heavier or more expressive mark is required or desired.

32b The Semicolon
The SEMICOLON is a heavy separator, often almost equivalent to a full stop, or period; compared to the comma, it is used very sparingly. It is used to separate certain clauses from each other, and occasionally even to set off phrases.

32c The Colon
The COLON is a very special punctuation mark, often avoided by beginning writers because they do not understand its expressive function. It is commonly used to precede lists (for example, after "the following:" or "as follows:") or to introduce long or formal quotations, but its possibilities in more everyday sentences are often overlooked. Put most simply, the colon looks forward or anticipates: it gives the

reader an extra push toward the next part of the sentence. In the preceding sentence, for example, the colon is intended to give the reader a little extra impetus, to set up a sense of expectation about what is coming. Another mark that could have been used in that spot, a semicolon, would in contrast have brought the reader to a screeching halt, leaving him to make, entirely on his own, the necessary connection between the two parts of the sentence. With the colon, however, the relation between the two parts (here, a relation in which the second part restates and further clarifies, with emphasis, what the first part said) is pointed out, even emphasized, making it easier for the reader to understand the writer's intention. (To be fully accurate, we should point out that a semicolon in that spot would not only be separating the two clauses; it would also be acting as a joiner, informing the reader that the two clauses were closely related to each other. Only a full stop, a period, would act as a complete separator.) Here is another example, a more common kind, where the anticipatory function of the colon can be seen more clearly:

> The garden contained only four kinds of flowers: roses, tulips, geraniums, and chrysanthemums.

Caution: Do not use a colon after a syntactically incomplete construction. For example:

> *Wrong:* He preferred such foods as: potatoes, corn, and spaghetti.

Here the colon is misused, since "He preferred such foods as" is not a syntactically complete construction: *such as* needs a noun to be complete. Had it been extended to "He preferred such foods as these," it would have been complete, and a colon following it would have been not only appropriate but necessary; without the addition of *these* or *the following,* no punctuation mark should be used before the list of foods. Here is another illustration of this common error:

> *Wrong:* His favourite pastimes are: fishing, hunting, swimming, and hiking.

Again, the colon should be removed, since the linking verb

are clearly needs a complement for the construction to be complete.

Here are some illustrations of the correct use of the colon:

> He wanted only one thing from life: happiness. (Note that, even with this common use of the colon, what follows it need not be an extended list.)
>
> It was a warm day: we soon removed our jackets and sweaters.
>
> Let me add just this: anyone who expects to achieve excellence must be prepared to work hard.
>
> His shortcomings were several: laziness, slovenliness, lack of talent, and a short temper.
>
> It was a lovely time of year: the trees were in blossom, garden flowers bloomed all around, the sky was clear and bright, and the temperature was just right.

Ms note: Practice varies regarding spacing with colons. Many writers insist on following a typed colon with *two* spaces, instead of only one, to mark it as special and to keep it from being mistaken for a semicolon. Whichever practice you adopt, be consistent. In any event, when a colon is used in a footnote or a bibliographical entry, or to precede the subtitle of a written work, only *one* space follows it.

32d The Dash

The DASH is a much-abused punctuation mark. Careless writers often use it as a hasty substitute for a comma, or where a colon would be better—probably because they feel insecure about colons. The best way to avoid inappropriate or sloppy use of the dash is to be sure that when you use it you have a definite reason for doing so. Like the colon, a dash in a sentence is a signal to the reader; like the colon, it sets up expectations in the reader's mind. The dash differs from the colon, however, in that the expectation it sets up is not simply an expectation that what is to follow will somehow explain, summarize, define, or otherwise comment on what has gone before. Rather, the expectation evoked by a dash is that what follows will be either emphatic or somehow surprising, involving some sort of twist or irony, or at least a complete break in syntax. The dash is an abrupt break, and induces a slightly prolonged pause; the colon, on the other hand, although it induces a similar pause, at the same time impels the reader onward. Consider the following sentence:

> What he wanted—and he wanted it very badly indeed—was to be well liked by everyone.

To set off that parenthetical clause with commas instead of dashes would not be "incorrect," but it would certainly be weak, for the content of the clause is clearly emphatic, and only dashes have the power to signal that emphasis; the dashes, therefore, are appropriate, whereas commas would not be, since they would be contradicting what the clause says. Here is another sentence:

> The teacher praised my wit, my intelligence, my organization, and my research—and failed the paper for its lousy spelling and punctuation.

Here the dash clearly adds to the punch of what follows it. It signals the reader, preparing him for the unexpectedness, even the irony, of the last part of the sentence. A comma, being a very light and neutral mark, could not do this; if a comma were used instead of the dash, the sentence would lose most of its force, and even sound odd, since the resulting matter-of-fact TONE would not be in harmony with the substance. Only the dash can convey the appropriate tone (see introduction to Chapter VII).

The dash is also used to attach a summarizing clause to a long and involved sentence, for example a sentence with a long series as its "subject":

> The laws of supply and demand, the health of the stock market, the strength of our currency, the world money market, the balance of payments, inflation, unemployment—all these and more go to shape our everyday economic lives, often in ways unseen or little understood.

Note that even here the emphasizing quality of the dash serves the meaning, though its principal function in such a sentence is to mark the abrupt and unusual syntactic break.

Ms note: A typewritten dash is composed of two hyphens, and is not preceded, followed, or interrupted by a space.

How to Use Commas, Semicolons, Colons, and Dashes

33 Between Independent Clauses

33a Generally, use a comma between independent clauses that are joined by one of the co-ordinating conjunctions (*and, but, or, nor, for, yet,* and sometimes *so*):

> The course proved very difficult, and she found herself burning a lot of midnight oil.
>
> It was a serious speech, but he included many jokes along the way, and the audience loved it.
>
> Jared could go into debt for the sports car, or he could buy the much cheaper economy car.
>
> He knew what he should do, yet he could not bring himself to take the first step.

If the clauses are short, or if only one of a pair of clauses is short, the comma or commas may be omitted:

> The road was smooth and the car was running well and the weather was perfect.
>
> The walls were crumbling and the roof was full of holes.

But sometimes even with a short clause a comma is advisable when a natural pause would make the sentence read more smoothly and clearly:

> The building was old, and the ivy had climbed nearly to the top of its three storeys.

Also, when the clauses are parallel in structure the comma may often be omitted:

> Art is long and life is short.
>
> He stood up and she sat down.

When the subjects of two clauses are the same, a comma is less likely to be needed between them:

> It was windy and it was wet. (Note also the parallel structure.)
>
> The play was well produced and it impressed everyone who saw it.

Caution: Independent clauses joined by the co-ordinating conjunction *but*, since it explicitly marks a contrast, will almost always need a comma between them. And when the co-ordinating conjunction *for* joins two clauses, it should always be preceded by a comma in order to prevent its being misread as a preposition:

> He was eager to leave early, for the restaurant was sure to be crowded.

33b You will sometimes want to use a semicolon between independent clauses, even though they are joined by a co-ordinating conjunction, when one or more of the clauses have other punctuation marks within them:

> Old as he was, my uncle, Abner, the best farmer in the district, easily won the ploughing contest; and no one who knew him —or even had only heard of him—was in the least surprised.

or when at least one of the clauses is unusually long:

> A politician may make long-winded speeches full of clichés and generalities and the sort of things it is obvious everyone wants to hear; but people will still vote for him because they like his face.

or when you want the extra emphasis provided by a stronger pause:

> He protested that he was sorry for all his mistakes; but he went right on making them.

33c Note that in the preceding example a similar and even better effect could be achieved by using a dash:

> He protested that he was sorry for all his mistakes—but he went right on making them.

If the conjunction were changed to the more neutral *and* a rhetorically different effect could be achieved, the dash taking over the contrasting function of the word *but:*

> He protested that he was sorry for all his mistakes—and he went right on making them.

Similarly, notice the slightly different effects of these two versions of the same sentence:

It may not be the best way, but it's the only way we know.
It may not be the best way—but it's the only way we know.

Of course, even a period could be used to separate such clauses. (There is nothing inherently wrong with using an *And* or a *But* to begin a sentence. It's just that because they are co-ordinating conjunctions, one expects them to join internally rather than begin. But even as the first word of a sentence, an *And* or a *But* is in fact still performing its joining function.)

Note: *So* as a co-ordinating conjunction is best avoided in formal writing.

33d Generally, use a semicolon between independent clauses that are not joined by one of the co-ordinating conjunctions.

33e Failure to do this results in a COMMA SPLICE. A semicolon
cs signals the reader that what is following is an independent clause; were only a comma used, the reader would be expecting some kind of subordinate sentence element, and if he encountered an independent clause instead, his train of thought would be derailed. In most such sentences, then, in order to avoid the very serious comma splice, semicolons must be used:

> It is clear that we understand each other; I am sure that we will get along.
> The student who works will gain his reward; the student who shirks will also gain his.
> The President of the United States is elected; the members of his cabinet are not.
> Vancouver, the largest city in British Columbia, is not the capital; Victoria has that distinction.

33f If the clauses are short, and especially if they are parallel in structure, commas rather than semicolons may be sufficient:

> She cooked, he ate.
> I came, I saw, I conquered.

33g Relatively short independent clauses in a SERIES of three or more, especially if they are grammatically parallel, may be separated by commas rather than semicolons:

> The water was calm, our luck was good, and the fish were biting.
>
> If you want to do well you must pay attention, you must read carefully, you must work diligently, you must write correctly, and you must keep your fingers crossed.

(Here a dash would have worked nicely instead of the last comma.) Sentences such as these should be the only exceptions you permit; here a comma is sufficient to splice the clauses together in the absence of co-ordinating conjunctions. In other sentences, the strength of a semicolon is needed to splice such clauses together. Joining them with a comma alone results in the disconcerting COMMA SPLICE.

33h Caution: Be sure to use a semicolon between independent clauses joined by a CONJUNCTIVE ADVERB. Some of the more common conjunctive adverbs are *therefore, however, besides, consequently, furthermore, moreover, likewise, still, nevertheless,* and *then.* Conjunctive adverbs often have the "feel" of subordinating or co-ordinating conjunctions, but they are not conjunctions; rather they are adverbs doing a joining or "conjunctive" job:

> The book's print was very small; therefore by the end of it she had a headache.

In this example, *therefore* works very much like *so;* but it nevertheless is a *therefore* and not a *so,* and consequently a semicolon must be used, rather than a comma, which would result in a comma splice.

> He felt well enough to go; however, his doctor ordered him to stay in bed.

Here *however* works very much like *but*; nevertheless, it is a conjunctive adverb, not a conjunction, and must therefore be preceded by a semicolon. (Note also that *however,* in this usage, must be followed by a comma; other conjunctive adverbs may on occasion be followed by commas, but *however* must be, in order to prevent its being misread as a regular adverb rather than a conjunctive adverb.) Note that conjunctive adverbs can be shifted around within a clause; you may find it helpful to apply that test if you are not sure whether a particular word is a conjunctive adverb or a conjunction.

Style Note: *However* often sounds stiff and awkward at the beginning of a sentence or a clause. Unless you want special emphasis on the word, equivalent to underlining it, it is better to place it at some appropriate place within the clause; delaying it just one or two words into the clause often works best:

> His doctor, however, ordered him to stay in bed.

33i Dashes and colons may also be used between independent clauses not joined by co-ordinating conjunctions: use a dash when you want stronger emphasis on the second clause; use a colon when you want its anticipatory effect—when the second clause explains or enlarges upon the first clause. For example:

> He was a bounder from head to toe: gentlemanly behaviour was the last thing one could expect from him.
> The proposal horrified him—it was unthinkable.
> He took the obvious way out: he turned and ran.
> It was a unique occasion—everyone at the meeting agreed on what should be done.

In most such sentences either a dash or a colon would be appropriate; the choice depends on the particular tone or emphasis one wishes to convey. Note also that in none of these examples would a comma be correct. A semicolon could be used, but it would be very weak and usually inappropriate (except perhaps in the first example). But note that a crisp and emphatic effect could be achieved, especially in the second and third examples, by using a period, turning each into two separate sentences.

33j
run-on
fs Failure to put any punctuation between independent clauses where there is also no co-ordinating conjunction results in a RUN-ON or fused sentence:

> Run-on: Philosophers' views did not always meet with the approval of the authorities therefore there was constant conflict between writers and the church or state.

A semicolon after *authorities* corrects this very serious error.

Exercise 33(1)

Insert whatever punctuation mark (other than a period) you consider desirable or necessary between the independent clauses in the following sentences. (You may decide that no punctuation is necessary.) Be prepared to explain your decisions.

1. The Beatles phenomenon swept the 1960's the four hirsute Liverpudlians took the world by storm.
2. Some people eat to live others live to eat.
3. She laughed she cried she tore her hair.
4. Easy come easy go.
5. The wolves came closer that winter than ever before it broke all records for low temperature.

Exercise 33(2)

Correct any comma splices, run-on sentences, and fragments in the following.

1. I had not been back since my childhood therefore I was very surprised at all the changes that had taken place.
2. The actual value of the reward is unimportant, it is the relative value that matters.
3. Throughout the poem Frost uses various techniques to get his point across, however, the literal sense is sufficiently clear.
4. But I heard nothing, everything around me was still and peaceful.
5. The rest of the syllables do not flow easily together, therefore the line slows.
6. Life in those days was a gruelling chore, but that was what made it satisfying. A satisfaction of knowing you were living independent of the rest of the world.
7. Industry was not very developed at this time, however, the world of commerce was hectic.
8. At last we pushed off from the shore, the canoes were buffeted by the rolling waves caused by the tidal flow.

9. It was a feeble attempt the defendant made no impression on the jury.
10. We finally gave up and walked back. Having exhausted ourselves trying to move the tree that blocked the road.

---

34 Between Independent Clauses and Subordinate (Dependent) Clauses

34a Generally, use a comma between an introductory subordinate clause and an independent (main) clause:

> If you think you can learn to write well without hard work, you are mistaken.
> After I had selected all the things I wanted, I discovered that I had left my wallet at home.
> Since he was elected by a large majority, he felt that he had a strong mandate for his policies.
> When the party was over, I went straight home.

When the introductory clause is short and when there would be no pause if the sentence were spoken aloud, the comma may often be omitted:

> When the party was over I went straight home.
> While you are out you can pick up a loaf of bread.
> Since he felt ill he decided to stay home.

34b When a subordinate clause follows an independent clause, a comma may or may not be required between them. If the subordinate clause is essential to the meaning of the sentence, there should not be a comma; if it is not essential, but contains only additional information or comment, then a comma is required. (See the discussion of *restrictive* and *nonrestrictive* modifiers below, #37.) Consider the following examples:

> I went straight home when the party was over.
> You are mistaken if you think you can learn to write well without hard work.
> He felt that he had a strong mandate for his policies because he was elected by a large majority.
> He simply could not succeed, however hard he may have tried.

> She did an excellent job on her second essay, although the first one was a disaster.

Note: Most such concluding adverbial clauses will be restrictive, necessary to the meaning of the sentence. If you are in doubt, try omitting the adverbial clause to see if the sentence still says essentially what you want it to. Consider the following pair of sentences:

> The conference was a success even though it began in wild confusion.
> The conference was a success, even though it began in wild confusion.

The meanings are basically different, depending on whether or not there is a comma.

Exercise 34

Insert commas where you think necessary in the following sentences. Indicate any places where you think a comma would be optional.

1. Although the hour was late he knew he had to stay up and finish the paper.
2. You can leave now if you want to.
3. You can leave whenever you wish.
4. The fruit crop is especially good this year because there was such a warm spring.
5. Because spring was so warm this year the fruit crop is unusually heavy.
6. Before you go to Greece you should read this book about the islands.
7. Travel by airplane is certainly fast though it is also very expensive.
8. You can often tell where commas are required by reading your sentence aloud and listening for the natural pauses.
9. After she had won the race she seemed oddly less confident than she had before the race began.
10. However you look at the problem you cannot find a simple answer.

---

35 Between Introductory or Concluding Elements (other than Subordinate Clauses) and the Rest of the Sentence

The principles governing the punctuation of various introductory and concluding words and phrases are similar to those governing the punctuation of subordinate clauses. Studying them separately, however, should enable you not only to grasp the principles more clearly, but also to become more aware of the syntactic variety available to you. In addition, there are special points relating to certain kinds of words and phrases.

35a Generally, use a comma to set off an introductory prepositional phrase that you think should be followed by a pause:

> After his fifteen years as leader of the party, he retired gracefully.
> Just like all the others in the office, she remained loyal through thick and thin.
> Toward the end of the year, he began to act rather strange.
> In 1971, they moved to Calgary.

More and more frequently, however, if the phrase is relatively short and if the absence of a comma poses no danger of misreading, commas after introductory prepositional phrases are omitted as unnecessarily impeding the sentence:

> In 1971 they moved to Calgary.
> Toward the end of the year he began to act rather strange.

In the first two examples, the commas should be retained, for the phrases are quite long, and the removal of the commas could result in misreading.

35b Always set off with a comma an introductory participial phrase that modifies the subject:

> Finding the course more difficult than he had expected, he began to worry.
> Feeling victorious, he left the room.
> Having been in prison so long, he scarcely recognized the world when he emerged.
> Puzzled, she turned back to the beginning of the chapter.

35c Always set off an introductory absolute construction with a comma:

> The doors locked and bolted, she went to bed feeling secure.

35d When such words and phrases occur at the end of a sentence, most—but not all—will be restrictive and therefore not set off by commas:

> He began to act rather strange toward the end of the year.
> They moved to Calgary in 1971.
> He retired gracefully after his fifteen years as leader of the party.
> He left the room feeling victorious.
> She remained loyal through thick and thin, just like all the others in the office.

Exercise 35

Insert commas in the following sentences where you think they are necessary. Be prepared to defend your decisions.

1. Unnoticed I entered the house by the side door.
2. At the end of the lecture I had no clearer understanding of the subject than I did when I came in.
3. Following the instructions I poured the second ingredient into the beaker with the first and shook them shutting my eyes in expectation of something unpleasant.
4. The dishes washed and put away I decided to relax with a good book.
5. Looking strained and intense the coach stared back at the referee without saying a word.

---

36 Either dashes or colons may be used to set off concluding summaries or appositives in a sentence. Some say that a dash should be used to set off a short summary or appositive and a colon to set off a long one. But in fact either a colon or a dash may effectively be used in either instance: the length of the concluding element is unimportant; what matters is its relation to the preceding part of the sentence. If its relation is straightforward, use a colon; if it is in some way emphatic or unexpected, use a dash. Consider one of the sentences used earlier to illustrate a use of the colon:

He wanted only one thing from life: happiness.

A dash could be used there instead of a colon, but only if the writer wants to impart a special emphasis to the word *happiness*. But note that the nature of the whole sentence, and the colon followed by the single word *happiness,* already convey a good deal of emphasis; it could be argued that any greater emphasis, such as that provided by a dash, would be unnecessary, even inappropriate to the ordinariness of the sentiment. But if we change the final word, the tone also is altered:

He wanted only one thing from life—money.

Here too a colon would be acceptable, and would convey a certain emphasis, as in the original version. But the idea of *money* as someone's single desideratum, because it is less expected, introduces more vigour into the expression than did the idea of happiness. The resultant tone of the sentence would not be as well served by the quietness of a colon as by the dash of a dash. The same principles apply to setting off longer concluding appositives and summaries, though the colon tends to be used more frequently; the dash should be used only when you wish to take advantage of its special flavour.

Note: Sometimes you will find a comma used instead of a colon or a dash in such instances. This is a practice worth avoiding, for a comma is unlikely to be as effective as the other marks, and often will even be temporarily misleading.

37 Between Nonrestrictive Elements and the Rest of the Sentence

A word or phrase or clause is said to be nonrestrictive when it is not essential to the meaning of the sentence; it should be set off from the rest of the sentence. This is usually done with commas, though dashes and parentheses can also be used (see #39). The most common restrictive modifiers are relative clauses. Appositives, though usually nonrestrictive, can also be restrictive (see #37b). As discussed earlier (#34b, #35d), other elements can also be either restrictive or nonrestrictive.

37a Always set off a NONRESTRICTIVE relative clause from the rest of the sentence; do not set off RESTRICTIVE relative clauses:

> She is a girl who likes to travel.

Clearly the relative clause "who likes to travel" is essential to complete the meaning of the sentence; it is therefore restrictive and not set off with a comma.

> Viola, who likes to travel, is going to Greece this summer.

In this sentence, the relative clause "who likes to travel" is merely additional—though explanatory—information: it is not essential to the identification of Viola, who has been explicitly named, nor is it essential to the meaning of the main clause. Being nonrestrictive, then, it must be set off by commas, as above, or by dashes or parentheses.

> Students, who are lazy, should not expect much from their education.

Punctuated as a nonrestrictive clause, the relative clause here applies to all students, and the sentence borders on the libelous. Punctuated as a restrictive clause, it applies only to those students who are in fact lazy, and the sentence becomes a statement of truth:

> Students who are lazy should not expect much from their education.

Now the relative clause *who are lazy* restricts the meaning of *students who . . . should not expect much* to those who are in fact lazy.

> The chair, which I admired, was badly damaged in the fire.

The relative clause *which I admired* is here punctuated as nonrestrictive. The chair being referred to is clearly the subject of discussion: there was only one chair in the room, or else the particular chair meant has already been identified.

> The chair which I admired was badly damaged in the fire.

With the commas removed, the clause becomes restrictive; it would then distinguish that chair from other chairs, as for example would be necessary if there were three chairs in the room, but the only one damaged was the one the speaker particularly admired.

> The book, which I so badly wanted to read, was not in the library.

The book, we must assume, has been clearly identified in a preceding sentence.

> The book which I so badly wanted to read was not in the library.

Punctuated thus, as restrictive, the relative clause must be seen as essential to the identification of the particular book meant: other books the library had in abundance, but the particular one the speaker wanted very much to read was not there.

Note: When the relative pronoun *that* is used, the clause is almost invariably restrictive:

> The book that I so badly wanted to read was not in the library.

Also, the relative pronoun *that* can often be omitted, in which case the clause is definitely restrictive:

> The book I so badly wanted to read was not in the library.

Similarly, if the relative pronoun *whom* can be omitted, the relative clause in question is, again, clearly restrictive and not set off by punctuation:

> The person [whom] I most admire is the one who works hard and plays hard.

37b Always set off a nonrestrictive appositive from the rest of the sentence; do not set off a restrictive appositive:

> Gus, our gardener, keeps the lawn mowed all summer.
> Karl—the man I intend to marry—is tops in all categories.
> Milton's *Paradise Lost* is a noble work of literature, one that will live in men's minds for all time.
> Hugh is going to bring his sister, Eileen.

In the last sentence, punctuating the appositive as nonrestrictive indicates that Hugh has only one sister. Without the comma it becomes restrictive, indicating that Hugh has more than one sister, and that the particular one he is going to bring is the one whose name is Eileen:

> Hugh is going to bring his sister Eileen.

Some appositives have become parts of names or titles and are not set off:

> William the Conqueror won the Battle of Hastings in 1066.
> The Apostle Paul wrote several books of the New Testament.
> Ivan the Terrible was the first czar of Russia.

Caution: Avoid awkwardly setting off titles of literary works and the like as nonrestrictive appositives. It's *the good ship "Lollipop,"* NOT *the good ship, "Lollipop."* There is, after all, more than one good ship.

> *Wrong:* In his poem, *Paradise Lost,* Milton tells of the fall of man.
> *Wrong:* In the novel, *Great Expectations,* Dickens's theme is that of growing up.

This punctuation makes it sound as if Milton wrote only this one poem and that Dickens's novel is the only novel in existence. Omit at least the first comma; after so short an introductory phrase, the second could also be omitted. If the context is clear, the explanatory words are often not necessary at all:

> In *Paradise Lost* Milton tells....
> In *Great Expectations* Dickens's theme....

See also #44g.

37c Caution: Adverbial clauses or phrases beginning with *because* (or sometimes *since* or *for*) can present a special problem.

> They don't trust him, because he is a foreigner.

The comma is probably necessary (in spite of what we have just said about not setting off restrictive elements) since the intended meaning is that the reason they don't trust the man is that he is a foreigner. If we remove the comma, however, the meaning changes:

> They don't trust him because he is a foreigner.

The intended meaning may still seem obvious, but strictly speaking the sentence now says that they do trust him, but for some reason other than his being a foreigner, so that we are inclined to ask, "Well, then why *do* they trust him?" The problem is caused by the explicit negative (*not*) in the independent clause preceding the *because* clause. If we remove the negative, but still retain the essential meaning of the sentence, the comma is no longer necessary:

> They distrust him because he is a foreigner.

Whenever you have a negative statement followed by a *because* clause or phrase, be sure to punctuate it so that it means what you intend it to mean:

> Mary didn't pass the exam, because she had stayed up all night studying for it: she was so sleepy she couldn't even read the questions correctly.
>
> Mary didn't pass the exam because she had stayed up all night studying for it. That no doubt helped, but her thorough grasp of the material would have enabled her to pass it without the extra work.
>
> He didn't like the man, because of his face.
>
> He didn't like the man because of his face. Rather he liked and respected him for his intelligence.

Exercise 37

Decide whether the italicized elements in the following sentences are restrictive or nonrestrictive and insert punctuation as required.

1. The student *who takes studying seriously* is the one *who is most likely to succeed.*
2. The novels *I like best* are those *that tell a good story.*
3. This movie *which was produced on a very low budget* was a popular success.
4. Whitehorse *the capital of the Yukon* is a cold place to spend the winter.

5. Cato *the Elder* was one of the principal Stoic philosophers.
6. Sentence interrupters *not essential to the meaning* should be set off with commas.
7. Women *who are not good drivers* should be kept off the highways.
8. The London *which is in Ontario* was named after the London which is the capital of England.
9. Raymond Massey *the actor* is the brother of one of Canada's governors general.
10. In the view of small-town newspaper editor *John Smith* the storm was nothing to get excited about.

---

38 Between Items in a Series

38a Generally, use commas between words, phrases, or clauses in a series of three or more:

> He sells books, magazines, candy, and tobacco.
> He promised the voters to cut taxes, to limit government spending, and to improve transportation.
> Carmen explained that she had visited the art gallery, that she had walked in the park, and that eventually she had gone to a movie.
> He stirred the sauce frequently, carefully, and hungrily.

38b Some writers prefer to omit the final comma, the one before the conjunction, especially when the items in the series are short; but they then trap themselves into being inconsistent, for sometimes it is necessary to include the comma before the *and* in order to prevent awkwardness or misreading. Consider the following sentences:

> For breakfast I like toast, coffee, ham and eggs.

Clearly this sentence needs either a comma after *ham* or, if "ham and eggs" is meant as a unit, an *and* before *ham* as well as after it.

> Besides good ideas, your teacher wants your essays to have good diction, good sentences, good paragraphs, good punctuation and mechanics, and good organization.

The comma after *mechanics* helps prevent confusion.

> They prided themselves on having a large and bright kitchen, a productive vegetable garden, a large recreation room with a huge fireplace and two fifty-foot cedar trees.

One might well be proud of a room that could contain huge trees. The ambiguity and the unintended humour are removed when a comma is inserted after *fireplace*. Look what the omission of the comma before *and* does to this sentence:

> The Speech from the Throne discussed foreign trade, improvements in transportation, slowing down the economy and the postal service.

It is more prudent always to include the comma before the *and,* for not only will your sentences then have a smoother rhythm (punctuate a sentence the way you want it to be heard), but also you will be able to be consistent, and you will never need to worry about awkwardness or ambiguity.

38c If the phrases or clauses in a series are long or contain internal punctuation, you will probably want to separate them with semicolons rather than commas:

> How wonderful it is to awaken in the morning when the birds are clamouring in the trees; to see the bright light of a summer's morning streaming into the room; to realize, with a sudden illuminating flash of joy, that it is Sunday and that this perfect morning is completely yours; and then to loaf in the sun without a thought of tomorrow.

> Saint John, New Brunswick; Victoria, British Columbia; and Kingston, Ontario, are all about the same size.

If you want to create emphasis and a slower rhythm, you can separate even short items in a series with semicolons:

> There are certain qualities we expect in our leaders: honesty; integrity; intelligence; understanding.

(The omission of the customary *and* before the final item stylistically heightens the effect, reinforcing the emphasis gained by using semicolons.)

38d One can also emphasize items in a series by using dashes to separate them; but this device should be used only very rarely and with great circumspection. The sharpness of the breaks provided by the dashes can considerably heighten the rhetorical effect of a sentence:

> Rising taxes—rising insurance rates—rising transportation costs—skyrocketing food prices: it is becoming more and more difficult to live decently and still keep within a budget.

Here again the omission of the customary *and* contributes, as does the repetition and the parallel structure, to the almost stridently emphatic tone of the first part of the sentence. Even the colon that ends the series adds its touch to the effect. But such dashes can also be used effectively in a quieter context:

> Upon rounding the bend we were confronted with a breath-taking panorama of lush valleys with meandering streams—flower-covered slopes—great rocks and trees—and, over-topping all, the mighty peaks with their hoods of snow.

38e Even colons can be used between items in a series, but even more rarely than dashes. Colons too provide a certain emphasis, partly because they are so unusual in such instances, but the distinguishing feature is rather that they assist in producing a cumulative effect; hence they are appropriate only in those rare circumstances where each item in the series leads to the next (again, the anticipatory function of the colon), building to at least a mild climax:

> He held on: he persevered: he fought back: and eventually he won out, regardless of the seemingly overwhelming obstacles.
> It blew: it rained: it hailed: it sleeted: it even snowed—it was a most unusual month of June.

(Notice how the dash sets one up for the final clause in the last example.)

38f Use commas to separate two or more adjectives in a series preceding a noun if they are co-ordinate, each modifiying the noun itself; do not separate adjectives in a series before a noun if they are not co-ordinate—that is, if each in effect modifies the group of words, consisting of adjective(s) and noun, following it.

> He is an intelligent, efficient, ambitious officer.

Here each of the three adjectives modifies the noun, *officer*.

> She is tall young woman.

Here *tall* modifies *young woman,* not just *woman.* It is a *young woman* who is *tall,* not a *woman* who is *tall* and *young.*

> She wore a new black felt hat and a long red dress with many gold, silver, and black sequins on it.

Here *new* modifies *black felt hat, black* modifies *felt hat,* and *long* modifies *red dress*; hence no separating commas are needed. *Gold, silver,* and *black* all separately modify *sequins,* and must be separated by commas. But it is not always easy to decide whether or not a series of adjectives is co-ordinate. There is one rule of thumb that will often help in difficult instances. Try putting the co-ordinating conjunction *and* between the adjectives. If it seems to work comfortably there, then the adjectives are probably co-ordinate and should be separated by commas; if *and* does not sound right then no commas are needed. Applying this to the last example, one would quickly realize that to say "a new and black and felt hat" or "a long and red dress" would be absurd, whereas to say "gold and silver and black sequins" would be quite natural; where an *and* will not go, a comma should not go— and the problem is solved.

It is partly also a matter of word order. We naturally say

> He was a tired old man.

and no comma is needed, since *tired* modifies *old man.* But if one wanted to depart from the natural order and say

> He was an old, tired man.

then a comma would be necessary. The *and* test verifies the punctuation of these two versions as well. But the natural word order is not always amenable to such changes. For example, it is natural to speak of a *new brick house,* but who would even consider referring to a *brick new house,* with or without a comma? Another hint to remember: it is usually correct to omit commas after numbers (*three blind mice*), and after common adjectives designating size or age (*long red dress; new brick house*). This is not foolproof, however, as *old, tired man* demonstrates; the matter of word order apparently takes precedence over this general rule.

There will no doubt be occasions when neither logic nor rules of thumb will seem to help. You must then rely on instinct or common sense, or both. For example, no hint or rule will help one to decide if commas are needed in a series of adjectives such as these:

> There was an ominous wry tone in her voice.
> What caught our eye in the antique shop was a comfortable-looking tattered old upholstered leather chair.

On such occasions, one can only try different arrangements and punctuations and settle on the one that sounds best or that seems best to fit one's intentions—or one can give up and rewrite the sentence.

Exercise 38
Punctuate the following sentences as necessary.

1. The things I expected from my education were better self-discipline a broader outlook on life and the arts and preparation for a possible career.
2. April May and June are my favourite months.
3. The handsome young man wore gray plaid slacks a yellow turtleneck sweater and a smartly tailored blue blazer with square brass buttons.
4. The nice cute little baby soon began to crawl and maul fall and squall.
5. The recital was over the audience began to cheer and applaud loudly and the pianist who was obviously pleased stood up and bowed.

---

39 How to Use Commas, Dashes, and Parentheses to Punctuate "Sentence Interrupters": The Punctuation Marks that Come in Pairs

Sentence interrupters can be of many different kinds, several of which have already been discussed under other headings. We have isolated interrupters here to stress two points: all in-

154 Punctuation

terrupters must be set off at *both* ends; and you can choose among three kinds of punctuation marks to set them off: a pair of commas, a pair of dashes, or a pair of parentheses.

39a Set off light, ordinary interrupters with a pair of commas:

> Boswell, the biographer of Samuel Johnson, was a keen observer. (nonrestrictive appositive phrase)
> This document, the lawyer says, will complete the contract. (parenthetical explanation)
> Grandparents, who are often far too indulgent, should not be allowed to spoil their grandchildren. (nonrestrictive relative clause)
> Could you be persuaded to consider this money as, well, a loan? (mild interjection)
> You may, on the other hand, wish to concentrate on the final examination. (transitional phrase)
> But the tuna, it now occurs to me, may after all be responsible for your discomfort. (afterthought)
> It was, all things considered, a successful concert. (absolute construction)
> At least one science course, for example botany or astronomy, is required of all students. (example)

39b Use a pair of dashes to set off abrupt interrupters that you wish to emphasize. An abrupt interrupter is one whose syntactical pattern is not related to the structure of the sentence in which it occurs. An interrupter that sharply breaks the syntax of a sentence will often be emphatic for that very reason, and dashes will be appropriate:

> This document—so says the lawyer, anyway—will complete the contract.
> The stockholders who voted for him—a quite considerable group—were obviously dissatisfied with our recent conduct of the business.
> He told me—believe this or not!—that he would never drink again.
> Samuel Johnson—the eighteenth century's most eminent man of letters—is the subject of James Boswell's great biography.

In this last example the appositive phrase could be set off with a pair of commas, but dashes seem more appropriate because of both the length and the content of the appositive; further, an appositive of that length coming so soon in the sentence, after only a proper name, does amount to an abrupt interruption, further justifying the dashes. In other instances where you want emphasis or a different tone, dashes can be used where commas would ordinarily serve:

> The best student—Roger Dalrymple—was elected class president.
> The modern age—as we all know—is a technology-ridden age.
> But since the steak was well done, he—of course—ate the whole thing.

In the last example, the interrupter *of course* could actually have been left unpunctuated; therefore the exaggerated pauses caused by the dashes produce a considerable tonal effect.

39c Use PARENTHESES to set off abrupt or other interrupters that you wish to de-emphasize:

> The stockholders who voted for him (a quite considerable group, by the way) were obviously dissatisfied with our recent conduct of the business.
> The best student (his name is Roger Dalrymple) was elected class president.

In these examples, interrupters that could be emphatic (see the preceding section) have been de-emphasized in order to emphasize the main parts of the sentences.

Dashes call attention to the intrusion; parentheses normally play down the intrusion.

> But since the steak was well done, he (of course) ate the whole thing.

Here, by de-emphasizing the slight interrupter, an effect is achieved similar to that achieved by emphasizing it with dashes, but this time by an ironic rather than an insistent tone. Here are some further examples of parentheses used to enclose explanations, qualifications, and examples whose syntax is not related to the syntax of the sentences in which they occur:

> It is not possible at this time (it is far too early in the growing season) to predict with any confidence just what the crop yield will be.

Speculation (I mean this in its pejorative sense) is not a safe foundation for a business enterprise.

Some modern sports activities (hang-gliding, for example) involve an unusually high element of danger.

Exercise 39

Set off the italicized sentence interrupters with commas, dashes or parentheses. Be prepared to defend your choices.

1. It was seven o'clock in the evening *a mild autumn evening* and the crickets were beginning to chirp.
2. No one *at least no one who was present* wanted to disagree with the speaker's position.
3. One Sunday morning *a morning I will never forget* the phone rang clamorously.
4. Since it was only a mild interjection *no more than a barely audible snort from the back of the room* he went on with scarcely a pause *but with a slightly raised eyebrow* and finished his speech.
5. And then suddenly *out of the blue and into my head* came the only possible answer.

---

40 Parentheses are also used to enclose cross-reference information:

As I said earlier (see p. 28), analyzing poetry can be fun.

(Note that if a comma or other mark is called for by the sentence, it comes after the parenthesis, not before it. And do not make the mistake of assuming that the parenthesis itself, since it requires a kind of pause, takes the place of the comma; it does not. Punctuation marks go inside the parentheses only if they are a part of what is enclosed, as with the exclamation point in the second paragraph below, or when an entire sentence or more is enclosed, as with the cross-reference at the end of the next paragraph—or as with this period right here.)

Note: If you have to put parentheses inside parentheses, change the inner ones to BRACKETS—i.e., square brackets. If you are careful, this should never be necessary, unless perhaps in a footnote or a bibliographical entry, where parentheses have particular uses. (See #74, footnote 3.)

Remember, punctuation marks that set off sentence interrupters come in pairs. No one who has put down an opening parenthesis is likely to omit the closing parenthesis (unless he is very careless!). It is just as wrong to omit the closing comma or dash. Of course, if one of these "interrupters" does not really interrupt, that is, if it comes at the beginning or end of a sentence, only one comma or dash is required (but two parentheses, of course—like this).

41 Other Conventions of Punctuation

41a Use commas between elements of an emphatic contrast:

> This is a practical lesson, not a theoretical one.

41b Use commas to indicate a pause where a word has been acceptably omitted:

> Ron is a conservative; Sally, a socialist.
> To err is human; to forgive, divine.

41c Use commas correctly with dates:

> He left on January 11, 1976, and was gone a month.

or

> On 11 January 1976 he left for a month's holiday.

With only month and year, either using or omitting a comma is considered correct—but be consistent:

> The book was published in October, 1971.

or

> It was published in October 1971.

41d Use commas correctly with geographical names and addresses:

> He left Fredericton, New Brunswick, and moved to Windsor, Ontario, in hopes of finding a better-paying job.

Her summer address will be 11 Bishop's Place, Lewes, Sussex, England.
The Library of Congress is in Washington, D. C.

Use commas after the salutation of informal letters (Dear Gail,) and the complimentary close of all letters (Yours truly,). In formal letters, it is conventional to use a colon after the salutation (Dear Sir:).

42 End Punctuation: The Period, the Question Mark, and the Exclamation Point

The end of every sentence must be marked with a period, a question mark, or an exclamation point. The PERIOD is the most common terminal punctuation; it ends the vast majority of sentences. The QUESTION MARK is used to end direct questions or seeming statements that are intended interrogatively. The EXCLAMATION POINT is used to end sentences that express strong emotion, emphatic surprise, or even emphatic query. Usually the appropriate choice of mark will be obvious, but sometimes you will want to consider just what effect you want to achieve. Note for example the different effects—provided entirely by the end punctuation—in the following sentences:

> You said that you didn't understand me. (simple statement of fact)
> You said that you didn't understand me! (emphatic assertion of speaker's belief)
> You said that you didn't understand me? (expression of speaker's disbelief)

In each instance, the end punctuation would dictate the necessary tone of voice and distribution of emphasis and pitch with which the sentence would be said aloud. Again:

> He succeeded. (matter-of-fact)
> He succeeded! (surprised or emphatic)
> He succeeded? (sceptical or surprised)

42a Use a period to mark the end of statements and unemphatic commands:

> It is much colder this winter than it was last winter.

Geoffrey Chaucer, the author of *The Canterbury Tales,* died in 1400.

Close the door on your way out, please.

Do not let yourself be fooled by advertising claims.

Note: A period can also be used after a polite question that is not really meant interrogatively:

You'll write to us soon, won't you.

Why don't you come over here and sit by me.

Use a period after most abbreviations:

abbr., Mr., Ph.D., Dr., Jr., B.A., Mt., Nfld., P.E.I., etc.

(Note: In England it is conventional to omit the period after abbreviations that include the first and last letter of the abbreviated word: Mr, Mrs, Dr, Bart, ft, Jr, St, etc.) Periods are not used after metric and other symbols (unless they occur at the end of a sentence):

km, cm, kg, C, Hz, Au, Zr

Periods are often omitted with initials of groups or organizations, especially if the initials are acronyms or thought of as a name and are all in capital letters:

UN, UNESCO, NATO, RCMP, RAF, NDP, TV, MLA, MP, STOL, ACUTE

If you are in doubt, consult a good dictionary. If there is more than one acceptable usage, be sure to be consistent: stick with the one you choose.

Note: Normally required punctuation marks follow the periods of abbreviations except when the abbreviation ends the sentence; in such an instance the abbreviation's period also marks the end of the sentence:

He gets up at 8 a.m., breakfasts at 9 a.m., and goes riding promptly at 10 a.m.

42b Use a question mark at the end of direct questions:

Who is the greatest philosopher of all time?

How many tons can you deliver?

Note that a question mark is necessary—and even more important—after questions that are not phrased in the usual interrogative way:

> You are going? (instead of "Are you going?")
> You want him to accompany you? (instead of "Do you want him to accompany you?")

A question may also appear as a sentence interrupter; it will still need a question mark at its end:

> I went back to the beginning—what else could I do?—and tried to get it right the second time through.
> The gentleman in the mackintosh (what was his name again?) took a rear seat.

Note that since these interrogative interrupters are necessarily abrupt, dashes or parentheses will be the appropriate marks with which to enclose them.

42c Use exclamation points after emphatic statements and after expressions of emphatic surprise, emphatic query, and strong emotion—that is, after exclamations:

> He came in first, yet it was only his second time in professional competition!
> What a fine actor!
> You don't say so!
> Isn't it beautiful today!
> Be careful! You might fall!
> Wow!

Caution: An exclamation point will seldom turn an otherwise ordinary sentence into an exclamation. The sentence should already *be* emphatic in order for the exclamation point to be appropriate. Of course there are exceptions to this: some sentences that a writer wishes to be read as exclamations will not in themselves appear emphatic, but rather than change a desirable wording the writer will simply settle for a final exclamation point to mark his intention.

Note: There are two other ways to end sentences, ways which occur occasionally in narrative fiction but rarely elsewhere. Dashes, or more commonly the three or four dots of ellipses—sometimes called suspension points—are sometimes used at the ends of sentences, especially in dialogue or at the end of a paragraph or a chapter, to suggest "and so on," a fading away, or an interruption, or to create mild suspense, so that the reader wonders what's going to happen next . . . .

43 Punctuation with Quotations

Q There are two kinds of quotation: dialogue or direct speech, as in a story, novel, or nonfiction narrative, or even in an essay that is not primarily a narrative; and verbatim quotation from a published work or other source.

43a Enclose all direct speech in quotation marks:

> "Henry, get your feet off the coffee table."

In dialogue, where there are two or more speakers, it is conventional to begin a new paragraph each time the speaker changes:

> "Henry," she said, a note of exasperation in her voice, "please get your feet off the coffee-table."
> "Oh, yes," he replied. "Sorry dear. I keep forgetting."
> She examined it for scratches. "Well, no harm done this time, I guess. But please try to remember."

Even when speeches are not complete, the part that is verbatim still must be enclosed in quotation marks:

> After only two weeks, he said he was "tired of it all" and that he was "going to look for a more interesting job."

43b Enclose in quotation marks all direct quotation from other sources when you run the quotation into your own text:

> According to Francis Bacon, "No pleasure is comparable to standing upon the vantage-ground of truth."

If a prose quotation extends to four or five lines or more, it is customary to indent it on both sides and single-space it; in a manuscript this represents what in a printed work would be an excerpt set in reduced type:

> As Milton puts it, in one of those ringing passages that make his *Areopagitica* so memorable:

I cannot praise a fugitive and cloistered virtue, unexercised and unbreathed, that never sallies out and seeks her adversary, but slinks out of the race where that immortal garland is to be run for, not without dust and heat.

Similarly, quotations of more than two or three lines of poetry should be indented and single-spaced:

In poetry, "The sound must seem an echo to the sense," as

Pope says in his *Essay on Criticism*. He then goes on to say,

demonstrating the while, that

Soft is the strain when zephyr gently blows,
And the smooth stream in smoother numbers flows;
But when loud surges lash the sounding shore,
The hoarse rough verse should like the torrent roar.

And there should be a *triple* line-space before and after such an inset quotation, for if you were quoting a single line of poetry, ordinary double spacing would make it look like the beginning of a new paragraph. For the same reason it is advisable to indent such quotations more than the customary five-space paragraph indention—say eight or ten spaces.

If you wish to quote more than one line of poetry and to run it into your own text rather than set it off with indention and single spacing, then the end of each line should be marked with a diagonal line, called a *slash* or *virgule,* with a space before and after it:

Wordsworth's comment in one of his sonnets almost two hun-

dred years ago could well be applied to the way we live today:

"The world is too much with us; late and soon, / Getting and

spending, we lay waste our powers: / Little we see in Nature

that is ours."

Note: The act of indenting and single-spacing is tantamount to using quotation marks; therefore no quotation marks are used. If, however, the original passage is itself in quotation marks, then these must be reproduced in your quotation of it:

Budgets can be important. As Dickens had Mr. Micawber say in *David Copperfield,*

> "Annual income twenty pounds, annual expenditure nineteen nineteen six, result happiness. Annual income twenty pounds, annual expenditure twenty pounds ought and six, result misery."

Note: If you quote a single paragraph or part of a paragraph and set it off from your text, do not include the paragraph indention. If your quotation takes in more than one paragraph, include the paragraph indentions. Also, if you are quoting two or more paragraphs that are in quotation marks in the original, put quotation marks at the beginning of each paragraph, but put them at the end of the final paragraph only.

Note: A quotation of less than four or so lines may be indented and single-spaced if you want it to receive special notice, to be slightly emphasized. A quotation of two lines or even a single line of poetry is often treated this way.

43c Use single quotation marks to enclose a quotation that occurs within something that is already enclosed by double quotation marks:

> "Well," said Noel, "when I got there I found a sign on the door that said 'Out to lunch.' "

This is the only time single quotation marks should be used.

43d When verbs of speaking or their equivalent precede a quotation, they are usually followed by commas:

> Adriana looked up and asked, "What time is it?"
> Helen said, "He will do exactly as I tell him."

If the quotation is short, however, a comma may not be necessary:

> He said "Not yet," so we waited a little longer.

Again, punctuate the sentence the way you want it to be heard; your sense of its rhythm should help you decide. On the other hand, if the quotation is long—especially if it consists of more than one sentence—or if the context is formal, a colon will probably be more appropriate:

> When dinner was over Oscar turned to his hostess and said: "Seldom have I enjoyed a meal more, my dear. The balance of courses was superb, and the wines were the perfect accompaniment."

If the introductory element is itself an independent clause, then a colon or a period must be used:

> Oscar turned to her and spoke: "A delicious repast, my dear."

Spoke, unlike *said,* is here an intransitive verb.

43e Colons are often used to introduce long and formal quotations that are set off by indention and single-spacing. If the quotation is worked into the syntax of your own sentence, however, it can be punctuated accordingly:

> In one of his *Devotions* John Donne wrote that
>
> > No man is an island, entire of itself; every man is a piece of the continent, a part of the main; if a clod be washed away by the sea, Europe is the less, as well as if a promontory were, as well as if a manor of thy friends or of thine own were; any man's death diminishes me, because I am involved in mankind; and therefore never send to know for whom the bell tolls; it tolls for thee.

The word *that* makes all the difference; if it were removed, a colon would be needed. The same applies to shorter quotations worked into your own syntax:

> It is often said that "Sticks and stones may break my bones, but words will never hurt me"—a singularly inaccurate notion.

43f If verbs of speaking or other such elements follow a quotation, they are usually set off by commas (or on occasion, as in the preceding example, by a dash):

> "The Great Lakes are extremely important to the commerce of the area," he said.
> "I think there's a fly in my soup," she muttered.

But if the quotation ends with a question mark or an exclamation point, no other punctuation should be added:

> "Have you read Margaret Laurence's latest novel?" she asked.
> "Mr. Chairman! I insist that I be heard!" he shouted.

Similarly, if a quotation is at the end of a sentence, its own terminal punctuation, whether period, question mark, or exclamation point, is also the terminal punctuation for the whole sentence; no extra period should be added.

If the phrase with the verb of speaking interrupts the quotation, it should be preceded by a comma and followed by whatever mark is called for by the syntax and the sense:

> "Since it's such a long drive," he said, "we'd better get an early start."
> "It's a long drive," he argued; "therefore I think we should start early."
> It's a very long way," he insisted. "We should start as early as possible."

43g Put quotation marks around words used in a special sense or for which you wish to indicate some qualification:

> What he calls a "ramble" I would call a twenty-mile hike.
> He had been up in the woods so long he was "bushed," as the saying is.
> "Competent" is hardly the word for it; I would call it magnificent!

Note: Some writers put quotation marks around words referred to as words, but it is better practice to italicize them (i.e., underline them in a manuscript):

> The dictionary defines <u>fulsome</u> as "distastefully excessive in an oily or insincere way."
> The word <u>aggravate</u> is commonly misused.

(See #49c.)

Caution: Do not adopt the practice of putting quotation marks around slang terms, clichés, and the like; if the word or phrase is so weak that you have to apologize for it, you should not be using it in the first place. Setting off such a word or phrase also calls attention to it, which is the last thing it needs. Moreover, this practice implicitly insults the reader's intelligence by presuming that he will not recognize a bit of slang when he sees it. Similarly, try to resist the temptation to use quotation marks for effects of comic irony:

> The "girl" behind the counter was forty if she was a day!

It is a cheap effect at best, and the snide tone often backfires upon the writer. And one final point: do not use quotation marks for emphasis; they do not work that way.

43h Put periods and commas inside closing quotation marks; put semicolons and colons outside them:

> "Knowing how to write well," he said, "can be a source of great pleasure"; and then he added that it had "one other important quality": he identified it simply as "hard work."

This is simply a printer's convention; the sample sentence exemplifies the dominant Canadian practice. Since it is also the standard practice in the United States, it could be called a North American convention. In England, however, it is conventional to place all four of these punctuation marks outside quotation marks. Some Canadians follow one method, some the other. In the interest of consistency, we recommend following the dominant North American practice. Whichever convention you choose, follow it consistently; do not punctuate one way on one page and the other way on the next.

Question marks, exclamation points, and dashes are put either inside or outside closing quotation marks, depending on whether they apply to the quotation or to the whole sentence:

> "What time is it?" he asked.
> Who said, "To be or not to be, that is the question"?
> Did you find out who shouted "God save the Queen!"?

43i Indicate any omission from quoted material with three spaced periods (ellipsis); if the omission includes the end of a sentence, add a fourth period. For example, if you wanted to quote only certain parts of the passage from Donne's *Devotions* quoted at length earlier (#43e), you might do it like this:

> As John Donne wrote: "No man is an island, entire of itself . . . any man's death diminishes me, because I am involved in mankind . . . ."

If the omission is from the beginning of the following sentence, do not leave a space before the first of the four periods, for it will then be the sentence period. A whole line of spaced periods is used to indicate the omission of a whole paragraph or of one or more lines of poetry. Do not indicate an ellipsis at the beginning of a quotation unless it could be mistaken for a complete sentence—for example, if the quoted portion of a sentence began with *I* or some other capital letter:

> One could say, echoing Donne, " . . . I am involved in mankind . . . ."

You need not use the dots at either end if your quotation is a mere word or phrase that could in no way be mistaken for a complete sentence.

Caution: Be careful not to omit material from a quotation in such a way that you distort what the author is saying, or destroy the integrity of his syntax. Similarly, do not quote unfairly "out of context"; that is, if an author qualifies a statement in some way, do not quote the statement bare, as if it were unqualified. If what you are quoting is a fragmentary part of a sentence, make sure that it conforms to the syntax of your own sentence.

43j Enclose in square brackets any editorial addition you make within a quotation. The passage from Milton's *Areopagitica* quoted earlier (#43b), for example, would be clearer with an added piece of information:

> As Milton put it:

>> I cannot praise a fugitive and cloistered virtue . . . that never sallies out and seeks her adversary, but slinks out of the race where that immortal garland [truth] is to be run for . . . .

The word *truth,* taken from a nearby sentence, identifies what "that immortal garland" refers to. Use this method also when it is necessary to change a word to make it conform to your syntax or tense:

> One of my friends wrote me that his "feelings about the subject [were] similar to" mine.

Similarly, use the word *sic* (Latin for *thus*) in square brackets to indicate that an error in the quotation occurs in the original:

> One of my friends wrote me: "My feelings about the subject are similiar [sic] to yours."

(For the use of quotation marks around titles, see #48 below.)

44 Some Common Errors in Punctuation to Guard Against

44a Do not put a comma between a subject and its verb unless some intervening element calls for punctuation:

> *Wrong:* His enthusiasm for the project and his desire to be of help, led him to add his name to the list of volunteers.

The comma after *help* intrudes between the compound subject ("enthusiasm . . . and . . . desire") and its verb, *led*. It is just as wrong as the comma in this sentence:

> *Wrong:* Edna, went to class.

But if some other element, for example an appositive or a participial phrase, intervenes between subject and verb, it must be set off:

> *Right:* His enthusiasm for the project and his desire to be of help, both strongly felt, led him to add his name to the list of volunteers.
>
> *Right:* Edna, the star student, went to class.

Here the sentence interrupters are properly set off by *pairs* of commas.

Occasionally, however, if a subject is unusually long or complicated or heavily punctuated, a comma after it and before the verb may be useful:

A student who comes to university looking not for an education but for a good time, to whom classes are a necessary evil and the weekend parties the really important occasions, and who feels that teachers and libraries are things to be avoided as much as possible, is not only likely to perform miserably but is fundamentally wasting his own and everyone else's time and money.

The comma after *possible,* while not essential, does make the sentence easier to read. Sometimes such a comma is required simply to prevent misreading:

The spirit of adventure and the openness to the unexpected sights, sounds, tastes, and people, give independent travellers a familiarity with a place that those on package tours could never have.

The last comma prevents *people* from being even momentarily mistaken for the subject of the verb *give.*

44b Do not put a comma between a verb and its object or complement unless some intervening element calls for punctuation:

Wrong: Jeremy found, that he could no longer keep his eyes open.

Here the noun clause beginning with *that* is the direct object of the verb *found* and should not be separated from it. Only if an interrupter requires setting off should there be any punctuation:

Right: Jeremy found, moreover, that he could no longer keep his eyes open.

Right: Jeremy found, as he tried once again to read the paragraph, that he could no longer keep his eyes open.

Another example:

Wrong: Ottawa's principal claim to fame is, that it is the national capital.

Here the comma intrudes between the linking verb *is* and its complement, the predicate noun consisting of a clause beginning with *that.* If there were an interrupter that required setting off, then a pair of commas (or dashes or parentheses) would be necessary:

> *Right:* Ottawa's principal claim to fame is, according to many, that it is the national capital.

44c Do not put a comma between the last adjective of a series and the noun it modifies:

> *Wrong:* How could anyone fail to be impressed by such an intelligent, outspoken, resourceful, fellow as Jonathan has proved himself to be?

The comma after *resourceful* is wrong, though it may momentarily sound right because a certain rhythm has been established and because there is no *and* before the last of the three adjectives; do not let yourself be trapped into this error.

44d Generally, do not put a comma between words and phrases joined by a co-ordinating conjunction; use a comma only when the co-ordinate elements are clauses:

> *Unnecessary:* The dog and cat circled each other warily, and then went off in opposite directions.
>
> *Unnecessary:* I was a long way from home, and didn't know how to get there.
>
> *Unnecessary:* He was not only intelligent, but also very industrious.
>
> *Unnecessary:* She was very tall, and pretty, and dumb.

All of the commas in these examples are unnecessary. Sometimes a writer will use such a comma to achieve a mild emphasis, but if an emphatic pause is desired, a dash would probably work better:

> The dog and cat circled each other warily—and then went off in opposite directions.
>
> She was very tall and pretty—and dumb.

Or the sentence could be slightly revised in order to gain the emphasis:

> He was not only intelligent; he was also very industrious.
>
> I was a long way from home, and I had no idea how to get there.

In the last example the comma is best, for the sentence now consists of two independent clauses; in this example, even though the subject remains the same, a comma is preferable to no punctuation. There are occasions, however, when commas in such places are appropriate, times when one desires a slight pause, or a mild emphasis, but yet does not want to call attention to it with a dash. (We have used two such commas in the preceding sentence.) When you do use such a comma, do so as the result of a conscious decision; mere instinct or a vague sense of rhythm can all too easily lead you into over-punctuation.

44e If the two elements joined by a conjunction involve an emphatic repetition, a comma is sometimes optional:

> I wanted not only to win, but to win overwhelmingly.

This sentence would be equally correct and effective without the comma. In the following sentence, however, the comma is necessary:

> It was an object of beauty, and of beauty most spectacular.

Again, sounding the sentence over to yourself should enable you to decide.

44f Generally, do not set off introductory elements or interrupters that are very short, that are not really parenthetical, or that are so slightly parenthetical that no pause is felt when reading them:

> *Wrong:* Perhaps, she was trying to tell us something.
> *Wrong:* But, it was not a case of mistaken identity.
> *Wrong:* We were asked to try it out, for a week, to see if we really liked it.
> *Wrong:* Therefore, he put on his raincoat.

When the pause is strong, however, be sure to set off the phrase:

> *Right:* It was only then, after dinner, that we could all relax.

Often such commas are optional. Writers who are insecure about their punctuation will often insert commas where they are not needed. Here are a few sentences in which a comma is optional, depending on the pattern of intonation the writer wants:

In Canada (,) the progress of the seasons is sharply evident.
In Canada (,) as elsewhere, money talks.
Last year (,) there was a record wheat crop.
In order to keep dry (,) therefore, he put on his raincoat.
It was one of those lovely days (,) in June (,) when everything seems perfect. (either two commas or none)
After dinner (,) we all went for a walk.
As she walked (,) she thought of her childhood on the farm.

Sometimes a comma must be used in order to prevent misreading:

> After eating, the dog Irene gave me jumped out the window.
> As she walked, past events in her life crowded before her mind's eye.
> We came to the door of the meeting room and opened it. Inside, a few students were standing about, three or four to a group.

44g Do not mistake a restrictive appositive for a nonrestrictive one.

> *Right:* According to Senator James Higginbottom, the economy is improving daily.

Few if any would put a comma after *Senator* in such a sentence. Yet all too often one comes across a sentence like this:

> *Wrong:* The proceedings were opened by union leader, John Smith, with remarks attacking the government.

The comma after *leader* is incorrect, since it is only his name, *John Smith,* that clearly identifies him and is therefore restrictive.

> *Right:* The proceedings were opened by the union's leader, John Smith, with remarks attacking the government.

In this version the definite article *the,* as well as the slightly different form *union's leader,* defines—restricts—the man; the name itself, *John Smith,* is only incidental information and is therefore *nonrestrictive.*

> *Wrong:* According to spokesman, James Higginbottom, the economy is improving daily.

Right: According to the spokesman, James Higginbottom, the economy is improving daily.

The definite article *the* makes all the difference, as again in the following:

Wrong: It was the stated belief of heavyweight champion, Muhammad Ali, that no one could beat him.
Right: It was the stated belief of the heavyweight champion, Muhammad Ali, that no one could beat him.

But even the presence or absence of the definite article is not always a sure test. Consider this sentence for example:

Right: One of the best-known mysteries of the sea is that of the ship *Mary Celeste,* the disappearance of whose entire crew has never been satisfactorily explained.

Here the phrase *the ship* is insufficient identification; the proper name is needed, and is therefore restrictive.

This error most often occurs when a proper name *follows* a defining or characterizing phrase. The proper name in such instances is usually restrictive, and therefore not set off with commas. Be careful not to confuse such appositives with appositives that occur in the reverse order (and include the definite article); these are nonrestrictive and set off with commas:

Right: James Higginbottom, the senator, said the economy was improving daily.
Right: Muhammad Ali, the heavyweight champion, often stated that he was unbeatable.

See also #37b.

44h Do not set off indirect quotations as if they were direct quotations:

Wrong: In his last chapter the author says, that civilization as we have come to know it is in jeopardy.
Wrong: If you ask Andrew he's sure to say, he doesn't want to go.

The commas in these two sentences are wrong because "the author" and "Andrew" are not being quoted directly; what they said is being reported indirectly. If Andrew is quoted directly, a comma before the quotation is correct:

> *Right:* If you ask Andrew he's sure to say, "I don't want to go."

See also #43a.

44i Do not use a question mark at the end of indirect questions; questions that are not quoted verbatim should end with a period:

> I asked what we were having for dinner.
> She wanted to find out what had happened the year before.
> What he asked himself then was how he was going to explain it to his boss.

44j Never put a comma or a semicolon or a colon together with a dash. Such combinations used to be common, but they are now avoided because they contribute little but clutter. Use whichever mark is appropriate.

Review Exercises: Chapter IV
(1) Correct any errors in punctuation in the following sentences.

1. It is a question of careful preparation, attentive reading, and review.
2. Many of his plays are about royalty, as in: *Richard II, Richard III,* and *Henry IV*.
3. With him too, she felt uncomfortable.
4. Therefore, Forster praises democracy as well for it allows variety and criticism.
5. As a person exercises the muscle of the heart becomes stronger; therefore, it can pump more blood while beating less.
6. The same word was used three times in the same paragraph; twice to describe different ideas altogether.
7. It was after all, exactly what he had asked for.
8. Eighteenth-century mathematicians, unlike their counterparts in the seventeenth century, were able to develop both pure and applied mathematics. Leonard Euler, a notable genius in both these fields contributed invaluably to every branch of mathematics.

9. It began to rain, nevertheless, since they were on the six-teenth fairway they went ahead and finished the round.
10. When company spokesman, Sidney O'Malley, rose to speak someone began to giggle.

(2) Here are some passages of prose written in the eighteenth century, when the conventions of punctuation were in some ways different from ours. How would you punctuate them if you had written them today? (You might also consider what other changes you would make.)

1. There are many accomplishments, which though they are comparatively trivial, and may be acquired by small abilities, are yet of great importance in our common intercourse with men. Of this kind is that general courtesy, which is called Good Breeding; a name, by which, as an artificial excellence, it is at once character-ised and recommended.

(*The Adventurer,* No. 87, 1753)

2. The philosophers of King Charles his reign were busy in finding out the art of flying. The famous Bishop Wilkins was so confident of success in it, that he says he does not question but in the next age it will be as usual to hear a man call for his wings when he is going a journey, as it is now to call for his boots. The humour so prevailed among the virtuosos of his reign, that they were actually making parties to go up to the moon together, and were more put to it in their thoughts how to meet with accom-modations by the way, than how to get thither. Every one knows the story of the great Lady, who at the same time was building castles in the air for their reception.

(*The Guardian,* No. 112, 1713)

3. By this original form, the usual station of the actors, in almost every scene, was advanced at least ten foot nearer to the audience, than they now can be; because, not only from the stage's being shortened, in front, but likewise from the additional interposition of those stage-boxes,

the actors (in respect to the spectators, that fill them) are kept so much more backward from the main audience, than they used to be: But when the actors were in possession of the forwarder space, to advance upon, the voice was then more in the centre of the house, so that the most distant ear had scarce the least doubt, or difficulty in hearing what fell from the weakest utterance: All objects were thus drawn nearer to the sense; every painted scene was stronger; every grand scene and dance more extended; every rich, or fine-coloured habit had a more lively lustre: Nor was the minutest motion of a feature (properly changing with the passion, or humour it suited) ever lost, as they frequently must be in the obscurity of too great a distance: And how valuable an advantage the facility of hearing distinctly, is to every well-acted scene every common spectator is a judge.

(*An Apology for the Life of Colley Cibber,* 1740)

4. My father had a small estate in Nottinghamshire; I was the third of five sons. He sent me to Emanuel-College in Cambridge, at fourteen years old, where I resided three years, and applied my self close to my studies: But the charge of maintaining me (although I had a very scanty allowance) being too great for a narrow fortune; I was bound apprentice to Mr. James Bates, an eminent surgeon in London, with whom I continued four years; and my father now and then sending me small sums of money, I laid them out in learning navigation, and other parts of mathematicks, useful to those who intend to travel, as I always believed it would be some time or other my fortune to do.

(Jonathan Swift, *Gulliver's Travels,* 1726)

5. It is justly considered as the greatest excellency of art, to imitate nature; but it is necessary to distinguish those parts of nature, which are most proper for imitation: greater care is still required in representing life, which is so often discoloured by passion, or deformed by wickedness. If the world be promiscuously described, I cannot see of what use it can be to read the account; or

why it may not be as safe to turn the eye immediately upon mankind, as upon a mirror which shows all that presents itself without discrimination.

(Samuel Johnson, *The Rambler,* No. 4, 1750)

(3) Punctuate the following sentences as you think necessary. Consider possible alternatives, and be prepared to defend your choices. (For all but the last ten, periods are supplied; for those ten, the terminal punctuation itself is part of the exercise.)

1. When the meeting ended he went to a pub and got drunk.
2. Fred went home to bed as soon as the meeting was over.
3. There was still much to be done but he decided to call it a night.
4. In 1971 he moved to Halifax Nova Scotia and bought a small business.
5. He felt uneasy about the trip yet he knew he had to go along.
6. I took the book that I didn't like back to the library.
7. Mary Winnie and Cora came to the party together.
8. He had a broad engaging smile.
9. Having heard all she wanted Bridget left the meeting.
10. But once you've taken the first few steps the rest will naturally be easy.
11. The poem was short the novel was long the poem was good the novel better.
12. Perhaps we can still think of some way out of this mess.
13. But Canadians don't think that way they prefer to sit back and wait.
14. Last summer we visited Hastings the site of the battle won by William the Conqueror in 1066.
15. It is not good policy to start writing right away because your work will probably be weak in organization coherence and unity.
16. There are only three vegetables I can't tolerate turnips turnips and turnips.
17. The doctor a specialist in family practice made house calls all morning.

p

18. August 1914 was when the world went to war.
19. He had to finish the novel quickly or he wouldn't be ready for class.
20. We arrived we ate we departed and that's all there was to the evening.
21. You must plan your budget carefully in times of inflation.
22. He is the only man I know who wears a tie every day whatever the season.
23. His several hobbies were philately woodworking chess and fishing.
24. The two opponents settled the question amicably at the meeting and then went home to write nasty letters to each other.
25. I enjoyed both the novel and the poem but the novel which was an adventure story was much easier to read.
26. It was a splendid old stone house surrounded by well-landscaped lush green lawns and approached by a long sweeping gravel driveway.
27. This new machine looking like a caricature of a human being may yet prove beneficial.
28. It was to prove a very important day for Richard the embattled king he having to decide which course to pursue.
29. One August afternoon it was the hottest day of the year he perversely decided to play tennis.
30. He enjoyed the work of Melville Hemingway and Twain even more than that of such a talented successful entertaining novelist as Dickens.
31. I found many mistakes in the paper which was a mess from beginning to end.
32. Because of the vast distances the extreme climate rapidly rising costs and far from least important the rights and needs of native peoples the matter of northern development is a difficult problem but more and more society's demand for energy and other resources dictates that some kind of action be taken that the north be increasingly opened up to technological exploitation.
33. Before I was even half-way through the job my boss told me I could have the rest of the day off.

34. They sat there glowing with pride in their accomplishments.
35. I drove my car which was splashed all over with mud down to the car-wash.
36. He found many mistakes in the paper which were quite serious.
37. It was a simple assignment for the student was asked to write only one page.
38. It was a long hot summer in fact it was so hot I got scarcely any work done.
39. To avoid error he proofread the paper carefully.
40. I kept my distance from Alfred feeling uneasy about his display of temper.
41. If winter is here can spring be far behind
42. As soon as the plane had landed I began to wonder would I be able to fly again without fear
43. Well can you beat that
44. Has anyone ever come up to you on the street and asked Where's the best place in town to eat
45. Later he thought of many things he could have done but at the moment of crisis only one way out occurred to him run like mad
46. Tell me Algernon whether you would write March 16 1962 or put it like this 16 March 1962
47. Wayne's tirade finished Anita said No one will be swayed by such behaviour
48. He said that he would try to calm down
49. I should think she remarked that you could see where your own best interests lie Can't you my dear
50. Then came the reply she'd been hoping for I'll do whatever you think is best

PART TWO
Mechanics

Chapter V Manuscript Conventions and Other Mechanical Conventions of Writing

45 Manuscript Conventions

45a A number of conventions govern the form of a manuscript
ms that is being prepared for submission. Unless directed otherwise you should carefully adhere to the following principles:

1. Use white bond paper, 21 by 28 cm or 8½ by 11 inches. Most instructors will ask you not to use erasable paper, since type, pencil, and ink all tend to smudge and blur badly on such paper. Do not submit work on paper torn out of a spiral notebook.

2. If you type your papers, use only a good black ribbon, a regular upright (i.e., not italic) typeface, and keep the type clean. Use unruled paper and double-space your text.

3. If you write your papers by hand, use medium- to wide-ruled paper and write on alternate lines. Use either black or blue-black ink. Never submit anything in pencil. Write legibly.

4. Use one side of the page only.

5. Leave generous margins, 3½ to 4 cm (1½ inches) at the left and probably at the top, and 2½ to 3 cm (1 inch) at the right and at the bottom.

6. Do not number the first page, or pages on which a new section begins (e.g., Notes or Bibliography), unless at bottom centre. Number all other pages consecutively with Arabic numerals in either the top right hand corner or at the top centre. Do not adorn the numerals with periods, dashes, slashes, circles, or other gizmos.

7. Centre the title about 5 cm (2 inches) down from the top of the first page. Leave at least one or two extra lines between the title and the beginning of the essay. For a long essay, such as a research paper, which is so bulky that it cannot easily be folded, it is customary to include a separate title page on which—centred or a little above centre—are the title, your name, the date, the course number, and the instructor's name. If you use such a title page, do not repeat the title on the first page of the essay.

8. Capitalize the title correctly (see #47m). Do not put the whole title in capital letters.

9. Do not underline your title or put it in quotation marks or put a period after it. If it includes the title of a poem, story, book, etc., or a ship's name, punctuate that part of it appropriately. Do not use the title of a published work by itself as your own title, though a work's title may be a part of your title. Here are some examples:

   Techniques of Irony in Swift's "A Modest Proposal"
   Thematic Imagery in *A Jest of God*
   How Are the Mighty Fallen: The Sinking of the *Titanic*

10. Never begin a line with a comma, semicolon, period, question mark, exclamation point, or hyphen. These marks of punctuation are attached to the words they follow, and therefore must occur at the end of a line rather than at the beginning of a new line. Occasionally a dash or the three or four dots of an ellipsis will fall at a line break; these *can* be put at the beginning of a new line, but even with these it is preferable—for clarity and ease of reading —to place them at the end of a line rather than at the beginning of a new line.

11. If you type, be sure to leave two spaces after any terminal punctuation; use two hyphens together to make a dash, with no space before or after them; and leave spaces before and after each period of an ellipsis. (But see #43i.)

12. Indent each paragraph five spaces (about 2 cm or an inch in handwritten papers). You need not leave extra space between paragraphs.

13. Be neat. If you make more than two or three emendations on a page, recopy the page. When you change or delete a

word or short phrase, draw a single horizontal line through it and write the new word or phrase, if any, above it. If you wish to insert an additional word or short phrase, place a caret (∧) below the line at the point of insertion and write in the addition above the line. If you wish to start a new paragraph where you have not indented for one, put the symbol ¶ where you want the paragraph to begin. If you wish to cancel a paragraph indention, put "No ¶" in the left margin. Avoid messy erasures, blots, and strike-overs.

14. Endorse your paper on the outside (usually at the top of the right-hand side of the back of the last page when the paper is folded vertically) with your name, the course number, the date, and probably the number of the assignment and the instructor's name. (See number 7 above.)

15. If necessary, fasten the pages of an essay together with a paper clip. Never use a staple or a pin. Long essays are often submitted in folders.

45b Syllabication and Word Division

syl
div
1. You should seldom need to divide a word at the end of a line; no one expects the right-hand margin of typed or hand-written material to be very straight. Therefore keep breaks to a minimum. If you must divide a word at the end of a line—perhaps because it is a very long word—be sure you divide it only between syllables. (Obviously, only words of two or more syllables can be divided.) If you are in doubt about where a word may be divided, consult your dictionary. Place a hyphen at the end of the line and the remainder of the divided word at the beginning of the next line.

2. Never separate a syllable consisting of only one letter from the rest of the word; if it were at the end of the word you would gain nothing, since the hyphen would occupy a space. Further, a single letter at either the beginning or the end of a line is often difficult to read as part of the rest of the word. It is even worth trying to avoid setting off syllables of only two letters; especially, do not separate a final *ed* from the rest of the word, even if it is a genuinely separate syllable.

3. Always try to begin the second part of the divided word with a consonant rather than a vowel. It makes for much easier reading. For example, divide *radical* so that the new line will begin with the consonant *c* rather than the vowel *i: radi-cal,* not *rad-ical.*

4. Try to avoid dividing words that are already hyphenated. If you must divide such a word, divide it only where the hyphen already stands.

Exercise 45b
Divide the following words according to their syllables. Consult your dictionary afterwards to see if you were correct. Indicate those syllabic breaks that should not be used to divide a word at the end of a line.

1. accommodated
2. apartment
3. appointed
4. befuddled
5. cannibalism
6. cigarette
7. commercialization
8. confused
9. counterirritant
10. differentiating
11. distinctly
12. Machiavellian
13. perspicacity
14. philosophical
15. prevaricated
16. sentenced
17. suggestion
18. tachometer
19. thoroughly
20. verisimilitude

---

46 Abbreviations

abbr Abbreviations are acceptable, even expected, in some special kinds of writing (technical and scientific writing, legal writing, business writing, reports, reference works, bibliographies and footnotes, tables and charts, and often in journalistic writing); in ordinary writing, however, only a few kinds should appear.

46a Titles before proper names, with or without initials or given names:

Mr. Johnson, Mrs. L. W. Smith, Dr. David Adams, St. John

46b In informal writing, titles before proper names with initials or given names:

> Prof. Roger Thomson (*but* Professor Thomson)
> Sen. I. C. Power (*but* Senator Power)
> Gen. John S. Hawkins (*but* General Hawkins)
> Rev. Matthew Markle (or, more formally, the Reverend Matthew Markle, the Reverend Mr. Markle)

These and similar titles should be spelled out in formal writing.

46c Titles and degrees after proper names:

> Timothy Johnson, Jr.
> David Adams, M.D. (but *not* Dr. David Adams, M.D.)
> A. Pullerman, D.D.S.
> Joseph McGregor, Ph.D., F.R.S.C.

Note: Academic degrees not following a name may also be abbreviated:

> Shirley is working toward her B.A.
> Abdul is studying for his M.A. examinations.

46d Standard words used with dates and numbers:

> 720 B.C., A.D. 231, the second century A.D., 7 a.m., 8:30 p.m., no. 17 (*or* No. 17)

Note that *A.D.* precedes a specific date whereas *B.C.* follows one.

46e Agencies and organizations commonly known by their initials:

> UNESCO, SIU, CBC, RCMP, NASA, CP Air

46f Some scientific, technical, or other terms (usually of considerable length) commonly known by their initials:

> BTU, DDT, DNA, ESP, FM, IPA, MLA, SST, TNT

46g Common Latin expressions used in English (in formal writing, it is preferable to spell out the English or, as with *versus,* the Latin equivalent):

i.e. (that is), e.g. (for example), cf. (compare), etc. (and so forth), vs. (*versus*), et al. (and others)

Notes:

1. If you use the abbreviation *e.g.,* use it only to *introduce* the example or list of examples; *following* the example or list, it should be written out:

> Some provinces—e.g., Alberta, Saskatchewan, and New Brunswick—felt that they had been poorly represented on the committee.
>
> Some provinces—Alberta, Saskatchewan, and New Brunswick, for example—felt that they had been poorly represented on the committee.

Note also that if you introduce a list with *e.g.* or *for example* or even *such as,* it is illogical to follow it with *etc.* or *and so forth.*

2. Use a comma after *i.e.* (just as you would to indicate the pause if you had written out *that is*). And usually use one after *e.g.* (test for it by reading aloud to see if you would pause after saying "for example").

3. The abbreviation *cf.* stands for the Latin *confer,* meaning *compare.* Do not use it, as so many carelessly do, to mean simply "see"; for that meaning the Latin *vide* (v.) would be correct.

Caution: Avoid using the abbreviation *etc.* lazily. Use it only when there are several items to follow and when they are obvious:

> Evergreen trees—cedars, pines, etc.—are common in northern latitudes.
>
> Learning the Greek alphabet—alpha, beta, gamma, delta, etc.—isn't really very difficult.
>
> *Wrong:* He considered several possible professions: accounting, teaching, farming, etc.

Further, if you do use *etc.,* do not write *and etc.,* since *etc.* (*et cetera*) already means "*and* so forth."

46h Terms used in official titles being copied exactly:

> Johnson Bros., Ltd.; Ibbetson & Co.; Smith & Sons, Inc.; Harper & Row; *Quill & Quire*

Caution: Never use the ampersand (&) as a substitute for *and*; use it only when copying a title of a company or publication exactly, as above.

47 Capitalization

cap All writers know that they should capitalize the first words of sentences and the pronoun *I*, but they are occasionally uncertain about some other uses of capitals. Here are the simple conventions governing capitalization.

Generally, capitalize proper nouns, abbreviations of proper nouns, and words derived from proper nouns, as follows:

47a Names and nicknames of real and fictional people:

> Lester B. Pearson, Barbara Ward, Bobby Orr, Rumplestiltskin

47b Names of real or fictional individual animals:

> Elsa, Rin Tin Tin, Lassie, King Kong, Dumbo

47c Titles when they are part of a name:

> Professor Jones (*but* I see that Jones is your professor.)
> Captain John Smith (*but* John Smith was a captain.)
> Rabbi David Small (*but* Mr. Small was our rabbi.)

Note: Normally titles that follow a name are not capitalized unless they have in effect become a part of the name: Joe Doaks, the senator; Bull Halsey, the admiral; *but* William the Conqueror, Peter the Hermit, Smokey the Bear. Some titles of particular distinction are customarily capitalized even if the person is not named:

> The Prime Minister will tour the Maritimes next month.
> The Queen visited Canada to open the Olympic Games.

47d Names designating family relationships when they are used as parts of proper names. When they are used in place of proper names, they are capitalized except when they follow a possessive:

> Uncle George (*but* I have an uncle named George.)
> There's my uncle, George. (*but* There's my Uncle George!)

I told Father about it. (*but* My father knows about it.)
I have always respected Grandmother. (*but* Juanita's grand-mother is a splendid old lady.)

47e Place names:

Alberta, Asia, Buenos Aires, the Amazon, the Andes, the Sahara, Japan, Vancouver Island, Hudson Bay, Kejimkujik National Park, Lake Ladoga, Moose Jaw, Rivière-du-loup, the Suez Canal, Trafalgar Square, Banff, Mt. Etna, Yonge Street, Québec, Niagara Falls

Caution: Do not capitalize *north, east, south,* and *west* unless they are part of specific place names (North Dakota, West Vancouver, South America) or are used to designate specific geographical areas (the frozen North, the East Coast, the Deep South, the Wild West, the Far East). Similarly, the seasons need not be capitalized: spring, summer, autumn, fall, winter.

47f Names of groups and organizations and of their members:

Canadian, Australian, Scandinavian, South American, Irish, Yankee, Toronto Maple Leafs, Progressive Conservatives, Catholic, Lions, Teamsters, Alcoholics Anonymous

47g Names of Institutions:

McGill University, Vancouver General Hospital, the Better Business Bureau, Lincoln Center, Le Reine Elizabeth

47h Names of deities and other religious names and terms:

God, the Holy Ghost, the Virgin Mary, the Bibie, the Dead Sea Scrolls, the Koran, Vishnu, Taoism, Islam, the Talmud

Note: Some people capitalize pronouns referring to a deity; others prefer not to.

47i Common nouns used as parts of proper nouns:

the Ottawa River, the Rocky Mountains, Fourth Street, the Pacific Ocean, Capilano College, the Eiffel Tower, the Mojave Desert, Canterbury Cathedral

47j Derivatives of proper nouns:

> Shakespearean, French Canadian, Confucianism, Haligonian, Celtic, Québecois, Christian, Miltonic, Vancouverite, Keynesian, Edwardian, Muscovite

Note: Some words derived from proper nouns—and some proper nouns themselves—have become so familiar, so commonly used, that they are no longer capitalized; for example: bible (in secular contexts), biblical, herculean, raglan, martial, quixotic, hamburger, frankfurter, french fries, champagne, burgundy, crapper, roman and italic, vulcanized, macadamized, galvanized, pasteurized, curie, volt, ampere, joule, gerrymander, denim, china, japanned, erotic, bloomers, jeroboam, jeremiad.

47k Abbreviations of proper nouns:

> NDP, CPR, TVA, CUPE, NATO, the BNA Act, P.E.I., B.C.

47l The pronoun *I* and the vocative interjection *O*.

47m In the title of any written work, including student essays, use a capital letter to begin the first word, the last word, and all other important words; leave uncapitalized only articles (*a, an, the*) and any conjunctions and prepositions that are less than five letters long (unless of course one of these is the first or last word in the title):

> | | |
> |---|---|
> | *A Jest of God* | *How to Win at Chess* |
> | *All About Eve* | *Of Thee I Sing* |
> | *In Which We Serve* | *Such Is My Beloved* |
> | *Victory Through Air Power* | *As for Me and My House* |
> | *As the World Wags On* | *Roughing It in the Bush* |

But be careful, for there can be exceptions: The relative pronoun *that* is usually not capitalized (*All's Well that Ends Well*), and in Ralph Ellison's "Tell It Like It Is, Baby," the preposition-cum-conjunction *like* demands to be capitalized.

Note: If the title includes a hyphenated word, capitalize the part after the hyphen if it is an important word:

The Scorched-Wood People
Murder Among the Well-to-do

Capitalize the first word of a subtitle, even if it is an article:

The Interior Landscape: The Literary Criticism of Marshall McLuhan

47n Always capitalize the first word of a sentence or of an acceptable fragment—of anything, that is, that concludes with terminal punctuation:

Modern art. Now there's a controversial topic. Right?

47o Also capitalize the first words of quotations that are intended as sentences or that are capitalized sentences in the original, but not fragments from other than the beginning of such sentences:

When he said "Let me take the wheel for a while," I shuddered at the memory of what had happened the last time I had let him "take the wheel."

If explanatory matter interrupts a quoted sentence, do not begin its second part with a capital.

"It was all I could do," she said, "to keep my head above water."

47p Capitalize the first word of a sentence in parentheses only if it stands by itself, apart from other sentences; if it is incorporated within another sentence, it is neither capitalized nor ended with a period (though it could end with a question mark or exclamation point; see #40 and #42b):

He did as he was told (there was really nothing else for him to do), and the tension was relieved. (But of course he would never admit to himself that he had been bested.)

47q An incorporated sentence following a colon may be capitalized if it seems to stand as a separate statement, for example if it is itself long or otherwise requires emphasis; otherwise it is best left uncapitalized:

There was one thing, he said, which we must never forget: No one has a right to a happiness that deprives someone else of deserved happiness.

It was a splendid night: the sky was clear except for a few picturesque clouds, the moon was full, and even a few stars shone through. (This *could* be capitalized, if the writer wanted particular emphasis on the details.)

It was no time for petty quarrels: everything depended on unanimity.

47r Although it is risky, and should not be done very often, a writer who has good control of tone can on occasion capitalize a personified abstraction or a word or phrase to which he wants to impart a special importance of one kind or another:

It was no longer a matter of simply getting along adequately; now it was a question of Survival.

Only when it begins to fade does Youth appear so valuable.

The filching fingers of the monster Inflation reach everywhere.

Sometimes the slight emphasis of capitalization can be used for a humorous or ironic effect:

Once he had popped The Question, she relented and let him catch her.

He insisted on driving His Beautiful Car: everyone else preferred to walk the two blocks without benefit of jerks and jolts and carbon monoxide fumes.

On occasion, but very infrequently, a writer can capitalize whole words and phrases or even sentences for a special sort of graphic emphasis:

When we reached the site, however, we were confronted by a sign warning us in no uncertain terms to KEEP OUT— TRESPASSERS WILL BE PROSECUTED.

When he made the suggestion to the group he was answered by a resounding NO.

Clearly in such instances no further indications, such as quotation marks or underlining, are necessary.

48 Titles

title Generally, titles of short works are enclosed in quotation marks; titles of longer works are italicized, i.e., underlined. (For the other uses of italics, see the next section; for the capitalization of titles, see #47m above.)

48a Put quotation marks around the titles of short stories, essays, short poems, chapters of books, and songs:

> Leonard Cohen's "Suzanne" is both poem and song.
> Poe's "The Cask of Amontillado" is one his most famous stories.

48b Use italics (underlining in a manuscript) for titles of written works published as units, such as books, magazines, journals, newspapers, and plays and movies:

> *Paradise Lost* is Milton's greatest work.
> Have you read Alice Munro's novel, *Lives of Girls and Women?*
> *Saturday Night* is a popular magazine.
> The scholarly journal *Canadian Literature* is published quarterly.
> I recommend that you see the Stratford production of *The Tempest.*
> I prefer *The Globe and Mail* to the *Winnipeg Free Press.*

Note: If the name of the city is printed as a part of a newspaper's name on the front page, it should be italicized (including the definite article): *The Vancouver Sun,* but *The Province, The Times* of London. Sometimes the definite article which often is part of a newspaper's name is not capitalized or italicized: *The New York Times* or the *New York Times.* This is especially likely if the name of the city necessarily intervenes: *The Citizen,* but the Ottawa *Citizen.* Some writers prefer never to consider the city as a part of the paper's name: the New York *Times;* the Edmonton *Journal.* Whichever practice you adopt, be consistent.

48c Titles of musical compositions (other than single songs), paintings, and sculpture are also italicized:

> Ravel's *Bolero;* Rembrandt's *The Night Watch;* Michelangelo's *David*

Caution: Be particularly careful with the definite article *the:* italicize and capitalize it only when it is actually part of the title: Margaret Laurence's *The Stone Angel;* Ethel Wilson's *Swamp Angel;* Pierre Boulle's *The Bridge on the River Kwai,* the *Partisan Review; The Encyclopaedia Britannica;* the *Atlas*

of Ancient Archaeology. Occasionally the indefinite article *a* or *an* bears watching as well.

48d Remember, do not italicize the titles of parts of publications; put quotation marks around them:

> The first chapter of Thoreau's *Walden* is called "Economy."
> "Shakespeare" is one of the poems in Irving Layton's collection *Nail Polish.*

There are exceptions, however. For example, a book by Robertson Davies, *Four Favourite Plays,* contains *Eros at Breakfast, The Voice of the People, At the Gates of the Righteous,* and *Fortune My Foe,* each of which as an individual play deserves to be italicized in its own right. Nevertheless, if you were to refer, for example in a footnote, to one of these plays as a part of this collection, you would enclose the title in quotation marks, not underline it. Italicizing a title means that the work being referred to was published separately. Some works, however, for example Coleridge's *The Rime of the Ancient Mariner* and Conrad's *Heart of Darkness,* although originally published as parts of larger collections, are fairly long and have attained a reputation and importance as individual works. Consequently most (though not all) writers feel justified in dignifying them with italics rather than consigning them to the relatively lesser regions indicated by quotation marks. Correct punctuation of titles can get quite tricky, and you must be careful. Consider for example the following:

> Northrop Frye's "Conclusion" to the 1965 *Literary History of Canada* is reprinted in his 1971 collection, *The Bush Garden: Essays on the Canadian Imagination,* where it is called simply "Conclusion to a *Literary History of Canada.*"

48e Another note on punctuating titles: If a book has a subtitle, it customarily appears below the title on the book's title page; usually there is no punctuation between title and subtitle. If you wish to include such a book's subtitle (as you would in a bibliographical entry), you must insert a *colon* between them, as we have done in the example above. (In this circumstance a single space following the colon is sufficient; the same is true for colons used in footnotes and bibliographical entries.)

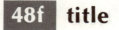

48f As in the last example cited in #48d, note that an essay title that includes a book title calls for italicizing part of what is enclosed in quotation marks. The reverse would be true if a book title included something that required quotation marks:

> *From Fiction to Film: D.H. Lawrence's "The Rocking-Horse Winner"*

Or, what is more common, when a book title includes something that itself would be italicized, such as a ship's name, another book title, or the name of a magazine, that secondary title is usually put in quotation marks:

> *The Nigger of the "Narcissus"*
> *Forum: Canadian Life and Letters 1920-1970: Selections from "The Canadian Forum"*

49 Italics

ital *Italics* are a special kind of slanting type; in typed or hand-written work, one represents italic type by underlining. The conventional uses of italics, other than for titles (see the preceding section), are as follows:

49a Italicize names of individual ships, planes, and the like:

> the *Golden Hind,* the *Erebus* and the *Terror,* the *St. Bonaventure,* the *Lusitania, The Spirit of St. Louis, Mariner IX,* the *Super Chief*

49b Italicize foreign words and phrases that are not yet sufficiently common to be entirely at home in English. English contains many terms that have come from other languages but that are no longer thought of as foreign and are therefore not italicized; for example: moccasin, wigwam, prairie, genre, tableau, bamboo, arroyo, corral, hara-kiri, chutzpah, spaghetti, goulash, hashish, eureka, litotes, hiatus, vacuum, and sic. There are also words which are sufficiently Anglicized not to require italicizing but which usually retain foreign accents, umlauts, and the like: cliché, naïf, cañon, façade, Götterdämmerung, fête champêtre. But English also makes use of many terms that are still felt to be sufficiently foreign to need italicizing; for example: *ad hoc, ad nauseam, au courant,*

chez, coup d'état, joie de vivre, Lebensraum, outré, per se, raison d'être, savoir faire, tempus fugit, vade mecum, verboten, Weltanschauung. Many such expressions are on their way to full acceptance into English. If you are at all unsure about a word, it is wise to consult a good up-to-date dictionary to find out if italics are necessary.

49c Italicize words, letters, and numerals referred to as such:

> The word *helicopter* is formed from Greek roots.
> There are two *r*'s in *embarrass.* (Note that only the *r* itself is italicized, and not the *s* which makes it plural.)
> The number *13* is considered unlucky even by many otherwise rational people.

49d Italicize words or phrases—or even whole sentences—that you want to emphasize:

> One thing he was now sure of: *that* was no way to go about it.
> Careful thought should lead one to the conclusion that *character,* not wealth or connections, will be most important in the long run.
> If someone tries to tell you otherwise, *don't listen to him.*
> Try to remember that *Fredericton,* not Saint John, is the capital of New Brunswick.
> He gave up his ideas of fun and decided instead to finish his education. *And it was the most important decision of his life.*

As with any typographical device, this method of achieving emphasis is worth trying to avoid in ordinary writing, for no merely mechanical means of emphasizing something can be as sound and, ultimately, as effective as punctuation, word order, and syntax. Such an easy method will often produce only a transitory effect. Consider the differences between the following sentences:

> Well, I felt just *terrible* when he told me that! (mere typographical effect, not helped by the exclamation point)
> I felt terrible, just terrible, when he told me that. (repetition—a little better)
> I can think of only one way to describe how I felt when he told me that: I felt terrible. (placement and punctuation—much better)

50 Numerals

num In technical and scientific writing, numerals are of course appropriate; newspapers sometimes use them to save space. But in ordinary writing certain conventions limit the use of numerals to express numbers.

50a Generally, spell out numbers that can be expressed in no more than two words; use numerals for numbers that would take more than two words:

> four; thirty; eighty-three; two hundred; seven thousand; 115; 385; 2120; three dollars; $3.48; five hundred dollars; $517

If you are writing about more than one number, say for purposes of comparison or giving statistics, then numerals are sometimes preferable:

> Enrollment dropped from 250 two years ago, to 200 last year, to only 90 this year.

Numerals are conventionally used for the following purposes:

50b For the time of day with *a.m.* or *p.m.*: 3 p.m. (*but* three o'clock)

50c For dates: November 11, 1918 *or* 11 November 1918

Note: *st, nd, rd,* and *th* can be used with numerals in dates, but only if the year is not given; also, the number may be written out:

> May 2, 1951; May 2nd; the second of May; May second

The year is almost always represented by numerals, and centuries written out:

> 1900 was the last year of the nineteenth century, not the first year of the twentieth century.

50d For addresses:

> 2132 Fourth Avenue; 4771 128th Street; P. O. Box 91; Apartment 8

50e For technical and mathematical numbers, such as percentages and decimals:

> 31 percent; 31%; 37°C; 37 degrees Celsius; 2.54 centimetres; 78 rpm

50f For page numbers and other divisions of a written work:

> page 27; p. 27; pp. 33-38; line 13; stanza 2; chapter 4; Chapter 4; section III; Part 2

50g A special form is used to refer to parts of a play:

> Act IV, scene ii, line 57 *or* (IV.ii.57)

Numerals are also often used to refer to parts of other literary works, especially in documentation (including parenthetical references); see #73.

> pages 3-4, (pp. 9-13), lines 3 and 5, (ll. 7-9), chapter 3, Chapter IV, Book IX of *Paradise Lost,* (IX, 120), 2 Samuel 22:3, II Samuel 19:1

(Note that books of the Bible are not italicized.)

50h Commas have long been conventionally used to separate groups of three figures in long numbers: 3,172,450; 17,920. As Canada proceeds to adopt the metric system, however, along with the rest of SI (Système Internationale, or International System of Units), such conventions change. Under SI (so abbreviated in all languages) groups of three digits on either side of a decimal point are separated by spaces rather than commas; with four digit numbers a space is optional:

> 3 172 450   3.1416 or 3.141 6   But: 3.141 59

This convention does not apply to addresses or amounts of money. For further information about SI consult the *Canadian Metric Practice Guide,* published by the Canadian Standards Association.

50i **Caution:** Do not begin a sentence with a numeral. Either spell out the number or rewrite the sentence so that the number does not come first:

Thirty to 40 percent goes for taxes. (Or rewrite to avoid the oddness: Taxes consume from 30 to 40 percent.)

Wrong: 750 people showed up to watch the chess tournament.
Right: As many as 750 people came to watch the chess tournament.
Right: The chess tournament drew 750 interested spectators.

Dates are sometimes considered acceptable at the beginning of a sentence:

1976 was a presidential election year in the United States.

But even this usage is worth avoiding, since some people object to it. Begin a sentence with a date only if you want a particular emphasis on it and can get it in no other way (see e.g. #50c) or if any rewritten version of the sentence sounds impossibly awkward.

Ms Note: When typing the Arabic numeral *one,* do not use a capital I, for that produces a Roman numeral. If your machine has no numeral *1,* use lower-case *l.*

Chapter Vl **Spelling**

For some writers, spelling seems to be the most troublesome convention of all; for others, it presents little or no difficulty. But even confident writers must look up a word in the dictionary now and again to check its spelling. If you are a poor speller, the dictionary may well be in a sense the best friend you have.

Spelling is not something to be taken lightly, to be shrugged off as not having any significant effect on a writer's ability to communicate a desired meaning. If you want a reader to respect what you write, you must show some respect for it yourself; sloppy spelling is visible evidence of a lack of such respect. Furthermore, correct spelling is not merely a conventional courtesy to the reader: judges have thrown cases out of court because of a misspelled name or a missing hyphen or apostrophe.

Unlike most other languages, English is rather capricious, sometimes even chaotic, in its spelling; often the same sound can be spelled in several ways (offer, fine, phone, cough; soap, sow, sew, so, beau, dough), or a single spelling element can be pronounced in several ways (cough, tough, dough, through, bough, fought; lot, tote, women, lost, tomb, fork, love). When such inconsistencies occur in longer and less familiar words, sometimes only a dictionary can help us. And remember, a dictionary does not offer *pre*scription but *de*scription: it is not commanding us to be correct, telling us what is "right" or "wrong," but simply recording as accurately as possible the conventions currently accepted by those who use the language—that is, by all of us.

The English language has changed a great deal over the centuries, and it is still changing. Old words pass out of use, new

201

words are added, conventions of grammar change, pronunciations change—and spelling changes, but not very fast; dictionaries can do a fairly good job of recording what is conventional, and therefore acceptable, and therefore "correct," right now. Words that are in transition are usually recorded as having more than one "correct" meaning or pronunciation or spelling. The word *pejorative*, for example, has several acceptable pronunciations (lexicographers will record them in what they consider to be the order of preference, with the most acceptable, or most common, first). Or consider the verb *dream*: its past tense can be either *dreamed* or *dreamt*. The past tense of *slide* has been *slid* since about the middle of the nineteenth century, before which it was *slided*; will the past tense of *glide* someday be "glid"? And consider *dove*: just a few years ago it was considered unacceptable, colloquial or dialectal at best, as the past tense of the verb *dive*; today it is almost as acceptable as the form *dived*. *Clue* is now the prevalent spelling, although for centuries it shared acceptability with *clew*. And so on.

In Canada we also have to contend with the influence of British and American spelling on ours. Some consider this a nuisance, but it can be thought of as a boon: we have greater choice than others. Broadly speaking, Canadian conventions—whether of spelling, punctuation, usage, pronunciation, or whatever—are more like American conventions than they are like British, and where they are changing they are changing in the direction of American conventions. Broadcast and print media by and large have chosen to adopt the usually simpler and more phonetic American spellings and pronunciations, and our closer proximity to the United States is gradually influencing the population at large in the same direction. We still say "leftenant" instead of "lootenant" although we spell it *lieutenant,* but we say and spell *aluminum* rather than *aluminium*. The last letter of the alphabet is still called *zed* rather than *zee* by most of us, though this difference is fading. (Long ago the letter *z* was called *izzard*—so you can see how far we have come!) Most Canadians write *centre* and *theatre* rather than, as Americans do, *center* and *theater*; but "skedule" is replacing "shedule" as the pronunciation of *schedule*. We usually write *connection* rather than *connexion* (though the influence of the British form apparently confuses some people into misspelling it *connextion*). Endings in *our* (colour, honour, labour, etc.) exist alongside those in *or* (color, honor, labor, etc.); either spelling is conventional in Canada. (Oddly enough, Americans prefer *glamour* to *glamor,* as do the British; many Canadians prefer *glamor.*) The same is true of endings in *ise* or *ize,* though in Canada the *ize* forms are clearly preferred. *Cheque* (bank) is far more common than *check,* and *racquet* (tennis) seems to be holding out against *racket*; but *draught* is losing ground to *draft,* and *program* is rapidly replacing *programme*; *judgment* and *judgement* are probably about even. And so on. (Should you ever wish to make an adverb out of the adjective *supple,* you may be pleased to discover that Canadians, like Americans, prefer the form *supplely* rather than the potentially confusing British form *supply.*)

Where alternative spellings exist, either is correct. But as in other areas where alternatives are available, you should try to be consistent; that is, if you spell *honour* thus, then you should also write *humour* and *colour* and *labour*; if you choose the form *analyze,* then you will also choose *paralyze* and *modernize*; if you choose *centre,* you will also choose *lustre* and *fibre.* And if do you use the *our* ending, watch out for the trap: if you write *humour, colour, vapour,* etc., then, when you add the suffixes *ous, ation,* and *ize* (or *ise*) to them, you must drop the *u* and write *humorous, coloration, vaporize.*

The point is, there is choice. In this book, for example, we have chosen to use the *our* rather than the *or* ending because we think it is still considered standard outside the popular media. And we have chosen the *ize* rather than the *ise* ending (where alternative possibilities exist) because we believe it to be the dominant form. If a particular form is clearly dominant or an acknowledged standard, we think it should be used: *catalogue, employee, furor,* and *syrup,* for example, are at present such forms. (We have included in the Spelling List at the end of this chapter some other words with alternative spellings that might occasionally be troublesome. The first form listed is at least slightly preferable.)

But such dilemmas, if they are dilemmas, are relatively infrequent. The real spelling difficulties, those shared by Canadian, British, and American writers, are of a different order.

51 Spelling Rules and Common Causes of Error

Many spelling errors result from carelessness or ignorance; self-discipline and a good dictionary are the only cures. Many other spelling errors, however, fall into clear categories. Weak spellers owe it to themselves and to the quality of their writing to familiarize themselves with the principles or "rules" that govern certain trouble spots. The material that follows provides the main rules and points out the main sources of spelling errors.

51a *ie* or *ei:*

The dilemma over whether to use *ie* or *ei* plagues many writers. The old jingle should help: Use *i* before *e* except after *c,* or when sounded like *a* as in *neighbour* and *weigh.*

> *ie:* achieve, believe, chief, shriek, fiend, field, siege, wield
> *ei* after *c:* conceive, deceive, receive, perceive, ceiling
> *ei* when sounded like *a:* neighbour, sleigh, weigh, veil, eight

When the sound is neither that of long *e* ($\bar{e}$) or long *a* ($\bar{a}$), the spelling *ei* is usually used:

> foreign, heir, height, counterfeit, their, forfeit

But there are several exceptions, which can only be memorized:

> seize, weird, leisure, either, neither, sieve, financier, friend

When in doubt, consult your dictionary.

51b *cede, ceed,* or *sede:*

A simple act of memorizing will prevent confusion among these endings. The *sede* ending occurs in only one word: *supersede.* The *ceed* ending is used for only three words: *exceed, proceed,* and *succeed.* All other words ending in this sound use *cede:* accede, concede, intercede, precede, recede, secede.

51c Final *e* before suffixes:

A *suffix* is one or more syllables added on to the end of a *root* word to form a new word, usually changing its part of speech. For example:

root	suffix	new word
appear (v.)	ance	appearance (n.)
content (adj.)	ment	contentment (n.)
occasion (n.)	al	occasional (adj.)
occasional (adj.)	ly	occasionally (adv.)

When the root word ends in a silent (unpronounced) *e,* however, certain rules generally apply. If the suffix begins with a vowel (a, e, i, o, or u), the final *e* of the root is usually dropped:

desire + able = desirable   forgive + able = forgivable
sphere + ical = spherical   argue + ing = arguing
come + ing = coming   allure + ing = alluring
continue + ous = continuous   desire + ous = desirous
sense + ual = sensual   architecture + al = architectural

Most words ending in *ce* or *ge* retain the final *e* in order to preserve the soft sound of the *c* (like *s* rather than *k*) and the *g* (like *j* rather than hard as in *g*un);

notice + able = noticeable
outrage + ous = outrageous

(Note the similar spelling of the words *vengeance* and *sergeant*.) This is true, however, only if the suffix begins with *a* or *o*; note for example that *dance + ing = dancing*. And note the spelling of *negligible*.

Similarly, words like *picnic* and *frolic*, which end in a hard *c*, must have a *k* added to preserve the hard sound before a suffix beginning with *e* or *i*: *picnicked, picknicking, frolicked, frolicking, politicking*; but: *tactical, frolicsome*. Exception: *arced, arcing*.

If the suffix begins with a consonant, the final *e* of the root word is usually not dropped:

definite + ly = definitely   involve + ment = involvement
effective + ness = effectiveness   mere + ly = merely
hoarse + ly = hoarsely   separate + ly = separately
immediate + ly = immediately   awe + some = awesome
immense + ly = immensely   woe + ful = woeful

Here there is a subgroup of words whose final silent *e*'s often are wrongly omitted before suffixes. In these words, the *e* in question is essential to keep the sound of the preceding vowel long:

livelihood	hopelessness	loneliness
remoteness	severely	completely
extremely	tasteless	

But again there are some important exceptions, so be very careful. These, for example, should be memorized:

awe + ful = awful   argue + ment = argument
due + ly = duly   true + ly = truly

Note that in these examples no consonant intervenes between the long vowel and the final *e* (the *w* in *awe* is a semi-vowel, not a true consonant).

51d Final *y* after a consonant before suffixes:
When the suffix is *ing,* the *y* is retained:

try + ing = trying   bully + ing = bullying

(Note: words ending in *ie* change it to *y* before adding *ing*:

die + ing = dying.)

When the suffix begins with something other than *i*, the *y* is changed to *i*:

happy + er = happier   duty + ful = dutiful
fancy + ful = fanciful   angry + ly = angrily
happy + ness = happiness

Exceptions: shyly, shyness; slyer or slier, slyly or slily, flyer or flier.

Caution: Do not carelessly omit the *y* before *ing:* not *worring,* but *worrying.*

51e Doubling of a final consonant before a suffix:
Double the final consonant of the root if

    (a)   that final consonant is preceded by a single vowel,

(b) the root is a one-syllable word or a word accented on its last syllable, and

(c) the suffix begins with a vowel.

One-syllable words:

fit + ed = fitted	fit + ing = fitting
	fit + er = fitter
shop + ed = shopped	shop + ing = shopping
	shop + er = shopper
bar + ed = barred	bar + ing = barring
hot + er = hotter	hot + est = hottest

Words accented on last syllable:

allot + ed = allotted	allot + ing = allotting
commit + ed = committed	commit + ing = committing
occur + ed = occurred	occur + ing = occurring
	occur + ence = occurrence
propel + ed = propelled	propel + ing = propelling
	propel + or = propellor

But note that when the addition of the suffix shifts the accent of the root word away from the last syllable, the final consonant is not doubled:

refer + ed = referred	refer + ing = referring	BUT *ref*erence
infer + ed = inferred	infer + ing = inferring	BUT *in*ference
prefer + ed = preferred	prefer + ing = preferring	BUT *pref*erence

Do not double the final consonant if that consonant is preceded by another single consonant:

faint + ed = fainted	faint + er = fainter
sharp + er = sharper	sharp + en = sharpen

or if the final consonant is preceded by two vowels:

fail + ed = failed	fail + ing = failing
stoop + ed = stooped	stoop + ing = stooping

or if the root word is more than one syllable and *not* accented on its last syllable:

benefit + ed = benefited	ballot + ed = balloted
parallel + ed = paralleled	paralleling parallelism

Note: For other words ending in *l*, even when they are of two or more syllables and not accented on the final syllable, the final *l* is often doubled; for example: *labelled* or *labeled; traveller* or *traveler*. Either form is correct, though in Canada the preference is for the doubled *l*. (Some even double the *l* at the end of *parallel,* in spite of the awkwardly present double *ll* preceding it.) The word *kidnap* is a similar exception, for the obvious reason of pronunciation. Either *kidnapped* or *kidnaped* is correct (and *kidnapping* or *kidnaping*). Another is *worship*: either *worshipped* or *worshiped, worshipping* or *worshiping*. In both instances, the doubled final consonant is preferred.

The final consonant should not be doubled if the suffix does not begin with a vowel:

commit + ment = commitment   hot + ly = hotly
defer + ment = deferment

51f The suffix *ly:*
When *ly* is added to an adjective already ending in a single *l,* that final *l* is retained, resulting in an *lly* ending for the new adverb; correct pronunciation of these and similar words will help prevent you from misspelling them.

accidental + ly = accidentally   mental + ly = mentally
incidental + ly = incidentally   natural + ly = naturally
official + ly = officially   cool + ly = coolly
political + ly = politically

If the root already ends in a double *ll,* one *l* is of course dropped: full + ly = fully, chill + ly = chilly, droll + ly = drolly.

Note: adjectives ending in *ic* add *ally,* not just *ly,* in becoming adverbs; again correct pronunciation will help avoid error:

basic, basically   dramatic, dramatically
enthusiastic, enthusiastically   drastic, drastically
symbolic, symbolically   scientific, scientifically

51g Prefixes

The more you know about how words are put together, the less trouble you will have with spelling. Many spelling errors, for example, occur because a writer does not realize that a given word consists of a root word with something stuck onto the front of it: a prefix. (*Pre* is from a Latin word meaning *before*; *fix* is a root, meaning *fasten* or *place*; the new word is *prefix*.) When a prefix ends with the same letter that the root begins with, the result is a double letter; be careful not to forget one of them:

ad + dress = address   mis + spell = misspell
com + motion = commotion   un + necessary = unnecessary

Similarly, one must be careful not to omit one of the doubled letters in certain compounds; for example:

beach + head = beachhead   room + mate = roommate

Many words have been formed by adding a prefix to a root whose first letter "pulls" the last letter of the prefix over, causing it to change, so that a double letter results. Writers unaware that a prefix is involved sometimes forget to double the consonant. The Latin prefix *ad,* meaning *to, toward, near,* is very commonly affected this way; for example, *ad* became *af* when it was added to the Latin *facere,* meaning *to do*; hence our word *affect* is spelled with two *f*'s. Here are some examples of this phenomenon occurring with *ad* and a few other prefixes:

ad >	an	in annul, annihilate
	ap	in apprehend, apparatus, application
	ac	in access, accept, acquire, acquaint
	al	in allusion
com >	con	in connect
	col	in collide
	cor	in correct, correspond
ob >	op	in opposed
sub >	suc	in success, succumb
	sup	in suppress

Note the structure of this frequently misspelled word: *accommodate*; both the *ac* and the *com* are prefixes, so the word must be spelled with both a double *c (cc)* and a double *m (mm)*. Errors can also result from mistaking the prefix. The writer who spells *arouse* with a double *r (rr)* doesn't realize that the prefix in this instance is simply *a*, not *ad>ar*. And the writer who spells *apology* with a double *p (pp)* is unaware that the prefix here is *apo*, not *ad>ap* (here awareness that the root involved is the Greek *logos*, "speech," would have helped prevent the error). It is helpful to be familiar with as many prefixes as possible. Here is a list of words with their prefixes printed in capital letters; each word is followed by a common misspelling that could have been avoided had the writers known their prefixes:

Right	*Wrong*	*Right*	*Wrong*
AFOREmentioned	aformentioned	MILLImetre	milimetre
BY-product	biproduct	MINIature	minature
CONTROversial	conterversial	PENinsula	penninsula
DEscribe	discribe	PERsuade	pursuade
DEstroy	distroy	PERvading	prevading
DIAlogue	diologue	PORtraying	protraying
DISappointed	dissappointed	PROfessor	proffessor
EXTRAordinary	extrordinary	Utopia	eutopia

51h Suffixes

Suffixes too can give trouble. For example, if you add *ness* to a word already ending in *n*, that original *n* must be retained, resulting in a double *n (nn)*:

> barren + ness = barrenness
> open + ness = openness
> stubborn + ness = stubbornness

This is true even when the final *n* is not pronounced:

> solemn + ness = solemnness

ful:

Remember that the correct suffix is *ful*, not *full*:

> spoonful, cupful, shovelful, bucketful, roomful, successful

51i Troublesome word-endings

Several groups of suffixes—here more conveniently thought of simply as word-endings—consistently plague bad spellers and sometimes confuse even good spellers. There are no rules governing them; pronunciation is seldom any help; one either knows them or does not. Whenever you are not absolutely sure of the correct spelling, consult your dictionary. The following examples will at least alert you to the potential trouble spots:

able, ably, ability; ible, ibly, ibility:

Many more words end in *able* than in *ible,* which should be a help; nevertheless, it is the *ible* endings that seem to cause the most trouble.

advisable	audible
comparable	deductible
debatable	eligible
desirable	flexible
immeasurable	forcible
indubitable	incredible
inevitable	inexpressible
laudable	irresistible
noticeable	negligible
quotable	plausible
respectable	responsible
syllable	tangible
veritable	visible

ent, ently, ence, ency; ant, antly, ance, ancy:

apparent	appearance
consistent	attendance
coherent	blatant
independent	brilliant
existence	concomitant
excellent	extravagant
inherent	flamboyant
persistence	irrelevant
permanent	maintenance
resilient	resistance
tendency	warrant

tial, tian, tiate; cial, cian, ciate:

confidential	beneficial

dietitian	crucial
existential	emaciated
expatiate	enunciate
influential	mathematician
martial	mortician
spatial	physician
substantial	politician

ce; se:

choice	course
evidence	dense
fence	dispense
presence	expense
pretence	phrase
voice	sparse

ative; itive:

affirmative	additive
imaginative	competitive
informative	genitive
negative	positive
restorative	sensitive

51j Some words require extra care because the spelling of their roots changes when they shift from one part of speech to another—sometimes because of a change in stress; for example:

clear, clarity	prevail, prevalent
despair, desperate	pronounce, pronunciation
exclaim, exclamatory	repair, reparable
maintain, maintenance	repeat, repetition

inherit, heritage, BUT heredity, hereditary

51k Spelling errors caused by faulty pronunciation

If you pronounce a word incorrectly, chances are you will also spell it incorrectly. Try to acquire the habit of careful and correct pronunciation; sound words to yourself, exaggeratedly if necessary, even at the expense of temporarily slowing down your reading speed. Here are some correctly spelled words followed by common misspellings; notice that mispronunciation is the likely culprit. Check your dictionary for any pronunciations you are not sure of.

Right	*Wrong*
academic	acedemic
accidentally	accidently
analogy	anology
approximately	approximently
architectural	architectual
athlete,	athelete,
athletics	atheletics
authoritative	authoratative
Britain	Britian
celebration	celabration
conference	confrence
congratulate	congradulate
controversial	contraversial
deteriorating	detiorating
detrimental	dentremental
dilapidated	delapitated
diphthong	dipthong
disastrous	disasterous
disgruntled	disgrunted
disillusioned	disallusioned
eerie	errie
elaborate	elaberate
emperor	emporer
environment	enviorment, enviroment
epitomize	epitemize
escape	excape
evident	evedent
excerpt	exerpt
facsimiles	facsimalies
film	filum
foliage	foilage
frailty	fraility
further	futher
government	goverment
governor	govenor
gravitation	gravatation
hereditary	heriditary
hurriedly	hurridly
immersing	emersing
incident	incedent
insurgence	ensurgence
interpretation	interpertation,
	interpratation

Right	Wrong
intimacy	intamacy
inviting	enviting
lightning	lightening
limpidly	lipidly
lustrous	lusterous
negative	negitive
nuclear	nucular
occasional	occational, occassional
optimism	optomism
original	origional
particular	peticular
peculiar	perculiar
permanently	perminently
phenomenon	phenomanon
philosophical	philisophical
predilection	predeliction
prevalent	prevelent
privilege	privelege
pronunciation	pronounciation
repetitive	repeditive
reservoir	resevoir
significant	signifigant
similar	similiar, simular
strength	strenth
suffocate	suffacate
surprise	suprise, supprise
temporarily	tempirarily, tempararily
ultimatum	ultamatum
village	villiage
villain	villian
visible	visable
vulnerability	vulnerbility
where	were
whether	wether
whines	wines

Sometimes changing the form of a word shifts its accent. For example, when the suffix *ical* is added to the word *technólogy,* the accent shifts to the third syllable: *technológical*; since the first *o* is no longer stressed, some writers change it, quite wrongly, to an *i* or an *a* (technilogical, technalogical). With such words, try to remember the spelling of the *root* word; it will almost always remain the same (except of course for its ending), even though the pronunciation may change when a suffix or a prefix is added.

Caution: Be careful not to omit the *d* or *ed* from such words as *used* and *supposed, old-fashioned* and *prejudiced,* which are often carelessly pronounced:

> I used to read a lot. (NOT use)
> She's a very old-fashioned girl. (NOT old-fashion)
> You were supposed to pick up a loaf of bread. (NOT suppose to)
> He seemed very prejudiced against Ontarians. (NOT prejudice against)

And don't write or copy so hastily that you omit whole syllables (usually near-duplications in sound). Write carefully—and proofread even more carefully, sounding the words to yourself. Here are some examples of "telescoped" words that occur repeatedly:

Right	*Wrong*
politician	politian
remembrance	rembrance
repetition	repition
criticize	critize
examining	examing
independent	indepent
convenience	convience
inappropriate	inappriate
institution	instution

511 Spelling errors caused by confusion with other words
Don't let false analogies and similarities of sound lead you astray.

A careless writer who thinks of a word like:	may make the error of spelling another word WRONG, like this:	instead of spelling it the RIGHT way, like this:
young	amoung	among
breeze	cheeze	cheese
conform	conformation	confirmation

diet	diety	deity
desolate	desolute	dissolute
exalt	exaltant	exultant
democracy	hypocracy	hypocrisy
discrete	indiscrete	indiscreet
ideal	idealic	idyllic
air, fairy	ordinairy	ordinary
ledge, knowledge	priviledge	privilege
size	rize	rise
religious	sacreligious	sacrilegious
familiar	similiar	similar
stupid	stupifying	stupefying
summer	summerize	summarize
prize	surprize	surprise
tack	tacktics	tactics
rink, sink	zink	zinc

51m Homonyms and Other Words Sometimes Confused

Some words are pronounced exactly like other words but mean different things and are spelled differently; these are called HOMONYMS. Be sure to distinguish such words from their sound-alikes. Here are some that have proved troublesome; look up in the dictionary any whose meanings you are not sure of, for this is a matter not just of spelling but of meaning as well (and see *Wrong Word, #57*).

aisle, isle	hail, hale
alter, altar	hanger, hangar
bear, bare	hoard, horde
birth, berth	hole, whole
border, boarder	holy, holey, wholly
born, borne	idle, idol, idyll
by, by-, bi-, buy, bye	incidents, incidence
callous, callus	insight, incite
canvas, canvass	its, it's
capital, capitol	led, lead
complement, compliment	mantel, mantle
cord, chord	naval, navel
council, counsel	paid, payed
course, coarse	past, passed
die, dying; dye, dyeing	patience, patients
discreet, discrete	peddle, pedal
forgo, forego	phase, faze

plain, plane	stationary, stationery
populous, populace	surf, serf
pray, prey	there, their, they're
precedence, precedents	to, too, two
presence, presents	vice, vise
principle, principal	waste, waist
roll, role	wave, waive
sight, site, cite	whose, who's
soul, sole	your, you're

There are also words which, although not pronounced exactly alike, are yet so similar that they are often confused. Be careful to distinguish between such words as these (and again, look up in the dictionary any whose meanings you are not sure of):

accept, except	finely, finally
access, excess	flaunt, flout
adopt, adapt, adept	forbear, forebear
adverse, averse	gantlet, gauntlet
advice, advise	genius, ingenious, ingenuous
allude, elude	Granada, Grenada
angle, angel	illusion, allusion, disillusion
bisect, dissect	impractical, impracticable
breath, breathe	incredulous, incredible
careen, career	later, latter
choose, chose	lineage, linage
censor, censure	liniment, lineament
climatic, climactic	loathe, loath
conscious, conscience	loose, lose
custom, costume	mitigate, militate
decent, descent, dissent	moral, morale
desert, dessert	persecute, prosecute
device, devise	predominate, predominant
discomfit, discomfort	prophecy, prophesy
elicit, illicit	quite, quiet
emigrate, immigrate	statue, statute
eminent, imminent, immanent	tack, tact
ensure, insure	than, then
envelop, envelope	verses, *versus*

Be careful also to distinguish between such words as the following, for although they sound the same, they function differently depending on whether they are spelled as one word or two:

already (adverb)	all ready (adverb plus adjective)
altogether (adverb)	all together (adverb plus adjective)
anybody (pronoun)	any body (adjective plus noun)
anyway (adverb)	any way (adjective plus noun)
awhile (adverb)	a while (article plus noun)
everyday (adjective)	every day (adjective plus noun)
everyone (pronoun)	every one (adjective plus pronoun)
maybe (adverb)	may be (verb)
nobody (pronoun)	no body (adjective plus noun)
someday (adverb)	some day (adjective plus noun)
sometime·(adverb)	some time (adjective plus noun)

51n One Word or Two Words?

The following words, among others, are always spelled as one unhyphenated word; do not spell them as if they consisted of two or three separate or hyphenated words:

background	nevertheless	spotlight
buildup (noun)	nonetheless	straightforward
countryside	nowadays	sunrise
easygoing	outshine	throughout
lifetime (noun or adj.)	setback	wrongdoing

Note: *Cannot* should almost always be written as one word. Write it as two words only when you want special emphasis on the *not,* as in "No, Johnny, you can *not* go out and play!"

The following words, on the other hand, should always be spelled as two words, unhyphenated:

a bit	any time	in order (to)
a lot	even though	in spite (of)
a part (noun)	every time	(on the) other hand
all right (NOT alright)	in between	(in) other words
any more	in front	time period

When in doubt consult your dictionary. You may find, as with *insofar, in so far,* that either form is acceptable.

51o Hyphenation

To hyphenate or not to hyphenate? That is often the question. There are some firm rules; there are some sound guidelines; and there is a large territory where only common sense and a good dictionary can help you find your way. Since the conventions are constantly changing, sometimes rapidly, make a habit of checking your dictionary for current usage; at least then you can be consistent. (For hyphens to divide words at the end of a line, see *Syllabication and Word Division,* #45b.)

Use hyphens in compound numbers from twenty-one to ninety-nine:

> Forty-three people came.
> He scored eighty-five out of a possible one hundred.

Use hyphens with fractions used as adjectives:

> A two-thirds majority is required to defeat the amendment.

When a fraction is used as a noun, however, many writers do not use a hyphen:

> Four fifths of the audience was asleep.
> The correct amount to use is about one fourth of the whole.

Use hyphens with compounds indicating time, when these are written out:

> seven-thirty, nine-fifteen

Use a hyphen between a pair of numbers (including hours and dates) which indicate a range, for example of pages or time:

> You will find the information on pages 73-78.
> The festival will be held June 20-26.

Note that the hyphen in these instances is equivalent to the word *to.* If, however, you use the word *from* to introduce the range, you should write out the word *to* instead of using a hyphen: "from June 20 to 26." Similarly, since you would not write "held between June 25 to July 2," neither should you write "held between June 25-July 2," but simply "held June 25-July 2."

Use hyphens with prefixes before proper nouns:

> all-Canadian   pre-Christian

anti-Fascist	pro-Tory
ex-Prime Minister	pseudo-Pindaric
non-Communist	semi-Gothic
post-Elizabethan	Trans-Siberian Railroad
Pan-Slavic	un-English

But there are some long-established exceptions; for example:

transatlantic   transpacific   antichrist

Use hyphens with compounds beginning with the prefix *self:* self-made, self-deluded, self-pity, self-confidence, self-esteem, self-assured, etc. Only a few words beginning with *self* are written without a hyphen: selfhood, selfish, selfless, selfsame; in these words *self* is the root, not the prefix. Hyphens are conventionally used with certain other prefixes, such as *all, ex* (meaning *former*), and *quasi:* all-important, ex-premier, quasi-religious. (It is usually preferable to use *former* rather than *ex.*)

Hyphens are conventionally used with most, but not all, compounds beginning with *vice* and *by:* vice-consul, vice-chancellor, vice-president, vice-principal, vice-regent, etc., BUT viceregal, viceroy; by-election, by-pass, etc., BUT bylaw, bygone, byroad.

Hyphens are used with the suffixes *elect* and *designate:* mayor-elect, ambassador-designate.

Hyphens are used in some words designating family relationships:

mother-in-law, father-in-law, son-in-law, daughter-in-law; great-grandfather, great-grandmother, great-granddaughter, great-grandson, great-aunt, great-uncle, great-nephew, great-niece, great-grandchild, great-grandparent;

but not in others:

grandmother, grandfather, grandson, granddaughter, grandparents, grandchild; stepmother, stepfather, stepdaughter, stepson, stepsister, stepbrother;

and still others are written as two words:

first cousin, second cousin, half sister, half brother.

Use hyphens to prevent a word's being mistaken for an entirely different word:

> He recounted what had happened after the ballots had been re-counted.
>
> If you're going to re-strain the juice, I'll restrain myself from drinking it now, seeds and all.
>
> Once at the resort after the bumpy ride, we sat down to re-sort our jumbled fishing gear.
>
> If you re-cover that chair before you sell it, you may be able to recover your investment.

Use hyphens to prevent awkward or confusing combinations of letters and sounds: anti-intellectual, photo-offset, re-echo, set-to, war-risk, doll-like.

Hyphens are sometimes necessary to prevent ambiguity:

> *Ambiguous:* The ad offered six week old kittens for sale.
> *Clear:* The ad offered six week-old kittens for sale.
> *Clear:* The ad offered six-week-old kittens for sale.

Another example:

> It will require two-hundred foot-pounds of energy to do the job.

Here, although *two hundred* would not normally be hyphenated, it is advisable in order to avoid the possible momentary misreading of *two hundred-foot*. And though one might refer to "forty odd dollars," one would be well advised to use a hyphen if referring to "forty-odd students." Here is another example:

> Some people think that what we need is a social evening out of benefits and responsibilities.

Simply hyphenating *evening-out* removes the possibility of misreading the sentence. (And using another word, such as *sharing* or *levelling,* would probably be even better.)

51p Compound Nouns

Some nouns composed of two or more words are conventionally hyphenated; for example: free-for-all, half-and-half, half-breed, man-eater, merry-go-round, old-timer, runner-up, safe-conduct, shut-in, tam-o'-shanter, trade-in, well-being. But many nouns that one might think should be hyphenated are not, and others that may once have been hyphenated, or even two separate words, have become so familiar that they are no longer separated by either a space or a hyphen. Usage is constantly and rapidly changing, and even dictionaries do not always agree on what is standard at a given time. Here for example is how six different dictionaries list the same words:

1.	pre-eminence	sheep-dog	waste-paper
2.	pre-eminence or preëminence	sheep dog	wastepaper or waste paper
3.	preeminence or pre-eminence	sheep dog	wastepaper
4.	preeminence, pre-eminence, or preëminence	sheepdog or sheep dog	wastepaper
5.	preeminence	sheep dog	wastepaper or waste paper
6.	pre-eminence	sheep dog	wastepaper

Here the dictionaries are cited in order of age, from the oldest (1) to the most recent (6). Though in general separate words and hyphenated compounds tend to give way to hyphenated and solid forms respectively, the pattern is not consistent, as you can see. Some dictionaries still record such old-fashioned and outdated forms as *to-night* and *to-morrow* as alternatives; be sure you use the preferred and newer forms *tonight* and *tomorrow*. Clearly one must consult a dictionary that is both good and up-to-date, and use the form it lists first.

51q Compound Modifiers

When two or more words are used together in such a way that they act like a single adjective before a noun, they are usually hyphenated: a well-dressed man, greenish-gray eyes, middle-class values, a once-in-a-lifetime chance, a three-day-old strike. But note that many compound modifiers are already listed as hyphenated words in the dictionary. One dictionary, for example, lists these, among others: first-class, fly-by-night, good-looking, habit-forming, matter-of-fact, open-minded, right-hand, short-lived, tongue-tied, warm-blooded, wide-eyed. These compound modifiers—already hyphenated—will of course remain hyphenated even when they follow the nouns they modify:

> Her performance was first-class.
> The tone of the speech was very matter-of-fact.
> The blossoms on this plant are very short-lived.

If the compound includes an *ly* adverb, however, it is not hyphenated, even when it precedes the noun it modifies:

> He is a happily married man.
> The superbly wrought sculpture was the centre of attention.

Exercise 51pq

What does your dictionary say about the following compounds? Should they be two separate words, hyphenated, or one solid word?

1.	boy friend	11.	power boat
2.	dumb waiter	12.	pre empt
3.	fish pole	13.	run around
4.	foot candle	14.	slip stream
5.	girl friend	15.	south bound
6.	half life	16.	stock pile
7.	half moon	17.	time out
8.	home stretch	18.	wine skin
9.	nail set	19.	world weary
10.	pocket book	20.	world wide

51r When two contrasting prefixes are used with one root, a "suspension" hyphen is used—even if the prefix would not normally be hyphenated:

> The audience was about equally divided between pro- and anti-Liberal listeners.
> You can either pre- or postdate the letter.

Note that some expressions can be spelled either as two separate words or as compounds, depending on what part of speech they are serving as; for example:

He works full time. (n.) He has a full-time job. (adj.)

If you get too dizzy you may black out. (v.) You will then suffer a blackout. (n.)

Call up the next group of trainees. (v.) The commander ordered a general call-up. (n.)

51s Verbs too are sometimes hyphenated. A dictionary will list most of the ones you might want to use; for example: baby-sit, pan-broil, pistol-whip, pole-vault, re-educate, second-guess, sight-read, soft-pedal, straight-arm, two-time.

Exercise 51o–s

Insert hyphens wherever they are needed in the following sentences. Consult your dictionary if necessary.

1. His broad jump record was twenty three and three quarters feet.
2. I would expect that two thirds of the members will be uncooperative.
3. The speech had a distinctly antiAmerican tone, and one of selfcongratulation to boot.
4. The all Canadian team proved too much for even the exchampions.
5. My half sister showed me an old tintype picture of her greatgrandmother.
6. She had bluish grey eyes, but they went well with her light blue dress.
7. The fully developed outline will be on your desk by midmorning.
8. The three youths, though well built, looked to me a run of the mill sort.
9. Summertime was only a golden memory.
10. There will be a two month delay.

51t Plurals

Most nouns add *s* or *es* to the singular to indicate plural number:

one girl, two girls   one wish, two wishes
one cat, two cats   one church, two churches
                       one box, two boxes

Add *es* rather than just *s* if forming the plural makes an extra syllable, as in the last three examples.

Nouns ending in *o* form their plural with either *s* or *es*. Some of these nouns use either plural form, but you should use the form listed first in your dictionary. Here are a few examples:

altos   tomatoes
echoes   buffaloes or buffalos
heroes   mottoes or mottos
noes   zeroes or zeros
potatoes

If the final *o* is preceded by a vowel, however, only an *s* is added:

arpeggios
cameos
embryos (*y* in this instance is a vowel)
studios

To form the plural of some nouns ending in a single *f* or an *fe*, change the ending to *ve* before adding the *s;* for example:

self, selves   life, lives
loaf, loaves   thief, thieves
leaf, leaves   knife, knives
shelf, shelves

But note:

beliefs   poufs
chiefs   still lifes
gulfs

Most words ending in two *f*'s simply add an *s:*

cliffs   sheriffs   puffs

Some words ending in *f* have alternative acceptable plurals:

wharfs or wharves   scarfs or scarves   dwarfs or dwarves

The plural of *hoof* can be either *hoofs* or *hooves*. *Roofs* is at present the only acceptable plural of *roof,* but someday, perhaps in only a few years, "rooves" will also be acceptable; one already hears it being pronounced that way.

Note: The well-known athletic group called the *Maple Leafs* is obviously a special case, a proper noun that does not follow the rules governing common nouns.

Nouns ending in *y* preceded by a consonant change the *y* to *i* and add *es:*

> one city, two cities
> one family, two families
> one country, two countries

Exception: Most proper nouns simply add *s:* There are two Marys and three Henrys in the group. Since 1949 there have been two Germanys. (But note that we always refer to the Rockies, and the Canary Islands are also known as the Canaries.) Nouns ending in *y* preceded by a vowel add *s* only:

> bays   guys
> valleys   buoys
> toys

Plurals of Compounds

Generally, form the plurals of compounds simply by adding *s:*

> backbenchers   man-eaters
> fire extinguishers   merry-go-rounds
> forget-me-nots   prime ministers
> great-grandmothers   second cousins
> major generals   shut-ins

But when the first part of the compound is a noun and the rest is not, or if the first part is the more important of two nouns, then that word is the one made plural:

> daughters-in-law   mayors-elect
> governors general   passers-by
> jacks-of-all-trades   poets laureate

But there are exceptions, and—as usual—usage is changing. Note for example these plural forms:

> spoonsfuls (*not* spoonsful; this is the pattern for all nouns ending in *ful*)
>
> courts-martial *or* court martials

A few compounds conventionally pluralize both nouns; for example:

> menservants
>
> ups and downs

And a few compounds are the same in both singular and plural; for example:

> daddy-long-legs, fancy pants, crossroads

Irregular Plurals

Some nouns are irregular in forming their plurals, but these are common and generally well known; for example:

> one child, two children
> one man, two men
> one foot, two feet
> one mouse, two mice

Some plural forms are the same as the singular; for example:

> one series, two series
> one deer, two deer
> one sheep, two sheep

The plurals of words borrowed from other languages (mostly Latin and Greek) can pose a problem. Words used formally or technically tend to retain their original plural forms; words used more commonly tend to form their plural according to regular English rules. Since many such words are in transition, you will probably encounter both plural forms. If you are in any doubt, use the preferred form listed in your dictionary. Here are some examples:

Words that have tended to retain their original plurals:

> thesis, theses
> stimulus, stimuli
> synthesis, syntheses
> parenthesis, parentheses
> basis, bases

> madame, mesdames
> oxymoron, oxymora
> crisis, crises
> kibbutz, kibbutzim

Words that are (apparently) in transition and have both forms of plurals (the choice often depending on the formality or technicality of the context):

> antenna, antennae (insects), antennas (radios and the like)
> apparatus, apparatus, apparatuses
> beau, beaux, beaus
> cactus, cacti, cactuses
> curriculum, curricula, curriculums
> index, indices, indexes
> memorandum, memoranda, memorandums
> referendum, referenda, referendums
> syllabus, syllabi, syllabuses
> symposium, symposia, symposiums
> terminus, termini, terminuses
> ultimatum, ultimata, ultimatums
> vertebra, vertebrae, vertebras

Words that now tend to follow regular English patterns in forming their plurals:

> bureau, bureaus
> campus, campuses
> genius, geniuses (*genii* for mythological creatures)

Note:

Data is plural; the singular is *datum*. Similarly for *strata* (*stratum*).

Kudos is singular and should not be used as if it were plural.

Trivia is plural and should not be used as if it were singular.

Media is the plural of *medium* and should not be used as if it were singular. (Note: *Mediums* is the correct plural for spiritualists who claim to communicate with the dead.)

Opinion, as well as usage, is divided on the spelling of the plurals of these and similar words. Many writers, for example, loathe *criterions* and *phenomenons,* preferring the original plural forms *criteria* and *phenomena*. On the other hand, they may not object to *data* as a singular noun. And *agenda,* originally the plural of *agendum,* is now simply a singular noun with its own plural, *agendas*.

Your dictionary should indicate any irregular plurals; if you are not sure of a word, look it up.

Exercise 51t

Write out what you think is the correct plural form of each of the following nouns. When you have finished, check your dictionary to see if you were right.

1. aide-de-camp
2. alley
3. ambassador-designate
4. analysis
5. bonus
6. bus
7. cloverleaf
8. embargo
9. fifth
10. focus
11. glass
12. goose
13. handful
14. wife
15. mongoose
16. moose
17. mosquito
18. museum
19. octopus
20. ox
21. plateau
22. radius
23. serf
24. society
25. solo
26. speech
27. staff
28. territory
29. town
30. yokefellow

51u Verbs in the third person singular present tense

The present tense inflection of verbs in the third person singular is usually formed by following the same rules that govern the formation of the plurals of nouns. For example:

I lift. The fog lifts.
I run. He runs.
I hate. She hates.
I lurch. It lurches.
They wish. He wishes.
I carry. He carries.
I try. She tries.
I portray. She portrays.
I buy. He buys.
I solo. He solos.
I brief him. She briefs me.

But be careful, for there can be exceptions:

I loaf. He loafs.

Exercise 51u
Supply the present tense, third person singular form of each of the following verbs.

1. atrophy
2. buy
3. chafe
4. choose
5. comb
6. condone
7. convey
8. echo
9. go
10. grasp
11. leaf
12. mouth
13. rally
14. reach
15. relieve
16. revoke
17. search
18. ski
19. swing
20. tunnel

51v Apostrophes

apos The *only* times an apostrophe can be used to form a plural is when it is used with an *s* to form the plurals of figures, symbols, letters, and words used as words:

> She knew her ABC's at the age of four.
> Study the three R's.
> It happened in the 1870's.
> Indent all ¶'s.
> *Accommodate* is spelled with two *c*'s and two *m*'s.
> There are four 7's in my telephone number.
> There are too many *and*'s in that sentence.

Note that when a word, letter, or figure is italicized, the *s* for the plural is *not*.

Note: Some people prefer to form such plurals without the apostrophe: Rs, 7s, ¶s, 1870s, *and*s. But this practice can be confusing, especially with letters and words:

> How many *is* are there in Mississippi? (looks like "is")
> Too many *his*s can spoil a good paragraph. (likely to be misread at first)

It is clearer and easier always to use the apostrophe. (Whichever method you use, it is best, in order to avoid ambiguity, to form possessives of abbreviations with *of* rather than with apostrophes: the opinion of the MLA; the opinion of the MLA's; the opinion of the MLAs.)

Use apostrophes to indicate omitted letters in contractions, and omitted (though obvious) numbers:

aren't (are not)	they're (they are)
can't (cannot)	wouldn't (would not)
doesn't (does not)	goin' home (going home)
don't (do not)	back in '63
isn't (is not)	the crash of '29
it's (it is)	the summer of '42
she's (she is)	

If an apostrophe is already present to indicate a *plural,* you can leave out the apostrophe that indicates omission:

the 20's   the 60's

51w Possessives

apos Some people neglect the simple mechanics of inflecting nouns for possessive case; such neglect can lead to confusion with the inflection for the plural. For correct and consistent usage, you should strictly follow these rules:

To indicate the possessive case of a noun—whether singular or plural—that does not end in *s,* add *'s:*

Emil's briefcase	a year's leave of absence
the girl's teacher	tomorrow's news
Alberta's capital city	children's books
the car's colour	the men's jobs
a day's work	the deer's hides

To form the possessive of compound nouns, use an apostrophe after the last noun:

The Solicitor General's report is due tomorrow.
Sally and Mike's dinner party was a huge success.

But be careful: if the nouns do not actually form a compound, each will need the apostrophe:

Sally's and Mike's lunches were markedly different.

To indicate the possessive case of most singular nouns ending in *s,* add *'s* to one-syllable words and also to words of more than one syllable for whose plural you would normally pronounce an extra syllable:

> the *cross's* symbolic significance
> the *class's* achievement as a whole
> the *congress's* interminable debates

To indicate the possessive case of plural nouns ending in *s* add an apostrophe only:

> the *girls'* sweaters   the *Smiths'* cottage
> the *cannons'* roar   the *Joneses'* garden

About some nouns, however, opinion is divided. Some writers feel that pronouncing an extra syllable would sound awkward, and therefore prefer to indicate the possessive case with only an apostrophe. Others feel that for consistency and clarity an *'s* should be added even to these words, in spite of the possibly awkward pronunciation:

> Jesus's birth *or* Jesus' birth
> Moses's miracles *or* Moses' miracles
> Dickens's novels *or* Dickens' novels
> Keats's poems *or* Keats' poems
> Jones's lawnmower *or* Jones' lawnmower
> Kansas's capital *or* Kansas' capital

Note that this problem seems to arise only with proper nouns, and often with those that end in two successive sibilants (*s* sounds). Simply pronounce the word yourself and then decide how you should form its possessive case. The problem can often be avoided (as it probably would be in speech, in order to avoid ambiguity as well as awkward sound) by simply rephrasing; instead of inflecting the noun for possessive case, use it in a prepositional phrase beginning with *of:*

> the novels of Dickens; the poems of Keats; the birth of Jesus; the price of success; the roar of the cannons; the roof of the house.

This manner of showing possession is often used with plural nouns to avoid stylistic awkwardness:

> the feelings of most Canadians (instead of *most Canadians' feelings*)

the voters of both parties (instead of *both parties' voters*)

(For information about prepositions and their objects, see #12.)

Caution: Do not use apostrophes in possessive personal pronouns:

NOT her's, but *hers*
NOT it's, but *its*
NOT our's, but *ours*
NOT their's, but *theirs*
NOT your's, but *yours*

Note: Although some people object to them, there is nothing wrong with double possessives, showing possession with both an *of* phrase and a possessive inflection. They are always used with possessive pronouns, and can be used similarly with common and proper nouns:

a favourite *of mine,* a friend *of hers,* a friend *of the family* or *of the family's,* a contemporary *of Shakespeare* or *of Shakespeare's*

And certainly the sentence "The story was based on an idea of Shakespeare" is at least potentially ambiguous, whereas "The story was based on an idea of Shakespeare's" is clear.

Exercise 51vw(1)
Insert apostrophes where necessary in the following sentences.

1. I dont know whether this book is his or hers, but theres no doubt its a handsome one, and its value on todays market, what its worth now, must surely be greater than its value as a new book, way back in the 1930s.
2. Clearly he doesnt know whats going on; itll take him a weeks study to catch up.
3. Our reports so far ahead of theirs that shell have to work nights to make ends meet.
4. It isnt whom you know but what you know that in the end seals the deal.

5. Dianas guess is closer than Seans, but the jars full and accurate count of beans wont be verified till Mondays announcement.
6. The teachers comments about Guys paper pointed out its errors.
7. Its sometimes a full days work to write a good paragraph.
8. It doesnt matter who wins the game; its rather its quality that counts.
9. When the childrens shouting got too loud, the Joneses neighbours had to shut their windows, but Alice left hers open.
10. Their approach was by ones and twos, whereas ours was a matter of charging in all at once.

Exercise 51vw(2)

In the following sentences, supply any missing apostrophes and correct any instances of their misuse.

1. Now we see wives who, by working and pooling their wages with their husbands, can purchase extra luxury items for the home and family.
2. Able people are often held back by societies structure.
3. The two main characters are each others foils.
4. He acted without a moments hesitation.
5. We will meet again in two days time.
6. Have you read H. G. Well's novel, *The Time Machine*?
7. The BNA Act is Canadas only constitution.
8. You can buy boys and girls jeans in any good department store.
9. The Smith's came to dinner.
10. In the Middle Ages, Latin was the universal language of Europes educated classes.

51x Spelling List
In addition to the words listed and discussed in the preceding pages, many other words often cause spelling problems.

Following is a list of frequently misspelled words. If you are at all weak in spelling, you should test yourself frequently on these words as well as those discussed earlier. These lists and examples, however, are not exhaustive; it is therefore very important that you keep your own list of misspelled words, especially recurrent ones, and that you practise spelling them correctly until you have mastered them.

absorption
acclaim
accumulate
acknowledgment or
    acknowledgement
acquaintance
additional
advertise
aesthetic or esthetic
adviser
affection
affidavit
aging
alternately
always
amour
analyze or analyse
analogy
anaesthetic
anonymous
anticipated
apartment
approach
architect
arctic
arithmetic
article
atmosphere
audience
automatically
auxiliary
axe or ax

beggar
beneficent

bizarre
botany
buoyant
bureau
burglar
buried

cafeteria
calendar
Calvinist
cameraderie
candidate
cannibal
captain
careful
carnival
cartilage
catalogue
category
cemetery
chagrin
challenge
changeable
chocolate
cinnamon
clamour or
    clamor
clothed
coincide
colossal
committee
comprise
comrade
concomitant
conqueror

conscious
consensus
conservative
consider
consumer
control
controlled
convenient
court
courteous
create
criticism
crucifixion
curiosity
cylinder

decorative
decrepit
defensive
desperate
develop
devastation
diameter
dilemma
diminution
dining
diphtheria
dispatch or despatch
dissipate
doctor
drunkenness

eclectic
ecstasy
efficient

electorate
elegiac
eligible
embarrassment
emancipation
emphasize
employee
emulate
encompass
encyclopedia
endeavour or endeavor
enforced
engraver
enterprise
envelop (v.)
envelope (n.)
epilogue
equip
equipment
equipped
erupt
euphonious
exalt
exaggerate
excel
exercise
exhausted
exhilarating
exuberant

facilities
fallacy
fascinating
fervour or fervor
filter
flippant
flourish
flyer or flier
focusses or focuses
foreign
foresee
fulfill
fundamentally
furor

gaiety
gauge
genealogy
gleam
goddess
gray or grey
grievous
guarantee
guard

harmonious
harass
height
heinous
heroine
hesitancy
hindrance
horseshoe
household
humorous
hygienist
hypocrite

illegal
illegitimate
illiterate
imagery
imagination
imitate
immediate
impious
implementation
importance
improvise
inadequacy
indefinite
industrialization
inevitable
influence
injuries
innocent
inoculate
inquire
integrated

interrupt
intimate

jealousy
jeweller or jeweler
judgment or
  judgement

knowledge
knowledgeable

laboratory
leeches
library
license or licence (v.)
licence or license (n.)
lieutenant
likelihood
lineage
liquefy
liqueur
liquor
luxury

mammoth
manoeuvre or
  maneuver
manual
manufactured
marriage
marshal
mattress
meant
medieval
melancholy
mineralogy
minuscule
mischievous
molester
monologue
monotonous
mould or mold
museum
mustache or
  moustache

necessary
nineteenth
nosey or nosy
nostrils
numerous

obstacle
offense or offence
omniscient
oneself
operator
ostracize

paralleled or parallelled
paralyze or paralyse
parliament
partner
peculiar
peddler
perseverance
personality
personify
personnel
persuade
pharaoh
phony or phoney
plagiarism
playwright
plough or plow
poem
pollution
porous
positioning
possession
practicality
practice (n.)
practise or practice (v.)
predecessors
prestige
pretense or pretence
procedure
proletariat
proscenium
psychiatry
psychology

pursue
putrefy
puzzled
pyjamas or pajamas

quandary
quantity
quatrain
quizzically

rarefied
reality
recognize
recommend
reflection
religious
reminisce
repel
resemblance
rhythm
ridiculous

sacrifice
safety
scandal
sceptic or skeptic
separate
sheik
shepherd
sheriff
shining
shiny
signifies
simile
siphon
simultaneous
skiing
skillful or skilful
smoulder or smolder
soliloquy
species
spectators
sponsor
storey or story (floor)

straddle
strategy
stretched
styrofoam
subconsciously
subsequent
subtly
succinct
sulphur or sulfur
superintendent
symbolic
symbolize
synonymous
syrup

tariff
temperament
temperature
territory
theory
therein
threshold
tragedy
tranquillity or
    tranquility
transferred
troubadour
tyranny
unavailing
undoubtedly
unmistakable
until
usefulness

vehicle
vilify

weary
whisky or whiskey
willful or wilful
wintry
wistfulness
woollen or woolen
woolly
writing
written

Review Exercise: Chapter VI
Below are 100 misspelled words. First spell them correctly,
and then try to decide which rule each one violates or which
classification of error each falls into. Remember, a given
error could belong in more than one classification. (For con-
venience, the misspellings are divided into four groups of 25
each.)

	A	B	C	D
1.	artisticly	surender	defered	exhorbitant
2.	hense	studing	vien	speach
3.	trailled	sofistication	marshmellows	bullit
4.	complextion	applys	polititian	interpretted
5.	incompatable	sentance	feasable	religous
6.	comparitive	procede	deliberatly	succomb
7.	dilemna	incidently	Elizabethian	primative
8.	exitment	excrutiating	fragrence	Heroshima
9.	inconcievable	mischievious	dilusion	backround
10.	disatisfaction	coherant	askes	ninty
11.	benifit	contemptable	proffessional	succeptible
12.	critisize	champian	reproachs	magestic
13.	indispensible	effecient	metaphore	inadvertantly
14.	unquardinated	repetative	devistated	successfull
15.	angery	familier	suspence	predjudice
16.	storys (tales)	exclaimation	denile	palacial
17.	menicing	striken	fourty	allys
18.	alure	absense	harmonous	accessable
19.	perfectable	repreive	foreigness	dependant
20.	prominant	monsterous	secretarys	fundemental
21.	grammer	dosent	opulant	permissable
22.	devide	concreate	representitive	listner
23.	substanciate	useable	realisticly	unforgiveable
24.	amature	reguarding	envelopped	finaly
25.	tryed	heavilly	wonderous	neice

PART THREE
Style and the Larger Elements of Composition

It is next to impossible to define style. For simplicity and directness—two of the most important qualities of good style—Jonathan Swift's attempt is probably the best: "Proper words in proper places make the true definition of style." In its broadest sense, STYLE consists of everything that is not the *content* of what is being expressed. It is the *manner* as opposed to the *matter:* everything that is a part of the *way* something is said constitutes its style. Although we generally separate style and content to facilitate discussion and analysis, this distinction is in some ways false, for the two are inseparably bound together; the way in which something is expressed inescapably becomes a part of what is being said. "I have a hangover" may seem to say essentially the same thing as "I'm feeling a bit fragile this morning," but the different *styles* of the statements create quite different effects. And it is the effect, finally, that counts, for the manner determines what the content means. The medium, then, if not the entire message, is at least a good part of it.

An important attribute of style is TONE, which is usually defined as the attitude of the writer toward his material and toward his audience. Tone in writing is analogous to tone in speech. We hear someone as speaking in a sarcastic tone of voice, or as sounding angry, or jocular, or matter-of-fact. Writing, like speech, can "sound" ironic, conversational, intimate, morbid, tragic, frivolous, cold, impassioned, comic, coy, energetic, phlegmatic, detached, sneering, contemptuous, laudatory, condescending, and so forth. The tone of a piece of writing—whether an essay or only a sentence—determines the feeling or impression the writing creates.

The style of a piece of writing, including its tone, arises from such things as syntax and point of view and even punctuation. It is also largely determined by diction: choice of words, figurative language, and even sounds.

Chapter VII   Diction

DICTION—a writer's choice of words—is obviously at the heart of effective writing and of style. No amount of correct grammar and rhetorical expertise can compensate for poor diction. This chapter isolates the principal difficulties writers encounter in choosing and using words, and offers some suggestions for overcoming these difficulties.

Use your dictionary. Become familiar with it; find out how it works and discover the variety of information it has to offer. Good college or desk dictionaries do not merely list the spelling, syllabication, pronunciation, and meaning of words; they also offer advice on usage, idioms, and synonyms and antonyms to help you decide on the best word for a particular context; they list any irregularities in the principal parts of verbs and in the inflection of adjectives and adverbs; they supply etymologies (knowing a word's original form and meaning can sometimes help you decide on its appropriateness for your purpose); they even tell you whether a word or expression is considered slang, colloquial, informal, or archaic. Don't waste your dictionary's resources by failing to take advantage of them.

52 Level

Use words appropriate to you, to your topic, and to the circumstances in which you are writing; that is, consider your occasion and your audience. Avoid any word or phrase that calls attention to itself rather than to the meaning you are trying to convey. Generally, avoid slang and colloquial or informal expressions at one extreme, and pretentious, overly formal language at the other. Of course there will be times when one or the other, or both, will be useful—for example to make a point in a particularly telling way, to achieve a humorous effect, or to make dialogue realistic. But it is usually preferable to adopt a straightforward, moderate style, a medium level of diction that neither crawls on its belly in the dirt nor struts about on stilts.

52a Slang

SLANG is diction that is at the opposite extreme from FORMAL. It therefore follows that, although we all use it in our speech and in informal contexts, slang is very unlikely to be appropriate in a formal context. Nevertheless, there is nothing inherently wrong with slang; it is in fact a lively and vigorous part of our language. But partly because it is so lively and vigorous, it is often faddish; some slang words remain in vogue only a few weeks, some linger on for a few years, and new ones are constantly popping up to take the place of those going out of fashion. Much slang is so ephemeral that dictionaries cannot keep up with it. The adjective *strapped,* for example, meaning out of money, has been around at least since the beginning of this century; one dictionary does not even list it, a second labels it *slang,* another calls it *informal* (i.e., colloquial), and yet another includes it but assigns no label, implying that it has entered the general vocabulary and become "respectable." A writer does well, therefore, to be careful—and conservative. The temptation to enliven one's writing with some pungent slang is often great, but too much spice can ruin the taste of something, especially something delicate—which in a way formal style is. In order to help you get the matter in perspective, here is a brief discussion of slang and a few examples culled from the thousands of slang terms that exist, or once existed.[1]

---

[1]The information in the following pages comes from our own experience and observation, and from the following books, to which we direct those readers interested in pursuing the subject further: Eric Partridge, *A Dictionary of Slang and Unconventional English,* 7th ed. (New York: Macmillan, 1970), and *Slang To-day and Yesterday,* 3rd ed. (New York: Bonanza, n.d.); H.L. Mencken, *The American Language,* 4th ed. (New York: Knopf, 1936); Walter S. Avis, et al., eds., *A Dictionary of Canadianisms on Historical Principles* (Toronto: Gage, 1967); and several general dictionaries, principally *Funk & Wagnalls Standard College Dictionary,* Canadian edition (Toronto: Fitzhenry & Whiteside, 1976), and the *Dictionary of Canadian English: The Senior Dictionary* (Toronto: Gage, 1973).

Clearly not all words which begin their lives as slang die out. Here are some which entered the language at least as long ago as the sixteenth and seventeenth centuries: *balderdash* has become not only standard but rather highfalutin; *budge, cocksure, to hedge, mob,* and *nincompoop* became standard long ago (i.e., in the eighteenth or nineteenth century); *blab* and *bolt* (depart quickly) became standard more recently; *bamboozle, to belt* (hit), *break the ice, chum,* and *clodhopper* are hovering between informal and standard; *brass* (impudence), *cocky, flame* (sweetheart), and *let on* (tell) are still considered informal (or colloquial; because many people confuse it with *dialectal,* some dictionaries no longer use the label *colloquial*); and *brass* (money) and *pinch* (steal) are still labelled slang. Many others have disappeared altogether; in fact, many more slang words die out than survive.

Here are some that arrived in the nineteenth century and that are still considered slang—insofar as they are at all current (how many of them do you even recognize?): *bats* or *batty, chin music, dough* (money), *frost* (failure), *gasser* (big success), *java, make the grade, perks* (perquisites), *Popsy-Wopsy* (a term of affectionate address), *shebang, stiff* (corpse), *sugar* (money).

Here are some other nineteenth-century slang terms that are still called slang; these, unlike the preceding group, are still fairly current (or do you not find them so?): *baloney, bang-up, beef, bender, bounced, flog, hang out, hold out, jug, kid* (fool), *lip, loony, pull, sack.*

Many nineteenth-century terms have become at least informal; for example: *backtalk, the blues, boom, boost, boss, break even, carry on, cave in, chip in, cram, dander, dig up, fix* (bribe, etc.), *freak* (but not *freak out,* which is recent slang), *game* (lame), *get the hang of, go the whole hog, hard up, has-been, in the clear, kid* (child), *rowdy, sleuth, smart aleck, splurge.* Others such as *get one's back up, go all out, land-slide* (of an election), *loafer* (and the verb *loaf,* formed from it), *nerve* (courage), and *shadow* (follow secretly), have attained respectability.

And linguistic inventiveness has not flagged in the twentieth century: *bat* (spree), *bawl out, beat it, big shot, broad, canned music, frame, guts, have someone taped, main drag, neck, pep, scram, scrounge, wonky*—all these originated early in the century, are still slang, and are probably familiar to you. Other slang terms from the same period have become at least informal: *to batch, break, buddy, cagey, chump, cold feet, date, double-cross, flu, grad, grouch, nerve* (audacity), *on the level, road hog*. Still others that were once slang, such as *dude* and *major* (as a verb), have been accepted into standard English. But still others that were once popular have all but disappeared and would sound very out-of-place today: *applesauce, balloon juice, banana oil, bean* and *loaf* (head), *the berries, the heebie-jeebies*.

The 1920's were rich in slang, but who now would dream of using—except facetiously—such words as *flapper* or *frail* for a girl, or such expressions as *the bee's knees, the cat's pyjamas,* or *twenty-three skiddoo*?

Canadian slang is particularly rich in what it shares with or has borrowed from the United States, England, and Australia. It also has its own colourful terms, like *sodbuster, crowbar palace, high muckamuck*. But to someone neither a player nor a fan of hockey, such terms as *cream, deke,* and *rink rat* would not be very meaningful.

Much slang begins as a kind of private language or lingo within a group or profession, among hoboes, thieves, circus people, actors, athletes, gamblers, sailors, students, and so on. Since much of the point of such lingoes is to keep outsiders from understanding, or simply to instil a feeling of being an insider, as soon as terms are picked up by others they are dropped by members of the group and replaced by new inventions—another reason for the short life-span of much slang. Nevertheless many slang terms come into general use from such specialized sources. From the world of crime, for example, come such terms as *bump off* and *knock off* and *rub out, hold up* and *stick up, racket, crook, bootlegger, hoodlum* (and from it *hood*), *copper* (and from it *cop*). From card playing come *pass the buck, four-flusher,* and *poker face*. Our language is full of nautical terms, among them such slangy ones as *on deck, hit the deck, bilge, chow, get spliced, pipe down,* and at least two for being drunk: *half-seas over* and *three sheets in the wind*.

Indeed, inebriety provides a good example of the vigour

and colourfulness of much slang and also of the astonishing number of words for one thing. Here are several others—some new, some very old, and many still in use: *blotto, boiled* (also *fried* and *stewed*), *bombed, canned, crocked, lacquered, oiled* (or *well-oiled*), *ossified, pickled, pie-eyed* (or *pied*), *pifflicated* (or *spifflicated*), *plastered* (or *stuccoed*), *snoggered, snozzled* (or *sozzled*), *soused, squiffed, stinko, tanked, tiddly, tight, tipsy, woozy.* Note also *tie one on* and *get bent out of shape* (from *bender*?).

The transitoriness of much slang makes it risky to use in writing; a phrase that is *hot* (or *cool*) when you write it may sound stale and dated soon after. Occasionally a slang term will fade out to reappear later. *Snafu,* for example, military slang from the Second World War, was little if at all known to the next generation, but has enjoyed a considerable vogue among the young just recently—and may (or may not) continue to do so; but an older reader encountering it in a new context would get associations the writer may not have intended.

Even more disconcerting is the way slang terms tend to shift their meanings or to have multiple meanings; to use slang is thus sometimes to risk complete misunderstanding. *Frazzled* is another slang word meaning "drunk," but it also has the standard meanings "frayed" and "tired, worn out." Yet another is *stoned,* but it is unlikely that in a contemporary context it would be taken to mean merely "drunk." Here are some other examples: *Chopper* used to refer to a machine gun, *mike* to a microscope, *sauce* to gasoline, *benny* to an overcoat, and *drag* to influence or to an unpopular girl. *Dude* used to apply specifically to a city-bred person or to a dandy. *Blab* used to mean "nonsense" or "camouflage talk," and a *sap* in the early nineteenth century was one who studied hard—perhaps the ironic source of its later meaning.

Fashions change, and it is all but impossible to keep up with them, however up-to-date one tries to be. *Coffin-nail* for a cigarette has been around since the nineteenth century; but for a while it was more common to ask for or offer a *fag* or a *weed*; later it was *cancer stick*; *dart* is a relatively recent arrival; and who knows what will be fashionable by the time you read this—or by next week, next month, or next year?

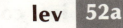

Would anyone nowadays seriously consider calling something *corny* or *groovy,* or someone a *noodnick* or a *drip* or a *jerk*? *Bread* for money and *threads* for clothing, so *with it* a decade or so ago, are now obsolescent; *wheels* for a car appears to have more staying power, but though it may seem fresh to some, others find it stale. Further, because slang is often not as universally understood as "standard" English, it may not convey the meaning you intend. Not only is it often confined to certain age-levels and groups, but it is also often regional. Consequently, rather than being pointed and vivid, in using slang you may only be confusing your reader.

But slang, because of its sharpness, vividness, and seeming timeliness, is always attractive. It can trap the unwary writer, and tempt even the wary, into sounding not only dated but also artificially chic and clever. Mixing even an occasional slang term with otherwise formal diction is always tricky, and nearly always damaging to a writer's effectiveness. Yet sometimes a slang term will seem the most economical way to say something, or even the only right way. Slang, therefore, is not to be avoided entirely; rather it is to be used only when it is the most appropriate means to a desired end—but used infrequently and with the utmost discretion. If tempted to write something slangy, then, think twice, or thrice—and consult not only a good dictionary but also your ear, your common sense, and your good taste.

Note: Remember, if you do decide to use a slang term, do not put quotation marks around it. (See #43g.)

Exercise 52a

List as many slang terms as you can think of for each of the following. Which are current in your vocabulary? Which if any would you consider using in an essay? In a letter to a friend? In conversation with someone of your own sex? In conversation with someone of the opposite sex?

1. criminal (n.)
2. mad (adj.)
3. intoxicated

4. cheat (v.)
5. cheat (n.)
6. court (v.)

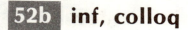

7. bore (n.)   12. boy
8. very good   13. girl
9. talk (v.)   14. beautiful
10. stupid person   15. ugly
11. bright person

52b Informal, Colloquial

It is often difficult to distinguish between slang and INFOR-MAL usage. Even dictionaries cannot agree. Slang terms are in one sense simply extreme examples of the colloquial or informal. Nevertheless, there are many words and phrases that can be labelled informal; although not slang, they do not belong in formal writing. For example, unless you are intentionally aiming for an informal level, you should avoid such abbreviations as *prof, gent, rev*; you should also avoid contractions (*can't, isn't, don't, wouldn't,* etc.), although such contractions are normal in spoken English.

Here are some examples of other informal or colloquial usages that most writers think should be avoided in formal writing:

Informal or Colloquial	*Acceptable equivalents*
absolutely	very; yes
a lot of, lots of, lots	much, many, a great deal of
and such	and so on, and things like that, and the like
anyplace, everyplace, noplace, someplace	anywhere, everywhere, nowhere, somewhere
around	about, approximately
awful	bad, ill, ugly, unpleasant, etc.
be sure and	be sure to
back of, in back of	behind
chance of + gerund (e.g., chance of getting)	chance + infinitive (chance to get)
enthused	was enthusiastic
expect (as in "I expect you want me to work overtime")	suppose, suspect
figure	think, believe, etc.
fix (verb or noun)	repair, prepare, etc; predicament, etc.

funny	odd, peculiar, strange, unusual
guess	believe, suppose, think
mean	bad, cruel, evil, etc.
most (as in "most everyone")	almost
nice	agreeable, attractive, pleasant, etc.
nowhere near	not nearly, not at all, not anywhere near
out loud	aloud
over with	ended, finished, done
phone	telephone
photo	photograph
plan on + gerund (e.g., plan on going)	plan + infinitive (plan to go)
quite, quite a bit, quite a few, quite a lot, etc.	somewhat, rather, many, a large amount, much, etc.
real, really (as intensive adverb)	very, greatly, surely, etc.
right away, right now	immediately
shape (good, bad, fine, etc.)	condition
show up	appear, arrive; prove better than, best (v.)
size up	judge, estimate the strength of, etc.
terrible, terribly (also as vague intensifiers)	unpleasant, uncomfortable, very, etc.
try and	try to
wait on	await, wait for
where (as in "I see where we're in for a storm")	that

In addition, many words have been so abused in movie and other advertising, used for gushy and exaggerated effect, that they can now seldom be used with precision in formal writing. For example:

> fantastic, marvellous, stupendous, terrific, tremendous, wonderful

Exercise 52b
Provide more formal substitutes for each of the slang or informal terms below. Use your dictionary as necessary. Compose sentences for at least ten of the terms, using them in

ways that you think would be acceptable in relatively formal writing.

1. bawl out	21. face the music
2. beef (n. and v.)	22. fall guy
3. booze	23. gamp
4. bunk	24. highbrow
5. cheapskate	25. hoofed it
6. chump	26. hoosegow
7. cinch (n.)	27. hunch
8. con (v.)	28. jerk
9. conniption	29. miss out
10. cook up	30. monkey business
11. crackdown	31. on the spot
12. crash pad	32. scram
13. crummy	33. scrounge
14. cuss (v. and n.)	34. slapdash
15. cute	35. slouch
16. died with his boots on	36. smarmy
17. ditch (v.)	37. southpaw
18. dope out	38. square
19. down the tube	39. stunner
20. egged on	40. truck (n.)

52c "Fine Writing"

Unnecessarily formal or pretentious diction is called "fine writing"—a term of disapproval here. Efforts to impress readers with such writing almost always backfire. Do not write "It was felicitous that the canine in question was demonstrably more exuberant in emitting threatening sounds than in attempting to implement said threats by engaging in actual physical assault," when all you mean is "Luckily, the dog's bark was worse than his bite." Do not write "I deem it unjust on the part of the professor to have refused passage to my latest expositional effort solely on the grounds that my orthography was in his judgement deficient" when you could say, more directly and effectively, "I don't think the teacher should have failed my last essay just because of my bad spelling." These are exaggerated examples, of course, but they illustrate how important it is to be natural (within reason) and straightforward. Writers who over-reach themselves often use

supposedly sophisticated and elegant terms incorrectly. The student who wrote "Riding majestically down the street on a magnificent float was the Festival Queen surrounded by all her courtesans" was striving for sophistication, but succeeded only in getting an undesired laugh from the reader who knew what *courtesan* really meant.

Exercise 52c

Provide one or more less formal, more common or natural equivalents for each of the following words. Use your dictionary as necessary. How many of these words do you consider to be in your own vocabulary? Mark any that you think should *not* be avoided as overly formal or pretentious in a normal context.

1. ablutions	25. gustatory
2. assiduity	26. habiliments
3. aviate	27. hebdomadal
4. bellicose	28. imbibition
5. cachinnation	29. impudicity
6. cinereous	30. jejune
7. circumambient	31. lubricity
8. collation	32. lucubrations
9. colloquy	33. matutinal
10. comminatory	34. mentation
11. compotation	35. objurgation
12. concatenation	36. obloquy
13. confabulate	37. oppugnant
14. conflagration	38. orthography
15. contumelious	39. otiose
16. crepuscular	40. pellucid
17. defenestration	41. penurious
18. divagation	42. peregrinations
19. doff	43. propinquity
20. egress	44. *raison d'être*
21. eleemosynary	45. rebarbative
22. equitation	46. refection
23. erstwhile	47. regurgitate
24. frangible	48. repast

---

53 Figurative Language

fig Strictly speaking, figurative language includes many "figures of speech," such as personification, synecdoche, metonymy, hyperbole (overstatement), litotes (understatement), and even paradox, irony, and symbolism. Generally, however, the term "figurative language" refers to metaphoric language, whose most common devices are the METAPHOR and the SIMILE. A SIMILE is an explicit comparison which is introduced by *like* or *as:*

> The river is *like* a snake winding through the flat landscape.
> She was as carefree *as* a wild canary.

A METAPHOR, on the other hand, is an implicit comparison; the things being compared are assumed to be identical:

> The river *is* a snake winding through the flat landscape.

Frequently a metaphor is condensed into a verb, an adjective, or an adverb. A condensed *verb* metaphor:

> The river *snakes* its way through the flat landscape.

A condensed *adjective* metaphor:

> The *serpentine* river meanders through the flat landscape.

A condensed *adverb* metaphor:

> The river winds *snakily* through the flat landscape.

Figurative language—in this instance, metaphors and similes—is an important element of good style. Writing that lacks it will be relatively dry, flat, and dull. It is important to remember, however, that a good metaphor does not merely enhance style; it also clarifies meaning. That is, one should use a metaphor not simply for its own sake, but rather to convey an idea or concept in a clearer or more effective way. For

example, to say that "the hillside was covered with a profusion of colourful flowers" is clear enough. But if one writes instead that "the hillside was a tapestry of spring blossoms," the metaphor not only enriches the style but also provides readers with an image (that of the tapestry) that helps them visualize the scene. In other words, an appropriate metaphor is another way of being more *concrete* (see the next section), the concreteness in this instance being a function of the explicit or implicit comparison embodied in the simile or metaphor.

53a But one must be careful not to force a metaphor upon a given expression merely to embellish one's style, for it will likely be inappropriate and call attention to itself rather than enhance the desired meaning. It will, to use a rather tired but still expressive simile, stick out like a sore thumb. For example, "the tide of emotion suddenly stopped" does not work, since tides do not stop; they ebb and flow. And a phrase like "bomb craters blossoming all over the landscape" contains an inherent discord. Writing something like "he ran like an ostrich in heat" only confuses the reader with inappropriate associations.

53b Another fault occurs when a writer becomes so fond of a supposedly clever metaphor that he extends it beyond the point where it can be of service, and allows it to take control of what is being said:

> When she came out of the surf her hair looked like limp spaghetti. A sauce of seaweed and sand, looking like spinach and grated cheese, had been carelessly applied, the red flower fastened in her tresses looked like a wayward piece of tomato, and the globs of mud clung like meatballs to the pasty pasta of her face. The fork of my attention hovered hesitatingly over this odd dish. Clearly I would need more than one glass of the red wine of remembered beauty and affection to wash it all down.

This may all be very clever, but after the first sentence—the spaghetti image itself being somewhat questionable—one quickly loses sight of the original descriptive intention and becomes mired in all the associated metaphors and similes; in short, the reader is likely to feel fed up, and to turn to something less fattening and overseasoned. Do not extend a metaphor beyond its usefulness.

53c One must also be on guard against dead metaphors and clichés (see #59e). The language is full of such dead metaphors as the *leg* of a table, *branching out, flew* to the rescue, and the like, which are perfectly all right since we no longer think of them as metaphors. But moribund metaphors, not yet dead but with little metaphoric force left, can be dangerous. Such hackneyed phrases as the *ladder of success, making mountains out of molehills, nipped in the bud, flog a dead horse,* and *between the devil and the deep blue sea* are muddying and soporific instead of enlivening and clarifying.

Occasionally, however, a dead or trite metaphor can be revivified, consciously used in a fresh and altered way. For example, the hackneyed phrase *bit off more than he could chew* was given a new life by the person who said of Henry James's writing that he "chewed more than he bit off." *Sound as a dollar* would these days be more appropriately rendered as "unsound as a dollar." Even a slangy phrase like *chew the fat* might be transformed and updated in a description of some overweight people sitting down to "chew the cholesterol." But be careful, for such attempts can misfire; like an over-extended metaphor, they sometimes call attention to their own cleverness at the expense of the intended meaning.

53d Be particularly careful to avoid incongruously MIXED METAPHORS. The person who wrote, of the Great Depression, that "what began as a zephyr soon blossomed into a giant," had obviously lost control of metaphor. The following paragraph about Shakespeare's *Othello* was written by a student who obviously began with the good intention of using metaphors to help describe the almost unbelievable evil of Iago, but who soon became lost in a self-created maze of contradictions and incongruities:

> Iago has spun his web and like a spider he waits. His beautiful web of silk is so fragile and yet it captures the souls of its victims

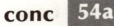

by gently luring them into his womb. Unsuspecting are those unfortunate creatures who sense the poisonous venom oozing through their veins. It has a tranquil effect, for it numbs the mind with its magical potion. The victims are transformed into pawns as they satisfy the queen's appetite and so they serve their purpose.

Here is another paragraph, again by a student, that not only successfully uses metaphor throughout to create its impression but that is also, in its entirety (note the title and the final clause), a single metaphor:

At the Movies

I remember once, as a kid, lying on my back watching clouds. Row upon row of factory-perfect models drifted along the assembly line. There went a nifty schooner, flag flying—and look, a snapping toy poodle with the most absurd cut! Next came chilly Greenland, with Labrador much too close for comfort. But the banana split was the best one of all. It reminded me how hungry I was, and how close to home. With a jump, I promised myself I'd catch the second feature on the next sunny day.

By all means, then, use figurative language. It can lend grace and charm and liveliness and—above all—clarity of meaning and greater effectiveness to your writing. But beware of its potential pitfalls: inappropriate, mixed, or over-extended metaphors.

54 Concrete and Abstract; Weak Generalizations

54a Concreteness

conc A concrete word denotes something tangible, physical, capable of being apprehended by the senses. Abstract words depict intangible things, like ideas or qualities. The more concrete your writing, the more likely your readers will be to respond to it, for it will provide handles for their imaginations to get hold of. Don't settle for an abstract or general term when you can be concrete and specific. Here are some expressions moving from the general to the specific:

> growing things—trees—evergreen—cedar, pine, spruce, etc.
> vehicle—car—sports car—Porsche—Porsche 911

moved—walked—pranced, sidled, slid, stumbled, staggered, swaggered, strode, etc.

creature—animal—dog—dachshund, St. Bernard, collie, fox terrier, etc.

saw, looked—glimpsed, spied, stared, glared, etc.

structure—building—house—bungalow, cottage, ranch house, mansion, etc.

Don't write "We experienced a hot day" when you could write more clearly "We sweltered all afternoon in the 35-degree heat" or "We enjoyed basking in the hot sun all afternoon." Don't write "I found him attractive" when you could write "I liked his handsome face and slim figure," or, better still, "I was enchanted by his curly blond hair and sharp blue eyes, his finely chiselled nose and determined chin, his muscular shoulders and arms." Do not write "He drove around the track very rapidly" when you could bring it alive by writing "He took every corner on two wheels and roared down the straightaways, shifting like a demon and never lifting his foot from the throttle."

The following passage makes sense, but its abstractness prevents it from being very memorable or effective:

> If one makes a purchase that a short time later proves to have been ill-advised due to the rapid deterioration of quality, then it is the opinion of this writer that one has every right to seek redress either by expressing one's displeasure to the individual who conducted the original transaction or, if it should prove necessary, by resorting to litigation.

Inexperienced writers often assume that this kind of language is better because it sounds more formal and sophisticated. But notice how much more vivid the revised version is:

> If you buy a car on Thursday and the engine falls out of it on Saturday, I think you should shout "Hey!" to the dealer who sold it to you, and hale him into court if necessary to get back the good money you paid for what turned out to be a pile of junk.

Of course abstract and general terms are perfectly legitimate and often necessary, for one can scarcely present all ideas concretely. Nevertheless, try to be as concrete and specific as your subject will allow.

54b Weak Generalizations

gen The most common weakness of student writing is an overdependence on generalizations. Merely stating a generalization or assumption is not enough. To be clear and effective—that is, convincing—the generalization must be illustrated and supported by specific evidence or argument. The amount of support needed will vary, but two pieces of support are more than twice as effective as only one and three pieces—often an optimum number to aim for—are probably twice as effective as two. "Women today are no longer content with their traditional roles in life." A reader who unquestioningly accepted such a general assertion would scarcely be a reader worth having, for the statement evokes all kinds of questions; it cries out for illustration, evidence, qualification: All women? In all countries? What "roles" in particular? Is such discontent really something new? And so on.

Here are two in-class essays on the same topic. Read the first one through:

> Travel can be a very broadening experience for people who go with the intention of having their eyes opened, which may often occur by unpleasant means. Culture shock can be a very unpleasant and hurtful experience to people who keep their eyes and minds closed to different attitudes or opinions. This problem of culture shock is an example of why people should prepare for the unexpected and try to learn from difficult experiences, rather than keeping a closed mind which will cause them to come away with a grudge or hurt feelings.

> Besides causing negative attitudes travel can also confirm the prejudices of people with narrow minds. For example, I once met an Englishman who had travelled around the world visiting the last vestiges of the British empire. He had even travelled to South Africa, and still come away with his colonialist attitudes.

> Even if one goes to a country with an open mind, one may still come away with a superficial perception of that country. It takes time to get to know a country and understand its people. The time one spends in a country will thus greatly affect one's perception of that country.

> Time is also needed before travelling begins, for people to read and learn about the area they will be going to. This

background will enable them to look for things they might otherwise never see, and they will appreciate more the things they do discover. If one knows something about the architecture of a country before one visits it, one can plan one's trip to include visits to buildings of special interest.

Thus an open, well-prepared mind will benefit from the experiences of travel, but otherwise travel is likely to have a very negative, narrowing effect on people's minds.

Now, without looking back at the essay, ask yourself what it said. Chances are you will remember something about a well-travelled but still narrow-minded Englishman, and perhaps something about the advisability of knowing something about foreign architecture; for those are the only concrete items in the essay. (Think how much more vivid and therefore meaningful and memorable the point about architecture would have been had it included a reference to a specific landmark, such as the Leaning Tower of Pisa or the Taj Mahal or the Parthenon or St. Paul's Cathedral!)

Now read the second essay, noting as you read how much clearer its points are, as opposed to the relatively unsupported generalizations of the first essay:

> Travel can be broadening. The knowledge gained in the areas of historical background, cultural diversity, and the range of personalities encountered in foreign lands gives us a more objective outlook on ourselves, on Canada and Canadian issues, and on our position as a cog in the great machine of civilization.

> The impact of history upon visitors to foreign lands is immense indeed. One cannot help but feel somewhat small when looking across valley upon valley of white crosses in France, coming face to face with the magnitude of death taking place in World Wars. Before long, one realizes that many of the events that took place years ago have an effect upon the way in which we live today. In some areas, scars such as the Berlin Wall remain, reminders to the visitor that the way he lives is not the same way people throughout the world live and that, indeed, many people live desperately frustrating lives, clinging to the dreams and aspirations of their forefathers and hoping beyond hope that one day they will be able to live without the threat of starvation, imminence of disease, or suppression of freedom.

This is not to say that there are not pleasant aspects of history as well. Sixteenth-century cobblestone lanes, usually less than ten feet wide, still remain in many old English villages, surrounded by Tudor cottages, complete with thatched roofs, oil lamps, and sculpted wrought-iron fences. Standing in such an environment and thinking about the writings of masters like Shakespeare brings out a much deeper and richer taste than merely reading about them in a cold classroom at home. And places like this remind us of how our ancestors lived, making it easier to understand the customs and ideas of the past.

In going through different foreign lands, one cannot ignore the great cultural diversity. This is best illustrated by contrasting Fiestas in Spain and *Oktoberfest* in Munich to our own celebrations. Many countries, besides having different languages (and dialects of those languages), also have their own dress, holidays, and religious beliefs. This variety is often startling to the tourist, used to the general homogeneity of such things back here and often taking it for granted that what is standard for him is also the norm throughout much of the rest of the world.

There is also a wide range of social habits within a country. This is especially true of Britain, which still rigidly clings to its class system. Many foreigners believe in the notion of nobility and common people, with a vast gulf between the two. A visitor from Canada may find it hard to understand such a system, not realizing that it is a centuries-old tradition; a son always does the same job as the father, whether knight or knave, and lives in the same place, and often dies there.

Above all, the differences among people from other countries is what leaves a visitor with the most lasting impression. From the beggar in the slums of Casablanca, to the well-dressed German walking briskly in the streets of Hanover, to the British businessman sipping his beer in "the local" on Hyde Street, there are myriad personalities as one travels through foreign lands. When we look at the world from this perspective, realizing that we are *not* all the same, we are better equipped to understand many of the problems throughout the world.

Even the next-to-last paragraph, with its feeble topic sentence, is at least partly saved by the examples that follow—even though they aren't very specific. The first essay is not devoid of meaning, for generalizations do have content;

but the similar meaning in the second is clearer, more forceful: a reader will better remember what it said simply because his mind has something concrete and specific to hang on to.

(Note also the different ways the two writers conclude: the first tacks on a perfunctory short paragraph, simply summarizing and restating the thesis, whereas the second ends by tying up the final substantive paragraph with a single strong sentence—much the better way, especially for so short an essay.)

In the second paragraph of the sample research paper(#74), the general statements of the first two sentences, the topic sentences, are backed up with several specific examples. Examine the rest of the sample research paper: Are any generalizations, assertions, or assumptions left unexplained or unsupported? If so, is such a generalization of a kind—for example a commonly accepted assumption—that doesn't need clarification or support? Or does its being left unsupported result in a weakness in the explanation or argument? Examine Sample Essays 1 through 5 (Chapter X), all on the same topic: Is there a noticeable difference in the amount and kind of detail their writers provide to support their generalizations? If so, is there any correlation between these differences and the effectiveness of the essays? The flabbiness of essay number 8 is largely a result of unsupported generalizations. Note also the amount and kind of evidence supplied in essay number 10, an argument; do you find any places where you think more evidence should have been provided?

It is also important to consider whether pieces of supporting evidence are matters of fact or of opinion. In an argument, for example, fact would clearly carry more weight than mere opinion. But are there other kinds of essays where opinion is sufficient? (Again, consider the sample essays.) And does it not matter—especially in an argument—just whose opinion is being cited? (See the sample research paper, for example.)

See also #64e.

Exercise 54(1)
For each of the following words, supply several increasingly concrete and specific examples.

1. furniture
2. car
3. answered
4. said
5. food
6. drink (v.)
7. drink (n.)
8. winged thing
9. seat
10. transportation

Exercise 54(2)
Rewrite this vague and abstract autobiographical paragraph. Try to make it sharp and vivid by supplying concrete and specific details wherever suitable.

When I was still fairly young it became necessary for our large family to move from a small prairie town to a large city. At first we were all a little sad, but after a while we settled into our new environment. When I had finished primary and secondary school, I enrolled in an institution of higher learning, and after pursuing my chosen course of studies for the required number of years I received my degree. With it in my possession, I began the search for suitable employment; however, for some time I met with no success, and I had to accept the help of others in order to get along. But finally I found the sort of thing I was looking for, and the people here seem to feel that I am the right person for the position, and even hint at rapid advancement. Consequently I look forward to a pleasant and rewarding career.

55 Connotation

Be careful of connotation: a word may DENOTE (literally mean) what you want it to, yet CONNOTE (suggest) something you do not want to include. For example, if you describe someone as "skinny" your reader will understand the meaning of "light in weight," but will also understand you to feel negatively about it; if you in fact approve of the condition (and the person), you should use a word like "slim" or "slender," for though they denote much the same thing as "skinny," their connotation is favourable rather than unfavourable. The denotations of *childlike* and *childish* are the same, but again one is favourable and the other unfavourable. And consider the differences in the connotations of these words: stink, stench, smell, odour, aroma, fragrance. Another example: If you say someone "harped" on a subject, you are implicitly criticizing him for doing so. If you say that he "insisted" on something, you are implying that you have a neutral attitude. If, however, you say that he "pleaded his case" or that he "repeatedly called attention" to the subject, you automatically suggest that you are on his side. As the old joke goes, "I am firm; you are stubborn; he is pig-headed": it's all a matter of the connotation of the words used.

Caution: Be careful when consulting a thesaurus or dictionary of synonyms: never assume that simply because words are listed together they are necessarily synonyms. They can be subtly different not only in denotation but—and this is where the danger lies—in connotation as well. Always distinguish very carefully among supposed synonyms; never use a thesaurus without using a dictionary in conjunction with it. A thesaurus is an excellent vocabulary-building tool; however, it should be used with extreme care, for it can all too easily trap the unwary into saying things they don't mean. As an example, consider the fact that many of the words in each group in the following exercise were listed in a thesaurus simple as synonyms.

Exercise 55

Label each of the following words as having a favourable (f), unfavourable (u), or neutral (n) connotation. If you think some could be labelled more than one way, depending on context, be prepared to explain. Use your dictionary if necessary.

1. earthy ribald obscene dirty nasty off-colour blue risqué bawdy coarse spicy vulgar
2. ingenuous simple naive stupid innocent candid ignorant shallow inept unthinking green artless
3. chunky heavy plump fat obese stout overweight corpulent beefy hefty buxom portly
4. slight underweight bony trim slender skinny svelte lean spare scrawny gaunt spindly
5. lithe limber rubbery willowy loose limp flaccid supple lissome floppy sapless pliant
6. flimsy delicate feathery fragile frail feeble slight dainty puny lightweight effeminate wispy
7. cherubic angelic goody-goody demure sanctimonious strait-laced narrow prim pious pietistic canting saintly
8. slimy oily greasy slippery unctuous smooth diplomatic suave insinuating clever artful wily
9. clothes duds attire dress costume apparel outfit get-up raiment garb garments trappings
10. scatterbrained confused mixed-up puzzled fuzzy uncertain irresolute undecided bewildered perplexed addled flustered
11. giggly frivolous frolicsome silly irresponsible capricious dizzy giddy volatile impulsive
12. stark bold naked straightforward undisguised plain clear forthright gross candid flagrant bare
13. power strength force ability impact clout influence pull drag sway high-handedness weight
14. boldness cheek impudence arrogance assurance presumption nerve effrontery gall chutzpah insolence audacity
15. intellectual egghead brain genius smarty sage scholar brainworker highbrow pundit bookworm pedant

---

56 Euphemism

EUPHEMISMS are substitutes for words whose meanings are unpleasant and therefore in certain circumstances socially or psychologically undesirable. Because as time passes certain words take on a pejorative quality, we tend to substitute others which in turn will be replaced. Women's underwear, for example, can be delicately referred to in the best of circles as lingerie, underclothing, or underthings. In social settings we tend to ask for the location not of the toilet, which is what we are really after, but of the restroom, the bathroom, the washroom, the powder room, the john, or even the little boys' or little girls' room. (The word *toilet* was itself once a euphemism.) Hearty words describing various bodily functions, words which once were generally acceptable, have now been replaced with euphemisms like bowel movement, passing water, sexual intercourse, intimate relations. In most instances such usage is commendable as a reflection of the degree of refinement and sensibility characteristic of our state of civilization.

However, the process is often abused. Euphemisms may be used, for example, to unnecessarily gloss over some supposed unpleasantness, or even to deceive. Someone who sweeps floors and cleans washrooms is sometimes called a "sanitary engineer" instead of a "custodian" or "janitor." A person who was once known simply as a salesman or a clerk is now often called a "sales representative" or even a "sales engineer." And some bank tellers are now known as "customer service representatives." What was once faced squarely as depression is now, in an attempt to mitigate its implications, termed at worst a recession, or even a mere economic downturn, or slowdown of the economy. A government official who has patently lied admits only that he misspoke himself. Someone who runs a sleazy boarding house is likely to advertise the fact with a sign in the window inviting "paying guests."

Such euphemisms imply a degree of dignity or virtue that is not always justified by the facts. Calling pornography mature entertainment seriously distorts the meaning of both "mature" and "entertainment." And how many sponsors or television stations are honest enough to refer to their ads as commercial *interruptions*? They are commonly referred to as commercial *breaks,* as if they were something to look forward to, like a coffee break. And how many are even honest enough to call them "commercials" rather than "messages"?

Other euphemisms help us to avoid the unpleasant reality of death, which we call "passing away," or "loss"; the lifeless body, the cadaver or corpse, we find less offensive as "remains." Such usage may be acceptable in certain circumstances; it may enable one to avoid aggravating the pain and grief of the bereaved. But in other circumstances, direct, more precise diction is preferable.

Euphemisms that deceive are obviously undesirable. Other euphemisms may be acceptable if circumstances seem to justify them; one must exercise taste and judgment. But generally speaking, call a spade a spade.

Exercise 56
Supply more straightforward equivalents for the following euphemisms and pretentious job-titles.

1. underdeveloped or developing countries
2. senior citizen
3. mortician
4. in the family way, expecting
5. realtor
6. underprivileged
7. social disease
8. impaired
9. lady of the night
10. untruth

---

57 Wrong Word

ww Any error in diction is a "wrong word," but there is a particular kind of incorrect word choice that one must guard against. Don't write *effect* when you mean *affect*. Don't use *infer* where the correct word is *imply*. (See the lists of often-confused words, #51l and #51m, and the Usage Checklist, #60.) But wrong words are not always the result of confusion between two similar words. People sometimes unthinkingly use words that do not convey the intended meaning or that will not work in the desired way. Here are some examples from student writing:

ww: Late in the summer I met my best friend, which I hadn't seen since graduation.

The pronoun *which* is wrong; the pronoun *whom* is the correct one for a person.

ww: Most men would have remembered spending several days in an open ship with little water and under the tropic sun as a terrible hardship, but Marlow recalls only that he felt he could "last forever, outlast the sea, the earth, and all men."

The word *ship* cannot be used to describe a small vessel like a rowboat or canoe; *boat* is the appropriate word here. *Boat* can be used to describe any size of water-going vessel, but *ship* can be used only for large ones.

ww: Many miles of beach on the west coast of Vancouver Island are *absent of* rocks.

The wrong phrase came to the writer's mind: *devoid of* was the one wanted. (See also the next section, *Idiom*.)

Exercise 57
Correct the wrong words in the following sentences.

1. The conference is intended to focus attention on the problems facing our effluent society.
2. Hamlet is filled with a desire to reek vengeance.
3. The representatives of the company claimed to be authoritarians on the subject.
4. Politicians try to maintain an impressionable image in the eyes of the public.
5. Lyell was a nineteenth-century geologist that was ahead of Darwin in some discoveries about evolution.
6. Some shoppers stopped buying coffee because they found the price so absorbent.
7. The Premier of Alberta led his party to the best of his possibilities.
8. He was deciduously on the wrong track with that theory.
9. It was an incredulous display of manual dexterity.

10. The cat was very expansive, weighing over twenty pounds.

58 Idiom

id A particular kind of incorrect word choice has to do with IDIOM. An idiom is an expression peculiar to a given language, one that may not make logical or grammatical sense but which is nevertheless customary, "the way it is said." The English expression "to sow one's wild oats," for example, if translated into another language, would not have its idiomatic meaning; but the French have an equivalent expression, *jeter sa gourme,* which would make little sense if translated into English. Here are some peculiarly English turns of phrase: to have a go at, to be down in the dumps, to be at sixes and sevens, to feel one's oats. You will notice that these idioms have a colloquial flavour about them, or even sound like clichés; but other similarly untranslatable English idioms are a part of our everyday language and occur in formal writing as well; for example: to do oneself proud, to take after someone, to get along with someone.

    Most errors in idiom result from using prepositions that are incorrect—unidiomatic—in combination with certain other words. For example, we get *in* or *into* a car, but we get *on* or *onto* a bus. One is usually angry *with* a person, but angry *at* a thing. One is fond *of* something or someone, but one has a fondness *for* something or someone. And so on. Errors in idiom are particularly likely to occur in the speech and writing of those whose native language is not English; they have to be especially careful. But experience has shown that being a native speaker of English is no guarantee that one's idioms will always be correct: one may have a tin ear for language, or never have encountered a particular usage, and therefore be prone to error. For example, even a native speaker of English could write something like this:

    In the beginning of the trilogy .... (should be *At*)

But when we use *beginning* to denote the start of a period of time and do not follow it with an identifying prepositional phrase, the preposition *in* is idiomatic:

> *In* the beginning was the Word.
> *In* the beginning he worked enthusiastically.

But when a defining phrase is added, *at* is idiomatic:

> *At* the beginning of his employment here he worked enthusiastically.

Here, from student papers, are some other examples of errors in idiom:

> France was at that time a close ally *to* Sweden. (of)
> He took the liberty *to introduce* himself to the group. (of introducing)
> He was screaming *of* how dangerous it was for me to walk so near the edge of the cliff. (about)
> It is pleasant to live in the dorms and be in close proximity *of* everything on campus. (to)
> The public knew very little about Carter and many Americans were *unsure of giving* the presidency to such an unknown person.

English usage will not allow *unsure of giving*. If one wishes to retain *unsure,* one would have to say "unsure whether to give"; if one wished to retain *giving,* one would have to say "hesitant about giving."

Idiom is a matter of usage and is not something which logic or grammar can help us with. Although most users of the language will automatically speak and write idiomatically, it nevertheless pays, as you read and listen, to be alert to the way things are expressed, for one needs continually to sharpen one's ear for the idioms of the language. One should maintain intimate familiarity with the spoken and written word, and know where to go for guidance when in doubt. A good dictionary can often help; for example, if one looks up *adhere,* one finds that it is to be used with *to,* so one would know not to write "adhere *on*" or "adhere *with*." And the writer of the first example in the above list could probably have inferred from a good dictionary that whereas one allies oneself, or is allied, *with* or *to* another, one is simply an ally *of* the other. Or, should you be worried about using the word *oblivious,* your dictionary will probably inform you that it can be followed by either *of* or *to.* (And see *agree* and *differ* in the Usage Checklist at the end of this chapter. Also see Chapter XI for more examples of idiomatic usage.)

Other references that help with idiom (and with other matters) are H. W. Fowler's *A Dictionary of Modern English Usage* (Second Edition, revised by Sir Ernest Gowers), which discusses usage in a most informative, interesting, and often amusing way; *The Oxford English Dictionary,* which always provides examples of a word used in various contexts; and Theodore M. Bernstein's *The Careful Writer,* which lists many verbs requiring certain prepositions.

Exercise 58
Correct the unidiomatic usages in the following sentences.

1. She has an unusual philosophy towards modern technology. [*on*] [*attitude*]
2. She was grieved of her lover's death. [*at*]
3. Last summer I was bestowed with a scrawny, mangy mutt. [*given*]
4. Desdemona had unquestioning faith of Iago's character. [*in*]
5. The concrete imagery gives the reader a better grasp at the expressed emotion.
6. The analysis is weak because it lacks in specific details.
7. These actions were the cause for his downfall.
8. He describes the scene so clearly that he must be serious about of what he's saying.
9. Higgins now walks around behind her and bellows out his indignation of her ignorance. [*at*]
10. Most intriguing for the spectator are the reasons behind each character's preference in one person and not the other. [*for*]
11. Recent findings on depression suggest that climate can influence one's mood.
12. He held strong beliefs against smoking and drinking. [*strong*]
13. My father demanded for me to go to university. [*that I*]
14. To hear a man standing in centre stage and holding a brick explain that he represents a wall is funny in the least. [*not*]
15. Lovers and poets create dream worlds in which only they can inhabit.

59 Wordiness, Jargon, and Associated Plagues

Any diction that decreases the precision, clarity, and effectiveness of expression is bad. Using too many words, or tired words, or fuzzy words can only be harmful. In this section several kinds of weaknesses in diction are discussed and illustrated. We have placed them all under this one omnibus heading, for they are related, sometimes even overlapping. For example, a phrase like "on the order of" could be labelled *wordy, trite, jargon.*

Not all the items listed in the following pages are so variously classifiable, but there is an inevitable family relationship among the several groupings—if only because one error frequently leads to, or is accompanied by, others. Considering them all together should give you a better sense of the kinds of weakness they produce than would considering them separately. No lists such as those that follow can be exhaustive, for new words and phrases are every day shoving their way (or being shoved) into these categories. Some of those we list are notorious, others borderline; the thing to do is to understand the principles, get a feeling in one's bones for the *kinds* of violations of the rules of good writing they represent. (If the reason for a given term's inclusion is not immediately apparent to you, the illustrations in the exercises should help to clarify the matter.)

59a Wordiness

w The fewer words you use to make a point the better. Useless words (deadwood) only clutter up a sentence; they may dissipate its force, cloud its meaning, blunt its effectiveness. The student who wrote the following sentence, for example, used many words where a few would have been much better:

> w: What a person should try to do when communicating
> by writing is to make sure the meaning of what he is trying to say is clear.

Notice the gain in clarity and force when the sentence is revised:

> A writer should strive to be clear.

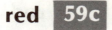

59b Repetition

rep Another kind of wordiness results from unnecessary repetition, which often produces awkwardness as well. Here is a student's sentence:

> rep: Looking at the general appearance of the buildings, you can see that special consideration was given to the choice of colours for these buildings.

The sentence is wordy in general, but one could begin pruning by cutting out the needless repetition of *buildings*. Here is another example:

> rep: She is able to make the decision to leave Manawaka and to abide by her decision.

It might be argued that the repetition of *decision* aids emphasis, but "make the decision" could be shortened to "decide," or the final "her decision" could be changed to "it."

59c Redundancy

red Another kind of wordiness is REDUNDANCY. ("Redundancy" can mean "excess" in general, but it is also used to designate the particular error known technically as "tautology.") Redundancy is also a kind of repetition, but of an idea rather than of a word. Something is redundant if it has already been expressed earlier in a sentence; here the word *earlier* is redundant, since the idea of *earlier* is present in the word *already*: repeating it is illogical and, of course, wordy. (Double negatives are a kind of redundancy, and plainly illogical: can't never, don't hardly, cannot but.) The student who begins a sentence with "In my opinion, I think ...." is already being redundant, for he could hardly do his thinking in anyone else's opinion. If you write that "Henry is a personal friend of mine," you are being redundant: Can a friend be other than personal? To speak of a "new innovation" is to be redundant, since the meaning of "new" is present in the word "innovation." And the person who wrote, in a letter to a prospective employer, that "an interview would be mutually helpful to both of us," probably did not get the job. Here are some other frequently encountered phrases that are redundant because the idea of one word is present in the other as well:

but nevertheless	general consensus
character trait	low ebb
close scrutiny	mental attitude
consensus of opinion	more preferable
continue on	new record
contributing factor	other alternatives
erode away	reason why
necessary prerequisite	refer back

One common kind of redundancy is called "doubling"—adding an unnecessary second word (usually an adjective) as if to make sure the meaning of the first is clear:

red: The report was brief and concise.

Either *brief* or *concise* alone would convey the meaning. Sometimes an insecure writer will go to even greater lengths:

red: The report was brief, concise, and to the point.

Further, people addicted to wordiness and jargon will prefer long words to short ones, and pretentious-sounding words to relatively simple ones. Try to be different: choose the shorter, the simpler, the more natural. In the following pairs of words, for example, the shorter forms are preferable:

analysis, analyzation
connote, connotate
courage, courageousness
existential, existentialistic
orient, orientate
preventive, preventative
remedy, remediate
symbolic, symbolical

On rare occasions the longer form of such a word may be preferable for reasons of euphony or rhythm. And if in a particular context there were any possibility of mistaking the verb *orient* for the noun *orient* or *Orient* (for example in reading aloud), then of course *orientate* would be the better choice.

Exercise 59c
Revise the following sentences to remove redundancy.

1. If enough food cannot be supplied for all the people in the world, man will have to deal with hunger, starvation, and wide-spread famine.
2. He is adventurous in that he likes a challenge and is willing to try new experiences, but he is not adventurous to the point of insanity, though.
3. Looking ahead into the future, the economist sees even worse conditions.
4. He approached the door with feelings of fear and dread.
5. The novel *Lord of the Flies* concerns a group of young children, all boys, who revert back to savagery.
6. If one doesn't thoroughly examine every part of the subject fully, one is almost sure to miss something that could be important.
7. Most people would rather flee away from danger than face it squarely.
8. Carol soon realized that she had to make a careful outline first, before she could expect an essay to be well organized.
9. She told him in exact and precise terms just what she thought of him.
10. The hangman in the story does not fit the stereotyped image of an executioner.

Exercise 59abc
Revise the following sentences to eliminate wordiness.

1. Time is a very powerful, strong image in this poem.
2. Davies attempts to divert attention away from himself by citing "them blacks" as the cause of the noises.
3. These were the very things that caused him his misery and his grief.
4. Advances in developments of modern technology greatly

contribute to making the equipment ~~necessary~~ for computerization ~~of~~ machinery ~~more and more~~ feasible ~~for~~ ~~potential~~ users.

5. Since he has both positive and negative qualities of human nature, Othello is far from perfect ~~and has many~~ faults.

59d Ready-made Phrases

"Prefabricated" or formulaic phrases that leap to our minds whole are almost always wordy. They are obviously a kind of cliché, and many also sound like jargon. Following are some examples; if you find yourself using any of them or others like them, check to see if they can be eliminated, or at least shortened (some shorter equivalents are given in parentheses):

a person who, one of those who
at the present time, at this time, at that time (now, then)
at the same time that (while)
by means of (by)
due to the fact that, because of the fact that, on account of the
    fact that, in view of the fact that (because)
during the course of, in the course of (during)
for the purpose of (for, to)
for the reason that, for the simple reason that (because)
in all likelihood (probably)
in all probability (probably)
in fact, in point of fact
in character
in colour
in height (high)
in length (long)
in nature
in number
in shape
in size
in the event that (if)
in the form of
in the light of (considering)
in the midst of (amid)
in the near future (soon)
in the not too distant future (soon)
in the neighbourhood of, in the vicinity of (about, near)
it is, there is, there are, there were

manner, in manner
on the part of
period of time (period, time)
personal, personally
previous to (before)
prior to (before)
seem, appear
tend, tendency
the fact that
up until, up till (until, till)
use of, the use of, by the use of, through the use of
with the exception of (except for)
with the result that

59e Triteness, Clichés

trite   Trite or hackneyed expressions, clichés, are another form of
wordiness: they are tired, worn out, all too familiar, and thus
contribute little to a sentence. Since they are by definition
prefabricated phrases, they are another kind of deadwood
that should be pruned away. Some trite phrases are
metaphors, once clever and fresh, but now so old and weary
that the metaphorical sense is, for some people, entirely
gone—which is why one sees such errors as "tow the line" instead of the original "toe the line," and "the dye is cast" instead of "the die is cast." Similarly, a student who weakly
settled for the cliché "time immemorial" was trapped into
confusing it with something else: "This is a problem with
which international relations have been plagued since time in
memoriam." Another carelessly asserted that a particular
poet's message to us was "that we should make hay while the
tide's in."

Some clichés are not only trite but redundant as well: first
and foremost, few and far between, over and above, each and
every, one and only, to all intents and purposes, ways and
means, various and sundry, all and sundry, part and parcel,
in this day and age (now, today), in our world today (now, today), in our modern world today (now, today), and so on.

Of course clichés serve a useful purpose, especially in
speech, enabling one to fill in pauses and gaps in thinking and
get on to the next point. Even in writing they can on occasion—simply because they are immediately recognizable, even

familiar—be the best way of saying something. And there is no denying their usefulness for an occasional humorous effect. In all such instances, however, they should be used consciously. It is not so much that clichés are bad in themselves but that the thoughtless use of clichés is weak. Generally speaking, then, they are to be avoided. No list can be complete, but here are a few more examples to suggest the kinds of expressions to avoid:

a bolt from the blue	it goes without saying
a heart as big as all outdoors	it stands to reason
a matter of course	lock, stock, and barrel
all things being equal	last but not least
as a last resort	love at first sight
as a matter of fact	many and diverse
as the crow flies	moment of truth
beat a hasty retreat	needless to say
brown as a berry	nipped in the bud
busy as a bee	no way, shape, or form
by leaps and bounds	off the beaten track
by no manner of means	on the right track
by no means	one and the same
clear as crystal (or mud)	par for the course
conspicuous by its absence	pride and joy
cool as a cucumber	raining cats and dogs
corridors of power	rears its ugly head
doomed to disappointment	rude awakening
easier said than done	sadder but wiser
fast as greased lightning	seeing is believing
from dawn till dusk	sharp as a tack
gentle as a lamb	slowly but surely
good as gold	smart as a whip
if and when	strike while the iron is hot
in a manner of speaking	strong as an ox
in one ear and out the other	when all is said and done
in the long run	wrong side of the tracks

Watch out also for the almost automatic couplings that occur between some adjectives and nouns. One seldom hears of a circle that isn't a vicious circle, or a fog that isn't a pea-soup fog, or a tenement that isn't a run-down tenement. Mere insight is seldom enough: it must be labelled penetrating insight. Here are a few more examples:

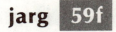

acid test	hearty breakfast
ardent admirers	heated opposition
budding genius	knee-jerk reaction
bulging biceps	natty dresser
blushing bride	proud possessor
consummate artistry	sacred duty
devastating effect	severe stress
drastic action	tangible proof
festive occasion	vital role

Some of these are clichés in the making; most have fully arrived. And several of the same sort are redundant as well:

advance planning	foreseeable future
advance warning	just deserts
blazing inferno	perfectly clear
cozy (little) nook	serious concern
end result	serious crisis
final outcome	terrible tragedy
final result	total (complete) surprise

59f Overuse of Nouns

The "noun disease" is another frequent source of deadwood; it is also a form of jargon. The focus of a sentence is its main verb; the verb activates it, moves it, makes it go. Too many nouns piled on one verb can slow a sentence down, especially if the verb is only a copula (*be* or another linking verb), or some other verb with little or no action in it. Consider the following:

> The opinion of the judge in this case is of great significance to the outcome of the investigation and its effects upon the behaviour of all the members of our society in the future.

The verb *is* in this sentence must do its best to move the great load of nouns and prepositional phrases along to some kind of finish. One could easily improve the sentence by reducing the proportion of nouns to verbs and making the verbs more vigorous:

> The judges' decision will inevitably influence how people act.

A particularly virulent form of the noun disease appears in the piling up of heavy Latinate *tion* nouns:

> The depredations of the conflagration resulted in the destruction of many habitations and also of the sanitation organization of the location; hence the necessitation of the introduction of activization procedures in relation to the implementation of emergency preparations for the amelioration of the situation.

This example is not as exaggerated as you might think. A simpler version of this monstrosity might be this:

> Since the fire destroyed not only many houses but also the water-treatment plant for the town, emergency procedures were quickly implemented.

The one verb of the original (*resulted*), a weak one at that, is here replaced by *destroyed* and *implemented*—some improvement, at least, especially since the two verbs have only one-third as much noun-baggage to carry. There is nothing inherently wrong with nouns ending in *tion*; the damage is done when they begin coming in clusters, usually resulting in wordy jargon.

Note: You should also try to avoid other unpleasant patterns of sound and rhythm, such as excessive alliteration or too regular a metrical pattern:

> At the top of the tree sat a bird on a branch.

or jarring repetitions of sound:

> They put strict restrictions on lending, which constricted the flow of funds.

or accidental rhyme:

> At that time he was in his prime; the way he later let himself go was a crime.

59g Nouns Used as Adjectives
One particularly insidious form of jargon is the awkward and unnecessary use of nouns as if they were adjectives. Many English nouns have long functioned as quite respectable adjectives, some even becoming so idiomatic as to form parts of compounds:

school board	schoolbook	schoolteacher
bathing suit	bath towel	bathtub
lunch hour	lunch box	lunchroom

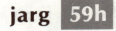

fire alarm	fire engine	firewood
space heater	space travel	spacesuit
business school	business card	businessman

Using nouns in this way is correct and normal, but it can be carried too far. "Lounge chair" is clearly preferable to "chair for lounging," but just as clearly "medicine training" does not conform to the usages of English as well as "medical training" or "training in medicine," nor "poetry skills" as well as "poetic skill" or "skill in poetry." In these last two examples, since there is a clear adjectival form available (*medical, poetic*), the simple nouns need not and should not be so used. But increasingly in recent years speakers and writers—especially those in government or other official positions, in business, and in the social sciences—have settled for or even actively chosen such noun-noun combinations. As a result, our language is becoming cluttered with such cumbersome phrases as *learning situation, resource person, cost factors, cash position, area man, profit outlook, opinion sampling, communication skills, leadership role, role model,* and so on and on. Even worse is the piling up of several nouns, as in something like Resource Management Personnel Training and Development Program.

Resist as much as possible the tendency to reduce the vigour of the English language to the flatness and awkwardness of such jargon. Do not speak, as we did a few sentences back, of people *in government positions,* but of those *in government* or *holding governmental office*; do not write, as a student did in a discussion of extracurricular activities, of their taking place "either in a school situation or a community-type situation"; don't talk of "emergency situations" or "crisis situations" but of *emergencies* and *crises* (and, obviously, try to avoid the word *situation* altogether).

59h Jargon

jarg JARGON in a narrow sense refers to terms peculiar to a specific discipline, such as psychology or chemistry or literary criticism, terms unlikely to be fully understood by an outsider; we prefer to use the word *jargon* in a broader sense, to refer to all the rubbish that tends to clutter contemporary expression. The private languages of particular disciplines or special groups are less dangerous to the general writer (and reader) than is the gobbledygook that so easily finds its way into the ears and minds and mouths and pens of most of us. As potential jargonauts, we must all be on guard against creeping sociologese and bureaucratese and the like, terms from other disciplines and from business and government that infiltrate layman's language. The unsophisticated, bombarded by such locutions, uncritically and even automatically use them in their own speech and writing; and so the disease spreads. If you write to communicate rather than to impress, you will avoid the pitfalls discussed and illustrated here; in that way, you will impress your readers in the best way.

The following list is a brief sampling of words and phrases that are virtually guaranteed to decrease the quality of your expression, whether spoken or written. The trouble with some should be obvious; others are fuzzy, imprecise, unnecessarily abstract; and still others objectionable mainly because they are overused, whether actually clichés or merely popular jargon. (We would succumb to the temptation to call some of these terms "buzz words" were this label itself not a voguish buzz word.)

affirmative, negative
along the lines of, along that line, in the line of
angle
area
aspect
at this point in time (now)
at that point in time (then)
background (especially as a verb)
basis, on the basis of, on a ... basis (see the Checklist)
bottom line
case
certain
circumstances
concept, conception
concerning, concerned
confrontation
connection, in connection with, in this (that) connection
considerable
considering, consideration, in consideration of
contact (especially as a verb)
cope

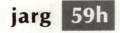

definitely
dialogue
escalate
eventuate
evidenced by
exactly
expertise
facet
factor
feedback
field
formulate
function
gap
hopefully (see the Checklist)
identify with
image
impact (especially as a verb)
implement (verb)
importantly
in relation to
infrastructure
instance
interface
in terms of (see the Checklist)
in the final analysis
input, output
involved
-ize verbs (finalize, concretize)
level
life-style
marginal
meaningful, meaningful dialogue
motivation
not at all (as an adverb: not at all well, not at all badly)
on stream
ongoing
parameters
personage
phase
picture, in the picture
position
posture
profile, low profile

realm
regarding, in regard to, with regard to
relate to
relevant
replicate
respect, respecting, in respect to, with respect to
scenario
sector
self-image
situated
situation
standpoint, vantage point, viewpoint
structure
time frame
type, -type (see the Checklist)
viable
-wise (see the Checklist)
worthwhile

Of course many of these words are perfectly legitimate and can be used in quite normal and acceptable ways. But even such acceptable words can be used as jargon, and those included in this list are the most likely offenders. For example, why say "He replied in the affirmative" when "He said yes" would do? *Angle* is a good and useful word, but in such expressions as "looking at the problem from a different angle" it begins to become jargon. *Aspect* has precise meanings, but they are seldom honoured; the student who wrote the following sentence certainly did not know them, but grabbed thoughtlessly at an all too familiar word: "Due to money aspects, many high-school graduates would rather work than enter university." Here *aspects* has no real meaning at all (and see *due to* in the Checklist, #60). A phrase like "For financial reasons" or "Because of a need for money" would be far better. Another student, analyzing a poem, fell into the jargon trap and wrote "The third quatrain develops the aspect of time." Attempting to revise the sentence the writer fell right back into the trap: "The third quatrain brings in the factor of time"; *factor* is nearly as bad here as *aspect*. Unless you use *case* to mean a box or container, a medical case, a legal case, a grammatical case, or in phrases like "in case of fire," you will be in danger of creating wordy jargon: "In most cases, students who worked hard got good grades.'' Why not "Most students who worked hard got good grades"? *Interface,* as a noun, has a precise technical meaning; but after social scientists adopted it for their purposes it began surfacing as jargon, used—even as a verb—by many who are evidently unaware of its meaning. *Realm* means a kingdom, and it can—or once could—be useful metaphorically in phrases like "the realm of poetry" or "the realm of ideas"; but it has for so long been so loosely and so widely applied that any thinking writer now will avoid it except when it does refer to a kingdom. And so on. If you read and listen carefully you will frequently find the terms listed, and other words and phrases like them, being used in ways that are offenses against clear and concise and precise expression. A few other specific items from this list are dealt with at length in the Checklist (#60). And you will find more examples in the exercises.

60 Usage: Checklist of Troublesome Words and Phrases

us In the following pages we list many words and phrases that have a history of being especially confusing or troublesome. You should study the whole list carefully, perhaps marking for frequent review any entries that you recognize as personal problem spots. Like any such list, this one cannot hope to be exhaustive; in fact, we have tried to keep it short. As with the list of frequently misspelled words, you should keep a list of your own errors of this kind for special study. You can supplement the information and advice provided below by consulting your dictionary. See also the lists under the following: Often Confused Words (#51l and m), Slang (#52a), Informal, Colloquial (#52b), Wordiness (#59a), Triteness, Clichés (#59e), Nouns (#59f and g), and Jargon (#59h).

above, below
Try to avoid the stiff references to something preceding or following in your essay. Say "for these (or those) reasons" rather than "for the above reasons." If you find yourself writing "as I said above" or "as I will explain below" and the like, you may well be the victim of your own poor organization; try revising your outline.

affect, effect

Affect is a transitive verb meaning *to act upon* or *to influence*; *effect* is a noun meaning *result, consequence*:

He tried to *affect* the outcome, but all his efforts had no *effect*.

Note: The plural noun *effects* can also refer to items of movable property, as in "household effects." And *effect* can also be a verb, but a relatively uncommon one, meaning *to bring about, to cause*: "The fertilizer *effected* rapid growth." *Affect* can also be a noun; its occurrence, however, is very uncommon and technical. It means, in psychology, something tending to arouse emotion rather than thought.

aggravate

Frequently misused to mean *annoy, irritate*. Properly speaking, something can be *aggravated* only if it is already bad; *aggravate* means *makes worse*:

His standing so long in the hot sun aggravated his headache.
The unexpectedly high tax bill aggravated the company's already serious financial condition.

agree to, agree with, agree on

Be careful to use the correct preposition with the verb *agree*. One agrees *to* a proposal or request or *to* do something; one agrees *with* another person on a question or opinion; a climate or certain foods agree *with* a person; one agrees *on* (or *about*) the terms or details of something settled after negotiation, or *on* a course of action.

alternate, alternative; alternately, alternatively

Some writers blur the useful distinction between these words. *Alternate* (adjective) means by turns, one following another, or every other one; *alternative* (adjective or noun) refers to one of a number of possible choices (usually two). Avoid using *alternate* when the sense has something to do with *choice*. The same distinction holds for the adverbial forms.

The squares on the board are alternately red and black.
In summer they could water their lawns only on alternate days.
The judge had no alternative: he had to dismiss the charges.
There is an alternative method, much simpler than the one you are using.
He could meekly resign or, alternatively, he could take his case to a higher authority.

The confusion perhaps arises from the legitimate use of *alternate* as a noun meaning a substitute or stand-by:

Each delegate to the convention had a designated alternate.

although, though

These are completely interchangeable, but *although* is usually felt to be more formal; and *although* usually sounds better at the beginning of a sentence, *though* elsewhere. Often the rhythm of a particular sentence will influence your choice.

amount, number

Use *number* only with countable things, *amount* only for something considered as a total or mass: a *number* of dollars, an *amount* of money; a large *number* of lumps of coal, a large *amount* of coal. *Number* can be either singular or plural, depending upon whether it refers to a collective *unit* or to a collection of distinct items; with the definite article it is usually singular, with the indefinite article, plural:

Singular: The *number* of unsolved crimes is appalling.
Plural: A large *number* of people object to his proposal.

See also *less, fewer,* and #7f.

and/or

To be avoided if possible. It is better to say "We'll get there on foot or horseback, or both," than "We'll get there on foot and/or horseback."

anxious

Does not mean *eager*; use it only where there is real anxiety, even to the point of suffering; think of the German word *Angst*.

anyways, anywheres, nowheres, somewheres

Dialectal errors for *anyway, anywhere, nowhere, somewhere.*

awaiting for

Awaiting does not require the preposition *for*; *waiting* does:

> I am *waiting for* the whistle to blow.
> I am *awaiting* the train's arrival.

as

To prevent ambiguity, do not use *as* in such a way that it can mean either *while* or *because*:

> As I was walking after dark I tripped over a sleeping dog.
> As I turned the flame up too high the grease caught fire.
> The car gathered speed quickly, as I pressed harder on the accelerator.

It is impossible to be sure whether the *as* in each of these means *while* or *because.* Many writers have banned *as* in the sense of *because* from their vocabularies; using it only in the sense of *while,* they are unlikely to commit an inadvertent ambiguity, for it is primarily when *as* is used to mean *because* (or *for* or *since*) that it leads to ambiguity. Watch out for another awkward use of *as*: In a sentence like "The book was considered *as* a threat to the authority of the church," the *as* should be omitted; not only is it unnecessary, but it also alters the essential meaning of the sentence at least slightly.

as far as . . . is (are) concerned, as far as . . . goes

This construction has a jargon-like air about it, but if you feel that you need to use it anyway, don't carelessly leave it unfinished, as in this example:

> As far as financing my education, I'm going to have to get a summer job.

This frequent error probably stems from a confusion of *as far as* with *as for.*

as to

A phrase worth avoiding; substitution or rephrasing will almost always improve matters.

> *Poor:* He made several recommendations as to the best method of proceeding.
> *Better:* He made several recommendations with respect to the best method of proceeding.
> *Still better:* He recommended several methods of proceeding.
> *Poor:* I was in doubt as to which road to take.
> *Better:* I was in doubt about which road to take.
> *Still better:* I was not sure which road to take.
> I did not know which road to take.

As to at the beginning of a sentence may seem more tolerable, but even there it can sound awkward; try changing it to *As for.*

bad, badly (See *good, bad, badly, well.*)

basis, on the basis of, on a ... basis

Basis is a perfectly good word, but these prepositional phrases using it are worth avoiding, for they are almost always wordy jargon.

> She made her decision *on the basis of* the committee's report.

This can easily be improved:

> She based her decision on the committee's report.

Again:

> He selected the furniture *on the basis of* its shape and colour. (by? for? according to? because of?)

The other phrase is even worse: *on a daily basis* is jargon for *daily*; *on a yearly basis* is jargon for *annually*; *on a temporary basis* is jargon for *temporarily*; *We'll do this for a week on a trial basis* is jargon for *We'll try this for a week*; *on a regular basis* is jargon for *regularly*; *on a political basis* is jargon for *politically* or *for political reasons*; and so on *ad nauseam.* See also *in terms of.*

beside, besides

Don't confuse these words. *Beside,* a preposition, means

next to; *besides* as an adverb means *also, too*:

> She stood *beside* her car.
> She knew she would have to pay the cost of repairs and the towing charges *besides*.

Besides can also be a preposition meaning *other than, in addition to*:

> Besides the cost of repairs, she knew she would have to pay towing charges.
> *Besides* this, what should I do?

between, among

Although even some good writers no longer strictly observe this rule, it is still usually best to use *between* only where two persons or things are involved, and *among* when there are more than two:

> They divided the cost equally *among* the three of them.
> There is almost no difference *between* the two products.

Don't let plurals trap you into error:

> There were the predictable differences *between* (not *among*) Liberals and Conservatives during the debate.

On occasion, however, *between* can be the more appropriate choice even for groups of three or more, especially if the emphasis is on the individual persons or things involved:

> At the end there remained little bitterness between the four men.
> It seems impossible to keep the peace between the nations of the world.

blame

Be careful with this word. As a verb it should not be followed by *on,* for one does not blame *something on* someone, but rather blames *someone for* something. One can of course *put* the blame for something *on* someone.

bust, busted

Slang or illiterate for *burst* (principal parts: burst, burst, burst), meaning *broken*.

can, may

Opinion and usage are divided, but in formal contexts it is still advisable to use *can* to denote *ability, may* to denote *permission* or *possibility*:

> "May I have some more soup, please?" " Are you sure you can eat another bowl?"
>
> He knew that he might leave if he wished, but he could not make himself rise from his chair.
>
> Things may turn out worse than you expect.

But *can* is frequently used in the sense of permission, especially in informal contexts and with questions and negatives (*Can I go? No, you cannot*) or where the distinction between *ability* and *permission* is blurred (*Anyone with an invitation can get in*)—a blurring which, inherent in the concepts, is making the two words increasingly interchangeable.

can't hardly, etc.

Barely, hardly, scarcely, only and *but* are considered negatives. Therefore do not use words like *can't* and *don't* and *couldn't* with them, for the result is an ungrammatical *double negative,* just as bad as writing (or saying) *don't never* or *wasn't never.* Use instead the positive form of the verb: I can hardly believe it. He could scarcely finish on time.

centre around

An illogical phrase. The meaning of the word *centre* (or *focus*) demands a different preposition:

> The discussion centred *on* the proposed amendment.

Or something can centre *in* or *at* something. One can of course say *revolved around, circled around,* and be quite logical.

compare to, compare with

Use *compare to* to liken one thing to another, to express a similarity:

> Shall I compare thee *to* a summer's day?
> He compared his job *to* that of a coolie.

Compare with means to examine for similarities or differences, or both:

> He compared the sports car *with* the compact car to see which one was the best for him.
>
> He compared favourably *with* the boy friend she had had the previous year.
>
> Compared *with* a desk job, farm work is more healthful by far.

(There is often an implication that, asked to compare *a* with *b*, you are being asked to look for similarities; that is true in the sense that you are expected to determine the extent of similarity, but one cannot easily do that without also discovering and pointing out the differences as well.)

comprise, compose

Confusion often arises from these words and the concepts they express. *Comprise* means *consist of, contain, take in*:

> The city comprises several separate communities.
>
> His duties comprise opening and shutting the shop, keeping the shelves stocked at all times, and running errands.

Compose means *constitute, form, make up*:

> The seven small communities together compose (constitute, make up) the city.

Here it would be incorrect to use *comprise*.

continual, continuous

Although these two words are very close to each other in meaning, there is an important distinction between them. *Continual* refers to something that happens frequently or even regularly but with interruptions; *continuous* refers to something that occurs constantly, without interruptions:

> Your *continual* harping on my faults has given me a *continuous* headache.
>
> The heckler *continually* tried to interrupt, but the speaker's voice went on in a *continuous* drone.

convince, persuade

Distinctions worth preserving: one is *convinced* by logic, proof, argument addressed to reason or intellect; one is *persuaded* by appeals to emotions, feelings, will. Note also the correct idiom: one is convinced *of* something, or *that* something is so and so, but one is persuaded *to* do something.

culminate

Since this verb is intransitive, it is incorrect to use it with a direct object or in a passive construction:

> *Wrong:* He culminated his remarks with a strong blast at the opposition.
>
> *Wrong:* The building was culminated by a revolving restaurant and television tower.

Instead, use it only intransitively and always with the preposition *in:*

> His speech culminated in a strong blast at the opposition.
> The building culminated in a revolving restaurant and a television tower.

decimate

Try to avoid using this in the hackneyed sense of causing great destruction and death. Strictly it means (or meant) to select and kill one out of every ten.

differ from, differ with

To differ *from* something or someone is to be unlike it or him in some way; to differ *with* someone is to disagree, to quarrel:

> He *differed from* his colleague in that he was less prone to *differ with* everyone on every issue.

different from, different than

From is the idiomatic preposition to use after *different*:

> Your car is noticeably different from mine.

Than, however, is becoming increasingly common, especially when followed by a clause and when it results in fewer words:

> The finished picture looks far different than I had intended.

But to avoid criticism and the label "colloquial," use the more acceptable construction with *from*:

> The finished picture looks different from what I intended.

disinterested

A much abused word, *disinterested* means *impartial, objective, free from personal bias.* Although often used sloppily as a synonym for *uninterested, not interested,* the distinction between the two should be retained:

> It is necessary to find a judge who is disinterested in the case, for he will then try it fairly; we assume that he will not also be uninterested in it, for then he would be bored by it.

due to

Rather than risk censure, use this only as a predicate adjective following a linking verb:

> The accident was due to bad weather.

Used to introduce an adverbial phrase at the beginning of a sentence, *due to* is considered awkward or incorrect; use *because of* or *on account of* instead:

> Because of (not *due to*) the bad weather, we had an accident.

each other, one another

In formal writing use *each other* for two, *one another* for more than two:

> The bride and groom kissed each other.
> The five boys traded hockey cards with one another.

either, neither

Use these only to refer to one or the other of *two* things, not more than two. Also, remember that *either* and *neither* are singular and take the singular form of a verb:

> Either of the two answers is all right.

For more than two, *any* or *any one* (two words) will usually suffice:

> Any (one) of the four proposals is acceptable.

enormity

Often incorrectly used to mean *great size, enormousness,* this word actually means *outrageousness, heinousness,* or *atrocity*:

> In pronouncing sentence, the judge emphasized the enormity of the arsonist's crime.

equally as

Avoid this awkward redundancy by dropping one or the other of the two words. In expressions like the following, *as* is unnecessary:

> Her first novel was highly praised, and her second is equally (as) good.
> He may be a good jumper, but she can jump equally (as) high, if not higher.

In expressions like the following, *equally* is unnecessary:

> In a storm, one port is (equally) as good as another.
> His meat pies were (equally) as tasty as hers.

ever

Not needed after *seldom* and *rarely.*

farther, further

Although this distinction is no longer widely observed, there is still sufficient reason to use *farther* and *farthest* to refer to actual physical distance, and *further* and *furthest* to refer figuratively to non-physical things like time and degree:

> To go any *farther* down the road is the *furthest* thing from my mind.
> Rather than delay any *further,* he chose the card *farthest* from him.

feels

Try to avoid using the word *feel* loosely when what you really mean is *think* or *believe; feel* is more appropriate to emotionally or bodily based ideas, *think* to intellectually based ones:

I feel the need of sustenance; I think I had better have something to eat.

I feel that we shouldn't start tonight; I think the road may be dangerous.

fewer (See *less, fewer.*)

firstly, secondly, etc.

Drop the old-fashioned and unnecessary *ly*; say simply *first, second, third,* etc.

following

It is a pretentious error to use *following* as a preposition meaning *after*: *Following the concert, we went home. Following* is a noun (*He had a large following; Study the following*) or an adjective (*Study the following rules; Following the hearse, we entered the cemetery*). It should not be used as a preposition to introduce an adverbial phrase.

former, latter

Use these only when referring to the first or the second of two things, and only when the reference is clear and unambiguous—that is, when it is to something immediately preceding. But, like *above* and *below*, they are worth avoiding if possible.

fulsome

Although frequently used as if it meant *full, abundant,* as in "fulsome praise," the word actually means *too full, excessive,* and therefore *disgusting, offensive, distasteful,* as in "fulsome flattery"; keep in mind that its meaning has been influenced by the word *foul* and you will likely not misuse it.

good, bad, badly, well

To avoid confusion and error with these words, simply remember that *good* and *bad* are adjectives, *badly* and *well* adverbs (except when *well* is an adjective meaning *healthy*). Troubles most often arise after linking verbs.

Helena looks good. (She is attractive.)
That suit looks bad on you. (It doesn't fit properly; do not use *badly* here.)
Nathan acted bad. (He did naughty things.)
Nathan acted badly. (His performance as Hamlet was terrible.)
I feel good. (I am happy.)
I feel bad. (I have a splitting headache.)
Herman feels badly. (An unlikely statement; it could only mean that he was feeling some object with his hands and doing it badly.)
Sophia looks well. (She looks healthy, not sick.)
This wine travels well. (It wasn't harmed by the long train journey.)
That steak smells good. (I look forward to eating it.)
Your dog doesn't smell well. (He is too old to hunt.)

hanged, hung

Use the past form *hanged* only when referring to an execution by hanging. For all other uses of the verb *hang,* the correct past form is *hung*.

He or she, his or her

Try to avoid using these cumbersome and cluttering locutions. And never sink to the abominable *he/she, his/her* device. If you are seriously intent on avoiding the pronouns *he* and *his* in their generalizing way of referring to either male or female, it is usually possible to find a way. For example,

Each student must bring his or her book to class.
If any member is late, he or she will not be admitted.

can easily be written as

All students must bring their books to class.
Members who are late will not be admitted.

healthy, healthful

Keep *healthy* as a word meaning *in a state of a good health,* and use *healthful* to mean *contributing to good health*:

To stay *healthy,* one should participate in a *healthful* sport like swimming.

hopefully

Although often used, especially in speech, *hopefully* as a sentence adverb, an adverb leading off (or sometimes ending) and modifying a whole sentence, is frowned upon by many who care about style.

> Hopefully, the economy will improve during the next few months.

What the writer means here is "I hope ..." or "One hopes ..." or "It is to be hoped that ..."; the economy, whether it improves or not, can scarcely be full of hope, yet there is nothing else for the word *hopefully* to attach itself to. Consider the following:

> Hopefully, many people will come to the prize drawing.

This would probably be understood as expressing the sentiments of the organizer or the person who gets a cut of the admission price. A careful writer who meant otherwise would have put it differently:

> Many people will come, full of hope, to the prize drawing.

Hopefully can be used correctly, of course; for example:

> Hopefully I undertook to reorganize the association's executive branch.
> "Some day," he said hopefully, "the service around here should improve."

But even when it is used correctly, its more frequent misuse can often make it sound ambiguous:

> Stephen was outside somewhere, hopefully looking for an empty cab.
> Hopefully, the coach has assigned his best quarterback for the crucial plays.

And since *hopefully* is almost certain to sound like jargon, many people avoid it simply because it is so sloppily overused.

in, into

In formal writing, *in* means *inside of* and *into* means *moving toward the inside of:*

He went *into* the hall to see if she was there, but she was *in* the kitchen.

We moved *into* our new home last Saturday.

individual

Not a synonym for *person.* The word *individual* should be used only when the meaning *distinct from others* is present:

The person (not *individual*) you are referring to is my aunt.

He is very much an individual in his behaviour. (That is, he behaves like no one else.)

You are always safe if you use it as an adjective rather than as a noun.

infer, imply

These two words give rise to frequent confusion and misuse; make every effort to learn to distinguish between them and to use them correctly. The very common error is to use *infer* where *imply* would be the correct word. As most people know, *imply* means *to suggest, hint at, indicate indirectly. Infer,* however, does not mean the same thing. Rather it means *to conclude by reasoning, to deduce.* What one person *implies* in a statement, then, a listener can *infer* from it:

Her speech strongly *implied* that she could be trusted.

I *inferred* from her speech that she was trustworthy.

in terms of

This phrase is another example of contemporary clutter. Note that it is similar, sometimes even equivalent, to those other offenders, *on the basis of* (see *basis*) and *-wise.* Do not write things like

He tried to justify the price increase in terms of [on the basis of] the company's increased operating costs.

In terms of experience [Experience-wise], she was as qualified for the post as anyone else applying for it.

In terms of fuel economy, this car is better than any other in its class.

He first considered the problem in terms of the length of time it would take him to solve it.

> When they planned the assault, they were clearly thinking in terms of how to minimize property damage.

when the ideas could so easily be much better expressed:

> He tried to justify the increase in price by citing the company's increased operating costs.
> She was as experienced as anyone else applying for the post.
> This car has the best fuel economy of any in its class.
> First he thought about how long it would take him to solve the problem.
> When they planned the assault, they were clearly thinking about how to minimize property damage.

And note the further family resemblance of this phrase to others like *along the lines of, in connection with, in relation to, in* [*with*] *respect to,* and *from the standpoint* [*viewpoint*] *of. Perspective* and *approach* are two more terms often used in a similar way.

irregardless

There is no such word. The prefix *ir* (not) is redundant, since the suffix *less* already expresses the "not." The correct word is *regardless.* (The error evidently stems from confusion of *regardless* with *irrespective.*)

is when, is where

Incorrect because a *when* or *where* adverbial clause cannot follow the linking verb *is;* a predicate adjective or predicate noun is required as complement after a linking verb:

> *Wrong:* A double play is when two base runners are put out during one play.
> *Right:* In a double play, two base runners are put out during one play.
> *Right:* A double play occurs when two base runners are put out during one play.

(Since *occurs* is not a linking verb, the adverbial clause beginning with *when* is all right.)

Note: This error is grammatically similar to that of *the reason* .... *is because* (see *gr* in Chapter XI).

kind of, sort of

Do not use these as adverbs, as in *kind of tired, sort of strange*. Do not follow with an article, as in "I had a bad kind of an afternoon" or "She was a rather peculiar sort of a guide." Even when used legitimately, these phrases are frequently awkward and unnecessary. Why not "I had a bad afternoon" and "She was a rather peculiar guide"?

less, fewer

Less should be used only in comparisons of things or amounts that are not being counted or considered as units; *fewer* refers to things that are countable:

> *fewer* dollars, *less* money
> *fewer* hours, *less* time
> *fewer* shouts, *less* noise
> *fewer* cars, *less* traffic
> *fewer* bottles of beer, *less* beer

See also *amount, number*.

lie, lay

If necessary, memorize the principal parts of these often misused verbs: *lie, lay, lain*; *lay, laid, laid*. *Lie* means *recline*, or *be situated*; *lay* means *put* or *place*; *lie* is intransitive; *lay* is transitive.

> I *lie* down now. I *lay* down yesterday. I *have lain* down several times today.
> I *lay* the book on the desk now. I *laid* the book on the desk yesterday. I *have laid* the book on the desk every morning for a week.

(In the sense of "prevaricate" the principal parts of *lie* are *lie, lied, lied*.)

like, as, as if, as though

In the following sentence, *like* is a *preposition*:

> Roger is dressed exactly like Ray.

But if *Ray* is given a verb, then he becomes the subject of a clause, and *like* is no longer functioning as a preposition:

> *Wrong:* Roger is dressed exactly like Ray is.

Like now functions as a conjunction—which in good usage it cannot be. Always use *as,* a perfectly good conjunction, when a clause follows:

> Roger is dressed exactly as Ray is.
> The steak is rare, as a good steak should be.

In slightly different constructions, either *as if* or *as though* is the correct form to use in place of the pernicious *like:*

> It looks like rain. (*not* It looks like it will rain.)
> OR
> It looks as if (or *as though*) it is going to rain.
> He stood there like a bronze Apollo. (*not* He stood there like he was a bronze Apollo.)
> OR
> He stood there as though (or *as if*) he were a bronze Apollo.

But be careful that, in an effort to avoid this error, you don't overcompensate; don't shun *like* for *as* when what follows it is *not* a clause:

> *Wrong:* Rover stood stiffly alert, pointing, head and tail down, as any well-trained dog.
> *Wrong:* Nicklaus, just as last year's winner, shot a stunning birdie on the final hole.

In each of these the *as* should be changed to *like.*

likely, liable, apt

Likely means *probable, showing a tendency, suitable*:

> A storm seems *likely*. He is *likely* to succeed. This is a *likely* spot.

Liable means *legally responsible, susceptible to something undesirable*:

> He is *liable* for damages. She is *liable* to headaches.

Confusion most often arises when either word would seem appropriate:

> If he isn't careful, he is *liable* to fall off that ladder.

Although *likely* ("showing a tendency") would seem right here, *liable* is preferable, in its sense of *susceptible to something undesirable.*

Apt is often used loosely as a synonym for both *likely* and *liable,* but it is best retained for those places involving a *habitual* tendency or inclination:

> Jimmy is *apt* to trip over his own feet.

literally, virtually, figuratively

Don't use these unthinkingly. *Literally* means *actually, really. Virtually* means *in effect, practically. Figuratively* means *metaphorically, not literally.* All too often they are used to mean the exact opposite of their real meaning:

> She was literally swept off her feet. (Hardly! What the writer really means is that the lady in question was *figuratively* or *virtually* swept off her feet.)
> They were caught in a virtual downpour. (It *was* a downpour! Who needs *virtual?*)

loan, lend

Some people still restrict *loan* to being a noun, but it is now generally accepted as a verb equivalent to *lend.*

mad

Only informally is *mad* a synonym for *angry.* Formal usage demands that *mad* be restricted to the meaning *insane.*

material, materialistic

Don't use *materialistic* when all you need is the adjective *material. Material* means *physical, composed of matter,* or *concerned with physical rather than spiritual or intellectual things*; it is often the sufficient word:

> The industrial West is a very *material* culture.
> His life is founded almost entirely on *material* values.

Materialistic is the adjectival form of the noun *materialist,* which in turn denotes one who believes in *materialism,* a philosophical doctrine holding that everything can be explained in terms of matter and physical laws. A *materialist* can also be one who is notably or questionably concerned with material as opposed to spiritual or intellectual things and values:

> He is very *materialistic* in his outlook on life.

But unless you intend the philosophical overtones, use the simpler *material*. There is an analogous tendency to use *relativistic* rather than *relative,* and *moralistic* rather than *moral.* Consult your dictionary.

See also *real, realism, realist, realistic.*

momentarily

Worth trying to keep as meaning *at the moment, at every moment*; do not use it to mean *in a moment, soon.* (See *presently.*)

number (See *amount, number.*)

of

Never needed after the prepositions *off, inside, outside,* and often unnecessary after the pronoun *all,* especially when countable items are not involved:

He fell off (or *from*) the fence. (not *off of*)
He found himself inside a large crate. (not *inside of*)
As requested, she remained in the hall outside the room for five minutes. (not *outside of*)
We had all the time in the world. (*of* not necessary)
All of the members were present. (*of* acceptable but not necessary)

Of is needed after *all* before some pronouns and usually before proper nouns:

Bring all of them. We travelled across all of Canada.

Note: In "He inspected the outside of the building," *outside* is a noun.

Also, do not make the mistake of unidiomatically using *of* after *remember:*

I remembered (not *remembered of*) all the things my mother had told me about the big city.

In addition, because of the way we speak, phrases like "would have," "should have," "might have," and so on often come out as contractions: "would've," "should've," "might've"; because of the way they *hear* such words, some people mistakenly assume that the *ve* is actually *of,* and then proceed to write "would of," "should of," "might of," etc. Do not make this illiterate error.

on

This preposition is sometimes awkwardly unidiomatic when used as a substitute for *about* or *of*:

id: She had no doubts *on* what to do next. (should be *about*)

id: I am calling my essay "A Study *on* the Effects of Automation." (should be *of*)

partially, partly

Since *partially* also means *with prejudice or bias,* using it in the sense of *partly* could be ambiguous. (*His decision was partially made.*) It is simpler and safer to use the shorter *partly.*

persuade (See *convince, persuade.*)

presently

Presently should mean *in a short while, soon*; it should not be used to mean *now, at the present.* But such is the confusion surrounding this word that it is best avoided altogether. Use the alternative words and your meaning will be clear. Besides, *presently* almost always sounds pretentious. (See *momentarily.*)

quote

This is a verb. Used as a noun, instead of *quotation,* it is colloquial, as is *quotes* instead of *quotation marks.*

raise, rise

Raise is transitive, requiring an object: *I raised my hand. He raises wheat. Rise* is intransitive, used without an object: *The temperature rises. I rise in the morning.* Learn the principal parts of these verbs: *raise, raised, raised*; *rise, rose, risen.*

real, realism, realist, realistic

Be careful to use these words correctly; it pays to consult your dictionary in order to be sure. The student who wrote

"Huxley's novel is not about realistic people" meant simply "*real* people." The one who wrote "He based his conclusions not on theory but on *realistic* observation" meant "observation of *reality*." See also *material, materialistic.*

relation, relationship

The longer word, *relationship,* is commonly used where it is not necessary; it is necessary only when speaking of family connections or where the desired meaning is analogous to that:

> What is the relationship between you two? (That is, how are you related to each other?) Are you sisters, cousins, or what?

Elsewhere the sense of the connection or state of being related is most often adequately expressed by the shorter word:

> I do not see any relation between your answer and the question I asked.
> The two countries have long enjoyed friendly relations.

sensual, sensuous

Sensuous means *pertaining to the senses, sensitive to beauty,* etc. *Sensual,* on the other hand, means *lewd, carnal, pertaining to the body and to the satisfaction of physical appetites*:

> Many Canadian poets, responding to the beauty of their natural environment, write sensuous poetry.
> The minister emphasized the spiritual quality of "The Song of Solomon" rather than its sensual features.

set forth

As an unwieldy, stiff substitute for *expressed* or *presented* or *stated,* this phrase is an attempt at sophistication that usually misfires.

since

Avoid in the sense of *because* when time is involved or when other ambiguities could result.

> *Ambiguous:* Since you went away, I've been sad and lonely.

so ... as

Prefer *so* or *so ... as* with *negative* comparisons, *as* or *as
... as* with *positive* comparisons:

Barbara was almost *as* tall *as* he was, but she was not *so* heavy.
He was not *so* light on his feet *as* he once was, but he was *as*
strong *as* ever.

state

A stronger verb than *say, state* should be reserved for
places where you want the heavier, more forceful meaning
of *assert, declare, make a formal statement.*

substitute

One thing cannot be *substituted by* or *with* another; the
correct verb there is *replace*:

Wrong: The french fries were substituted by (or *with*) a tossed
salad.

Wrong: The term paper was substituted by (or *with*) three
smaller reports.

Right: The french fries were replaced by (or *with*) a tossed
salad.

Right: The term paper was replaced by (or *with*) three
smaller reports.

Used correctly, *substitute* usually takes the preposition *for*:

The waitress kindly substituted a tossed salad for the greasy
french fries.
This year you may substitute three short reports for the term
paper.

Substitute can also be used intransitively:

Because he is off his game this season, Randolph has only
substituted.

suspicion, suspect, suspicious

Suspicion is a noun; *suspect* is the verb (though it can also
be a noun). Though *suspicious* can mean *arousing suspicion,* it is sometimes safer to reserve it for the person in
whom the suspicions are aroused, using the adjectival sense
of *suspect* for the object of those suspicions; otherwise ambiguity may result (unless the context makes everything
clear):

ambig:	He was a very suspicious man.
clear:	I thought his actions suspect.
clear:	He was suspicious of everyone he met.
clear:	All of us were suspect in the eyes of the police.

though (See *although, though.*)

thusly

A pretentious-sounding error for *thus,* as is *muchly* for *much.*

too

Used as an intensifier, *too* is illogical; use *very*:

I don't like my cocoa too hot. (Well, of *course* you don't!)
I don't like my cocoa very hot.
She didn't care for the brown suit too much. (How *could* she care *too* much!)
She didn't care for the brown suit very much.

See also *very.*

toward, towards

These are interchangeable, but *toward* is usually preferred to *towards,* just as *afterward* is preferred to *afterwards,* and *forward* to *forwards.*

true facts, etc.

An attempt to be emphatic that backfires into illogic. If there are such things as "true facts" or "real facts," then what are "false facts" or "unreal facts"? Let the word *facts* mean what it is supposed to; trying to prop it up with *true* or *real* only makes a reader suspect it of being weak or insincere.

type, -type

In any but a technical context, the word *type* almost always sounds like jargon, even when followed by the obligatory *of.* Without the *of* it is colloquial at best. In general writing, if you *can* substitute *kind of* for *type of,* do so—but even then check to make sure you really need it, for often it is unnecessary: He is an intelligent [kind of] man. As a hyphenated suffix, *-type* is similarly often unnecessary, as well as being one of the worst results of the impulse to turn nouns into adjectives: "This is a new-type vegetable slicer," or "He is a patriotic-type person." Avoid it.

unique, necessary, essential, perfect, empty, wrong, round, square, etc.

These and other such adjectives cannot logically be compared. Since by definition something that is *unique* is the *only one of its kind,* then clearly one thing cannot be "more unique" than another, or even "very unique"; in other words, *unique* is *not* a synonym for *unusual.* Similarly with the others: one thing cannot be "more necessary" than another. Since *perfect* means *without flaw,* there cannot be degrees of perfection. A thing is either round or not round; one tennis ball cannot be *rounder* than another. And so on. (Note that we get around this semantic limitation by speaking of one thing as, for example, *more nearly perfect, more nearly round,* or *closer to round* than another.)

usage, use, utilize, utilization

Usage (noun) is most appropriate when you mean customary or habitual use (*British usage; the usages of the early Christians*) or a particular verbal expression being characterized in a particular way (*an ironic usage, an elegant usage*). Otherwise the shorter noun *use* will usually do. *Use* (verb) should suffice nearly all the time; *utilize,* which is often pretentiously employed instead, should carry the specific meaning *put to use, make use of, turn to practical or profitable account.* Similarly with the noun *utilization*: simply the noun *use* will usually be more appropriate. Phrases like *use of, the use of, by the use of,* and *through the use of* tend toward jargon and are almost always wordy.

verbal, oral

These are not synonyms. If you mean *spoken aloud,* then *oral* is the right word. *Verbal* regularly means *pertaining to words,* which could be either written or spoken. (In some special contexts *verbal* is customarily used to mean *oral* as opposed to written: *verbal contract, verbal agreement.* But for general writing keep the distinction between *verbal* and *oral* clear.)

very

Do not overuse *very* as a lame intensifier. You will often find that where you have used *very* you could just as well have omitted it; sometimes it even detracts from the force of the word it modifies, or is a lazy and vague substitute for a more precise adverb or adjective:

> It was very sunny today. (magnificently sunny? torturously sunny?)
>
> I was very tired. (exhausted?)
>
> He was very intoxicated. (falling-down drunk?)
>
> Her embarrassment was very obvious. (It was either obvious or it wasn't; drop *very,* or change it to something like *excruciatingly.*)

Note: Before some past participles, it is idiomatic to use another word along with *very*:

> You are *very much* mistaken if you think I'll agree without an argument.
>
> Sharon is *very well* rehearsed for the role.

well (See *good, bad, badly, well.*)

while

As a subordinating conjunction, *while* is fine as long as it is restricted to meanings having to do with time:

> While I cut the lawn she raked up the grass clippings.
> She played the piano while I prepared the dinner.

When it is not intended to refer to time it can be imprecise at best, ambiguous at worst:

> *While* I agree with some of his reasons, I still think my proposal is better.

Here the meaning would be better served by *although.*

> The Liberals want a new freeway, *while* the Conservatives favour some form of rapid transit.

Here the meaning would be better served by *whereas.*

> The winning team guzzled champagne, *while* the losers sat and sulked.

Here either an *and* or a *but* would make a sharper statement.

-wise

Do not add this suffix—in its sense of "with respect to" or "in terms of"—to nouns; find a way to say what you want without using jargon.

> not: Grammarwise, Stephen is not doing well.
> but: Stephen is not doing well with grammar.
> not: Insurance-wise, I believe I am well enough protected.
> but: I believe I have enough insurance.
> not: This is the best car I've ever owned, powerwise.
> but: This car has more power than any other I have owned.

See also *in terms of*.

worthwhile

Try to find a more precise and concrete way to express the desired meaning. "It was a very worthwhile experience" tells one very little (nor does the *very* succeed in propping up the weak *worthwhile*). Skip the vague statement; instead, describe or explain just what was so worthwhile about the experience. See also *Concreteness, #54*.

Review Exercise: Chapter VII

Correct the errors, strengthen the diction, and normalize the usage in the following sentences.

1. Her refusal to express her feelings caused her to store her problems within herself, which added to her visible instability.
2. They are a close-knit unit that functions on a collective basis.
3. Poetry during this time period did not pay very well.
4. Because this particular word occurs frequently throughout the course of the play, it achieves a certain importance.
5. In the winter even less tourist dollars are spent.
6. His striving to be a perfectionist was evident in his business.

7. The scientist grew his sample bacteria in a test-tube situation.
8. He was ignorant as to the proper use of the tools.
9. As is so often the case, one type of error leads to another.
10. The selection of bishops was based chiefly on political grounds.
11. His metaphors really bring out a sinister feeling which one feels while reading it.
12. Eliot sees his poetry as occupying a kind of niche in a long conveyor belt of accumulated knowledge and poetry.
13. She has him literally at her beckon call.
14. He found himself in a powerless situation.
15. I resolved to do my best in terms of making friends and working hard.
16. The hulls of the tankers were ripped open in a majority of cases, dumping countless barrels of oil into the ocean.
17. She suspicioned that he was not sincere.
18. This poem is concerned with the fact that one should grasp an opportunity quickly.
19. They try hard, but the answers they search always seem to elude them.
20. A grave problem concerned with overpopulation besides the food crisis is the inability for our civilized world to educate the people of underdeveloped countries.
21. As he gave me so much money I thanked him profusely.
22. The overall impression of the place was so overwhelming that within two weeks I had decided to stay for an indefinite period of time, and make a decision concerning departure at a later date.
23. People in watching these shows or movies may develop a love for violence as a result of watching this type of program.
24. It seems like he is rather mad at her for daring to try and deceive him.
25. In Olympic sports nationalism is increasingly becoming a more important factor.
26. When he speaks, it is to reassure her; therefore he speaks gently and reassuringly.
27. In the following stanza Donne tries to make his wife proud of their relationship by comparing it to "dull sublunary lovers' love whose soul is sense."

28. Frodo continuously fretted about the Ring.
29. The author cites that in one of Macaulay's speeches on the First Reform Bill he said, "Reform, that you may preserve."
30. At the end of the story Hardin comes up with a baffling solution to which the reader knew nothing about until then.
31. The general shape of this particular hockey stick is no different than that of any other.
32. The contribution of the coalition to the passage of the legislation was capitalized on by the opposition.
33. As to getting a job, in some cases it has been shown that being in the right place at the right time is all that is required.
34. These instructions are contingent to your acceptance.
35. She was anxiously awaiting for some response from the government.
36. One must judge the various proposals on an equal basis.
37. The ad claims that this tonic is doctor-recommended.
38. Iago is regarded by all as an honest, pure man.
39. The character of Nicholas is recognizable to people who really exist in the world.
40. His heroic deeds were awarded with medals.
41. In Elizabethan time, love was the dominant theme of poetry.
42. There were artists which continued to study and produce classical works and there were artists which developed new ideas in their fields.
43. Pope and Dryden shared that idea in common.
44. After going only a hundred miles the ship was forced to return to its point of origination.
45. The chairman insisted that the company must be better organized if it was to make any profit.
46. The new program will cost in the realm of five million dollars.
47. He was advised to keep his feelings on a spiritual plain for a while yet.
48. The minister said that he would not want to be categorized with respect to a reply to that statement.
49. Prospective teachers are required to take a Written Expression Competency Examination.

50. There was a general consensus in the neighbourhood that ambulance service in the area was frequently inadequate regarding response time.

Omnibus Review Exercise

Here are some sentences containing various errors and weaknesses. Test yourself by finding out how easily you can spot and correct them. Label them with appropriate correction symbols. Note: Many of these sentences contain more than one error.

1. I was playing my typical type of game.
2. There was a clear increase in strength of Protestant power, especially in England and Prussia who had benefitted from the treaty of Utrecht.
3. In today's world it is becoming increasingly more difficult to find relatively inexpensive ways to use your leisure time.
4. It was difficult being a foreigner and try to comprehend the obsession of the army in Israel.
5. The nature of his errors were not serious.
6. New-wise, there is not much under the sun.
7. As for ancient man, being civilized was of no concern to one who was battling the many forces of nature such as hunting wild animals for food and shelter from the weather.
8. My landlord, as did most of the people in the district, spoke both French and English.
9. The reason their cars don't live as long is because most people have no idea of how to properly look after their cars.
10. Sam, my dog, is no exception as she provides me with enjoyment, companionship and protection.
11. Our apartment was not more than a ten minute walk away from the Opera House and if I weren't going to a concert on a Saturday evening, I was going to an Opera.
12. For those who are not gifted they are happy there because they can see that others are like them.

13. He was charged of embezzling over ten thousand dollars.
14. Though this fork is small and lifeless, on close examination, it gives forth the impression of something powerful and threatening.
15. She fears being thought of as a fool by everyone.
16. The poem's strange theme states that one is better off dying at a young age rather than growing old.
17. Eliza is understandably nervous, for this is her first lesson and she is wearing different clothes as well as being in strange surroundings.
18. I had truly scarred her while she had only embarrassed me.
19. In 1681, architect Sir Christopher Wren was being as creative as ever, as he was working on the famous Tom Tower, at Christ Church, in Oxford, which he had designed and was building.
20. He is only in town on a once-in-a-while basis.
21. A hobby such as playing music in a band gives more than just enjoyment, it gives relaxation, self-satisfaction, it is educational, and it is competitive.
22. He did not seem to care to the least of his reputation.
23. I spent the afternoons partcipating in workshops such as, the newspaper, theatre, choir, painting, gymnastics and folk dancing.
24. I felt a sudden needle like pain.
25. Based on her findings, she concluded that comedy was more healthful than tragedy.
26. It may take a long time for it is not an easy task.
27. There are many arguements with respect to the importance of a university education in today's society.
28. In this modern day and age it is not unusual to find people who are ignorantly unaware of the technology of how things in our society work.
29. She had so many assignments over the holiday that she felt bogged under.
30. The police act against violators of this minor law only on a complaint basis.
31. They substituted butter with margarine in the belief that it was healthier.
32. For the children's sake he hoped he could find some acceptable substitute to television.

33. The silver mentioned at the beginning and the end of the story not only symbolize freedom but they foreshadow a better future.
34. My grandfather was a very introspective-type individual.
35. He is one of those people, (and there are many of them) who does not understand economics.
36. In Margaret Laurence's *A Jest of God* there is a symbol used throughout the novel which represents what Rachel's life is like at the time.
37. He prepared a dish that was a feast not only for the eyes but a treat for the palate as well.
38. Failure to produce efficiently together with failure to reduce imports have had serious economic consequences.
39. He was told that if he persisted on complaining he would soon find himself without a job.
40. There's so many good things on the menu that it's difficult to make a choice.
41. The government permits the sale of surplus material abroad on an intermittent basis.
42. I hope you will forgive me pointing out certain weaknesses in your argument.
43. The potatoes smelled so badly that I had to throw them out.
44. The laws were made by the parliament and enforced by a police force, which is a similar system to the present.
45. The room was furnished with the new chrome and plastic furniture but it wasn't very attractive.
46. With an increasing number of cars on the road there is a greater demand for cars to respond efficiently in emergency situations.
47. A poorly maintained car uses much more oil and gas than it should. This is not only expensive, but with the energy crisis on, we need all the fuel we can save.
48. The English aristocracy, which was mainly comprised of wealthy landowners, did not however, in spite of their comfortable lifestyle, know the manners and etiquette that seemed to elevate the French aristocracy.

49. He promised that he would take me to the movies, in spite of how much work that he hasn't finished yet, but has to do.

50. The adventurer struggles with his inner conflict between society and adventure.

Chapter VIII   Elements and Principles of Composition: A Brief Survey

The principles of composition apply with equal validity to the essay as a whole and to each of its parts: what holds true for the essay as a whole also holds true for its paragraphs and its sentences. Just as the sentence is the basic unit of expression, so the paragraph can be considered the basic element of composition; paragraphs make up an essay just as sentences make up a paragraph. To be effective, a sentence must be unified, coherent, and emphatic: it must be about a single thought; its parts (especially if it is other than a simple sentence) must cohere; and its main point must be appropriately emphasized. The same tenets apply to a paragraph and to an essay. We have examined sentences in detail in earlier chapters; here we will discuss briefly the basic principles of composition that apply to paragraphs and essays, outline the major points to remember about paragraphs, and provide a step-by-step guide to planning and writing an essay.

61 Unity

u   Like a paragraph or a sentence, an essay must be unified; that is, it must be about one subject, and everything in it must contribute to the elucidation of that subject. If your paragraphs themselves are coherent and unified, and if you make sure that the first sentence of each paragraph refers explicitly (or implicitly but unmistakably) to the overall subject, then your essay will be unified.

316

62 Coherence, Transition

coh
tr There must be coherence not only between words within sentences (see #31) but also between sentences and between paragraphs. Coherence is often provided by a transitional word or phrase, or by repetition of or direct reference to some preceding word or idea. But unless there is an inherent connection between one part and the next (a function of the unity of a sentence or paragraph or essay), even an explicit transition will be ineffective. Here are a few examples of words and phrases that are useful in making connections and transitions:

and	moreover	another
in addition	also	furthermore
similarly	yet	thus
but	for example	then
on the other hand	for instance	as a result
nevertheless	in other words	hence
however	that is	although
still	therefore	even though
on the contrary	consequently	of course

A demonstrative adjective (*this, that, these, those*) and a repeated noun or noun phrase from a preceding sentence or paragraph can effect a good transition. Using a pronoun which automatically refers back to a preceding noun, its antecedent, is another common method. Parallel syntax can also tie successive sentences together. Sometimes simply a paragraph's structure, for example comparison or contrast, or alternating between negative and positive, will provide the necessary coherence. But the writer must supply explicit transitions, such as those listed above, if nothing else is doing the job. Whatever works is good. It is difficult—but possible—to overdo transitions. If a writer feels so insecure about coherence that he adds transitional words and phrases slavishly to nearly every sentence, whether required or not, his writing will be stiff and awkward.

63 Emphasis

emph As in a sentence, the most emphatic position in an essay or paragraph is its end and the second most emphatic position its beginning. That is why it is important to be clear and to the point at the beginning of an essay, usually stating the thesis explicitly, and why the topic sentence is so important a part of a paragraph. Similarly, a conclusion can make or break an essay or a paragraph: the last thing a reader sees is what will remain most vivid in his mind. Paragraphs and essays, therefore, often build to a climax; that is, they begin with the simpler and less important points and end with the most important. (See for example the sample research essay, #74.)

Another thing to remember about emphasis: the amount of space devoted to any part of an essay should be reasonably proportional to its relative importance. A careful writer avoids giving peripheral issues, however interesting, more space than he gives principal points.

64 Paragraphs

64a Kinds of Paragraphs

There are two kinds of paragraphs: substantive and non-substantive. The substantive paragraph is the more common, consisting of some kind of development or other treatment of a specific topic. Non-substantive paragraphs comprise introductory paragraphs, concluding paragraphs, and transitional paragraphs. Introductory and concluding paragraphs will often also develop a topic somewhat, but their principal function is to introduce and conclude; often, however, the most effective introductions and conclusions are not separate paragraphs but only a sentence or two, or even just part of a sentence, at the beginning or end of an otherwise substantive paragraph. (See #74, paragraphs 1 and 22, 5 and 14.)

64b Length of paragraphs

Paragraphs vary in length. In narrative or dialogue especially, one word can constitute a paragraph; sometimes a single paragraph continues for pages (although such long paragraphs seldom occur in modern writing). Most substantive paragraphs, however, consist of at least three or four sentences, and probably not more than nine or ten; and most paragraphs contain between 100 and 200 words. Transitional paragraphs are usually short, often only one sentence. Introductory and concluding paragraphs will be of various lengths, depending on the complexity of the material and on

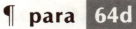

the techniques of beginning and ending that the writer is using.

And sometimes, if a particular point deserves special emphasis, it can be put into a one-sentence paragraph—like this one.

64c Parts of paragraphs

A normal substantive paragraph consists of three parts: a topic sentence, the body of the paragraph, and the conclusion. Some paragraphs include a fourth part, a second sentence which partly restates the topic and partly leads into the body of the paragraph.

64d Topic Sentences

Almost all substantive paragraphs have explicit topic sentences. (Transitional paragraphs do not have topic sentences; introductory or concluding paragraphs may or may not have topic sentences, depending on the extent to which they also serve as substantive paragraphs.) The topic sentence is usually the first sentence in a paragraph. Occasionally, and by conscious design, the topic sentence can come at the end, or even elsewhere in the paragraph. And—very rarely—a paragraph's topic may not be stated at all but only implied. (A strong topic sentence can sometimes effectively govern two or even three paragraphs; the second or third paragraph will not have its own topic sentence, but must begin in such a way that the continuing relation to the topic of the preceding paragraph is sufficiently clear. This most often happens when a narrative element is present in an essay.)

A good opening topic sentence will perform three functions:

It will refer explicitly to the subject of the essay.

It will provide a transition from the preceding paragraph.

It will state the topic to be developed by the paragraph.

Caution: Do not make the mistake of trying to include transitional material in the last sentence of a paragraph. The work of transition should be done by the first sentence of the next paragraph; tampering with a final sentence merely for transitional purposes usually destroys a paragraph's effect.

A topic sentence, like other sentences, should be efficient. Here is one that is not:

> The poet uses a great deal of imagery throughout the poem.

The topic of the paragraph—the poem's imagery—is clearly announced, but that is saying very little; the paragraph might well consist of no more than a list of images, which would mean that it was not really a paragraph at all. In revising this weak topic sentence, the writer inserted the adjective *good* before *imagery*; the paragraph now at least promises to have something to say about the images—but not very much. A better topic sentence should not only say more in itself but also suggest the approach the paragraph will take. For example:

> The most striking feature of this poem is its imagery.

or

> The poem's imagery, most of it drawn from nature, helps to create not only the poem's mood but its theme as well.

A subsequent topic sentence from the same essay is again extremely inefficient:

> In the second stanza the poet continues to use images.

The attempted revision,

> In the second stanza the poet continues to use excellent images to express his ideas.

is little better. Again, what is needed is something sharper, more specific:

> The imagery of the second stanza continues in the same vein (as that of the first).

or

> In the second stanza, the poet uses images which provide a contrast with those of the first.

or

> In the second stanza, images of death begin the process that leads to the poem's ironic conclusion.

A good topic sentence should be more than just a label on a box; it should itself be a part of the contents of the box.

See also A Note on Beginnings, #65h.

64e Body—Development of the Topic
dev The body of a paragraph must be long enough to develop a topic well; merely restating or summarizing the topic is not enough. Inexperienced writers often settle for paragraphs that are too short to develop their topics sufficiently. Sometimes several related short paragraphs can be integrated to form one substantial paragraph. Whatever their length, make sure that your paragraphs actually go somewhere, and do not just tread water.

There are many methods of development; the method or methods you use in a given instance will be determined by the nature of the topic and by what you want to do with it. Here are some of the more common methods used to develop a topic within a paragraph:

> definition
> illustration and example
> narrative as illustration
> analogy as illustration
> explanation
> analysis
> comparison and contrast
> from general to particular (or vice versa)
> from abstract to concrete (or vice versa)
> from cause to effect (or vice versa)
> from minor to major, small to large, etc.

A narrative paragraph generally follows a chronological order, a descriptive paragraph a spatial order (left to right, up to down, distant to near, etc.). It is important to remember that you can use two or more methods in combination to develop a paragraph. (See also #54b.)

64f Conclusion
The conclusion of a paragraph will sometimes be a separate sentence that summarizes its content, restates its topic, or provides an expository punch line to bring the paragraph to a

satisfactory close. But often the best way to end a paragraph is simply to let it stop, naturally and unobtrusively, once its point is made. Too often explicit conclusions seem anti-climactic and destroy the effectiveness of otherwise good paragraphs. (The same is true of laboured, overly obvious conclusions to essays.)

As a rule, it is poor tactics to end a paragraph with a quotation—especially a long or block quotation that is indented and single-spaced. Even if a writer carefully introduces a quotation, if it is left dangling at the end of a paragraph it almost inevitably leaves a "so what?" feeling in the reader's mind. Therefore make it a practice to complete such a paragraph with at least a brief comment on the quotation which explains it, justifies it, or re-emphasizes its main thrust. (See #74, paragraph 21.)

65 The Steps in Planning and Writing an Organized Essay

No respectable essay can be a mere random assemblage of sentences and paragraphs. It must have a shape, a design, even if only a simple one. The minimum requirement is that it start somewhere and by an orderly process arrive somewhere else.

It is better not to think of Introductions and Conclusions as "parts" of essays. In fact, in order to avoid the stiffness so often found in over-formal "Introductions" and "Conclusions," you might try to acquire the habit of calling them Beginnings and Endings instead. You may then more easily avoid beginning a final paragraph with "In conclusion"; coming upon that phrase is like encountering a piece of bone sticking out through the skin.

It is the *body* of the essay that must be thought of as starting somewhere, proceeding through its development, and arriving somewhere else. How does one get from the zero of a blank mind to the desired finished product? The steps that any writer must follow, whether consciously or not, are these:

1. Finding a subject
2. Limiting the subject
3. Gathering data

4. Classifying the data
5. Ordering the data
6. Constructing an outline
7. Writing the essay

It is wise for any relatively inexperienced writer to follow them rigorously, particularly if the projected essay is long or complicated, like a research paper.

65a Finding a subject

If a subject has not been assigned, you must find one for yourself. Some people think this is among the most difficult parts of writing an essay, but it need not be, for subjects are all around us and inside us. A few minutes with a pencil and a sheet of paper, jotting down and playing around with any ideas that pop into your head, will usually lead you at least to a subject area, if not to a specific subject. Or look around you and let your mind wander over whatever comes into your field of vision. Or scan the pages of a magazine or a newspaper to stimulate a train of thought; the editorial page and the letters page are usually full of intriguing subjects to write about, perhaps to argue about. Or think about people, your friends (or enemies), your immediate family and other relatives; your hobbies, or favourite sports. The possibilities are almost endless. Obviously, try to find a subject that you will enjoy writing about; do not, in desperation, pick a subject that bores you—for then you will almost certainly bore your reader as well.

65b Limiting the subject

Once you have selected a subject, limit it; narrow it down so that you can develop it adequately within the length of essay you want or have been asked to write. For example, you might decide you want to write about animals, but "animals" is far too broad a category. "Domestic animals" or "wild animals" is narrower, but still too broad. "Farm animals," perhaps, or "farm animals I have known"? Better, but still too large, for where would you begin? How thorough could you be in a mere 500 or even 1000 words? When you find yourself narrowing your subject to something like "Homer, the spoiled pig on my uncle's farm" or "my pet dachshund, Rex" or "the experience of living next door to a noisy dog" or "why a cat makes a better pet than a dog" or "the day Dobbin kicked the barn door down"—then you can with confidence look forward to developing the subject with sufficient thoroughness.

65c Gathering data

One cannot, or should not, write in a vacuum. A good essay must be composed of facts, details, particulars, not just vague generalizations and unsupported statements and opinions. Whatever his subject, a writer must gather material somewhere, by reading, talking to others, or—especially if the subject draws on his personal experience—simply reflecting on it. It is a good idea to collect as much information as you can, even two or three times as much as you can possibly use, for then you can *select* the best and discard the rest.

65d Classifying the data

With the data collected, the next step is to sit down with a pencil and a large sheet of paper. Begin jotting down facts, ideas, suggestions, whether from gathered notes or from your own head; do this jotting as rapidly as you can. Soon you will begin to see connections between one item and another, and before long you will find yourself with several groups of items. You will then have classified your material according to some principle which arose naturally from it. During this process you will also probably have discarded the weaker or less relevant details and kept only those which best suit the subject as it is now beginning to take shape.

For a very short essay you may have only one group of details, but for an essay of even moderate length (750 words or more) you should have several groups. Always try to classify your material in such a way that you end with at least three groups (or three details in the single group) and not more than, say, six or seven: an essay composed of more than seven parts is likely to be unwieldy for both writer and reader; and an essay with only two parts is not likely to be smooth and coherent.

65e Ordering the data

The next step is to arrange these groups into some kind of order. Rather than accept the first arrangement that comes to mind, consider as many different arrangements as are appropriate to the particular material you are working with. There are many possibilities. The order could be spatial, moving from one place to another; it could be temporal, moving in time, whether chronological or not; it could be from least important to most important, or from least specific to most specific, or from abstract to concrete, or from negative to positive, or from personal to impersonal or vice versa. The point is that unless you consider a number of possibilities you may adopt one that is less than the best. It is important to decide on a scheme of ordering and not simply to let things line up by chance; whatever the order, the reader should feel that it is necessary rather than arbitrary. Ideally, the order you finally decide on should grow out of your material; the groups and their details should speak to you, as it were, demanding to be arranged in a particular way because it is the most effective way.

During this process you will probably have formulated at least a tentative THESIS, a statement of what you want to say about your subject. This thesis is the starting point for the next step in the process.

65f Constructing an outline

Now, with the groups arranged in a good order and a probable thesis in mind, you should put your material into the form of an outline. The thesis statement will start the outline, the groups will become main headings under Roman numerals (I, II, III, etc.), and the details that make up each group, if they are not simply absorbed by the main heading, will become subdivisions of it in various levels of subheading (A, B, C, etc.; 1, 2, 3, etc.).

Those who think outlining a waste of time and effort are mistaken, for a good outline actually saves both time and effort: the actual writing is easier and smoother because it follows a plan; moreover, a good outline enables a writer to avoid pitfalls like repetition, digression, and awkward and illogical organization. It is much easier to do things right the first time than to go through laborious revisions in an attempt to undo error—if the writer is even aware of the errors, for without an outline he might never know they are there. One should no more start writing an essay without a carefully prepared outline than begin a trip into unfamiliar territory without a good road map. An outline keeps the traveler from taking wrong turns, wandering in circles, or getting lost altogether.

Outlining of some kind is a prerequisite for a good essay. The more complicated the essay, the more important the outline. A short, relatively simple essay can be outlined in your head or with a few quick jottings; but even a short essay is usually easier to write if you have made a careful written outline first. The method of outlining you use may be your own choice or it may be dictated by your instructor or by the nature of the assignment. Some people like the topic outline, with brief headings and subheadings for the various parts of the essay. Sometimes a paragraph outline will work well enough, one that simply lists the topic sentences of the successive paragraphs that will eventually form the essay. But the one method of outlining that consistently recommends itself is the sentence outline, for it is virtually foolproof.

Every entry in a sentence outline is a complete sentence. Because a complete sentence is a completely formulated thought, it is impossible to fool yourself into believing that you have something to say about a topic when in fact you do not. For example, a topic outline for an essay comparing various cuisines might have "Chinese food" as a heading. If the writer in question had little or no experience of Chinese food, it might happen that when he sat down to write the essay he would find that he had nothing to say about Chinese food. If, however, his outline had been a sentence outline, the writer would have been forced to make a statement about Chinese food, perhaps to mention its positive and negative qualities—for example, "Although Chinese food sometimes seems strange to Western tastes, it never fails to be interesting." With even such a vague sentence before him, the writer will more easily be able to begin supplying corroborative particulars to develop his idea; the very act of formulating the sentence guarantees that he has at least some ideas about the topic of Chinese food.

Another virtue of a sentence outline is that it is, when properly handled, self-constructing. A sentence like "Although Chinese food sometimes seems strange to Western tastes, it never fails to be interesting," automatically supposes two subheadings: A. Chinese food sometimes seems strange to Western tastes. B. Chinese food never fails to be interesting. (This kind of repetition is natural to a good sentence outline. It may seem stiff and clumsy, but it guarantees coherence and unity within each part of the essay, as well as in the essay as a whole.)

Any good outline must begin with an indication of the subject of the essay and what is to be said about it. This should be a complete sentence, usually called a Thesis Statement or Thesis Sentence. This Thesis Statement, or T. S., if properly formulated, will also predict the main headings of the outline which follows it; for example: "Each of the principal exotic cuisines familiar to most people, Chinese, Mexican, Italian, and Greek, has both positive and negative qualities." The outline which follows will then have its four main headings prescribed: Chinese, Mexican, Italian, and Greek cuisines; and each of the main headings will say something about positive and negative qualities and in that way dictate its subheadings. Another main heading might go like this: "Greek cooking's lack of variety is compensated for by the consistent piquancy of its flavours."

There are several rules which you must follow to write a good sentence outline. First, make every item from the Thesis Statement down to the last sub-subheading a single complete major sentence. Second, use only simple or complex sentences; do not use compound sentences. (A compound sentence, by its very nature, could be split into two sentences, which means that two headings could be masquerading as a single one, and thus lead to awkward problems of organization. If you find yourself writing a compound sentence, such as "Chinese food sometimes seems strange to Western tastes, but it never fails to be interesting," try to rephrase it as a complex sentence. In this instance it is easy: "Although Chinese food . . . ." But if for some reason you cannot turn a compound sentence into a simple or a complex one, rethink the whole matter: some revision or reorganization is necessary.)

Third (and this holds true for any kind of outline), you must supply at least two subheadings if you supply any at all. If under I you have an A, then you must also have at least a B, and so on with all subheadings. Fourth, the headings or subheadings at each level should be reasonably parallel with each other; that is, I, II, III, etc. should have about the same importance. The same is true of subheadings A, B, C, etc. under a given main heading, and of 1, 2, 3, etc. under each of these. One way to ensure this balance is to make the sentences at any given level syntactically parallel—that is, the same kind of sentences and sentence patterns. (A and B under I should be parallel, but an A and B under II or III need not be parallel with those under I, though they may well be.)

Fifth, seldom does an outline need to go beyond the first level of subheading. If an essay is unusually long or complicated, however, you may find it helpful or necessary to break things down to a second or even third level of subheading. Remember that headings and subheadings in an outline should mostly state ideas, propositions, generalizations; the supporting facts can be supplied in the essay-writing stage of composition. For example, if we had a subheading saying that "Though many people think of Mexican food as impossibly fiery, the heat can easily be reduced, making the tangy, earthy flavours capable of being enjoyed by anyone," the next step would almost have to be some specific instances to illustrate the point, examples that need not appear in the outline. In fact, if you find yourself including several levels of subheading, you may already be at the level of facts and details; although this is not necessarily wrong, it can be wasteful (you may find yourself thinking of different details when you actually begin writing), and can lure a writer into producing a mechanical-sounding essay.

Sixth, it is a good practice not to label main headings of an outline "Introduction" or "Conclusion." By definition these are not substantive parts of an essay. If at the outline stage you already have in mind a possible way to begin your essay, by all means jot it down in a sentence or two—even labelling it "Introduction" if you want to—after which you can proceed to Roman numeral I, the first main heading. Similarly, after the outline is complete, you could summarize a possible conclusion.

Finally, remember that an outline is not meant to be a straitjacket. If, as you write, you think of a better way to organize a part of your essay, or if some part of the outline proves clumsy when you try to set it down in paragraphs, or if you suddenly think of some new material that should be included, by all means do what you think best and revise your outline accordingly. The virtue of the outline in such an instance is that, rather than drifting about rudderless, you are in complete control of any changes in course you might make. Without an outline, a writer can be lured unaware into digressions and irrelevancies; but when you make changes in an outline, you cannot help making them consciously and carefully—and you will also have a record of them if you want to recheck them later.

Here is a sample pattern showing the mechanical structure of an outline, its indention and punctuation (for purposes of illustration, part I goes to five levels of subheading):

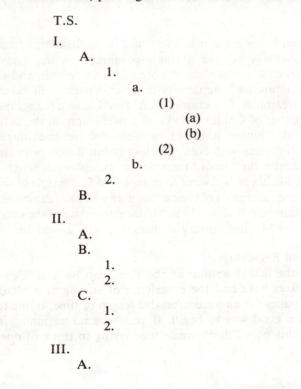

T.S.

I.

    A.

        1.

           a.

              (1)

                (a)

                (b)

              (2)

           b.

        2.

    B.

II.

    A.

    B.

        1.

        2.

    C.

        1.

        1.

        2.

III.

    A.

```
            1.
            2.
                a.
                b.
            3.
        B.
```

See also the outline for the sample research essay, #74.

65g Writing the essay

With the outline before you, drafting the essay should be almost effortless; sometimes one feels that, with a good outline to follow, the only work left is supplying good transitions between parts and paragraphs. But of course the point is that, with the shape of the whole laid out, one can concentrate on the real job of writing: finding the right words, generating the right kinds of sentences, and constructing good paragraphs.

Note: Sometimes a main heading and its subheadings from the outline will become a single paragraph in the essay; sometimes each subheading will become a paragraph; and so on. The nature and the density of your material will determine its treatment. For example, one could have a paragraph on the virtues of Chinese food and a paragraph on the deficiencies of Chinese food, or one could have one longer paragraph dealing with both. Another point: it may be possible to transfer the Thesis Statement to the essay unchanged, but more likely you will want to change it to fit the style of the essay; the requirements of the outline may well have demanded a stark statement that would sound inappropriate in the essay itself. See #74, commentary on paragraphs 1, 2, and 14.

65h A Note on Beginnings

Starting the actual writing of the essay can be a problem: most writers have had the experience of staring at a blank sheet of paper for an uncomfortable length of time, trying to think of a good way to begin. If you have no beginning in mind at this point, don't waste time trying to think of one.

Plunge right into the body of the essay and write it as rapidly as you can. When the first draft is finished, you will of course know what you have written—and therefore you will know precisely what it is that needs to be introduced. You can then go back and do the necessary introducing with relative ease. In fact, writers who write their introductions first frequently discover that they have to discard their original introduction and write a new one to fit the essay as it finally took shape.

Just as it is not a good idea to begin a final paragraph with "In conclusion," so it is generally not good practice to open a first paragraph with something like "In this essay I will discuss" or "This essay is concerned with." Rather than beginning by informing readers of what you are going to say (and then concluding by reminding them of what you have said), begin your essay by saying something substantial and if possible attention-getting (and conclude it with something similarly sharp and definitive). Occasionally, however, when an essay is unusually long or complicated, it can be helpful to explain in advance, to provide readers with what amounts to a brief outline (just as it is then often necessary to provide some summary by way of conclusion).

However you begin, it is always necessary to identify your subject (and perhaps also to define your thesis) somewhere at or near the beginning—almost never later than the first paragraph. For example, even if your title is something like "Imagery in Donne's 'The Flea,' " you must still, preferably in your first sentence, mention both the author and the title of the poem. The title of your essay is not a part of its content; the essay must be able to stand on its own. Further, be as direct and smooth and economical as you can. Here are three ways in which such an essay could begin; note how differences in order, punctuation, and wording make each one better than the preceding one:

1. In the poem "The Flea," by John Donne, there is a great deal of imagery.
2. John Donne, in his poem "The Flea," uses imagery to . . . .
3. The imagery in John Donne's "The Flea" . . . .

Here is the beginning of an essay on one of Shakespeare's

sonnets. The writer cannot seem to get his engine warmed up:

> William Shakespeare, famous English poet and writer of plays, has always been known for the way he uses imagery to convey the point he is making in a particular piece of work. Shakespeare's Sonnet 65 is no exception to this, and this is one of the better examples of his work that I have studied, for illustrating his use of imagery.
>
> The best example in the sonnet comes in lines four and six, where Shakespeare compares a "summer's honey breath" and a "wrackful siege of battering days."

Compare this with another student's beginning on the same topic:

> Shakespeare's Sonnet 65 expresses its meaning through imagery. The poet appeals to a person's knowledge of visible properties in nature in an attempt to explain invisible properties of love and time.

Rather than vacillating as the first writer has done, this writer has taken control of his material immediately. Even though no particular image has yet been mentioned, the second writer, in two crisp sentences, is far beyond where the first writer still is, though well into a second paragraph.

Here is another example of a weak beginning. That the writer was in difficulty is shown by the jargon, awkwardness, and poor usage in the first sentence, the cliché and the illogicality in the second sentence, and the vague reference and the wordy emptiness of the third:

> With all aspects considered, a person's graduating year from high school is a very unique experience. It is filled with a seemingly endless variety of memories, dreams, and emotions. I would imagine this is experienced by almost everyone and I most certainly am not an exception.

The writer's own crisp and provocative revision proves that the difficulties were merely the result of trying too hard to make a beginning; had the beginning been written after the essay was complete, it might well have taken this form in the first place:

> There are few things in life that can match the significance of a person's high-school graduation year. At least that is the way it seems soon after you complete it.

The Final Steps

Earlier we referred to the product of rapid composition as a first draft—which of course is all it is. It is very unlikely that it can be considered a finished product. This means that there are two more steps—call them 8 and 9—to be taken before the essay should be considered finished.

65i Revising

Revision (re-vision: literally "scrutinizing again") is an extremely important stage of writing, far too often neglected by inexperienced (or lazy) writers. Writers who care at all about the quality of their work revise a piece of writing at least two or three times. Many writers revise their work five or ten times before they consider it finished, some even as many as thirty times. In fact, the process of revision could be said to be never-ending, for one can almost always find something to improve.

Revise carefully, slowly, with an eye to anything that could improve what you have written; do not proofread just to correct errors made in haste, but also to improve diction, sentence structure, punctuation, coherence, paragraphing, and so on. Some writers find that going through an essay for only one thing at a time is effective—for example, going through it looking only at paragraphing, then going through it again looking only at sentences, then at punctuation, and then at diction, and so on. Weaker writers should require themselves to revise in this careful way, concentrating on one thing at a time. When you are revising, pretend that you are a hypercritical reader looking for weaknesses and errors. (In order to do this effectively, it helps to wait as long as possible between the writing and the revising—at least two or three days—so that you can look at your own work with some objectivity.)

You should find the Omnibus Checklist (Chapter XII) helpful during your revisions.

65j Proofreading

Proofreading, the final essential step, will have been taking place during revision, naturally; but when what you consider to be the final copy of your essay is ready, go over it again. Rarely will this final proofreading not prove worthwhile;

despite earlier careful scrutiny, you will probably discover not only typographical errors but also hitherto unnoticed errors in spelling, punctuation, or grammar. Do your proofreading with exaggerated care. Read each sentence, as a sentence, slowly; but also read each word as a word; check each punctuation mark, and consider the possibility of adding some or removing some or changing some. Particularly when you proofread for spelling errors, do so as a separate process, and do it by starting at the end of the essay and reading word by word, backward; then you are unlikely to get so caught up in the flow of a sentence that you overlook an error.

When you have done all these things conscientiously and carefully, you should be able to submit your finished essay with pride and confidence.

PART FOUR
The Research Paper

**Chapter IX   The Process of Writing a
Research Paper**

If you need to consult only one or two outside sources in order to write an essay—for example some critical comment on a literary work—it will be easy enough to keep track of your sources and the notes you take from them so that you can provide the necessary documentation (see *ack* and *doc* in Chapter XI). But when you are writing a full-fledged research paper, one depending predominantly on outside sources, the task of keeping things straight can be formidable. The following chapter outlines briefly the mechanical process of writing such a paper and points out the precautions one must take to work efficiently and accurately.

But first, just what is a "research" or "library" paper or essay? At one extreme, it can be simply the culmination of a fact-finding process: the writer locates information about a subject and presents it in a coherent report. At the other extreme, it can mean that the writer consults a number of outside sources, interprets and evaluates the information and arguments they offer, and then produces an essay which is a piece of original thinking; though it is based on or begins with the information gathered by research, it is nevertheless an expression of a new attitude toward the subject. Most research papers fall somewhere in between these two extremes. A particular assignment or occasion will usually call for a particular kind of result. But it is a good rule to try to make the resulting essay represent the writer's independent thought as much as possible, however much it may be based on facts and ideas gathered from outside sources; the writer of a research paper should always try to draw his own conclusions. The worst—and dullest—kind of "research paper" presents gathered data in a mechanical way; such a paper is merely a pastiche, a cut-and-paste job, which has involved the writer's own intelligence only in deciding what data to present and in what order.

A student who is assigned or chooses an unfamiliar research topic, and who explores that topic conscientiously, may eventually produce a dull report—nevertheless that student will have learned a good deal in the process. (Only a graduate student writing a dissertation is really expected to produce a substantial and original contribution to knowledge.) And our hypothetical student, in the process of exploring a subject new to him and writing about it, will also learn a good deal about how to do research and present the results. For the undergraduate, or for any inexperienced writer, learning about method is very important. The chapter which follows is intended to make that learning easier than it might otherwise be. It also provides examples of footnotes and bibliography. Finally, there is a sample research essay—an actual essay by a student—which, with the comments provided, will repay your close attention as an illustration of the matters discussed in the body of the chapter.

66

Chapter IX   The Process of Writing a Research Paper

An essay based on library research is still an essay: it should conform to the principles governing any good essay. But research essays also require writers to follow certain procedures which are not a part of writing other kinds of essays. This chapter outlines the process of writing a research essay, isolating and discussing and illustrating the various steps and the details that must be kept in mind in order to do a good job with a minimum of wasted time and effort. All the matters discussed below are important. They are not intended merely to show you things you *can* do, but rather to show you the kinds of things you *must* do in order to put together a good essay without wasting time and energy and without risking serious error. Some of these steps and details may seem almost absurdly mechanical, and some of them may look like unnecessary fiddling, but all of them are nevertheless important, and all of them have proved useful to many writers.

Note: The system outlined below is of course not the only possible system, but it is a tested one. An instructor may wish you to follow a different system, for example to make out note or bibliography cards in a different way or to cross-reference material in a special way. Indeed, after some experience you may yourself devise or discover different or additional methods of safeguarding accuracy and increasing efficiency. No one system is sacrosanct: the important thing is to *have* a system. The alternative is likely to be confusion, error, and wasted effort.

66   The Library and Its Resources

Learn your way around your library: whether on a conducted tour or all on your own, explore its layout, its reference facilities, its other holdings, its catalogues, its whole system—in a word, its resources. Don't be afraid to ask the librarians for help when you need it. Once you feel reasonably at home in what may be a vast and complex building, you can begin to use the library as it is intended to be used.

66a The Card Catalogue

Except in those libraries that use microfiche systems, a library's holdings are listed on cards, one item to a card (an "item" may consist of several volumes), and kept in drawers in the "card catalogue." Usually these cards are organized according to more than one system. If you know only the author of a book, look in the section called the Author Catalogue; if you know the title, look in the Title Catalogue. These two are often combined in one catalogue. If you are not seeking a specific book but are interested in a particular subject, look in the Subject Catalogue. In some libraries, parts of the subject catalogue, such as the names of writers, are combined with the author and title catalogues. In a small library, all three catalogues may be entirely combined. Some libraries also have a Shelf Catalogue, in which the cards are arranged by CALL NUMBERS and are therefore in the same order as the books on the shelves. Such a catalogue may also double as a location file, if the library has branches.

66b Reference Books

The reference section contains many sources of information. Here is a sampling of the kinds of reference books usually available and of some of the more useful items in each category. Before you begin work on any particular project, it is a good idea to browse through some of these, familiarizing or at least acquainting yourself with them. Since these lists are necessarily incomplete, you should find out for yourself what other reference aids are available in your library. In addition, as you explore you will find that often an article in an encyclopedia or a book on a given subject will itself include bibliographical information; by following such leads you can often save much of the time you might otherwise spend searching for sources.

Bibliographical Aids and Reference Guides (General)

Bibliographic Index: A Cumulative Bibliography of Bibliographies. 1937–.

Gates, Jean Key. *Guide to the Use of Books and Libraries.* 3rd ed. 1974.

Winchell, Constance M. *Guide to Reference Books.* Rev. Eugene Paul Sheehy. 1976.

Dictionaries and Other Word Books

Brewer's Dictionary of Phrase and Fable. Rev. Ivor H. Evans, 1970.

Dictionary of Canadian English: The Senior Dictionary. Rev. 1973.

Evans, Bergen, and Cornelia Evans. *A Dictionary of Contemporary American Usage.* 1957.

Fowler, H. W. *A Dictionary of Modern English Usage.* 2nd ed. Rev. Sir Ernest Gowers. 1965.

Funk & Wagnalls New Standard Dictionary. 1965.

Dictionary of Foreign Phrases and Classical Quotations. Ed. H. P. Jones. 1949.

Nouveau Petit Larousse Illustré. 1972.

The Oxford English Dictionary. 13 vols. 1933.

Partridge, Eric. *A Dictionary of Slang and Unconventional English.* 7th ed. 1970.

The Random House Dictionary of the English Language. 1973.

Webster's Third New International Dictionary. 1976.

Wentworth, Harold, and Stuart Berg Flexner. *Dictionary of American Slang.* 1967. Supps. to 1975.

Quotations

Bartlett, John. *Familiar Quotations.* 14th ed. Rev. Emily Morison Beck. 1968.

Colombo's Canadian Quotations. Ed. John Robert Colombo. 1974.

The Oxford Dictionary of Quotations. 2nd ed. Rev. 1974.

Newspaper and Other General Indexes

Alternative Press Index. 1973–.

The Book Review Digest. 1905–.

Book Review Index. 1965–.

British Humanities Index. 1962–.

Comprehensive Index to English-Language Little Magazines. 1890–1970. Ed. Marion Sader. 8 vols.

Essay and General Literature Index. 1900–.
French Periodical Index. 1973–.
Guide to Indian Periodical Literature. 1964–.
Index to Jewish Periodicals. 1963–.
Index to The Times (London). 1906–.
Indian Press Index. 1968–.
International Index to Periodicals. 1907–1960. This then went
    through changes:
    International Index. 1960–1965.
    Social Sciences and Humanities Index. 1965–1974.
    Social Sciences Index. 1974–.
    Humanities Index. 1974–.
Le Monde: Index Analytique. 1967–. (Covers from 1944.)
The New York Times Index. 1851–.
Poole's Index to Periodical Literature. 1802–1906.
Readers' Guide to Periodical Literature. 1905–.
Répertoire analytique d'articles de revues de Québec. 1972–.
The Wall Street Journal Index. 1958–.

General Encyclopedias

Collier's Encyclopedia. 24 vols. 1972.
Encyclopedia Americana. 30 vols. 1972.
Encyclopaedia Britannica. 15th ed. 30 vols. 1974. (Also
    useful is the 11th ed., 29 vols., 1910–1911.)
The New Columbia Encyclopedia. 1975.

Collections of Facts and Opinions; Yearbooks

The Americana Annual. 1923–.
The Annual Register: A Record of World Events. 1758–.
Britannica Book of the Year. 1938–.
Editorials on File. 1970–.
Facts on File. 1940–.
Gallup Opinion Index. 1965–.
Information Please Almanac. 1947–.
World Almanac and Book of Facts. 1868–.

Specialized Reference Books:
Biography

Biography Index. 1946–.
Current Biography. 1940–.

Dictionary of American Biography. 12 vols. 1964.
Dictionary of National Biography (British). 22 vols. and supp. 1921–1922.
The International Who's Who. 1935–.
Webster's Biographical Dictionary. 1972.
Who's Who (British). 1849–.
Who's Who in America. 1899–.

History and Politics

Arctic Bibliography. 1953–.
Australian Public Affairs Information Service; Subject Index to Current Literature. 1945–.
Cambridge Ancient History. 3rd ed. 12 vols. 1924–1958.
Cambridge History of the British Empire. 2nd ed. 8 vols. 1963.
Cambridge Medieval History. 2nd ed. 8 vols. 1966.
A Current Bibliography on African Affairs. 1962–.
Geographical Abstracts. 1966–.
Harvard Guide to American History. 2 vols. Rev. 1974.
Heimanson, Rudolph. *Dictionary of Political Science and Law.* 1967.
Historical Abstracts. 1955–.
International Bibliography of Historical Sciences. 1926–.
International Political Science Abstracts. 1951–.
Johnson, Thomas H. *The Oxford Companion to American History.* 1966.
Langer, William L., ed. *An Encyclopedia of World History.* 5th ed. 1972.
Morris, Richard B., and Graham W. Irwin. *Harper Encyclopedia of the Modern World.* 1970.
The New Cambridge Modern History. 2nd ed. 14 vols. 1968.
The Oxford Classical Dictionary. 2nd ed. 1970.
Peace Research Abstracts Journal. 1964–.
Plano, Jack C. *Dictionary of Political Analysis.* 1973.
Political Handbook of the World. 1927–.
Public Affairs Information Service. 1915–.

Philosophy, Religion, Mythology

Chamberlin, Roy B., and Herman Feldman. *The Dartmouth Bible.* 1950.

Cross, F.L., and Elizabeth A. Livingstone. *The Oxford Dictionary of the Christian Church*. 2nd ed. 1974.

Edwards, Paul, ed. *The Encyclopedia of Philosophy*. 8 vols. 1967.

Ferm, Vergilius. *An Encyclopedia of Religion*. 1945.

Hastings, James, ed. *Encyclopedia of Religion and Ethics*. 13 vols. 1917–1927.

The Interpreter's Bible. 12 vols. 1951–1957.

Landman, Isaac, et al., eds. *The Universal Jewish Encyclopedia*. 10 vols. 1939–1943.

Larousse World Mythology. 1965.

Leach, Maria, and Jerome Fried, eds. *Funk & Wagnalls Standard Dictionary of Folklore, Mythology, and Legend*. 1972.

McDonald, William J., et al., eds. *New Catholic Encyclopedia*. 15 vols. 1967.

McKenzie, John L., S.J. *Dictionary of the Bible*. 1965.

The Mennonite Encyclopedia. 4 vols. 1955–1959.

Nelson's Complete Concordance of the Revised Standard Version Bible. 1957.

Parinder, Geoffrey. *A Dictionary of Non-Christian Religions*. 1971.

The Philospher's Index. 1967–.

Rose, H.J. *A Handbook of Greek Mythology*. 6th ed. 1958.

Roth, Cecil, ed. *The Standard Jewish Encyclopedia*. Rev. 1962.

Spence, Lewis. *An Encyclopedia of Occultism*. 1960.

Strong, James. *The Exhaustive Concordance of the Bible*. 1890.

Urmson, J.O., ed. *The Concise Encyclopedia of Western Philosophy and Philosophers*. 2nd ed. 1975.

Weiner, Philip P., et al., eds. *Dictionary of the History of Ideas*. 5 vols. 1973–1974.

Social Sciences; Education

Abstracts in Anthropology. 1970–.

Current Index to Journals in Education. 1969–.

Deighton, Lee C., ed. *The Encyclopedia of Education*. 10 vols. 1971.

The Education Index. 1929–.

Freides, Thelma K. *Literature and Bibliography of the Social Sciences*. 1973.

Gould, Julius, and William L. Kolb, eds. *A Dictionary of the Social Sciences*. 1964.

The Harvard List of Books in Psychology. 4th ed. 1971.

Hoselitz, Bert F., ed. *A Reader's Guide to the Social Sciences*. Rev. 1972.

Indian Behavioural Sciences Abstracts. 1970–.

International Bibliography of Sociology. 1951–.

Mitchell, G. Duncan, ed. *A Dictionary of Sociology*. 1968.

Psychological Abstracts. 1927–.

Psychological Index. 1894–1935.

Royal Anthropological Institute Index to Current Periodicals. 1963–.

Sills, David L., ed. *International Encyclopedia of the Social Sciences*. 17 vols. 1968.

Sociological Abstracts. 1953–.

White, Carl M., et al. *Sources of Information in the Social Sciences*. 2nd ed. 1973.

Science and Technology

Agricultural Index. 1916–1964.

Applied Science and Technology Index. 1958–.

Besançon, Robert M., ed. *The Encyclopedia of Physics*. 2nd ed. 1974.

Biological and Agricultural Index. 1964–.

Challinor, John. *A Dictionary of Geology*. 4th ed. 1973.

Considine, Douglas M., ed. *Van Nostrand's Scientific Encyclopedia*. 5th ed. 1976.

Gillispie, C.C., ed. *Dictionary of Scientific Biography*. 1970.

The Engineering Index. 1884–.

The Environment Index. 1971–.

Gray, Peter, ed. *The Encyclopedia of the Biological Sciences*. 2nd ed. 1970.

Hines, Theodore O., ed. *McGraw-Hill Basic Bibliography of Science and Technology*. 1966.

International Encyclopedia of Chemical Science. 1964.

Jenkins, Frances B. *Science Reference Sources*. 5th ed. 1969.

King, Robert C. *A Dictionary of Genetics*. 2nd ed. 1974.

Lasworth, Earl J. *Reference Sources in Science and Technology*. 1972.

McGraw-Hill Encyclopedia of Science and Technology. 4th ed. 15 vols. 1977.

Newman, James R., et al. *Harper Encyclopedia of Science.* 4 vols. Rev. 1967.

Sarton, George. *A Guide to the History of Science.* 1952.

Smith, Roger C., and Malcolm W. Reid, eds. *Guide to the Literature of the Life Sciences.* 8th ed. 1972.

Universal Encyclopedia of Mathematics. 1964.

The Zoological Record. 1864–.

Economics and Business

Business Periodicals Index. 1958–.

Economic Abstracts. 1953–.

Greenwald, Douglas. *The McGraw-Hill Dictionary of Modern Economics.* 2nd ed. 1973.

Munn, Glenn G. *Encyclopedia of Banking and Finance.* 7th ed. Rev. F.L. Garcia. 1973.

Seldon, Arthur, ed. *Everyman's Dictionary of Economics.* 2nd ed. 1976.

Sloan, Harold S., and Arnold J. Zurcher. *A Dictionary of Economics.* 5th ed. 1970.

Art

Art Index. 1929–.

Encyclopedia of World Art. 15 vols. 1959–1968.

Myers, Bernard S. *Encyclopedia of Painting.* 3rd ed. 1970.

Osbourne, Harold, ed. *The Oxford Companion to Art.* 1970.

Osbourne, Harold, ed. *The Oxford Companion to the Decorative Arts.* 1975.

The Praeger Encyclopedia of Art. 5 vols. 1971.

Music

Apel, Willi. *Harvard Dictionary of Music.* 2nd ed. 1969.

Baker, Theodore. *Biographical Dictionary of Musicians.* 5th ed. Rev. Nicolas Slonimsky, 1972. Supp. G. Shirmer, 1965.

Chujoy, Anatole, and P.W. Manchester. *The Dance Encyclopedia.* Rev. 1967.

Ewen, David. *Encyclopedia of the Opera.* 1963.

Grove, Sir George. *Dictionary of Music and Musicians.* Ed. Eric Blom. 10 vols. 1955. Supp. 1961.

Hindley, Geoffrey, ed. *The Larousse Encyclopedia of Music.* 1974.

The Music Index. 1949–.

The New Oxford History of Music. 11 vols. 1954–.

Scholes, Percy A. *The Concise Oxford Dictionary of Music.* 2nd ed. Ed. John Owen Ward. 1964. Rev. 1977.

Scholes, Percy A. *The Oxford Companion to Music.* 10th ed. Ed. John O. Ward. Rev. 1970.

Thompson, Oscar. *The International Cyclopedia of Music and Musicians.* 10th ed. 1975.

Literature and Drama; Language

Altick, Richard D., and Andrew Wright. *Selective Bibliography for the Study of English and American Literature.* 5th ed. 1975.

Baugh, Albert C., ed. *A Literary History of England.* 2nd ed. 4 vols. 1967.

Bell, Inglis F., and Jennifer Gallup. *A Reference Guide to English, American, and Canadian Literature.* 1971.

Benét, William Rose. *The Reader's Encyclopedia.* 2nd ed. 2 vols. 1965.

Bond, Donald F. *A Reference Guide to English Studies.* 2nd ed. 1971.

Contemporary Authors. 1962–.

Dramatic Index. 1909–1952.

Fiction Catalog. 1908–.

Fleischmann, Wolfgang Bernard, ed. *Encyclopedia of World Literature in the 20th Century.* 4 vols. 1967–1975.

Gassner, John, and Edward Quin. *The Reader's Encyclopedia of World Drama.* 1969.

Grigson, Geoffrey, ed. *The Concise Encyclopedia of Modern World Literature.* 1971.

Hart, James D. *The Oxford Companion of American Literature.* 4th ed. 1965.

Hartnoll, Phyllis, ed. *The Oxford Companion to the Theatre.* 3rd ed. 1967.

Harvey, Sir Paul. *The Oxford Companion to Classical Literature.* 2nd ed. 1969.

Harvey, Sir Paul. *The Oxford Companion to English Literature.* 4th ed. 1967.

Harvey, Sir Paul, and J. E. Heseltine. *The Oxford Companion to French Literature.* 1959.

Language and Language Behavior Abstracts. 1967–.

Linguistic Bibliography. 1939–.

Matlaw, Myron. *Modern World Drama: An Encyclopedia.* 1972.

McGraw-Hill Encyclopedia of World Drama. 4 vols. 1972.

New, William H., comp. *Critical Writings on Commonwealth Literatures: A Selective Bibliography to 1970, with a List of Theses and Dissertations.*

The New York Times Film Reviews. 1913–.

The Penguin Companion to Classical, Oriental, and African Literature. 1969.

Preminger, Alex, Frank J. Warnke, and O. B. Hardison, Jr. *Princeton Encyclopedia of Poetry and Poetics.* New ed. 1974.

Short Story Index, 1953–.

Spevack, Marvin. *A Complete and Systematic Concordance to the Works of Shakespeare.* 8 vols. 1968–1975.

Steinberg, Sigfrid Henry. *Cassell's Encyclopedia of World Literature.* Rev. J. Buchanan-Brown. 3 vols. 1973.

Watson, George, ed. *The New Cambridge Bibliography of English Literature.* 4 vols. 1972.

The Year's Work in English Studies. 1919–.

The Year's Work in Modern Language Studies. 1929–.

Canadian Subjects

Brown, George W., et al., eds. *Dictionary of Canadian Biography, 1000–1880.* 10 vols. 1966–1972.

Canada Yearbook. 1886–.

Canadian Annual Review of Politics and Public Affairs. 1971–.

Canadian Essay and Literature Index. 1973–.

Canadian News Facts. 1967–.

Canadian Newspaper Index. 1977–.

Canadian Periodical Index. 1929–.

The Canadian Who's Who. 1910–.

Encyclopedia Canadiana. 10 vols. 1975.

Klinck, C. F., et al., eds. *Literary History of Canada.* 2nd ed. 3 vols. 1976.

Letters in Canada. 1935–.

Story, Norah. *The Oxford Companion to Canadian History and Literature.* 1967. Supp. ed. William Toye, 1973.

Wren, Sheila, comp. *Short Story Index.* 1967.

67 Collecting Data: Sources

67a Once you have decided on or been assigned a subject, the first step in gathering information is to compile a PRELIMINARY BIBLIOGRAPHY. By consulting various sources (for example periodical indexes, essay indexes, general and particular bibliographies, encyclopedias, and of course the card catalogue), make a list of possibly useful sources of information about your topic. Next, look in the appropriate card catalogues to find out which items on your list are available in your library, and record the call number of each one (you will already have done this for items you first found in the card catalogues).

67b When you begin looking at the actual books and articles on your list, there are two things you should do. First, as soon as you locate an actual book or article, make out a BIBLIOGRAPHY CARD for it. It is best to use the small eight-by-twelve-centimetre or three-by-five-inch index cards. Using cards enables you to keep track of material easily: you can keep them in handy alphabetical order, insert new cards as you find new sources, and put aside any cards for sources you think are of no use to you. *Caution:* Do not throw away such cards. At a later stage you may decide to use some of them after all. In fact, do not throw away anything: keep all your notes, jottings, scribblings, lists, and drafts, for they may prove useful later in checking back on something.

You will save time if you record the bibliographical information exactly as it will appear later in your bibliography (see #73c). Make sure that you record this information accurately and completely. Double-check spellings, dates, page numbers, and so on. Record the information from the actual book or article; do not simply copy it onto your cards from your preliminary list.

Note: Some writers prefer not to make a list but instead to enter each item on a card as soon as they come across it in a bibliography or other source. This does save one step, but if you choose to follow such a method, be careful: as soon as you come upon the actual book or article, check your card against it for accuracy, because bibliographies and the like sometimes contain errors, for example in spelling or punctuation or even dates. One could argue, then, that copying the information from the actual source onto a card also saves a step.

Second, peruse the book or article to find out how useful it promises to be, and jot down, on the card, a quick note to yourself about its worth as a source. For example, note whether it is promising or appears to be of little or no use, or whether it looks good for a particular part of your project, or whether one part of it looks useful and the rest not. Be as specific as you can, for a glance at such a note may later save you the trouble of a return trip to the library. You may also want to write a label, called a SLUG, on each card, indicating what part of your subject it pertains to; this information too could save you extra trips. For the same reason, you might note on a card just how thorough your examination of the source was; that is, if you just glanced at it, you may want to return to it, but if you found it so interesting that you read it carefully and even took notes, then you will know that you need not return to it later. And, in case you do want to return to a source, save yourself time by recording the call number of each item; the lower left-hand corner of the card is a good place for this.

Here are three sample bibliography cards that go with the sample research paper later in this chapter. Note the arrangement and completeness of the bibliographical information, the slugs in the upper right-hand corners, the writer's notes to herself in the lower right, and the library call numbers in the lower left. (One card has no slug; its several essays applied so widely that separate cards were later made out for each one used.)

III-Concl

Bowman, James S. "Public Opinion and the
Environment: Post-Earth Day Attitudes
Among College Students,"
Environment and Behavior, 9 (1977),
385-416.

HM 206	- includes 3 pages of
E 59	references!
B 5	

III ?

Calef, Charles E. "Not out of the
Woods." Environment, 18, No. 7
(Sept. 1976), 17-20, 25.

T D	- read through; made notes
A l	on proposed "energy
E 5 8	plantation."

McBoyle, G. R., and E. Sommerville, eds.
_Canada's Natural Environment: Essays
in Applied Geography._ Toronto:
Methuen, 1976.

HC	- title sounds limiting, but maybe
120	"geographers" have more to do with
E5	it than I thought. Theberge on
C 34	parks looks promising, and
1976	Jackson on government action.

68 Taking Notes

When you have compiled your preliminary bibliography and begun consulting the items it lists, you will also be taking some notes—a process that will accelerate as you go along, until your collection of bibliography cards is complete and you are only taking notes. Your preliminary research should be relatively casual, for you will still be exploring your subject, investigating and weighing its possibilities, and attempting to limit it (see #65b) as much as necessary. You should now be able to construct a preliminary outline (see #65f)—which of course will be subject to change as you go along.

At first you may be uncertain about the usefulness or relevance of some of the material you come across. Be generous with yourself: take many notes. If you toss aside a book that doesn't look useful now, you may discover later that you need it after all; it is better to spend a few minutes taking some careful notes than to spend an hour or two on a return trip to the library only to find that the book has been borrowed by someone else. Use it while you have your hands on it.

For your notes you will need a separate stack of index cards. If you use the same size card as you used for your bibliography, use a different colour so that you can easily distinguish between them. Or use the larger ten-by-fifteen-centimetre or four-by-six-inch cards, especially if your writing is large. On each NOTE CARD you will include at least three things: the note itself, the exact source, and a label or slug indicating just what part of your subject the note pertains to.

68a The Note Itself

1. Include only one point on each card. The reason for using cards in the first place is that it is easy to shuffle them around, to arrange them as you see fit at various stages. If you try to cram too much information onto one card, you will not be able to move it so easily; you may even have to recopy part of the material onto other cards so that you can shift it to where you want it. You may be able to include two or three closely related points on one card, but do so only if you are certain that they will occur together in your essay.

2. Be as brief as possible. If for some reason your note must extend beyond one side of a card—if for example it is an unusually long summary or quotation—it can be continued on the back of the card. If this happens, be sure to write a large OVER in the bottom right-hand corner so that you cannot forget that there is more to the note than appears on the front side. Or, to be even safer, continue the note on another card. If it is ever necessary to use more than one card for a single note (it should not happen often), be sure to repeat the listing of the source, and number the cards. For example, if a note extended to three cards, card one should say *1 of 3,* card two *2 of 3,* and the last card *3 of 3.*

3. Distinguish carefully between direct quotation and paraphrase or summary (see #71). Generally, use as little direct quotation as possible, but when you feel that you must quote directly, be exaggeratedly careful to quote accurately: your quotation must exactly reproduce the original, including its punctuation, spelling, and even any peculiarities that you think might be incorrect (see item 10 below); do not "improve" or in any way alter what you are copying. In fact, it is a very good idea to double-check your copying for absolute accuracy, at least once, immediately after doing it, and then to mark it as checked (a check mark, or double check mark, perhaps in red, at the right-hand edge will do). When you do quote directly, put exaggeratedly large quotation marks around the quotation so that you cannot possibly later mistake it for summary or paraphrase. This is particularly important when a note is part quotation and part summary or paraphrase.

4. If a note consists of a combination of summary or paraphrase or quotation and your own interjected thoughts or explanations or opinions, enclose your own ideas in square brackets—or, to be even safer, in double square brackets [[ ]]; you might even want to initial them. This will prevent you from later assuming that the ideas and opinions came from your source rather than from you.

5. As much as possible, express the material in your own words when taking notes. The more you can digest and

summarize information at the note-taking stage, the less interpreting you will need to do later—and it will never be fresher in your mind than at the time you are taking the note. If you fail to assimilate it then, you may well have to return to the source to find out just why you quoted it in the first place. It is all too easy to forget, over a period of days, weeks, or even months, just what the point was.

6. When you quote, or even paraphrase or summarize, do so from the original source if possible. Second-hand quotation may be not only inaccurate but misleading as well. Seek out the most authoritative source—the original —whenever possible, rather than accept somebody else's reading of it. Similarly, if more than one edition of a source-book exists, use the most authoritative or definitive one.

7. Distinguish between facts and opinions. If you are quoting or paraphrasing a supposed authority on a subject, be careful not to let yourself be unduly swayed. Rather than note that "aspirin is good for you," say that "Dr. Jones claims that aspirin is good for you." Rather than write that "the province is running out of natural resources," say that "the Premier believes, based on the results given him by his investigative committee, that the province is running out of natural resources." The credibility of your own presentation may well depend on such matters. (See #74, commentary on paragraph 3.)

8. When you are quoting (or even just summarizing or paraphrasing), be careful with page numbers. If a quotation runs over from one page to another in your source, be sure to indicate just where the change occurs, for you may later want to use only a part of the material, and you must know just which page that part came from in order to provide an accurate footnote. A simple method is to indicate the end of a page with one or two slashes (/ or //). (See #74, commentary on paragraph 21.)

9. Whenever you insert explanatory material into a quotation use square brackets (see #43j).

10. When there is something in a quotation that is obviously wrong, whether a supposed fact, a spelling, or a point of grammar or punctuation, insert [sic] after it (see #43j).

11. Whenever you omit something from a quotation, use three spaced periods (suspension points) to indicate ellipsis (see #43i).

68b The Source

In the upper left-hand corner of each note card, identify the exact source. Usually the last name of the author and a page number will suffice. But if you are using more than one work by the same author, you must include at least a shortened title of the particular work from which the note comes. Indeed, it is a good idea always to include the title, for later in your note-gathering you may come across a second work by an author you are already using; with a title on each card, no confusion can possibly arise. If the note covers more than one page, indicate the inclusive page numbers; the note itself will indicate just where the page changes (see #68a, item 8). (Some people, when the bibliography is complete, number the bibliography cards, if only to make it easier to put them back in order if they are dropped or otherwise mixed up. But it is not always safe to use merely this number to identify the source of a particular note. It is best to be cautious and use the author's name and a short title.)

68c The Slug

In the upper right-hand corner of each note card, write a slug, a word or brief phrase indicating just what part of your essay the note belongs in, and be as specific as possible: this slug will be helpful when it comes to organizing the cards before writing the essay. If you have prepared a good outline, a key word or two from its main headings and subheadings will be the logical choice to use as a slug on a card. It may be advisable to write the slug in pencil, for you may discover later that you want to rework your outline or use a particular note in a different place.

Caution: Except for the slug, use ink or type everything on your note cards and your bibliography cards. Pencil writing can easily become smudged and illegible. You may want to write even the slug in ink; if you leave enough space on the card the slug can be crossed out and a new version written below it. Further, guard against the natural impulse to invent private code symbols and abbreviations; they may make the writing of notes easier at first, but over even a short time you can all too easily forget what they mean. Except for standard abbreviations (but not even these in material you are quoting), write everything out in full. Similarly, if you do not type, be sure to write with exaggerated legibility.

68d Depending on the complexity of your project, you may want to devise some system for cross-referencing closely related note cards, or even ones you think might later prove to be closely related. One way to do this is to number the cards, probably at the centre of the top, when you are through taking notes. Indeed, it is important, when the cards are all arranged, to number them consecutively; imagine how long it would take, should you drop a stack of a hundred or so cards, to put them back into the correct order without the aid of such numbers. Be sure that your cards are organized according to your outline, or that your outline has been changed to conform to the organization of your cards.

68e In addition to taking notes from other sources, preserve your own ideas, insights, and flashes of inspiration as you go along, however fragmentary or tentative they may seem at the time; they may well turn out to be valuable at a later stage. Even if you suddenly have so strong an idea about something that you feel sure you will remember it forever, write it down; otherwise there is a good chance you will forget it, for another strong idea may dislodge it just a few minutes later. As with regular notes, restrict these to one idea per card. Even though there will be no indication of source in the upper left-hand corner, take the extra precaution of initialling such a card, or of putting double square brackets around the note, so that you cannot possibly later wonder where it came from. And of course put an appropriate slug in the upper right-hand corner.

For sample note cards illustrating these points, see #74 below.

69 Writing the Essay

When your research is complete and all the note cards you intend to use are in the desired order, you are ready to begin the actual writing of the essay. If your note-taking has been efficient—that is, if you have kept quotation to a minimum, assimilating and interpreting and judging as much as possible as you went along, and if you have included among the cards a sufficient number containing only your own ideas—then the essay will almost write itself; you will need to do little more than supply the necessary transitions as you move from card to card and follow your outline. (Of course the usual process of revision and proofreading must follow the writing of the first draft, as described in the preceding chapter; see #65i and j.)

69a As you write, proceeding from card to card, include in your text the information that will eventually become part of your footnotes. That is, at the end of every quotation, paraphrase, summary, or direct reference, put at least the last name of the author and the relevant page number or numbers—and also a title, if you are using more than one work by the same author; you can abbreviate these, but be clear, so that no confusion can possibly arise later. Do not insert footnote numbers at this stage, for you may well find yourself re-arranging material, or adding new material where you did not originally plan to use it—either of which would necessitate completely renumbering the notes. To avoid this needless and tedious task, do not put numbers in yet, not even in a rough draft. As you revise, copy the footnote information into each successive draft. It is also a good idea to put this data not just in single parentheses but in double or triple parentheses, so that you cannot possibly overlook any of them when you come to number them. When you are ready to prepare the final copy, number your footnotes consecutively throughout the draft.

Note: If footnotes are gathered together in a list at the end of an essay instead of being put at the bottom or "foot" of each page, they are of course not really *foot*notes. Such a list should be labelled "Notes." However, to avoid confusion with the word *notes* as used for facts and ideas taken from sources and put on note cards, we here use the word *footnotes* to designate these items of documentation wherever they may appear.

70 Acknowledgment of Sources

ack The purpose of documentation is three-fold: first, it acknowledges the writer's indebtedness to particular sources; second, it lends weight to a writer's statements and arguments by citing authorities to support them; third, it enables an interested reader to follow up by consulting cited sources (or to check the accuracy of a reference or a quotation, should it appear questionable). For these reasons it is essential that documentation be complete and accurate.

70a For the same reasons, it is not necessary to provide documentation for facts or ideas or quotations that are well known, or "common knowledge"—such as the fact that Shakespeare wrote *Hamlet,* or that Hamlet said "To be or not to be," or that Sir Isaac Newton formulated the law of gravity, or that the story of Adam and Eve is in the Bible, or that the moon is not made of green cheese. But if you are at all uncertain whether or not something is "common knowledge," play safe: it is far better to over-document and appear a little naive than to under-document and commit plagiarism.

One rule of thumb sometimes adopted is that if a piece of information appears in three or more different sources, it qualifies as "common knowledge" and need not be documented. For example, such facts as the elevation of Mt. Logan, or the population of Peterborough in a given year, or the date of the execution of Louis Riel, can be found in dozens of reference books. But it can be dangerous for a student, or any non-professional, to trust to such a guideline when dealing with other kinds of material. For example, there may be dozens of articles and books referring to or attempting to explain something like a quark, or the red shift, or discoveries at the Olduvai Gorge, or Freudian readings of "The Turn of the Screw," or deep structure in linguistic theory, or neo-Platonic ideas in Renaissance poetry, or the origin of the name *Canada*; nevertheless, it is unlikely that a relatively unsophisticated writer will be sufficiently conversant with such material to recognize and accept it as "common knowledge": if something is new to *you,* and if you have not thoroughly explored the available literature on the subject, it is far better to acknowledge a source than to try to brazen it out and slide something past the reader.

When the question of "common knowledge" arises, ask yourself: common to whom? Your reader will probably welcome the explicit documentation of something that he himself does not realize is, to a few experts, "common knowledge." Besides, if at any point in your presentation you give your reader even the slightest cause to question your data, you will have lost his confidence. Be cautious: document anything about which you have the least doubt.

71 Quotation, Paraphrase, Summary, and Plagiarism

QUOTATION must always be exact, verbatim. PARAPHRASE, on the other hand, reproduces the content of the original, but in different words. Paraphrase is a useful technique because it enables writers to make use of source material while still using their own words and thus to avoid too much quotation. But a paraphrase, to be legitimate, may not use significant words and phrases from an original unless they are inside quotation marks. A paraphrase will usually be a little shorter than the original, but it need not be. A SUMMARY, however, is by definition a condensation, a boiled-down version that expresses only the principal points of an original passage.

Direct quotation must obviously be documented: a reader of a passage in quotation marks will expect a footnote explaining who and what is being quoted. But it is important to know and remember that paraphrase and summary must also be fully documented. Some writers make the serious error of thinking that only direct quotations need to be documented; failure to document summaries and paraphrases is PLAGIARISM, a form of theft. When you paraphrase or summarize, you must acknowledge your debt to the original source. To illustrate, here is a paragraph, a direct quotation, from Rupert Brooke's *Letters from America* followed by (a) legitimate paraphrase, (b) illegitimate paraphrase, (c) combination paraphrase and quotation, (d) summary, and (e) a comment on plagiarism.

> Such is Toronto. A brisk city of getting on for half a million inhabitants, the largest British city in Canada (in spite of the cheery Italian faces that pop up at you out of excavations in the street), liberally endowed with millionaires, not lacking its due share of destitution, misery, and slums. It is no mushroom city of the West, it has its history; but at the same time it has grown

immensely of recent years. It is situated on the shores of a lovely lake; but you never see that, because the railways have occupied the entire lake front. So if, at evening, you try to find your way to the edge of the water, you are checked by a region of smoke, sheds, trucks, wharves, storehouses, "depôts," railway-lines, signals, and locomotives and trains that wander on the tracks up and down and across streets, pushing their way through the pedestrians, and tolling, as they go, in the American fashion, an immense melancholy bell, intent, apparently, on some private and incommunicable grief. Higher up are the business quarters, a few sky-scrapers in the American style without the modern American beauty, but one of which advertises itself as the highest in the British Empire; streets that seem less narrow than Montreal [sic], but not unrespectably wide; "the buildings are generally substantial and often handsome" (the too kindly Herr Baedeker). Beyond that the residential part, with quiet streets, gardens open to the road, shady verandahs, and homes, generally of wood, that are a deal more pleasant to see than the houses in a modern English town.[1]

[1] Rupert Brooke, *Letters from America* (London: Sidgwick and Jackson, 1916), pp. 80-81.

(For more information about quotations, especially about punctuating them, see #43.)

71a   During his 1913 tour of the United States and Canada, Rupert Brooke sent back to England articles about his travels. In one of them he describes Toronto as a large city, predominantly British, containing both wealth and poverty. He says that it is relatively old, compared to the upstart new cities further west, but that nevertheless it has expanded a great deal in the last little while. He implies that its beautiful setting is spoiled for its citizens by the railways, which have taken over all the land near the lake, filling it with buildings and tracks and smell and noise. He also writes of the commercial part of the city, with its buildings which are tall (like American ones) but not very attractive (unlike American ones); one of them, he says, claims to be the tallest in the British Empire. (He pokes fun at Baedeker for being over-generous with his comments about the city's downtown architecture.) The streets he finds wider than those of Montreal, but not too wide. Finally he compares Toronto's pleasant residential areas favourably with those of similar English towns.[1]

This is legitimate paraphrase. Even though it uses several exact words from the original (*British, railways, tracks, American, British Empire, streets, residential, English town*[s]), they are a small part of the whole; more important, they are common words that it would be difficult to find reasonable substitutes for without distorting the sense. And, even more important, they are used in a way that is natural to the paraphraser's own style and context. For example, had he written "in the American style" or "the entire lake shore," the style (and words) would have been too much Brooke's. Paraphrase, however, does not consist in merely substituting one word for another, but rather in assimilating something and restating it in your own words and your own syntax.

The footnote number, even though it comes at the end of the paragraph, is clear because the paragraph begins by clearly identifying its overall subject and because the writer has carefully kept Brooke's point of view apparent throughout by including him in each independent clause (a technique which also establishes good coherence): *Rupert Brooke, he describes, He says, He implies, He also writes, he says, He pokes fun, he finds, he compares.*

71b An illegitimate paraphrase of Brooke's paragraph might begin like this:

> Brooke describes Toronto as a *brisk* kind of city with nearly *half a million inhabitants,* with some *Italian faces popping up* among the British, and with both *millionaires and slums.* He deplores the fact that the *lake front* on which *it is situated* has been *entirely occupied by the railways,* who have turned it into *a region of smoke* and *storehouses* and the like, and *trains that wander back and forth, ringing their huge bells.*[1]

Even the footnote does not protect such a treatment from the accusation of plagiarism, for too many of the words and phrases and too much of the syntax are Brooke's own. The words and phrases that we have italicized are all "illegitimate": a flavourful word like *brisk*; the intact phrases *half a million inhabitants* and *Italian faces*; *popping up,* so little different from *pop up*; and so on. Changing *the railways have occupied the entire lake front* to the passive *the lake front ... has been entirely occupied by the railways,* or *trains that wander up and down* to *trains that wander back and forth,* or *tolling . . . an immense . . . bell* to *ringing their huge bells,* does not make them the writer's: they still have the diction, syntax, and stylistic flavour of Brooke's original, and therefore constitute plagiarism. Had the writer put quotation marks around "brisk," "Italian faces . . . pop[ping] up," "millionaires" and "slums," "lake front," " it is situated," "occupied," "a region of smoke," "trains that wander," and "bell[s]," the passage would, to be sure, no longer be plagiarism—but it would still be illegitimate, or at least very poor, paraphrase, for if so substantial a part is to be left in Brooke's own words and syntax, the whole might as well have been quoted directly: the writer has done little more than slightly "edit" the original.

71c A writer who felt that a pure paraphrase was too flat and abstract, who felt that some of Brooke's more striking words and phrases should be retained, might choose to mix some direct quotation into a paraphrase:

> In *Letters from America,* Rupert Brooke characterizes Toronto as "brisk," largely British, and as having the usual urban mixture of wealth and poverty. Unlike the "mushroom" cities farther west, he says, Toronto has a history, but he notes that much of its growth has nevertheless been recent. He notes, somewhat cynically, that the people are cut off from the beauty of the lake by the railways and all their "smoke, sheds, trucks, wharves, storehouses, 'depôts,' railway lines, signals, and locomotives and trains" going ding-ding all over the place.[1]

This time the context is very much the writer's own, but some of the flavour of Brooke's original has been retained through the direct quotation of a couple of judiciously chosen words and the cumulatively oppressive catalogue. The writer is clearly in control of the material, as the writer of the preceding example was not.

71d A summary, whose purpose is to substantially reduce the original, conveying its essential meaning in a sentence or two, might go like this:

> Brooke describes Toronto as large and wealthy, aesthetically marred by the railway yards along the lake, with wide-enough

streets and tall but (in spite of Baedeker's half-hearted approval) generally unprepossessing buildings, and a residential area more attractive than comparable English ones.[1]

71e Had one of the foregoing versions of the passage not mentioned Brooke, nor included quotation marks, nor been footnoted, it would have been guilty of outright PLAGIARISM, passing off Brooke's words or ideas, or both, as the writer's own, whether intentionally or not. Do not, either through design or through carelessness, commit plagiarism. If you have any doubts whatever about what does or does not constitute plagiarism, ask your instructor about it: it is too serious a matter to remain uncertain about.

See *ack* and *doc* in Chapter XI.

On Avoiding Plagiarism

Be careful when you study. For example, suppose you want to write an essay on a particular literary work. Do not rush off and read half a dozen critical essays on the work and then use their ideas in an essay without footnotes, merely listing the secondary sources in a bibliography. Be scholarly: take careful notes as you read, identify the source of any ideas other than your own, and explicitly acknowledge those ideas as you use them in the essay. A "covering" bibliography may protect you from a charge of outright dishonesty, but it will not exonerate you of plagiarism if ideas from those sources appear in your essay without footnotes. If you label your bibliography "List of Works Cited," you may more easily remember that you must explicitly cite or quote those works in the essay itself and provide footnotes.

Exercise 71

Here are two more paragraphs from Rupert Brooke's *Letters from America*. For each, write a paraphrase, a paraphrase with some quotation mixed in, and a summary.

1. Ottawa came as a relief after Montreal. There is no such sense of strain and tightness in the atmosphere. The

British, if not greatly in the majority, are in the ascendancy; also, the city seems conscious of other than financial standards, and quietly, with dignity, aware of her own purpose. The Canadians, like the Americans, chose to have for their capital a city which did not lead in population or in wealth. This is particularly fortunate in Canada, an extremely individualistic country, whose inhabitants are only just beginning to be faintly conscious of their nationality. Here, at least, Canada is more than the Canadian. A man desiring to praise Ottawa would begin to do so without statistics of wealth and growth of population; and this can be said of no other city in Canada except Quebec. Not that there are not immense lumber-mills and the rest in Ottawa. But the Government farm, and the Parliament buildings, are more important. Also, although the "spoils" system obtains a good deal in this country, the nucleus of the Civil Service is much the same as in England; so there is an atmosphere of Civil Servants about Ottawa, an atmosphere of safeness and honour and massive buildings and well-shaded walks. After all, there is in the qualities of Civility and Service much beauty, of a kind which would adorn Canada. (pp. 54–55)

2. Winnipeg is the West. It is important and obvious that in Canada there are two or three (some say five) distinct Canadas. Even if you lump the French and English together as one community in the East, there remains the gulf of the Great Lakes. The difference between East and West is possibly no greater than that between North and South England, or Bavaria and Prussia; but in this country, yet unconscious of itself, there is so much less to hold them together. The character of the land and the people differs; their interests, as it appears to them, are not the same. Winnipeg is a new city. In the archives at Ottawa is a picture of Winnipeg in 1870—Mainstreet, with a few shacks, and the prairie either end. Now her population is a hundred thousand, and she has the biggest this, that, and the other west of Toronto. A new city; a little more American than the other Canadian cities, but not unpleasantly so. The streets are wider, and full of a bustle

which keeps clear of hustle. The people have something of the free swing of Americans, without the bumptiousness; a tempered democracy, a mitigated independence of bearing. The manners of Winnipeg, of the West, impress the stranger as better than those of the East, more friendly, more hearty, more certain to achieve graciousness, if not grace. There is, even, in the architecture of Winnipeg, a sort of *gauche* pride visible. It is hideous, of course, even more hideous than Toronto or Montreal; but cheerily and windily so. There is no scheme in the city, and no beauty, but it is at least preferable to Birmingham, less dingy, less directly depressing. It has no real slums, even though there is poverty and destitution. (pp. 102–03)

72 Further Advice on Footnotes

72a Partial Footnotes

Notice that the foregoing paraphrases and the summary (#71 abcd) begin by referring to Brooke explicitly. Version (a) uses his full name, as should be done the first time he is mentioned; subsequent references to him can then cite only his surname. Mentioning a source's name in this way is a convenient way of indicating the source and the point of view of a sentence or two, or even of a whole paragraph. When an author's name is given in the text, the footnote need supply only the rest of the information about the source. If the text supplies both the author and title, as in version (c), the footnote need not repeat them, though some writers prefer to repeat the title, for clarity. If for some reason you do not want to bring the author's name into your text (for example if you were surveying a variety of opinions about Toronto and did not want to clutter your text with all their authors' names) then your text might read in part like this:

> Toronto was once described as "brisk," large, and encumbered with railways and tall but ugly buildings.[1]

Your footnote would then of course have to be complete.

72b Subsequent References (see also #73b below)

When at some later point in an essay you cite something else from a source already referred to, the second or subsequent footnote should not repeat all of the information; the author's last name and the relevant page number suffice:

> ⁷ Brooke, p. 82.

If another footnote referring to the same source immediately precedes, then the form

> ⁸ Ibid., p. 80.

is acceptable, but current practice favours using the author's name instead of *ibid*. If you are using more than one work by the same author, such subsequent references must also include at least a short version of the title of the work being cited. In an essay on Brooke which was also discussing his works of poetry, for example, a footnote might look like this:

> ⁹ Brooke, *Letters,* p. 75.

72c Major Sources; Parenthetical References

If you are writing an essay which refers exclusively or predominantly to one particular source, such as a novel or a play, you can reduce the number of footnotes by including all but the first reference in your text. When you first quote or refer to the work, provide a complete footnote, and add an explanatory note, something like this: "Subsequent references to this work will be included in the text." Then, in an essay discussing Brooke's views of Canada, your subsequent references would take this form:

> Brooke calls Toronto a "brisk city" (p. 80).

Note that any necessary punctuation comes after the parentheses. Supply a period or other necessary mark even if the quotation ends with a question mark or exclamation point. If, however, the quotation is a longer one set off by indenting and single spacing, the period comes before the parentheses:

> It is impossible to give [Toronto] anything but commendation. It is not squalid like Birmingham, or cramped like Canton, or scattered like Edmonton, or sham like Berlin, or hellish like New York, or tiresome like Nice. It is all right. (pp. 83-84)

Parenthetical references can also be used for more than one source, especially if the information is brief. If an already identified author's name is given in the text, for example, a page number in parentheses will usually be preferable to a footnote with only a page number in it. In order to reduce the number of footnotes even further, writers sometimes put authors' names and even titles in such parenthetical references. (See the sample research paper, #74, for illustrations of parenthetical references.)

72d Consolidated Footnotes

In order to minimize the number of footnotes, consolidate them whenever possible. Suppose for example that in one sentence, or even in one paragraph, you refer to or quote more than one source. Rather than provide a separate footnote for each, use one footnote at the end of the sentence or paragraph, listing all the sources, in the relevant order—but be particularly careful: use consolidated footnotes only when you can do so without confusing your reader about just what came from where. Use only one number to signal such a footnote; do not put [9, 10, 11] to refer to separate footnotes or to the parts of a consolidated footnote.

72e Covering Footnotes

When your use of a source is not specific, use a single "covering" footnote to express general indebtedness to a particular source; for example:

> [1] In preparing this biographical sketch, I have used the system of classification recommended by Jacques Barzun and Henry F. Graff in *The Modern Researcher,* 3rd ed. (New York: Harcourt Brace Jovanovich, 1977), chapter 8.

> [1] I am indebted to Cleanth Brooks and Robert Penn Warren, *Understanding Poetry,* 4th ed. (New York: Holt, Rinehart and Winston, 1976), p. 202, for suggesting this approach to the poem.

The number that signals such a footnote sometimes occurs at the very end of an essay, but it is more logical to put it near the beginning. Some writers insert it after the title of an essay, but others think that looks odd. It can often conveniently and logically be placed at the end of the first sentence, or at the end of the first paragraph. And sometimes such a footnote is simply added to the first footnote supplied for any other reason.

72f Discursive Footnotes

Occasionally a writer will want to add a comment to a footnote, or include some tangential information or discussion that would be out of place in the text. But such footnotes, since they temporarily distract the reader from the flow of the main text, should be kept to a minimum. Usually, such a comment, if it is relevant, can be worked into the text.

72g Placement of Footnote Numbers

Try to so arrange things that a number indicating a footnote occurs at the end of a sentence rather than somewhere near the beginning or the middle of it. But if it is necessary to quote or paraphrase something, and then to follow it in the same sentence with added facts or comments of your own, the number should immediately follow the citation, especially if there is any possibility that your comment could be mistaken for material from the source.

72h Mechanics of Footnotes

Footnote numbers are *superscript* numbers—*written above* the line about half a space, not even with it or below it. No space precedes the number. In the footnote itself, the number is also written slightly above the line, and a space follows it. The footnote number is not followed by a period, not enclosed in parentheses, and not circled. A footnote number follows all punctuation marks except the dash. Footnotes may be single-spaced, but double-space between them. Indent each footnote five spaces.

73 Documentation: Footnotes and Bibliography

doc There are certain prescribed forms for footnotes and bibliographical entries. The examples below are based on the forms recommended by *The MLA Style Sheet,* 2nd ed. (1970), and followed by most writers in the humanities. Other disciplines, such as the sciences and some of the social sciences, use different formats; when preparing papers for

them, find out what forms and methods of documentation are required and adhere to them.

The forms of documentation are simple: the pattern of a footnote or an entry in a bibliography is straightforward, constant, and sensible. However, many books and other sources include anomalies and complexities that can be puzzling when one tries to account for them in an item of documentation. If you encounter an instance not covered by any of the following examples, try to work it out by applying common sense and the general principles outlined below.

The basic pattern of a footnote is as follows: author's name in normal order, title of work, publication data in parentheses, and page number. For example:

> [1] Colin M. Turnbull, The Mountain People (New York: Simon and Schuster, 1972), p. 167.

The corresponding bibliographical entry contains the same information and looks like this:

> Turnbull, Colin M. The Mountain People. New York: Simon and Schuster, 1972.

The differences between the two are obvious and easy to remember: A footnote is meant to read like a sentence; therefore it gives the author's name in normal order, puts the publication data in parentheses to de-emphasize it, and is punctuated with commas. A bibliographical entry is in a relatively stiff and technical form, with reverse indention and author's last name first (so that entries can be listed alphabetically) and periods, rather than commas, between the parts. Similarly, a footnote gives only the information necessary to identify a citation; secondary information, such as subtitles, introductions by someone other than author or editor, and general editors of extended series, need not be included in footnotes. Such things must, however, be included in bibliographical entries, for a bibliography is a reference tool. In instances where no bibliography is to be provided, such information would have to be included in the footnotes. And sometimes—but only when there is a bibliography— footnotes do not even identify the publishers of cited works; but it is more common practice to include them in all footnotes.

Since many sources do not present a simple and straightforward set of facts to record, examine closely the following examples, which include the more common kinds of sources and some of the more common variations. When necessary, refer to these samples for models. (Bibliographical entries for these works are given in #73c. See also the footnotes and bibliography in the sample research paper, #74.)

Caution: Always take the information for a footnote or a bibliographical entry only from the title page of a book, and if necessary (for example the date of publication) from the reverse of the title page (the copyright page); do not take it from the book's cover or from the running title at the top of the book's pages. Similarly, for an article in a periodical, take the author and title from the actual article, not from the cover or a table of contents, for they often use shortened or otherwise varied forms of names and titles.

73a Sample Footnotes: First References

A book with one author:

> ¹ Robertson Davies, <u>One Half of Robertson Davies</u> (Toronto: Macmillan, 1977), p. 138.

> ² William Zinsser, <u>On Writing Well</u> (New York: Harper & Row, 1976), p. 36.

Note that no comma precedes the parentheses, and that each footnote ends with a period, just as a sentence would.

A later or revised edition:

> ³ Albert C. Baugh, <u>A History of the English Language</u>, 2nd ed. (New York: Appleton-Century-Crofts, 1957), p. 171.

A book with two or three authors:

> ⁴ E. H. Carter and R. A. F. Mears, <u>A History of Britain</u>, 2nd ed. (Oxford: Oxford Univ. Press, 1948), pp. 821-22.

Note that such abbreviations as *Univ.* are acceptable; note also that only the last two digits of a three-digit page number are given to locate the end of a cited passage. This edition was printed in 1953, but the date of its first

printing, 1948, is the one used, since the book was not revised but merely reprinted.

A work with more than three authors:

> 5 Raymond Breton et al., "The Impact of Ethnic Groups on Canadian Society: Research Issues," in Identities: The Impact of Ethnicity on Canadian Society, ed. Wsevolod Isajiw, Canadian Ethnic Studies Association series, Vol. 5 (Toronto: Peter Martin Associates, 1977), p. 193.

The subtitle and series editor are not mandatory in a footnote, but the subtitle at least is useful information and so was included. One could use "and others" instead of the Latin *et al.*

A collection of pieces by one author:

> 6 Leonard Cohen, Selected Poems 1956-1968 (Toronto: McClelland and Stewart, 1968), p. 200.

A specific work in a collection of pieces by one author:

> 7 Peter C. Newman, "Noises from the Attic," in his Home Country: People, Places, and Power Politics (Toronto: McClelland and Stewart, 1973), pp. 229-31.

Again, the subtitle seemed useful. This book has an introduction by Hugh MacLennan, but that need be recorded only in the bibliography.

A book with one author and an editor:

> 8 Thomas Carlyle, Reminiscences, ed. James Anthony Froude (New York: Harper, 1881), p. 260.

A work in a collection by several authors, with an editor:

> 9 Douglas Bush, "Stephen Leacock," in The Canadian Imagination, ed. David Staines (Cambridge, Mass.: Harvard Univ. Press, 1977), p. 143.

This book has a subtitle, but it need not appear here; it is included, however, in the bibliography. *Mass.* is added to the city's name to avoid confusion with Cambridge, England. Harvard University Press also has an office in London, England, but that need not be recorded here; Cambridge is listed first, and it is also the likely origin of the book used in Canada; if the publisher had also had an office in, say, Toronto, that would have been the logical city for a Canadian to include in the footnote. David Staines also wrote an introductory essay for this book, but that need not be noted either here or in the bibliography. However, should one wish to quote or refer to that introduction, one could use a footnote like this:

¹⁰ David Staines, "Canada Observed," editor's Introd. to <u>The Canadian Imagination</u> (Cambridge, Mass.: Harvard Univ. Press, 1977), p. 15.

If the introductory matter were not titled but merely labelled, one would use Introd., Pref., or Foreword, neither italicized nor in quotation marks.

A piece reprinted in a collection of essays by several authors:

¹¹ Northrop Frye, "The Typology of <u>Paradise Regained</u>," <u>Modern Philology</u>, 53 (1956), 227-38; rpt. in <u>Milton: Modern Essays in Criticism</u>, ed. Arthur E. Barker (New York: Galaxy-Oxford Univ. Press, 1965), p. 436.

Anthologies and casebooks such as this have become common in recent years. Even though you are using such a collection, it is a courtesy to give the reader all the data you can pertaining to an essay's original publication; this information is customarily provided in the anthologies. This footnote also illustrates how to treat the name of a paperbound series; "Galaxy" books are published by Oxford. See also footnote 31 below.

A reprint of an earlier edition (often in paperback):

¹² Robertson Davies, <u>The Diary of Samuel Marchbanks</u> (1947; rpt. Toronto: Clarke, Irwin, 1966), p. 57.

¹³ Harold Nicolson, <u>Some People</u> ([London], 1927; rpt. New York: Vintage, 1957), p. 72.

Here, since the book originally appeared in a different country, the city's name is included; it was not given in the paperback, however, but deduced from the original publisher's name; it is therefore enclosed in square brackets.

A book with more than three editors:

¹⁴ Alexander W. Allison et al., eds. The Norton
Anthology of Poetry, rev. ed. (New York: Norton, 1975),
pp. 799–800.

Again, one can use the English "and others" instead of
the Latin abbreviation *et al.* The abbreviation *rev. ed.*
means "revised edition"; in this instance, the edition is
not numbered (cf. footnotes 3 and 4 above). And here
obviously all three digits of the second page number must
be included.

An anonymous book, for example a reference work:

¹⁵ Dictionnaire des Gallicismes les Plus Usités
(Paris: Payot, 1951), p. 120.

A translation:

¹⁶ Carlos Fuentes, Where the Air is Clear, trans. Sam
Hileman (New York: Ivan Obolensky; Toronto: George J.
McLeod, 1960), p. 328.

Some books, like this one, are published simultaneously
in different places by different publishers; when possible,
include this information. (This does not apply when a
book is published in different places by the same
publisher; see footnote 9 above.) If the work of the
translator were being discussed, his name would come
first.

A book that is one of a series:

¹⁷ William Wycherley, The Plain Dealer, ed. Leo
Hughes, Regents Restoration Drama Series (Lincoln: Univ.
of Nebraska Press, 1967), p. 120.

The name of the general editor is reserved for the
bibliography. It is customary to include the state or
country of less well-known cities like Lincoln, but here it
was unnecessary, since "Univ. of Nebraska Press" identifies the publisher's location clearly enough.

¹⁸ Paul Hiebert, Sarah Binks, New Canadian Library,
No. 44 (1947; rpt. Toronto: McClelland and Stewart,
1964), p. 68.

¹⁹ I. A. Richards, "Literature for the Unlettered," in
Uses of Literature, ed. Monroe Engel, Harvard English

Studies, 4 (Cambridge, Mass.: Harvard Univ. Press, 1973), p. 212.

Such series are open-ended; sometimes, however, a number of works are published over a period of years, but are nevertheless part of a set that has or will come to a definite end. The next footnote illustrates such a work.

A book that is part of several volumes:

> [20] Ian Jack, <u>English Literature 1815-1832</u>, Vol. X of <u>The Oxford History of English Literature</u> (Oxford: Oxford Univ. Press, 1963), p. 313.

If you refer generally to a multivolume work, use this form:

> [21] Margot Asquith, <u>An Autobiography</u>, 2 vols. (New York: Doran, 1920).

If you refer to a specific place in one of the volumes, this form:

> [22] Margot Asquith, <u>An Autobiography</u> (New York: Doran, 1920), II, 98-101.

This refers to pages 98–101 of the second volume of the two-volume set. Note that since the volume number is given, the abbreviations *pp.* and *vol.* are omitted; when both are present, one cannot be mistaken for the other. This work's two volumes were published simultaneously, in 1920. When referring to a multivolume set that was published over a number of years, one must use a slightly different form:

> [23] Samuel Pepys, <u>The Diary of Samuel Pepys</u>, ed. Robert Latham and William Matthews, III (London: Bell, 1970), 214-15.

Note that, once again, since the volume number is included, *pp.* is omitted. Since the volumes were not published all at the same time, the volume number precedes the publishing data, and the year given is the publication date of that particular volume. If one wanted to refer to the work of the editors rather than to Pepys's work, their names would come first:

> [24] Robert Latham and William Matthews, eds., <u>The Diary of Samuel Pepys</u>, VII (London: Bell, 1972), 277n.

The *277n.* means that the material quoted or referred to occurs in a footnote on page 277. A general reference to the whole set would look something like this:

> 25 All quotations from Pepys are from <u>The Diary of Samuel Pepys</u>, ed. Robert Latham and William Matthews, 9 vols. (London: Bell, 1970-76). Subsequent references appear in the text.

With such a covering reference to a major source, further footnotes to it are unnecessary; instead, references can be included in your text following each quotation, like this: (III, 214–15).

A book with a corporate author:

> 26 Fellowship of Australian Writers, <u>Australian Writers Speak: Literature and Life in Australia</u> (Sydney: Angus and Robertson, 1943), p. 27.

A government publication:

> 27 Department of External Affairs, <u>Canada from Sea to Sea</u>, rev. ed. (Ottawa: Queen's Printer, 1963), p. 44.

An article in an encyclopedia or similar reference work, signed or unsigned:

> 28 P[eter] C[halmers] M[itchell], "Evolution," <u>Encyclopaedia Britannica</u>, 11th ed. (1910).

> 29 "Halifax," <u>The New Columbia Encyclopedia</u>, 1975.

Since such articles are arranged alphabetically, no volume or page numbers need be given. The article on evolution is signed "P. C. M.," but the name for which the initials stand is listed at the front of the volume; as information supplied from outside the actual article, therefore, the added letters are placed in square brackets. Note the spelling of *Encyclopaedia Britannica.*

A work without complete publication data:

> 30 William Kirby, <u>The Golden Dog: A Romance of Old Quebec</u> (Toronto: Musson, n.d.), p. 128.

The abbreviation *n.d.* stands for "no date"; similarly, if the place of publication is not provided, put *n.p.* (no place) before the colon; if the publisher is not identified, put *n.p.* (no publisher) after the colon. If the pages of a work are not numbered, put *n. pag.* (no pagination) at the end of the footnote. If such missing information can be found, even if it is only the country of publication, it should be included in square brackets.

Quotation at second hand:

> [31] Sir Charles Lyell, Life, Letters, and Journals of Sir Charles Lyell, ed. Mrs. Katherine Lyell (London: John Murray, 1881), II, 436, as quoted in Loren Eiseley, Darwin's Century (1958; rpt. Garden City, N.Y.: Anchor-Doubleday, 1961), p. 107.

If the data for the original source can be found, they should be included, as here. Note that it is all right to abbreviate the state, N.Y., but not the city.

Reference to the Bible:

> [32] Hebrews 13:8.

Books of the Bible are not italicized. Lower case Roman numerals can be used for the chapter, but Arabic are becoming more common.

Reference to a play:

> [33] Shakespeare, Othello V.i. 19–20.

Shakespeare's name was not given in the test; the first name of such a well-known author is unnecessary in a footnote. Note that, as with the Bible, no comma is needed following the title. The Roman numerals are still common for plays; upper case *V* indicates act five; lower case *i,* scene one; and 19-20, the quoted lines. A footnote such as this would be proper only if an earlier footnote or the text had indicated the edition being used.

A weekly or bi-weekly magazine:

> [34] Norman Cousins, "The Mysterious Placebo: How Mind Helps Medicine Work," Saturday Review, 1 Oct. 1977, p. 10.

A monthly magazine:

> [35] Veronica Thomas, "The Hutterites of Canada," Gourmet, Nov. 1976, p. 36.

This and many other magazines have volume and issue

numbers; but unless one is referring to scholarly periodicals, these numbers need not be included; compare 39, 40, and 41 below.

A newspaper article:

³⁶ "Budworm Spray Opponents Meet," Ottawa <u>Citizen</u>, 8 Dec. 1977, p. 20, col. 1.

The column number could be omitted. Sometimes writers include the particular edition of a newspaper. The definite article *The* is customarily omitted from the title of the newspaper (see also footnotes 37 and 42 below).

A newspaper editorial:

³⁷ "Bodies and Minds at the New U of T," Editorial, Toronto <u>Globe and Mail</u>, 9 March 1978, p. 6, col. 2.

An interview:

³⁸ Barbara Ward, Interviewed by Peter C. Newman in <u>Maclean's</u>, 17 May 1976, p. 4.

An article in a journal with continuous pagination throughout annual volumes:

³⁹ Robert Cuff and J. L. Granatstein, "The Rise and Fall of Canadian-American Free Trade, 1947-8," <u>Canadian Historical Review</u>, 58 (1977), 473.

Note that the volume number is given in Arabic numerals. The additional information—that this was in No. 4 of the 58th volume, and that it appeared in December—is not necessary. And though such journals usually have one or more listed editors, these editors' names are never included in footnotes or bibliographies.

An article in a journal with separate pagination for each issue:

⁴⁰ Naim Kattan, "Space in the Canadian Novel of the West," <u>Ariel: A Review of International English Literature</u>, 4, No. 3 (1973), 105.

The separate pagination in each issue necessitates that the number of the issue be given. As in the preceding footnote, the presence of the volume number means that *p.* is not needed.

A signed review; a journal that numbers only issues:

> [41] Herbert Rosengarten, "Urbane Comedy," rev. of <u>Lady</u>
> <u>Oracle</u>, by Margaret Atwood, <u>Canadian Literature</u>, No. 72
> (Spring 1977), p. 85.

With no volume number, the abbreviation *p.* is required. The word *Spring,* like months for other journals, is not necessary, but it (or Summer, Fall, Winter) is often provided as a possible aid to the reader.

An unsigned review:

> [42] "The Dispossessed Americans," rev. of <u>Bury My Heart</u>
> <u>at Wounded Knee</u>, by Dee Brown, <u>Times Literary Supplement</u>,
> 21 July 1972, p. 830.

The fact that this weekly publication numbers its pages consecutively throughout a year, or that this is issue number 3,673, is irrelevant.

73b Sample Footnotes: Second and Subsequent References

Second or subsequent references are short. Once a first and full footnote has identified a particular source, usually all that a second or later reference need contain is the author's last name and a page number; this is now the most common practice. It is better—and easier—not to bother with such Latin abbreviations as *op. cit.* and *loc. cit.*, although *ibid.* (short for *ibidem,* "in the same place") is still sometimes used. Following are sample footnotes illustrating subsequent references to some of the works listed in the full footnotes in #73a above.

> [43] Zinsser, p. 40.
>
> [44] Carter and Mears, p. 719.
>
> [45] Ibid., p. 725.

Here *Ibid.* means that this is another reference to Carter and Mears; if you use *ibid.,* remember that it refers only to the footnote immediately preceding. One could almost as easily have repeated the authors' names; then a reader would not have to look back at the preceding footnote to see what *ibid.* referred to. (Since *ibid.* is an abbreviation, it must be followed by a period; it is not necessary to italicize it in a footnote.)

⁴⁶ Breton et al., p. 194.

⁴⁷ Ibid.

Here *Ibid.,* without a page number, means that footnote 47 documents another reference to page 194 of the work of Breton et al.; a page number after *Ibid.* is not necessary if the reference is to the same page cited in the preceding footnote.

⁴⁸ Bush, p. 143.

This refers to the same work referred to in footnote 9. Should one wish to refer to a different essay from the same book, some information would have to be repeated to identify the source clearly for the reader:

⁴⁹ Margaret Atwood, "Canadian Monsters: Some Aspects of the Supernatural in Canadian Fiction," in Staines, ed., The Canadian Imagination, p. 103.

Subsequent references to this essay would then simply cite Atwood and a page number.

⁵⁰ Davies, Diary, p. 63.

Since two works by Davies are cited earlier (see footnotes 1 and 12), it is necessary to repeat the title of the one being referred to a second time. Note that a shortened version of the title is sufficient if it is clear.

⁵¹ Davies, One Half, p. 117.

⁵² Ibid., pp. 75-76.

Since *Ibid.* refers only to the immediately preceding footnote, the title need not be repeated.

⁵³ Allison et al., eds., The Norton Anthology of Poetry, p. 308.

This form would be used if the name of the author and the title of a cited poem were included in the text. The first

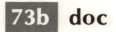

editor's name and page number alone would not make a very clear reference. In such an instance, also, the title of the anthology could come first; one could even omit the editor's name. If you did decide to use only the editor's last name and a page number for such a footnote, you would not include *ed.* or *eds.*

54 Dictionnaire des Gallicismes, p. 98.

The shortened title of an anonymous work is sufficient. Such a form would serve also for second references to the sources cited in footnotes 26 and 27.

55 Asquith, II, 149.

Even though the reference is to the same volume as in the earlier footnote (22), the volume number must be included.

56 Ibid., I, 84.

This refers again to Asquith's work, but to the first volume. Similarly, in a subsequent reference to a multivolume work whose volumes were published over several years (see footnotes 23–25), the volume number must be given:

57 Pepys, Diary, III, 120.

If, however, you cite a different volume from such a set, the date of publication of that newly cited volume must also be included:

58 Pepys, Diary, V (1971), p. 117.

The title alone of an unsigned encyclopedia entry is sufficient:

59 "Halifax."

Second and subsequent references to periodicals are handled similarly:

60 Cousins, p. 8.

61 "The Dispossessed Americans," p. 831.

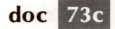

73c Sample Bibliographical Entries

Following are sample bibliographical entries that correspond to the sample footnotes in #73a. As in an actual bibliography, the items are listed in alphabetical order.

Allison, Alexander W., et al., eds. <u>The Norton Anthology of Poetry</u>. Rev. ed. New York: Norton, 1975.

Asquith, Margot. <u>An Autobiography</u>. 2 vols. New York: Doran, 1920.

Atwood, Margaret. "Canadian Monsters: Some Aspects of the Supernatural in Canadian Fiction." In <u>The Canadian Imagination: Dimensions of a Literary Culture</u>. Ed. David Staines. Cambridge, Mass.: Harvard Univ. Press, 1977, pp. 97-122.

Baugh, Albert C. <u>A History of the English Language</u>. 2nd ed. New York: Appleton-Century-Crofts, 1957.

"Bodies and Minds at the New U of T." Editorial. Toronto <u>Globe and Mail</u>, 9 March 1978, p. 6, cols. 1-2.

Breton, Raymond, et al. "The Impact of Ethnic Groups on Canadian Society: Research Issues." In <u>Identities: The Impact of Ethnicity on Canadian Society</u>. Ed. Wsevolod Isajiw. Canadian Ethnic Studies Association series, Vol. 5. Toronto: Peter Martin Associates, 1977, pp. 191-213.

Brooke, Rupert. <u>Letters from America</u>. Pref. Henry James. London: Sidgwick & Jackson, 1916.

"Budworm Spray Opponents Meet." Ottawa <u>Citizen</u>, 8 Dec. 1977, p. 20, cols. 1-2.

Bush, Douglas. "Stephen Leacock." In <u>The Canadian Imagination: Dimensions of a Literary Culture</u>. Ed. David Staines. Cambridge, Mass.: Harvard Univ. Press, 1977, pp. 123-51.

Carlyle, Thomas. <u>Reminiscences</u>. Ed. James Anthony Froude. New York: Harper, 1881.

Carter, E. H., and R. A. F. Mears. <u>A History of Britain</u>. 2nd ed. Oxford: Oxford Univ. Press, 1948.

Cohen, Leonard. <u>Selected Poems 1956-1968</u>. Toronto: McClelland and Stewart, 1968.

Cousins, Norman. "The Mysterious Placebo: How Mind Helps Medicine Work." <u>Saturday Review</u>, 1 Oct. 1977, pp. 8-16.

Cuff, Robert, and J. L. Granatstein. "The Rise and Fall of Canadian-American Free Trade, 1947-8." <u>Canadian Historical Review</u>, 58 (1977), 459-82.

Davies, Robertson. The Diary of Samuel Marchbanks. 1947;
     rpt. Toronto: Clarke, Irwin, 1966.

-----. One Half of Robertson Davies: Provocative Pro-
     nouncements on a Wide Range of Topics. Toronto:
     Macmillan of Canada, 1977.

Department of External Affairs. Canada from Sea to Sea.
     Rev. ed. Ottawa: Queen's Printer, 1963. .

Dictionnaire des Gallicismes les Plus Usités. Paris:
     Payot, 1951.

"The Dispossessed Americans." Rev. of Bury My Heart at
     Wounded Knee, by Dee Brown. Times Literary Supplement,
     21 July 1972, pp. 829-31.

Eiseley, Loren. Darwin's Century: Evolution and the Men
     Who Discovered It. 1958; rpt. Garden City, N.Y.:
     Anchor-Doubleday, 1961.

Fellowship of Australian Writers. Australian Writers
     Speak: Literature and Life in Australia. Sydney:
     Angus and Robertson, 1943.

Frye, Northrop. "The Typology of Paradise Regained."
     Modern Philology, 53 (1956), 227-38. Rpt. in Milton:
     Modern Essays in Criticism. Ed. Arthur E. Barker.
     New York: Galaxy-Oxford Univ. Press, 1965, pp.
     429-46.

Fuentes, Carlos. Where the Air is Clear. Trans. Sam
     Hileman. New York: Ivan Obolensky; Toronto: George
     J. McLeod, 1960.

"Halifax." The New Columbia Encyclopedia. 1975.

Hiebert, Paul. Sarah Binks. Introd. by A. Lloyd Wheeler.
     New Canadian Library, No. 44. Ed. Malcolm Ross.
     1947; rpt. Toronto: McClelland and Stewart, 1964.

Jack, Ian. English Literature 1815-1832. Vol. X of The
     Oxford History of English Literature. Ed. John
     Buxton and Norman Davis. Oxford: Oxford Univ.
     Press, 1963.

Kattan, Naim. "Space in the Canadian Novel of the West."
     Ariel: A Review of International English Literature,
     4, No. 3 (1973), 103-10.

Kirby, William. The Golden Dog: A Romance of Old Quebec.
     Toronto: Musson, n.d.

M[itchell], P[eter] C[halmers]. "Evolution." Encyclopaedia Britannica. 11th ed. (1910).

Newman, Peter C. "Noises from the Attic." In <u>Home Country: People, Places, and Power Politics</u>. Introd. Hugh MacLennan. Toronto: McClelland and Stewart, 1973, pp. 229-31.

Nicolson, Harold. <u>Some People</u>. [London], 1927; rpt. New York: Vintage, 1957.

Pepys, Samuel. <u>The Diary of Samuel Pepys</u>. Ed. Robert Latham and William Matthews. 9 vols. London: Bell, 1970-76.

Richards, I. A. "Literature for the Unlettered." In <u>Uses of Literature</u>. Ed. Monroe Engel. Harvard English Studies, 4. Cambridge, Mass.: Harvard Univ. Press, 1973, pp. 207-24.

Rosengarten, Herbert. "Urbane Comedy." Rev. of <u>Lady Oracle</u>, by Margaret Atwood. <u>Canadian Literature</u>, No. 72 (Spring 1977), pp. 84-87.

Shakespeare, William. <u>Othello</u>. Ed. M. R. Ridley. The Arden Edition of the Works of William Shakespeare. London: Methuen, Arden Shakespeare Paperbacks, 1965.

Staines, David. "Canada Observed." Editor's Introd. to <u>The Canadian Imagination: Dimensions of a Literary Culture</u>. Cambridge, Mass.: Harvard Univ. Press, 1977, pp. 1-21.

Thomas, Veronica. "The Hutterites of Canada." <u>Gourmet</u>, Nov. 1976, pp. 32-36, 94-97, 102-06.

Ward, Barbara. Interviewed by Peter C. Newman. <u>Maclean's</u>, 17 May 1976, pp. 4-8.

Wycherley, William. <u>The Plain Dealer</u>. Ed. Leo Hughes. Regents Restoration Drama Series. Ed. John Loftis. Lincoln: Univ. of Nebraska Press, 1967.

Zinsser, William. <u>On Writing Well</u>. New York: Harper & Row, 1976.

73d Points to Remember About Bibliographical Entries:

Mechanics: Author's or editor's last name comes first; if there is more than one author or editor, only the first one is reversed: Carter, E.H., and R.A.F. Mears. Complete title, and subtitle if any, are provided. Periods separate main parts, each followed by two typed spaces, and the entry ends with a period. Only one space follows a colon. The second and all subsequent lines of an entry are indented. Entries are listed

alphabetically by authors' last names or by the first significant word (ignore *The, A,* and *An*) of the titles of unsigned
works. When more than one work by an author is listed,
those after the first begin with a long dash—that is, a row of
anywhere from five to ten hyphens, amounting to "ditto";
see the entries for Davies. Bibliographical entries are not
numbered. Like footnotes, bibliographical entries may be
single spaced, but leave double spaces between them.

A source such as the Bible need not be included in the
bibliography, unless one was using one or more particular
editions for a particular purpose, such as comparing transla-
tions or citing and discussing commentary.

Unlike in footnotes, page numbers for references are not
given. But note that entries for essays and articles from larger
works or from periodicals end with the inclusive page
numbers—the first and the last—of each piece (and columns,
for newspaper articles).

The name of a university press must be given in full, but
other publishers' names are given in short but clear forms.
That is, "Scribner's," not "Charles Scribner's Sons"; "Norton," not "W.W. Norton & Co., Inc."; "McClelland and
Stewart," not "McClelland and Stewart Limited."

When only one or two pieces from a collection are cited, as
with the entries for Breton, Frye, Newman, and Richards,
those individual pieces are usually the ones listed in a
bibliography. But when as many as three pieces from a collection are cited, as with the entries for Atwood, Bush, and
Staines, a writer may wish simply to list the collection itself as
a source, not listing the individual pieces in the bibliography
at all:

> Staines, David, ed. The Canadian Imagination: Dimensions
> of a Literary Culture. Cambridge, Mass.: Harvard
> Univ. Press, 1977.

A bibliography, when it consists—as it usually does—of a
list of sources actually cited in the text and footnotes, is
customarily labelled "Works Cited" or "List of Works
Cited." On occasion, one may wish to add a list of "Works

Consulted." Sometimes a large bibliography is divided into sections, such as "Primary Sources" and "Secondary Sources, " or "Books" and "Periodicals."

Some abbreviations commonly used in documentation:

anon.	anonymous
c., ca.	(Latin *circa*) about
cf.	(Latin *confer*) compare
ch.; chs.	chapter; chapters
col.; cols.	column; columns
comp.; comps.	compiled by, compiler; compilers
diss.	dissertation
ed.; eds.	editor, edited by, edition; editors, editions
et al.	(Latin *et alii*) and others
fig.; figs.	figure; figures
ibid.	(Latin *ibidem*) in the same place
introd.	introduction, introduced by
l.; ll.	line; lines
ms; mss	manuscript; manuscripts
n.d.	no date of publication
n.; nn.	note (footnote); notes
no.; nos.	number; numbers
n.p.	no place of publication, no publisher
n. pag.	no pagination
p.; pp.	page; pages
passim	(Latin) throughout
pref.	preface, preface by
q.v.	(Latin *quod vide*) which see
rev.	revision, revised, revised by, review
rpt.	reprint, reprinted by
st.; sts.	stanza; stanzas
supp.; supps.	supplement; supplements
trans.	translated by, translator
v.	(Latin *vide*) see
vol.; vols.	volume; volumes

74 Sample Research Paper with Comments

This sample essay was selected less because it is a model research paper—though it is clearly a good one—than because it conveniently illustrates many of the details discussed in the preceding pages. The combined essay and commentary will repay your close attention.

Title Page: The information could all have been grouped in the upper part of the page, but the arrangement opposite, with only the title and author at the top and the rest lower down (all centred, of course), presents an attractive and balanced appearance.

Since a title page is used, the title itself is not repeated on the first page. Notice also that the first page is not numbered. If a first page or a page beginning a new section, such as outline, notes, or bibliography, is to be numbered at all, it should only be at the bottom centre. The outline page, then, could have been numbered at bottom centre with a small Roman numeral *i*. The title page is not counted as a page for numbering purposes, and pages containing preliminary material such as outlines and prefaces are not considered part of the regular pagination but are instead numbered, if at all, with small Roman numerals.

Note that, on page 1, the text begins about a quarter of the way down, presenting a cleanly balanced beginning page—and one that is obviously a beginning page, even without a number.

The Environment: Ours to Do with What We Will

by

Janice Elnor

English 100

Professor Smith

April 7, 1978

Note that the outline goes only to the first level of subheading. An obvious 1, 2, and 3 could easily have been supplied under each A, B, and C; for example, under I-B could come

1. Industry pollutes.
2. Industry wastes energy.
3. Industry harms wilderness and wildlife.

But these are so obvious as to be unnecessary.

Organization and emphasis: Note that paragraph 2 of the essay corresponds to section I-A of the outline. The three subjects (pollution, energy, and wilderness) are covered in one paragraph, as also in paragraphs 3 and 4. The writer had more data, but decided not to include them. When she reached part II, however, she began to break some of the material into separate paragraphs. And though III-A becomes two paragraphs (15 and 16) and III-B only one (17), at III-C the whole pattern changes: the individual's importance is represented by this section's turning into several paragraphs in which pollution, energy, and wilderness are all woven together. All of this corresponds to the writer's desired emphasis on the need for greater action (part III occupies the last half of the paper) and especially on the need for changed attitudes (part III-C occupies the last quarter of the paper). That is, the essay builds to a climax.

Part II-A of the outline is spread over two paragraphs (6 and 7). Part II-B is given three (8, 9, and 10), continuing the expansion and consequent emphasis on solutions after stating the problem. One result of this is shorter and less satisfactory paragraphs in part II; paragraph 8, for example, is shorter even than paragraph 5, which is merely transitional. By part III, however, the section given most space, the writer gets back to longer, more fully developed paragraphs.

Outline

Thesis Statement: Since man is responsible for environmental damage, and though he is trying to help, he must change his attitudes and work harder to save the environment and himself.

Beginning: "Environmentalism" is something new, though the problem is not: "The Problem Is People."

I.   The problem: Man as government, industry, and individual causes environmental deterioration.
       A. Lacking foresight, governments cause pollution, the waste of energy, and damage to wilderness.
       B. Profit-oriented industry causes pollution, wastes energy, and destroys wilderness.
       C. Through laziness and carelessness, individuals cause pollution, waste energy, and damage wilderness.

II.   Government, industry, and individual are currently working to repair the damage and prevent further harm.
       A. Through legislation and example, governments help to control pollution and save energy and wilderness.
       B. Largely under compulsion, industry helps to cut pollution, save energy, and preserve wilderness.
       C. Alone and in groups, individuals work to cut pollution, save energy, and preserve wilderness.

III.   Government, industry, and individual must all do more if we and our environment are to be saved.
       A. Government must act to control pollution and to promote the saving of energy and wilderness.
       B. Industry must change its priorities to halt pollution, save energy, and preserve wilderness.
       C. People must change their attitudes to stop pollution, save energy, and halt the destruction of wilderness.

Ending: The essential for the future is changed attitudes. We and our environment are interdependent, and we must behave accordingly.

Paragraph 1: The first paragraph is partly introductory and partly substantive. From two opening sentences which state and substantiate the newness of our environmental

(continued on next page)

Footnote 2: This book was out of the library, but the writer felt that the title alone was too good to pass up. She of course had to trust the accuracy of a bibliographical listing and the card catalogue.

Footnote 3: This is a discursive footnote, though the material could have been included in the text. The documentary part at the end is enclosed in parentheses, which means that square brackets must replace the usual internal parentheses. The dots do not indicate ellipsis but are part of the title; typing them without spaces is a device used by some writers to indicate that they are in the source, not added by the writer. Compare this footnote with the original source and with the version that appeared on the relevant note card to see how the information was successively boiled down. The source:

> Ecosystems represent a standing crop of energy and minerals that are stored in plants, animals, and soils. It is this standing crop that is utilized by man. If the removal of the crop, either wholesale or selective, proceeds at a rate greater than the recuperating processes operating in the ecosystem, in the absence of artificial fertilization, then ecosystem degradation, or landscape pollution, is inevitable.

Edgell, p. 49. "ecosystem" - Introd. or I ?

says that "Ecosystems" amount to "a standing crop of energy and minerals that are stored in plants, animals, and soils." If man removes the "crop" "at a rate greater than the recuperating processes" of the ecosystem can restore it, "in the absence of artificial fertilization, then ecosystem degradation, or landscape pollution, is inevitable." [' use as part of definition of the 'problem'?]]

In recent years there has been rapidly growing concern
about the environment. A 1975 encyclopedia contains an entry
on "environmentalism," whereas its predecessor of 1963 does not.[1]
We hear about the environment every day: pollution is bad,
energy resources are being depleted, and the wilderness is
dwindling. The problem is not new, as the title of a recent
article points out: "Pollution Begins in Prehistory: The
Problem Is People."[2] But as population and technology grow,
the troubles multiply, until now we are in the midst of a crisis.
And clearly it is a man-made crisis. Any time he moves a rock
from one place to another, or cuts down a tree for fuel, or
kills an animal for its pelt, man is altering a natural balance:
He is interfering with an "ecosystem."[3] In Pollution: Canada's

[1] The New Columbia Encyclopedia, 1975; cf. The Columbia
Encyclopedia, 3rd ed., 1963.

[2] T. Cuyler Young, in Man in Nature, ed. Louis D. Levine
(Toronto: Royal Ontario Museum, 1975).

[3] M. C. R. Edgell, in "Landscape Pollution," defines an
ecosystem as consisting of "energy and minerals that are stored
in plants, animals, and soils" and describes environmental
deterioration as the result of man using up the "crop" faster
than it is able to regenerate without artificial help (in
Pollution: What It Is...What It Does...What Can Be Done About
It, ed. W. J. Maunder [Victoria: Evening Division, Univ. of
Victoria, 1969], p. 49).

awareness, the writer moves quickly and economically to introduce the three elements—pollution, energy, and wilderness—that run throughout the essay. The rest of the paragraph, while continuing to provide background and definition, also states and restates the part of the thesis covering man's responsibility. The final sentence also makes explicit the part of the thesis that serves as an organizing principle throughout the essay. The rest of the thesis is not stated here but left until the second and third parts begin. By naming Morgan and his book's title (which itself helps state part of the thesis), the writer implies that he is an important source. Morgan's statement could have been paraphrased, but the writer felt that his words were distinctive and that a direct quotation was appropriate here in the opening paragraph.

Footnote 4: Since the author's full name and the book's title are in the text, they are not repeated here. The name of the editor of the series is reserved for the bibliography.

Footnote 5: This covering footnote, expressing general indebtedness, appears at the end of the first paragraph; the tripartite division mentioned in the last sentence is part of what is being credited. The subtitle of the first book is omitted here. The work by Ferguson gave no city as the place of publication; rather than put *n.p.*, however, the writer chose to accept the library's tentative suggestion in the card catalogue—" [Vancouver?]"—and included this logical guess in square brackets in her footnote.

Footnote 6: This "See for example" footnote indicates that Bell is only one of several sources that discuss the matter. This form is less direct documentation of material from Bell than it is a way of informing the reader that the subject is a common one and telling him of at least one place where he can find out more about it, a method which here is preferable to simply assuming that a widely mentioned matter is "common knowledge." The book edited by Maunder is fully identified in footnote 3, but rather than just say "Maunder, pp.

(continued on next page)

Critical Challenge, Frank Morgan says that "When man mismanages his environment, man pays, sometimes with his livelihood, always with some part of his way of life."[4] Man alone is responsible for environmental damage, whether he acts as an individual or through the industries he creates and the governments he elects.[5]

Governments, through lack of foresight, have contributed to the deterioration of the environment. All levels of government want growth, whether of a nation, a province, or a city, but in the past they have given little thought to the ecological implications of rapid growth. Municipal governments, for example, responding to the needs of their citizens, have been major polluters of water, land, and air because of poor planning of sewage and garbage disposal systems.[6] We were asleep at the energy switch as well. It took the Arabs and the oil crisis of the 1970's to alert governments and everyone else to the need for conserving our dwindling supplies of conventional fuels. And wildlife and wilderness areas have suffered because govern-

---

[4] *Shaping Canada's Environment*, No. 4 (Toronto: Ryerson, Maclean-Hunter, 1970), p. 2.

[5] Some of the parts and organization of this paper were suggested to me--or rather my inclinations toward them were strengthened--by C. I. Jackson, "Environmental Policy and Environmental Planning in Canada," in *Canada's Natural Environment*, ed. G. R. McBoyle and E. Sommerville (Toronto: Methuen, 1976), and Cherry Ferguson, *Efforts by the Citizen, Labatt Breweries, and Government to Achieve Environmental Quality in B. C.* ([Vancouver]: Labatt Breweries, 1971).

[6] See for example M. A. M. Bell, "Waste Management and Environmental Quality in Victoria, B.C.," in Maunder, ed., *Pollution*, pp. 87-101.

Paragraph 3: It is safe enough to say in the second sentence that "Industry is one of the two main sources" rather than to hedge with something like "is said to be" or "is claimed to be." Footnote 10 covers the second sentence. The third sentence clearly draws on the writer's own experience, the fourth sentence is transitional, and footnote 11 covers the specific citation of the fifth sentence. Since the point of view

(continued on next page)

87–101,'' the writer decided to use not only the name but also *ed.* and a short title because of the possible confusion which could arise later (see footnote 10). The page numbers given are inclusive, indicating that the whole article is relevant to the point being made.

Footnote 7: The edited book was fully identified in footnote 5; here the abbreviation *eds.* is not needed. *Passim* indicates that the points referred to occur here and there throughout Kitchen's article; this is slightly different from what footnote 6 tells us about Bell's article.

Footnote 8: Here the writer cites three specific points as the sources for the information referred to; as you see in the paragraph, the information is more specific than that documented in footnotes 6 and 7.

Footnote 9: The first reference to this source requires a complete footnote, though the writer again decided that it was not necessary to include the book's subtitle in the footnote.

Footnote 10: This consolidated footnote, its parts separated by a semicolon, refers to the two main parts of the sentence. The writer could find no model for the first reference to Maunder's essay in his own edited book, which had already been referred to; applying her common sense, she came up with this form. Note that repeating *ed.* after the second instance of his name keeps his functions as author and editor distinct (see also footnotes 6, 14, 33, and 40). Note that since the title of Maunder's article ends with a question mark, no comma follows it (see also footnotes 27 and 38).

3

ments have not adequately controlled highways, subdivisions, and industrial developments, to name a few of the manifestations of progress which are replacing the natural environment.[7] Governments establish lovely parks, but exploitation of the land--for example urban development in Banff, logging in Pacific Rim, and also in Algonquin, where it has reduced the deer population-- continues, and is sometimes written into the agreement which created the park in the first place.[8] And defoliants sprayed on roadsides have, when carried further afield by unexpected winds, transformed green areas into virtual deserts.[9]

Government has also been at fault in failing to control industry, whose effects on the ecology are sometimes massive. Industry is one of the two main sources of water pollution (the other being municipal sewage systems), and several other sources of man-made pollution are industry related, such as smokestack emissions, demolition and construction operations, and manufacturing processes in general.[10] No one who has seen the brownish foam floating on the Fraser River near Prince George,

[7] Cameron M. Kitchen, "Ecology and Urban Development: The Theory and Practice of Ecoplanning in Canada," in McBoyle and Sommerville, pp. 217-40, passim.

[8] John B. Theberge, "Ecological Planning in National Parks," in McBoyle and Sommerville, pp. 195, 201, 211.

[9] M. J. Dunbar, _Environment and Good Sense_ (Montreal: McGill-Queen's Univ. Press, 1971), pp. 46-47.

[10] Morgan, p. 4; W. J. Maunder, "What is Pollution?" in Maunder, ed., _Pollution_, p. 2.

of each sentence is therefore clear, the reader does not wonder about sources and documentation. Note how in the sixth sentence the writer has turned a weakness, the scarcity of useful information, into a strength by tying a different kind of environmental damage, the killing of fish, to her point about wasted energy.

Paragraph 4: Footnote 14 could have been omitted; it would be hard to find many things more "common knowledge" than auto exhausts and littered streets. Nevertheless the writer did encounter a specific mention of these and decided that the point would be stronger if documented from an authority.

(continued on next page)

Footnote 11: Commoner's book was out of the library; the writer therefore had to take Hohenemser's word for what it said in chapter 7. Since the words quoted in the text are Hohenemser's, not Commoner's, it would be wrong to say "quoted by Hohenemser"; the word *cited*, which can mean "quoted" but can also mean "mentioned," is correct. *Environment* is a monthly magazine, but since it has volume and issue numbers and is specialized, the writer decided to treat it like a learned journal. Note that when the volume number is given, no *p.* precedes the page number.

Footnote 12: The superscript number *12* could logically be placed after the word *fish.* But in line with the principle that footnote numbers should when possible come at the ends of sentences, that is where it is placed here; the final clause is reasonably clearly the writer's, and the form "See Morgan" also suggests that he is to be consulted for the evidence of dead fish, not the conclusion about wasted energy. It would not, however, be wrong to put the number after *fish,* for then the reference would be completely unambiguous; the footnote would then read simply "Morgan, pp. 6-7."

4

B. C., or breathed the air on a foggy morning in Duncan, can
doubt the influence of the pulp and paper industry on the local
environment. Wasted energy is another of industry's contributions to the general deterioration of the environment. The
"profit motive" even leads industry to install equipment that
is "less energy-efficient" than what it replaces.[11] Evidence
of energy-wasting practices is hard to find, but if heated water
around industrial plants is killing fish, then energy is being
wasted somewhere.[12] As for wilderness, though industry is not
often directly responsible for the destruction of wildlife,
indiscriminate logging and mining practices are detrimental to
animals' habitats and food sources.[13]

Man in his private role also accounts for some of the
ecological problems he encounters. Automobile exhausts and
littered streets are two major kinds of pollution to which the
individual contributes.[14] Few people think about the beer bottle
they toss from their boat or the cigarette butt they drop on the
street, but such acts pollute the environment, and also suggest
a poor attitude toward the problem of the environment in general.

[11] Barry Commoner, The Poverty of Power (New York: Knopf,
1976), ch. 7, cited by Kurt H. Hohenemser, "Energy: Waste Not,
Want Not," Environment, 18, No. 7 (Sept. 1976), 4.

[12] See Morgan, pp. 6-7.

[13] Dunbar, p. 39.

[14] Maunder, p. 2.

The rest of the paragraph is in fact her own information, her own thinking, and can also be claimed to be common knowledge. The final sentence, however, would have been strengthened by some specific examples of endangered and extinct species, accompanied by documentation of authoritative sources.

Paragraph 5: This is a transitional paragraph, a bridge between sections I and II of the outline. The quotation from Ferguson is very convenient in that it reminds the reader of the three-part structure of each section. (It is also fairly obviously one of the reasons Ferguson is cited in footnote 5.) The parenthetical reference following the quotation is sufficient since the author of the already footnoted work is named. Note that the period comes after the parentheses.

5

Individuals waste energy through laziness (driving short distances) and indifference (turning up the heat instead of putting
on a sweater; leaving lights on in unused rooms). Man's "I can't
be bothered" attitude reflects an egocentric desire to save
personal time and effort at the expense of his surroundings.
And egocentric man the "sportsman" and outdoorsman does his
share of damage to the wilderness and its wildlife through carelessness and indiscriminate hunting and fishing, even to the
extent of adding to the list of endangered and extinct species.

5   The problem, then, is the destruction of the natural
environment at the hands of man. What is man doing to repair
the damage and to prevent further harm? Since man created the
problem, it is only logical that he work to correct it. And as
Cherry Ferguson says, "effective environmental quality management is the product of a co-operative effort involving the
citizen, industry and government" (p. 1). Indeed, all three are
now working to slow down most and to eliminate some of the
environmental deterioration in Canada.

6   Since 1966, the federal government has enacted legislation
aimed at preventing and cleaning up pollution, conserving energy,
and preserving parklands. The Canada Centre for Inland Waters
was established in 1967, a research facility which provided much
of the information necessary to start the cleanup of the Great
Lakes. In 1970, the government created Environment Canada and
drew up such pollution-oriented legislation as the Canada Water
Act and the Clean Air Act. Canada participated actively in

Paragraph 6: Footnote 15 documents the single source for all the data in the paragraph up to that point. The next sentence, about Habitat, is from the writer's own experience; though sources could easily be found, they are unnecessary. Footnote 16 documents the information in the final sentence.

Paragraph 7: Footnote 17 documents the data in the first sentence, and 18 the data in the second sentence. The third sentence, however, is documented by a parenthetical reference, since the author is named and has already been documented in an earlier footnote (number 7). Identifying Kitchen as a geographer is perhaps marginally useful, but it might have been worth remarking that Morgan, a principal source, is news editor for a medical journal. Whenever possible, identify cited authorities as indeed having some authority.

Footnote 17: A first reference to a newspaper article. Note that the definite article is usually omitted from a newspaper's name. Like many newspapers, this one has sections (A, B, C, etc.) which must be included as part of the page number. Identifying the column number or numbers is not essential, but is nevertheless a courtesy to the reader.

6

international conferences dealing with man and his environment, such as the UN Conference on the Human Environment (Stockholm, 1972) and the Law of the Sea Conference (Caracas, 1974-75).[15] And Canada sponsored the Habitat conference in Vancouver in 1976. Provincial and municipal governments help by establishing pollution control boards which regulate industry and by being more conscientious about regional planning.[16]

7

In order to conserve energy, governments are considering rapid transit systems to replace private cars as the main method of everyday travel; they are encouraging research into new energy sources; and they are leading the way to active energy conservation, for example with the federal government's "Save 10" program and the B. C. Energy Commission's programs to reduce energy consumption.[17] Wildlife and wilderness areas are also getting more attention from town planners (greenbelts and parks), provincial governments (agricultural land and parks), and also the federal government, as in the operations of Parks Canada and the Canadian Wildlife Service.[18] And more care precedes development now: Cameron M. Kitchen, a geographer, analyzes three case studies-- of a subdivision, a zoo, and a highway by-pass, all in Ontario--

[15] Jackson, pp. 247-60.

[16] Morgan, p. 19.

[17] Michael Harcourt, "Where to Start Saving Energy," Vancouver Sun, 25 Nov. 1977, p. A6, cols. 5-6.

[18] Theberge, pp. 197-98, 208.

Paragraph 9: The writer decided that the first two sentences needed no documentation, since this fact is so widely known and discussed. Nevertheless, the reader might have appreciated a "see for example" footnote, especially about the more specific matter of solar energy. The fourth sentence is clearly the writer's own speculation. Here is how the information from Calef's article looked on a note card, with the writer's own idea enclosed in double square brackets:

Calef, pp. 17, 18   Industry + energy   II B

–reminds us that burning wood for fuel is really a "solar technology, depending only upon the inexhaustible radiant energy from the sun." (p. 17)
– U.S. proposal of a huge "energy plantation" – ca. 149,000 acres of trees (p. 18)

[[Wouldn't this work well in Canada, with all our trees ?!]]

Note that in order to change the singular "energy plantation" of the original into a plural for the purposes of her own sentence, the writer added an *s* in square brackets.

Footnote 21: Note how a comment can be added to a documenting footnote. Harcourt's point is relevant, but would, the writer felt, be obtrusive in her text. Note also the parenthetical documentation of Harcourt's remark, and its punctuation: the period follows the parentheses.

7

as examples of the "pre-development ecology" or "ecoplanning"
which has been lacking in the past (pp. 221-37).

Industry, too, is becoming more conscious of the environment. Government and individuals have forced this awareness on
industry, but as time goes by, industry is taking more responsibility upon itself. Tax breaks and subsidies encourage industry
to install pollution control equipment--though some industries
do not think these incentives great enough. But some industries
are even sponsoring public-awareness programs and providing
money for research and planning.[19]

Industry's main efforts are directed at reducing energy
consumption and finding new sources of energy. Power companies
and others are working on alternatives and additions to hydro
power and fossil fuels; solar energy is a major example. In the
United States some people are proposing huge "energy plantation[s]"
of trees, claiming that burning wood is actually a "solar technology."[20] Such an idea might work well in Canada, with all
its woodlands. And scientists are even beginning to work on
nuclear fusion.[21] There is also research into recycling energy,
and the government offers tax breaks to industries installing

[19] Ferguson, p. 38 and passim.

[20] Charles E. Calef, "Not Out of the Woods," Environment,
18, No. 7 (Sept. 1976), 17-18.

[21] Dieter Hohenberger, "Is Fusion the Answer? It Wouldn't
Hurt to Ask," Maclean's, 3 April 1978, p. 70. Harcourt, however,
says that fusion "is at least 30 years off" (col. 3).

Paragraph 10: The final sentence is the writer's own idea. Here is how she recorded it on a note card, complete with double square brackets, at the moment it occurred to her:

what "industry" does – II B

[[Reforestation: industry helps itself by also helping the environment — chicken and egg? which came first?]]

Footnote 22: As also in the preceding footnote, since Harcourt's entire article appears on one page, A6, there is no need to repeat the page number every time.

Footnote 23: Such a fragmentary sentence is permissible in this kind of footnote, though it could easily have begun with "See" or "Note" or "We have all seen" or the like.

8

heating equipment which can re-use energy.[22] Industry is even
trying to educate the public in ways to conserve energy--with
an emphasis, of course, on saving money.[23]

Although industry's interest in conserving wilderness and
wildlife is largely government imposed, new restrictions on sites,
methods, and tools are having the desired effects. Land developers
are paying more attention to the ecology; consequently they produce better developments which are readily approved by local
governments.[24] Industry is also helping to develop new methods
that will, it is hoped, eliminate the need for chemical insecti-
cides.[25] And reforestation is a prime example of how industry
looks out for its own interests while helping to maintain
natural ecological balance.

Public outcry and the work of citizens' groups are probably
the most effective ways individuals can help to preserve their
environment. The number of groups is rising, and though many
problems have limited their success to date--poor facilities,
low budgets, lack of active participation, poor communication
with other groups as well as with government and industry--these

[22] Harcourt, col. 5.

[23] For example the frequent "public interest" TV spots,
magazine ads, and even billboards by power companies, oil
companies, and automobile manufacturers.

[24] Kitchen, p. 239.

[25] Dunbar, pp. 44-46.

Paragraph 11: The material in the last two sentences stems from the writer's own awareness and not from anything she read about these affairs in the sources. Nevertheless, one would think that she could without too much trouble have found one or two sources (for example in newspaper articles) in order to strengthen and document this point.

Paragraph 12: Unlike the points in the preceding paragraph about tankers and pipeline, those in this paragraph are obviously generally known. Sources for such data could be found, but documentation here would be superfluous.

Paragraph 13: Here is how the writer recorded on a note card one of the ideas that became a part of this paragraph:

what "people" do - II C

[[Individuals help by helping the experts — supporting, with contributions, such groups as Greenpeace and the Sierra Club.]]

Footnote 27: The writer chanced upon the review documented in this footnote when she was nearly through revising her essay, and felt that it would make a good discursive footnote to add depth and particularity to the paragraph's opening statement. The comment had to go into a footnote, she felt, for if put into the text it would destroy the already established flow and integrity of the paragraph.

problems are resolvable.[26] And there are more frequent public

hearings into potentially harmful projects. Plans for oil

tankers to dock at Kitimat, for example, and for a Mackenzie

Valley Pipeline, were met with public demands to know more

about their ecological implications.

12   Citizens' groups tend to concentrate on pollution and wild-

life conservation, but the individual is also helping to conserve

energy. People are insulating their houses better, and buying

smaller cars; they are recycling glass and paper and metal; and

some refuse to buy such energy-hungry items as self-cleaning

ovens. Although some of these acts are economically motivated,

they nevertheless indicate changing attitudes.

13   The increase of public interest in outdoor activities such

as camping, hiking, climbing, and cross-country skiing has also

increased the individual's awareness of his environment.[27]

Interest in conserving wildlife and recreation areas is growing,

and with the aid of such groups as Greenpeace and the Sierra

Club, this interest is turning into action. Though the individual

may feel powerless to save a whale or preserve natural woodland,

his contributions help organizations that have the ability to

[26] Ferguson, p. 1.

[27] One indication of the growing interest in and respect
for the wilderness is the large number of books and articles
about it that are pouring out these days. See Diane Johnson,
"Ah, Wilderness!" rev. of The Last Cowboy, by Jane Kramer, and
Coming into the Country, by John McPhee, New York Review of
Books, 23 March 1978, pp. 3-6. Johnson discusses the phenomenon
and mentions several other works.

Paragraph 14: Note how this short transitional paragraph neatly sums up section II and then introduces section III with the appropriate part of the thesis.

Paragraph 15: The number for footnote 18 had to be placed early in the sentence, since only the opening clause derived from the source. Note also that the parenthetical reference to Morgan's book comes as soon as possible after his name rather than at the end of the sentence; this is the usual practice when the material is paraphrased or summarized rather than quoted (cf. the parenthetical references in paragraphs 5, 7, 11, 19, and 20, and in footnote 21).

Footnote 28: A first reference to an article in a scholarly journal with continuous pagination throughout the issues that make up each annual volume. The issue number is not necessary. Note the Arabic numeral for the volume number, and that no *p.* is included when the volume number is given.

accomplish something tangible.

14 Obviously some good results have been achieved, but man cannot yet sit back on his laurels with a satisfied smile. As industrialization and urbanization continue to grow, new environmental problems arise. The work must not only continue, therefore, but also be intensified if we are to preserve our quality of life.

15 Government control over industries must be tightened. Since voluntary controls have a way of not working,[28] there must be new legislation which includes mandatory measures, such as limits on the chemical contents of industrial discharges, and there must be large fines for those who contravene the regulations. Governments must also try to make it attractive for industry to obey the laws. By providing funds for research into new equipment and alternative materials and methods, governments would be viewed less as disrupters of the status quo than as active contributors to a clean environment. Morgan (p. 3) advocates that environmental programs be under federal control but be carried out by the provinces, and that they cover all the different kinds of possible damage to the environment. But such programs can work only if governments get together and agree to make them work.

16 Conservation also requires more attention from governments. Not only should they set good examples; they also have a respon-

[28] Daniel J. Koenig, "Additional Research on Environmental Activism," _Environment and Behavior_, 7 (1975), 475.

Paragraph 17: It would have been preferable to translate the obscure jargon of the quotation from Morgan into simpler, more comprehensible English. In contrast, the quotation from Novick on page 12, long enough to be indented and single-spaced, would be difficult to paraphrase effectively and is better left in the author's own words. Note that, for the sake of clarity, the writer herself inserted the year, in the obligatory square brackets. And note the four dots of the ellipsis at the end. Note also how the quotation is introduced with a complete sentence followed by a colon.

Footnote 29: Rather than cite a whole list of other sources, the writer merely calls attention to the fact that the subject of educating the public is a common one among her sources. She could probably have used a "see for example" footnote here, but perhaps felt that adding a comment would be stronger.

Footnote 31: A secondhand source. Identifying Pépin's position in this way adds authority to his ideas. If he were, say, a taxi driver, his thoughts on these matters would not carry so much weight.

sibility to educate the public.[29] By making people aware of
energy problems, government can lessen public resistance to
conservation measures; by imposing higher taxes on luxury items
such as big cars, government can discourage the use of energy-
draining extras; and by subsidizing improved insulation, government can encourage homeowners to save energy.[30] And educating
the public about the use and value of parkland and wilderness
areas is essential for effective land and animal conservation.

17

    If education, legislation, and leadership are the key roles
for government, responsibility and unselfishness must increasingly
motivate industry. Most of the environmental problems created
by industry are the result of our profit-oriented system. One
expert proposes a plan that would require that we consider
"natural resources as economic assets. Their use should be
expressed in terms of an equation combining elements of cost-
profit and the individual-community--and all within a perspective
of relativity of both time and space."[31] Industry must
re-examine the relative values of profit and environmental
despoliation. Stopping pollution costs money, but pollution
itself can be expensive:

    [29] Morgan, p. 133. Many other authorities also mention
this need.
    [30] Harcourt, cols. 4-5.
    [31] Pierre-Yves Pépin, of the Urban Institute of the
University of Montreal, as summarized by Morgan, p. 133.

Paragraph 18: The passage from Morgan on page 13 is much more quotable than that from Winham; Winham's is pedestrian and passive, whereas Morgan's has a distinctive rhetorical flavour that it would be a pity to lose by paraphrasing. All but perhaps the last few words of Winham's would better have been paraphrased. Note how the first quotation is introduced with a brief subordinate clause followed by a comma. The quotation begins with a capital *G* as it does in the source. Since the sentence following the block quotation continues with material from Winham and—which is important—repeats his name so that the point of view remains clear, no footnote number is needed at the end of the block quotation; it can wait until the end of the next sentence, when the writer is finished with Winham. The quotation from

(continued on next page)

Footnote 34: Since the author's full name (or as full as was available) is given in the text, it is not included in the footnote. Here is how the note card for this paraphrase looked:

> Winham, p. 389   *public opinion—III C*
>
> "Public attitudes are seldom the principal component of public policy, yet they are a factor which is weighed in the decisions of popularly elected leaders."
>
> [To lead into conclusion about the importance of people's attitudes toward their environment and their lives?]]

Footnotes must always begin on the page where the material they document occurs, and should if possible be completed on that page. Occasionally, however, as they do here, the exigencies of spacing and numbering require that a footnote be continued at the beginning of the footnotes on the next page.

(continued on next page)

12

> Toward the end of June [1976], businessmen antici-
> pating heavy summer tourist trade in the famed
> Thousand Islands region of the Saint Lawrence
> Seaway were shocked to find themselves facing
> several months of shore cleanup in the wake of a
> barge grounding which released about 2.5 million
> gallons of toxic fuel oil into the seaway . . . .[32]

In the long run pollution may well cost more--not only in money, but also in health and happiness--than would steps taken now to prevent it.[33] It may cost more to install energy-recycling units, and it may be less efficient to operate in a location which does not interfere with wildlife, but industry must realize that its own survival hangs in the balance along with everyone else's.

Industry is in a sense an unfortunate scapegoat, for it is after all a manifestation of man's desire for "progress" and material well-being. And government is equally unfortunate in that it is pulled in two directions. As G. Winham observes,

> Government officials today are pressed by the public
> to reduce environmental pollution. At the same time
> they are also expected to maintain high growth rates
> and to increase employment opportunities. Too often
> these demands are simply inconsistent.

Public opinion, as Winham notes, may not often be the primary influence, but it is an influence and can affect legislation.[34]

[32] Sheldon Novick, "Spectrum" (a monthly newsletter), _Environment_, 18, No. 7 (Sept. 1976), 22-23.

[33] See for example Maunder, pp. 5-8.

[34] "Attitudes on Pollution and Growth in Hamilton, or

Morgan is also introduced with a short clause and a comma; this quotation, however, begins with a lower case *t* because it does not start at the beginning of a sentence in the source. Note that an opening ellipsis (...) is not necessary, since beginning with the lower case letter makes it clear that it is not from the beginning of a sentence. Note also that when a parenthetical reference follows a block quotation, it comes after the period rather than before it.

When this occurs, type or draw a line about one third of the way across the second page two or three spaces below the text, as here, to separate text from continued footnote. Otherwise, since the continued footnote does not begin with a raised number and a five-space indention, it could momentarily and confusingly be mistaken for part of the text. Notice the single quotation marks inside the usual double quotation marks.

Footnote 35: Strictly speaking, *The Gallup Poll of Canada* is the title of the annual bound volumes of reports; since it is given in the text, the writer does not repeat it in the footnote. She also decided that the Canadian Institute for Public Opinion was the corporate author rather than the publisher, and otherwise handled this difficult footnote with commendable common sense.

13

In any event, man's attitude is at the root of the problem, and must be modified if we are to be successful in our fight to preserve the environment. As Morgan concludes,

> the degree of national, international and even global commitment to control will depend finally on our own concern for the condition of the street on which we live, the river in which we fish and swim, the town in which we spend our time and money. (p. 133)

The Gallup Poll of Canada reported that on March 25, 1970, 91 percent of the people surveyed professed an awareness of pollution, and 69 percent of them regarded it as "very serious." A similar poll on February 26, 1975, showed 93 percent awareness—but only 57 percent considered the problem very serious.[35] The decline in concern over five years may be attributable to improved environmental protection mechanisms, or it may be due to complacency. In any event, the initial furor of the late 1960's and early 1970's seems to be dying down, while oil spills and air pollution continue.

19

The media, once credited with increasing public awareness, have recently come under fire for misleading the public about environmental issues,[36] and it seems, of late, that only items

---

'There's an Awful Lot of Talk These Days About Ecology,'" Canadian Journal of Political Science, 5 (1972), 389.

[35] The Canadian Institute of Public Opinion, "Concern with Pollution Drops Among Canadians," Gallup Report of 26 Feb. 1975; cf. 25 March and 2 Dec. 1970.

[36] Jacqueline Cernot, quoted by Robert Wielaard, "News Media Augment Ignorance of Ecology, Ottawa Official Says," Winnipeg Free Press, 1 Dec. 1977, p. 6.

Paragraph 19: The writer inserted *sic* in square brackets in the quotation from Koenig lest she be accused of herself misspelling *despoliation.* This is strictly correct, since quotation is supposed to be verbatim. Most writers, however, would consider an error like this too minor to be concerned about, and would simply perform a silent correction as they transcribed the sentence. They would reserve *sic* for serious errors, such as errors of fact or stylistic errors that are obviously more than a slip. For example, note that we decided to include a *sic* in our long quotation from Rupert Brooke (see #71); the correction—inserting "those of" before the word *Montreal,* or adding *'s* to it—was more than we felt we should do silently. If you are not sure which course to take, use *sic*; it is better to risk being thought a pedant than to be accused of tampering unduly with a quotation. Note that after the three dots of the ellipsis the writer has inserted a comma—inside the quotation mark—for the purpose of punctuating her own sentence. Note too how smoothly she has worked Koenig's words into the syntax of her own paraphrase. The parenthetical reference at the end clearly covers all the material from Koenig; a reference or footnote number after the first quotation as well is unnecessary since the paragraph obviously continues to draw on Koenig.

Paragraph 20: All the specific details of this paragraph are the writer's own. Note how neatly the paragraph is framed by the two sentences quoted from Harcourt, and how the first quotation is handled. Note also how the second sentence is a kind of second topic sentence (see #64c).

Footnote 37: Here the writer, by means of a discursive and consolidated footnote, turns a point that could probably have been treated as common knowledge into something emphatic.

of great international interest (the Brittany oil spill, for example) receive major coverage. As Daniel J. Koenig remarks, "Individuals may be quickly aroused by sudden and visible environmental despoilation [sic] in their immediate environment . . . ," but most people, he believes, remain passive "until it is too late." People may be getting bored by all the talk about the environment, but if they ignore it, matters will only get worse. Koenig fears that if people continue to submit passively, "the environmental rapists will quickly realize the lack of genuine resistance to their advances," and continued environmental destruction will be inevitable (pp. 473-74).

20

"The first thing Canadians should do," writes Michael Harcourt, "is recognize that they are the most wasteful, head-in-the-sand nation on the face of the earth" (col. 3). Clearly, people will have to accept "an associated reduction in the standard of living" if they really want to conserve energy.[37] This may well mean smaller and fewer cars, less travel by jet, fewer labour-saving but energy-consuming gadgets, more clothes and less heat, and even a--perhaps welcome--decrease in the amount of plastic in our lives. It also means higher prices for manufactured goods, and probably higher taxes to support government programs. The individual is also going to have to

---

[37] Hohenemser, p. 4. Most authorities agree on this commonplace; see for example Winham, pp. 400-01, and James S. Bowman, "Public Opinion and the Environment: Post-Earth Day Attitudes Among College Students," Environment and Behavior, 9 (1977), 394-95

Paragraph 21: Note how footnote 38 comes at the end of three sentences derived from the same source. Only one footnote is needed; do not make the mistake in such instances of providing three separate footnotes. The final clause before the number is clearly the writer's, and the number can come at the end of the sentence. Again with footnote 39 (next page), one footnote is sufficient, even though a reader cannot tell, without going to the source, just what part of the material comes from each of the three cited pages. Here is how one of the note cards from Bowman looked. Note that the writer was careful to write the hyphenated word *pro-environmental* all on one line; had *pro-* been written at the end of a line, she might have wondered later if the word was hyphenated in the source or merely in her note. Always be thus careful with hyphenated words in quoted notes:

Bowman, p. 393   III-C or (concl.)

" ... student attitudes are decidedly
pro-environmental."

In the long quotation from Loney on the next page, note that in the third ellipsis there is no space before the first of the four dots; this indicates that it is the period and that the ellipsis occurs at the beginning of the next sentence, which thus begins with a lower case *i.* Some writers would change it to a capital *I* in square brackets, to mark the beginning of a new sentence, but others feel that that would be awkward and unnecessary. The long quotation from Jackson (next page), as footnote 41 reveals, comes from two widely separated places in his article; the full line of dots indicates this unusually large ellipsis. Here is how the note card for the second part of the quotation looked:

learn to enjoy his wilderness trips without the motor-home or
the trailer, to get back to tents and hiking so that green areas
may be spared the carnage of roads and artificially created
campsites. Such sacrifices are not great, though they may sound
somewhat less attractive than what we are used to. But unless
such changes take place, changes--for the worse--in our health
and the future quality of our lives are inevitable. As Harcourt
puts it, "We are all going to have to change our ways, either
wisely and voluntarily, or in a panic as an emergency reaction to
the crisis that looms a few years ahead" (col. 3).

21   We can only speculate about what will happen. One group of
American researchers concludes that since public concern about
pollution is a relatively "new phenomenon," it may turn out to
be no more than a "fad." They note that publicity in the media
had failed, in the town they surveyed, to stir up anti-pollution
sentiment. Yet they also remark that young people show more
concern than their elders, which offers some hope.[38] Indeed,
another sociologist suggests that students' attitudes may be the
most important ones because students did so much to bring
environmental matters to public attention with such affairs as
the Earth Day demonstrations in 1970, because they are less
likely than older and less-educated people to be bound by
tradition, and because they are likely to be the leaders of

[38] Marvin C. Sharma, Joseph E. Kivlin and Frederick C.
Fliegel, "Environmental Pollution: Is There Enough Public
Concern to Lead to Action?" Environment and Behavior, 7 (1975),
467-68.

> Jackson, pp. 260-61   the future, optimism; concl.
>
> "... the concern in Canada and the rest of the world that // marked the late 1960's has left a permanent and substantial legacy. The sheer volume of legislative change during that period, combined with the creation of major departments of government concerned with environmental matters, should alone ensure that the momentum
>
> [OVER]

Observe that the double slash (//) indicates where the quotation went from page 260 to page 261; had the writer carelessly omitted that mark when taking the note, she would have had to make a trip to the library to find out from the source—if it was still available—on just which page or pages was the part she wanted to use. And note the important OVER to remind her of the few further words on the back of the card. Note that she lifted the phrase "the late 1960's" from earlier in the passage and substituted it—in square brackets to indicate her editorial tampering with the original—for the otherwise obscure "that period" in the part quoted. Note also that whereas the preceding paragraph ended effectively with a brief quotation, the writer here, knowing that long quotations make poor paragraph endings, managed to follow it with an expressive brief comment to end the paragraph effectively. Identifying Loney as a municipal planner and Jackson as working in a relevant federal ministry is good tactics, for it lends weight to their statements. (See paragraph 7.)

Footnote 41: Jackson has been referred to before, but the writer wanted to add the brief comment, and felt it would be silly to have both a parenthetical reference and a discursive footnote at the same point (although some writers do combine the two, putting the footnote number after the parentheses).

tomorrow. He concludes from his survey that students are
"decidedly pro-environmental" and that we need "to make the
transition from a negative attitude to a positive one" in order
to "actuate the widespread environmental concern that exists
today."[39] T. W. Loney, a municipal planner, sees some hope:

> Public opinion . . . does change, and . . . cultural
> patterns today seem to be undergoing changes at an
> ever-accelerating rate. . . . if the causes and
> effects of pollution can be objectively measured
> and put before the people, they may be willing to
> support a much greater degree of control over, and
> investment in, the environment than is now generally
> accepted.[40]

And C. I. Jackson, of the Ministry of State for Urban Affairs,
in Ottawa, is also guardedly optimistic:

> there seem to be adequate grounds for believing that
> Canadians, and their legislators and administrators,
> recognize the importance of environmental concerns
> and are prepared to give them adequate attention.
> . . . .
> The sheer volume of legislative change during [the
> late 1960's], combined with the creation of major
> departments of government concerned with environmental
> matters, should alone ensure that the momentum is
> maintained.[41]

Let us hope that this optimism is justified.

[39] Bowman, pp. 386-87, 393, 409.

[40] "Pollution and Planning in Victoria, B. C.," in
Maunder, ed., _Pollution_, p. 86.

[41] Pp. 245, 261. Jackson insists that he is expressing
his own views, not necessarily those of the government.

74

Paragraph 22: Notice how this finishing paragraph grows smoothly out of the point about changing people's attitudes that has recurred during the last half of the essay, especially toward the end. It therefore manages to sound not only like a conclusion but also like a logical substantive continuation of what has gone before.

Footnote 42: A quotation at second hand. Compare the handling of the additional comment here and in footnote 37 with the much weaker handling of a similar instance in footnote 29.

Footnote 44: Although this documents the same source as footnote 43, the two cannot be consolidated, because 44 must refer to Peterman citing Commoner, not to Peterman alone. For the same reason, although this is the only place in the essay where two successive references are to the same source, neither could one use an *ibid.* in footnote 44. Peterman gives no source other than Commoner's name; the writer therefore could not provide further information, since Commoner's books were out of the library.

17

22

Man as a whole is responsible for what has happened and is happening to our environment, and man as a whole must continue and increase his efforts if the damage is to be repaired, the environment--and ourselves--saved. As one student put it, "The basic key to helping the environment is to change people's attitudes."[42] If we can accept the philosophical fact that we are a part of nature, not separate from it; if we can bring ourselves to believe in "organism" rather than "dualism," we will not irreparably destroy our environment but rather use it intelligently.[43] "Everything," as Barry Commoner's "first law of ecology" puts it, "is connected to everything else."[44] People as individuals, as builders and users of industry, and as electors and members of governments, must work together in honouring this natural interdependence.

[42] Quoted by Bowman, p. 406. Many make this point: see for example I. Burton, "The Quality of the Environment," in Vegetation, Soils and Wildlife, ed. J. G. Nelson and M. J. Chambers (Toronto: Methuen, 1969), p. 360.

[43] William A. Peterman, "Nature: A Democracy of Trees," Environment, 18, No. 7 (Sept. 1976), 41.

[44] Cited by Peterman, p. 40.

The page on which a new section begins need not be numbered, but it can, as here, be numbered at bottom centre. The label "Works Cited" is usually preferable to the less precise "Bibliography." Note that a page beginning a new section has a wider margin at the top.

In bibliographical entries, as in footnotes, only one space follows a colon, whatever a writer's practice may be elsewhere. But note that the standard two spaces follow each period. Some people prefer to underline only the separate words of a title, claiming that one cannot italicize a space; to others this seems unnecessarily meticulous and choppy looking, and they feel, as well, that a continuous underlining gives a better graphic representation of the wholeness of a title.

Note that entries for articles in periodicals give inclusive page numbers—and inclusive column numbers for the newspaper article in the eighth entry. The page numbers in the third entry indicate that Calef's article concluded on a page that was not in consecutive sequence with its first pages, a common practice in some magazines.

The fourth entry is alphabetized according to "Canadian," the first significant word; the definite article "The" is ignored for the purposes of alphabetizing. The sixth item, an anonymous article in an encyclopedia, is alphabetized according to its title.

Although the third and tenth items are both from the same issue of the same journal, the complete data for that issue must be included in each entry.

The thirteenth entry, the last on the page, lists Maunder's edited book as a source; the individual essays from it—by Edgell, Loney, and Maunder himself—are not listed, since there are as many as three of them. *Maunder* is alphabetized before *McBoyle* (see next page), although some people, using the system adopted by telephone books, would put all *Mc*'s and *Mac*'s ahead of other names beginning with *M*.

Works Cited

Bowman, James S. "Public Opinion and the Environment: Post-Earth Day Attitudes Among College Students." *Environment and Behavior*, 9 (1977), 385-416.

Burton, I. "The Quality of the Environment." In *Vegetation, Soils and Wildlife*. Ed. J. G. Nelson and M. J. Chambers. Toronto: Methuen, 1969, pp. 347-60.

Calef, Charles E. "Not Out of the Woods." *Environment*, 18, No. 7 (Sept. 1976), 17-20, 25.

The Canadian Institute of Public Opinion. *The Gallup Poll of Canada*. 1970, 1975.

Dunbar, M. J. *Environment and Good Sense: An Introduction to Environmental Damage and Control in Canada*. Montreal: McGill-Queen's Univ. Press, 1971.

"Environmentalism." *The New Columbia Encyclopedia*. 1975.

Ferguson, Cherry. *Efforts by the Citizen, Labatt Breweries, and Government to Achieve Environmental Quality in B. C.* [Vancouver]: Labatt Breweries, 1971.

Harcourt, Michael. "Where to Start Saving Energy." *Vancouver Sun*, 25 Nov. 1977, p. A6, cols. 1-6.

Hohenberger, Dieter. "Is Fusion the Answer? It Wouldn't Hurt to Ask." *Maclean's*, 3 April 1978, p. 70.

Hohenemser, Kurt H. "Energy: Waste Not, Want Not." *Environment*, 18, No. 7 (Sept. 1976), 3-5.

Johnson, Diane. "Ah, Wilderness!" Rev. of *The Last Cowboy*, by Jane Kramer, and *Coming into the Country*, by John McPhee. *New York Review of Books*, 23 March 1978, pp. 3-6.

Koenig, Daniel J. "Additional Research on Environmental Activism." *Environment and Behavior*, 7 (1975), 472-85.

Maunder, W. J., ed. *Pollution: What It Is...What It Does... What Can Be Done About It*. Victoria: Evening Division, Univ. of Victoria, 1969.

18

The first item on this page has two editors. Note that only the first editor's name is reversed, surname first, for the purpose of alphabetizing; the second name is written in normal order. As in the preceding entry, since as many as three articles from this book were cited (those by Jackson, Kitchen, and Theberge), the book itself is listed as a source and the individual articles are not.

In the second entry, the name of the editor of the series is included; it was not necessary in the footnote (number 4). It is unnecessary to record that Morgan's book includes an introduction by Forrester; had the introduction been by someone else, however—neither author nor editor, neither Morgan nor Forrester—his name would have had to be included, along with *Introd.* or *Introd. by.*

In the fifth entry on this page, note again that only the first of the three authors' names is reversed; the other two are written in normal order.

In the sixth entry, the fact that the "Ottawa official" is Jacqueline Cernot is not included; it was, however, necessary in the footnote (number 36) since Wielaard was quoting her. The column number or numbers for a newspaper article are not essential, though they are often included as a courtesy to the reader; the writer neglected to make a note of them for this article and so could not include the information here.

The final entry, though listing an item the writer never saw, must be included since she did directly cite its title. A work cited at second hand, such as Barry Commoner's in footnote 11, should not be included in a bibliography. The footnote (number 2) did not have to include the subtitle of Levine's book, but the bibliographical entry must.

Ms note: Like footnotes (or notes collected at the end of an essay), bibliographical entries are often single-spaced, as here, with double spaces between them. If you or your instructor wish, however, they can be double-spaced throughout.

19

McBoyle, G. R., and E. Sommerville, eds. _Canada's Natural Environment: Essays in Applied Geography_. Toronto: Methuen, 1976.

Morgan, Frank. _Pollution: Canada's Critical Challenge_. Shaping Canada's Environment, No. 4 Ed. James Forrester. Toronto: Ryerson, Maclean-Hunter, 1970.

Novick, Sheldon. "Spectrum." _Environment_, 18, No. 7 (Sept. 1976), 21-24.

Peterman, William A. "Nature: A Democracy of Trees." _Environment_, 18, No. 7 (Sept. 1976), 38-41.

Sharma, Marvin C., Joseph E. Kivlin, and Frederick C. Fliegel. "Environmental Pollution: Is There Enough Public Concern to Lead to Action?" _Environment and Behavior_, 7 (1975), 455-71.

Wielaard, Robert. "News Media Augment Ignorance of Ecology, Ottawa Official Says." _Winnipeg Free Press_, 1 Dec. 1977, p. 6.

Winham, G. "Attitudes on Pollution and Growth in Hamilton, or 'There's an Awful Lot of Talk These Days About Ecology.'" _Canadian Journal of Political Science_, 5 (1972), 389-401.

Young, T. Cuyler. "Pollution Begins in Prehistory: The Problem Is People." In _Man in Nature: Historical Perspectives on Man in His Environment_. Ed. Louis D. Levine. Toronto: Royal Ontario Museum, 1975, pp. 9-26.

PART FIVE
Sample Essays, Correction Symbols, and Omnibus Checklist

Chapter X Sample Student Essays with Comments and Grades

The sample essays which follow are actual essays written by students. Some were written in response to specific assignments; others were on freely chosen topics under some such general instruction as "Write a description" or "Write an argument." The essays vary in length, kind, and quality. The marginal comments may differ from those that other instructors would make, but we believe that they are generally accurate and fair. Similarly, the grades we have assigned may not be exactly what others would have given, but we think that they are reasonably accurate and that most instructors would agree with them. Since grading methods vary from institution to institution, here is a chart to show how our letter grades would translate into other systems:

A	I	80-100%	Very Good to Excellent
B	II	65-79%	Fairly Good to Good
C	Pass	50-64%	Passably Weak to Fair
D	Fail	40-49%	Poor to Unsatisfactorily Weak
F		0-39%	Very Poor

Some comments on the individual essays:
The first five essays were written in response to the same assignment and represent a range of quality. Essay 4, which we have failed with a D, could be considered a borderline case; for example, had it been written early in the academic year, it might have been awarded a C-. Similarly, essay number 1, had it been written late in the year, could be considered worth only an A-. Essay 5 is counted a very poor

failure largely because of its style and mechanics; an instructor who wished to emphasize this might—especially if it were early in the year—decide to give it a "split" grade, such as C+/F, the C+ indicating the quality of content and the presumed promise of the writer, the F indicating the very careless performance. If the student in question improved in subsequent papers, the F component of the early grade could be effectively ignored in reckoning a final grade. Essay 6 is a brief description. Essay 7 might be considered borderline between A– and B+, but if one objectively gauges the actual performance rather than the strong potential demonstrated by the writer, the lower grade is accurate. Number 8, an essay in definition, is graded C, but a case could be made for giving it a C+, depending on variables such as the time of year and the student's past performance. Number 9, on the other hand, another attempt at definition, contains almost nothing to redeem its badness. Essay 10 is a straightforward and well-handled argument. Number 11 is also an argument, but of a special kind: it was written in response to a request for an argument using irony in the manner of Jonathan Swift's "A Modest Proposal." Since the student chose to commit deliberate errors as a part of the characterization of the speaker, those errors had to be labelled in the margin so that they would not be blamed on the student himself. Essays 12 through 15, unmarked and ungraded, are included for the purposes of practice and discussion.

Some teachers, rather than mark virtually all the errors and weaknesses in an essay, as we have done here, prefer to mark selectively so as not to smother a paper with symbols and comments and thereby possibly unduly discourage a student. Your instructor will inform you if such a method is being used—and if it is, you should make it your added responsibility to try to discover any further errors and weaknesses when an essay is returned to you. If your essay is to be resubmitted, your corrections and revisions of unmarked errors and weaknesses will make it an even better product, and will also impress your instructor.

(Essays 6, 10, and 13 were written by second- and third-year university students for a course in advanced composition; the rest were written by freshmen.)

Sample Essay No. 1

The Days of the Pioneers

Good opening ⁋ The first Canadian was a hardy man from France.
He worked all day for bread. Today's Canadian works
half the day for cake. The pioneers worked to lay
the foundations. We work to add the playroom and
the bar.

The _fermier_ paid very little for his estate.
He built his home without blueprints. His prime
tools were the axe, the saw, and the hammer. When
the house was ready, he did not sit in his den and
read his newspaper. He had to clear the land so
he could <u>eat and feed his children.</u> *ambig. Rephrase to avoid cannibalism!*

He got up at four in the morning, when it was
pitch black outside. No streetlights lit his
pathway to the out-buildings where his animals
were. He worked for three hours until breakfast.
His breakfast was not habit, but necessity. He ate
oatmeal, pancakes, and bacon, and drank coffee with
thick cream. His daily routine varied with the
season, not the time of the fiscal year. In spring, *p. necessary?*
he cleared the land, then plowed and planted. He
helped his animals have their young. In summer he
p. necessary? cleared more land, and cultivated his crops. In
autumn he harvested. Winter brought some resting
time, but the _fermier_ still had many chores to do.

The man and his wife worked as a team on the

---

farm. Togetherness came naturally. They did not
have to strive for it. The children came, for
family planning was unheard of. They were made a
part of the working unit. They cleaned the chicken
coop, hoed the garden, and watched the inevitable
baby. The family was united, for they needed each
other. The nearest neighbor was often miles away.

co-ord.

Use ;

agr, shift

preferred sp

Family loyalty was only one of the fermier's
loyalties. He was a lover of his land, working
with it until he died. He remembered his mother
country, holding dear her language and customs. He
was loyal to his Church, loving the priest and
attending the masses.

Good
// sr

This man, this pioneer, experienced days of
discouragement, days when his crops failed, days
when his children died. He experienced days of
hardship, when the elements raged. But he had a
goal, a purpose, which was immediate and urgent.
He earned his bread. The Canadian of today does
not have this immediate goal, and his cake is
sometimes tasteless.

Good
// sr

A

Your simple expression and crisp utterance,
varied when the need arises to prevent choppiness,
give this essay clarity, elegance, and charm. Very
well done indeed. Familiarize yourself with the
meaning of the semi-colon; its use here would have
added just that extra bit of finesse. Some of the
paragraphs are suspiciously short, but each has unity
and is sufficiently developed. Very nice opening and
closing image.

Sample Essay No. 2

The Days of the Pioneers

As I read through well-thumbed history books about the great North American pioneers of a century ago, I often disregard the important names, dates ~comma?~ and places which must be memorized, and I ⊙read ~unnecessary Q~ between the lines⑤ trying to imagine what the ~art. necessary?~ ordinary, day-to-day life was like in those times. I think it could be favorably compared to our ~sp.~ ~weak. d. here~ present-day life, where we often become so involved in the mad rush of living that we miss the real meaning, the essence of life.

In pioneer days life was simple. The one goal everyone was working for was survival, so all ~w. w? toward?~ activities were directed towards the achievement ~inf. coord. conj. Try co-ordinating with a semi-colon.~ of that goal. From the pre-dawn waking hours until the last chores were finished at night; the work was tedious and physically exhausting. But the pioneer knew that it had to be done in order for his family to survive. As all activities were ~d. (us)~ simple and elemental, the pioneer was not afflicted ~w. comb? id.~ by insomnia, ulcers, or migraine. These ailments ~logic? Can you be sure?~ are derived from the constant worry about success or failure, so were not familiar to the pioneer. ~awk.~ To him, life was reduced to its most simplest form: ~gr. Check inflection for degree.~ ~lc~ Success meant survival; failure, extinction.

As the pioneer worked hard, so too he played, ate, and slept with simple enthusiasm. The secondary activities of eating and sleeping were considered as necessary parts of the plan of survival. The pioneer reasoned that food and sleep were necessities if he was to be able to continue working in order to survive. According to that belief the foods were simple, filling, and nourishing. Gourmet dishes were unknown in those days and everyone's health probably profitted from this ignorance. Pleasures were simple and few in the days of the pioneers, but they were always enjoyed enthusiastically. The industrious pioneer usually tied pleasure in with work, and such things as barn-raisings and quilting-bees were made into social events.

The life of the pioneers was hard and exhausting, but, ultimately, it was more satisfying and rewarding than our present life.

illog. //

unnec. word

log — is this really a matter for the mind?

ref.

sp.

red?

Perhaps, but hardly proven. Rather too sweeping for an effective ending.

B

Stylistically good, but your "most simplest" is "the most unkindest cut of all". Apart from that and the odd slip in idiom and diction, this is well executed. Consider the logic, however, at the places marked. The third paragraph contains some confusion and implicit contradiction. There is a tendency to wordiness throughout. As for substance, there is very little implicit comparison here of the kind the assignment asked for. Trying to do all the comparing in the last sentence of the first paragraph, and of the paper, doesn't work well.

Sample Essay No. 3

The Days of the Pioneers

If the North American people of today were to suddenly go back in time, to the days of the pioneers, they would find life very hard to endure. The pioneers did not have all the modern conveniences of today. They travelled in covered wagons, had to hunt for their food, and slept outdoors with only a canvas roof over their heads.

They were constantly travelling. Because of this they led very insecure and uncertain lives. Education was limited because there were no schools, and the children, at an early age were expected to assist in the daily chores. Survival depended on each person in the family doing his utmost in whatever job he was expected to do.

They led very simple lives. There were no motion pictures they could go to for entertainment, no laundromats to take the clothes to when there were too many clothes to be washed at home, no restaurants to go to when mother was too tired to cook dinner. Because they had no electricity, everything was done by manual labor. Since they worked so hard and because there were no beauty parlors, make-up, or face cream, the women grew haggard at an early age. The men also aged quickly because of

Handwritten marginal annotations:
- p. unnecessary
- w
- log? only some?
- W. red
- really?
- weak ref.
- dev.; cl?
- vague; log. of d?
- p
- id.
- ref. remote
- rep. w.
- f. p. //
- log?
- pas sp
- misleading //
- log

vague   the worries and hardships of life. The family   *coh*

worked together as a closely knit unit. The children

cl?   had no <u>outside</u> activities <u>outside</u> of the family,   *awk. rep.*

ref.   <u>which</u> kept them from seeing each other for days at

a time. <u>Because of this closeness</u>, there was no   *coh, log –*

sp. × log. awk.   juvenile deliquency or teen-age crime which is so   *you've just*

ref.   rampant today.   *said they didn't*

see each other

The pioneer's sole worry was survival. He did   *for days*

climactic   not have to even think of such things as the atomic   *at a time!*

order?   bomb, politics and frustrations at the office. His   *p, ambig*

id?   time was <u>occupied by</u> protecting himself and his family

from Indians and wild animals, and providing enough

p, awk   // food to eat, and enough fuel to keep them warm.

(If) a person of today were to go back in time   *awk –log*

to the days of the pioneers, (one) wonders (if), in spite   *ss*

of the hardships, the simplicity of pioneer life

× ∧   would make him basically happier person than he is

in the modern world.

— Why end on so vague a note? Why not discuss
this and provide a positive conclusion?

C   *Although you are reasonably careful with mechanics, and*
although you do bring in some contrasts, you fail to provide
the vivid detail and close development that could make
your commentary interesting. Is "face cream" and the like
really worth bringing in? You do demonstrate some sense
of form, but your handling of "facts" is often awkward
and incorrect. There is also a strong flavour of cliché
about much of the thinking and writing (e.g. "at an
early age" applied to both children and women becomes a
meaningless phrase). The ending is very weak. Illogicality
and poor coherence plague this paper throughout. Be careful
with loose reference of words like "this" and "which."

Sample Essay No. 4.

Reaching Maturity~~O~~ *No period*

The early pioneers were a hardy breed of people. They had to be in order to survive the harsh and dangerous life they lived. Their lot was not made easy by modern technology. They didn't have urban redevlopments and traffic control signals. Indeed, in those times there was little traffic, and very few roads for it to use anyway.

Would these have made their lives easier?
X sp

log? Is this an attempt at humor?

w
More than what?
Incomplete comparisons

Life was more a calculated gamble. There was more danger in the pioneer's life. There were no police forces and men were more reliant on there own strength, rather than on the strength of a society, for their survival.

sp !

What do these mean?
do these necessarily, "sully" life "one word"
p.
rephrase to make || with preceding sent. d? p

Sophistication and complex life had not yet evolved. Life was of a simple nature unsullied by modern mass production, eye shadow, freeways, continental suits, and split-level housing. We today can not understand the appreciation of these people of the past, of a log cabin; crude unpainted, warm and secure. We would not appreciate a heavy homespun shirt to keep a body warm.

log? where? w, p. d.

The "of" phrases make awk. ||
p.v.

The deep thick evergreen tree and sentinal mountain peak were the dominant features of a man's environment. He lived more with nature and did not depend on a bloodless machine in a grey smoke-vomiting factory for his existence. He was

sp
what if he were home-steading in Saskatchewan?

Try for more
vigour, conc.

Comb?

air he breathed?

independent of the production line. The sky above
d. - fouled? polluted
the pioneer was not <u>grey</u> with <u>an</u> oppressive industrial *& an*
waste. It was clear. A man produced his crops or
cut his timber for his own profit and for his own

Is this what
modern man
does do?

survival. He did not <u>push his buttons</u> from eight *Log. Did*
to five for E. P. Taylor's pocketbook. *he have*
buttons?

Is this specific
comment
appropriate here?

The pioneer days were times of <u>innocent infancy</u> *awk. id?*
<u>of our civilization</u>. Life's simplicity and man's *Is this true*
?
independence and self-reliance were <u>the characteristics</u> *Too*
of our nation's childhood. *exclusive.*
Surely there were
other characteristics?

D   Your style here is unimpressive. Except for
a few specific details, your essay has a "dead"
feeling about it. You should try to find more
effective ways to express your ideas. The points
you raise are pertinent and could have been
useful to you if you had developed them
more fully with concrete detail and if you
had expressed them in a more vigorous style.
Watch idiom and wordiness. The incomplete
comparisons, though implicitly clear, are nonetheless
awkward as expressed. Weak logic and diction also
damage the effect. The introduction and conclu-
sion are both very poor. You have a reasonably
good grasp of sentence structure, but in other respects
your execution is very uneven.

Sample Essay No. 5

THE DAYS OF THE PIONEER FARMER — *MS: not all caps*

lc - passim   The Pioneers in Alberta led an exciting and adventurous farming life as compared to the quiet

log - are farmers not domesticated"?   domesticated life the people lead now. Inconveniences of farmers in Pioneer days seems unsurmountable *agr* / *sp* to us with all our conveniences. *d ?*

weak, red   ←   Although there are many aspects of this life, *ref? ambig.*

weak d, id   the farming life has the most vivid impression on

"makes"?   my imagination.

awk, dm   Starting in the spring when the crops must be / *al*

PV shift   sowed, the farmer did not sit on a tractor an pull *×* a seeder over his land; he hitched eight or twelve horses to a seeder and walked every stretch of land, *id? means?*

d, us   as the horses did. As time was a precious period in *no meaning.*

p   seeding, he worked from dawn to dusk; unlike the *Say what you*

sp - passim   present-day farmer. The work went slowly; the *mean.* present day farmer can accomplish five times what *only?* *cl* the Pioneer farmer accomplished. In the mid-day, *in the same*

break the Pioneer had his dinner, but before he was *time?*

verb form?   eating he had to first go through the ritual of *split* *ww?*

Are you sure?   unhitching, watering and feeding his eight horses. *P* *×* After his meal the horses must be re-hitched, and *PV shift,* the slow work continued. Present day farmers come *t*

d?   in with the tractor, give it gas and grease, and in

agr   no time at all he is returned back to the field. *ut form;*

Once the Pioneer had his seeding completed he had *red*

Do present-day farmers do differently?

ambig ref

ref

to wait till summer, while nature provided for his *weak d*

crops. If locusts should strike or choking weed *plural?*

invade his fields he would be helpless in defending

them. It was not a matter of spraying his fields

to insure its results. A dry year would mean a poor

yield; there was no irrigation to guarantee a

successful crop. If his crop survived the trials *ambig.*

of nature, he had a harvest in August.

// wo

also

x

this? coh?

August not only meant the harvest of his crop

but a spell of long hot days, if the weather agreed. *with what?*

Now by had he cut his crop, and with his hands he

bound the sheaves. A job which would take the Pioneer *t?*

farmer from August to mid-October, takes the present *p*

farmer four to six weeks.

Why not simply "with nature"? Are modern farmers exempt from such "natural" problems?

x

Not only did the Pioneer farmer have to cope *d*

with Nature's trial but also there was a constant *p*

menace of the Indians; a ridiculous thought of the *id meaning badly garbled. Say what you mean*

farmer of today. He had to protect his crops from

fire set by the Indians or even protect himself from

harm. At nights it was maybe a matter of hustling

to the fort for protection within the high walls; *p*

where as todays farmer relaxes in front of a tele- *sp (apos)*

vision set. It could be that todays farmer has the *sp (apos)*

conveniences but he certainly does not have the *p*

sp excitment and adventure of the Pioneer.

F I'm afraid this is entirely inadequate. You must carefully review the conventions of punctuation and the elements of English syntax; you must also make some attempt to master English idiom. Consider your sentences before you write. Spelling errors and other errors resulting from carelessness must be avoided. When you are writing you should also be thinking. Many of your details are good ones potentially, but so badly handled that this essay must fail.

Sample Essay No. 6

My Special Place

Not far away is a special place I visit when
I want to feel quiet. From my park bench overlooking
the harbour, I see the flickering layout of North
Vancouver stretching from the cluster of lights on
the Grouse Nest to the reflections in the water.
Tug lights silently slip up the inlet and under the
span of lights known as Second Narrows Bridge. In
front of me, loading cranes stretch starward like
man-made redwood trees.

In this context sound patterns like alliteration are good. ✓

Distantly, an engine grumbles as it pulls a line
of boxcars. Near me, a cat rustles through tangled
berry bushes. From behind, I hear the inconsistent
sound of leaves leaving their branches, sidestepping
down to the grass. Footsteps quicken on the sidewalk
as a dog erratically protests against a trespasser.

good // sentence rhythm

Intentional, I hope; effective.

nice fig

As I watch and listen, a cool mask of rain
lightly covers my face. This, and the cold, hard
bench slats persuade me to leave my special place.

good ref back to #1 (sight) and #2 (sound).

P

Excellent patterning throughout Details well organized in each paragraph.

A

This mistaken comma almost ruins the otherwise excellent effect you've created. Without that slip, this descriptive piece would have been virtually perfect.

Sample Essay No. 7

What _am_ I _doing_ _here_?   *MS - caps*

Years ago, two men were helping to build a cathedral.
A passerby stopped and asked: "What are you doing here?"
"I am just laying bricks," the first man grumbled. The
second replied, "I am building a monument to God's glory."

Unnecessarily drab, jargon-like. In the present situation, the student is like the two
workers. When he asks himself the question, "What am I

P ↵ doing here?", he may reply in one of two ways. His *an unnecessarily vague sentence*
answer depends on the range of his view of life. *and unfortunately the next ¶ ex-*

Probably better not to start a new ¶ here. The student may be "Just laying bricks." Plodding *pounds on*
through work without any connective thought or unifying *the vagueness*
goal, he has only a short view of his efforts. He finds as *rather than*
little satisfaction as the first worker, labouring without *on some-*
plan or point at an aimless, backbreaking task. On the *thing*
other hand, the student may be building a memorial. He sees *specific.*
a point to his work beyond the confusion of courses, ex- *It lacks*

P_comma would help. periences and years. The student is laying a foundation *concrete-*
for his life. Looking beyond the immediate job, he is able *ness.*
to see a goal, to recognize a purpose to his work.

The answer to "What am I doing here?" holds the key to
satisfying living. If the student, indeed any person, *Two differ-*
recognizes his own end, he will not just be laying bricks; *ent and*
he will be building a memorial. He will not merely be *unfortunate*
existing; he will find satisfaction in getting nearer his *connotations*
goal. He will know why he is here. *suggested by*

B+ You have chosen an interesting basis *this phrase*
for your discussion of this question. *besides the*
Well organized, clear; good strong ending. *meaning you*
Marred, however — mainly by that central *intended. "purpose"?*
vagueness.

444   Sample Student Essays

Sample Essay No. 8

Responsible Government

[margin: p. unnecessary] Here, in Canada, we enjoy the benefits of
responsible government. In responsible government
the cabinet, or governing body, is directly
[margin: ambig.] responsible to the elected representatives of the *[margin: in ?]*
legislature, who, in turn, are responsible to their *[margin: p needed ?]*
[margin: plu ?] elector, the people. Through this transfer of
[margin: comp: than what ?] responsibility, a greater control can be exerted *[margin: wo ambig.]*
on the machinery of government by the populace.

In this country, we become more aware of the
workings of responsible government when a minority
government is in power. The term "minority govern-
[margin: p] ment," means that the combined votes of the opposi- *[margin: cast by or for them ? ambig.]*
tion parties exceed the number of votes of the party
in power. Then, if the legislature does not agree
[margin: caps] with the cabinet and it is defeated, the prime *[margin: ambig. ref.]*
minister is required to submit the question in
dispute to the people; that is, call a general *[margin: ss "he must"]*
[margin: ref. vague at best. Weak ¶ conclusion.] election. This clearly shows how the prime minister *[margin: caps]*
and his cabinet are directly responsible to the
legislature.

There are many benefits of this system of
government. We, as citizens of Canada, are assured
of our control over the affairs of our country. No
[margin: w.w. ?] leader can become authoritarian or radical because *[margin: log p]*
[margin: are these words necessarily antithetical ?]

guaranteed?
Never self-
serving?

he is always answerable for his actions. <u>Therefore</u>,   *P log.*

the governing body, the cabinet, <u>always</u> has the good
interests of the people in mind when planning and
executing governmental business. <u>They</u>, <u>themselves</u>,   *p unnecessary*

Ms ⌒   were elected by the people ⌒--⌒ not appointed as the
cabinet is in the United States where the government
Ms ⌒   is only representative, not responsib<u>le</u> -- and so
must be directly concerned for the welfare of the
people.

P   We have seen<u>,</u> how, in responsible government,   *stiff*
conclusion
the great mass of people exert power over the chosen
ones who govern them and how these few, <u>in turn</u> <u>are</u>   *P- 2 commas*
or none.
responsible to them. In this system democracy <u>is</u>   *weak*
<u>in</u> its most <u>complete</u> form.

meaning? What of Switzerland? ancient
Athens?

C

*For the most part you form sentences well
and provide variety in structure. As for the
content here, you frequently express your
sentiments rather uncritically, and sometimes
ambiguously. You need to work on your
punctuation.*

Sample Essay No. 9

The Dignity of Man

The word? or the quality?

*P - ital
(passim)*

no p

Dignity had its origin in a Latin word meaning
worth. Nowadays this meaning is only occasionally
employed. But, if we could step outside this world
and watch men playing out their lives in the passage
of time, we would use the original meaning to
describe the stature of these men.

*"stand back
from"?
not very
clear.*

*ref: all
men? some?
certain?*

d?

sp

"How dignified he looks." The remark is often
passed. Such an unconsequential statement may well
have lead to the modern corruption of the word
dignity. One might apply it to many Greek statues.
One of demosthanes immediately springs to mind.
There is a certain elevated stateliness about it,
which is neither elated nor despondent energetic
nor lethargic. It possess all the loft immovable
qualities of stone itself.

*sp begs
the question
necessarily?*

ref?

*cap; sp
trite*

p

× ×

*Identify it?
d - means?*

*ref - al?
al - can
qualities be
lofty or
immovable?*

One might well ask why its neighbouring statue
is so fat and ugly. True Socrates was an ugly man,
but his ideas and actions have transended time. In
time the great orator Demosthanes is dwarfed by the
great phylosopher. Although I have seen a statue
of Socrates; I must confess I think of him in my
minds eye as a tall slender figure who carries his
majestic head high. Although I think I know the
difference academically, I am conditioned to reflect

*of Socrates?
P
sp
sp*

sp

*the one referred
to above? or
another? all
very confusing.
meaning?*

sp p

on this dignified figure in the modern sense, in the
corrupted sense.

True worth then is what elevates a man in time. *ambig.*
ital.

log { I avoid the word history because the light of human
cl { dignity has shone from many men without it ever
{ being recorded. I think of a relative of mine whose

contribution to other peoples lives has been tremen-
sp (apos)

d dous. To those who know her, in passing she is *p misplaced*
Co-ordinate simply a humble woman. To those who know her well
with a semi-
colon. she is a saint.

Dignity may also be covered over by some querk *sp*
of nature. It was this dignity in Hamlet which *ref.*
caused his dying assailant to call him "noble
Hamlet. *O* *× Q*

log y So the dignity of a man is physically invisable *sp*
fc } and is sometimes perceivable. And we of this earth
Use the
right } are therefore limited because we can only judge what *log not*
conjunction we can see. *fully clear*

F You are not defining the dignity of man. You
deal with only a part of it — a rather abstract
and difficult part — and you do not succeed in clarifying your meaning precisely enough. The number and
nature of mechanical errors in this paper are
appalling: it is no courtesy to your reader to
present him with something so carelessly done as
this. You have a high potential, intellectually,
for excellent work, but you must learn to put your
intellectual children into neater, cleaner, more
appropriate clothes.

Sample Essay No. 10

Handle _With Care_   *could be l. c.*

Consider reversing order?

Patent _medicines_ and _vitamins_ are bought in increasing quantities by people every day. They are placed on open shelves in stores to be bought without prescription by individuals who have little knowledge of what the chemical

awk. wo effects (will be on their bodies) Many of the drugs are potentially harmful; they should be removed from the

p unnecessary shelves, and their sale X more strictly controlled. To be sure, many of the drugs that are so readily available to consumers are helpful in relieving irritating conditions, and are not harmful if administered properly. But people have come to believe that many drugs on the shelves are not harmful at all. Certain medicines have become so commonly used that they are taken as panaceas and administered for any discomfort. The drug universally known under one brand name, "aspirin," is an obvious example. People take one, or two, or several aspirin tablets for headaches, stomach pains, insomnia, nervous and emotional upsets-- the whole range of disturbances--and many parents use aspirin to dose their children at the first sign of hyper-activity! These common cures are not safe when used in excess or when taken without being needed. Medicines are *W -*
drugs, and when used incorrectly, drugs can be poison. *"unnecessarily"*

Of course one might say that the government cannot be expected to pass regulations protecting people from them-

Comb? // ? , *that*

selves. Individuals are expected to exercise their own
intelligence when using drugs. However, this reasoning *better wo?*
assumes that the public is given information that will
help it to act wisely. Unfortunately, that is not so.
Most of the information received by society today is
transmitted through popular media. What the public hears
about patent medicines is conveyed via radio and television
in the form of advertising. Drug companies have launched
extensive campaigns designed to tell people how accessible
✓ drugs are and how little they cost. The advertisements are
little more than popularity contests between brands. To
∿ ? (ok)
the consumer, what is the value of a film clip showing a
famous actor loading a shopping cart with fancy packages
picked off a shelf in a drug store? It is all very well
P to be told that in a conveniently located store, the prices
are always "right," but that says nothing about the drugs.
The message is to buy.

Of course, some may say that instructions about dosage
are on the package of every medicine. Moreover, individual
drug companies often warn the public about misuse of their
products. But in an advertisement, the warning against
the detrimental effects of the drug is cleverly disguised.
For example, there are several medicines on sale that are
too strong for children's use. When one company says
(boasts) that its product is "not even recommended for
children," the message somehow gets mixed up. Adults are
made to feel that they are part of an exclusive class of

3

people who can, and therefore should, rush out and buy the
product. No one would rationally accept this line of
reasoning, but this kind of advertising appeals to the
emotions, and people think what they are made to feel.

Still, one must admit that many of these products are
helpful in controlling ailments or in maintaining proper
health, and that more stringent control of sales would

ambig ref cause prices to rise. This may be so, but after all,
medicines are used by many people who do not need them.
If these drugs--including vitamins--were less available
or cost more, people would find alternative, more natural
ways of maintaining good health. For instance, exercise

✓ can cure many ailments as quickly as aspirin; and regular *good P.*
exercise is a better preventive medicine than regular *for emph.*
doses of patented, bottled cure-alls. Moreover, many
people would soon discover that the body functions very
well on a proper diet without daily vitamin supplements.
Indeed, the body is designed to assimilate what it needs
from good food. In this age of technology, people are
beginning to forget that the human race survived for
generations before nourishment was compressed into little
capsules, and the entire daily requirement swallowed with
a drink of water in one gulp.

I will concede that there are individuals who do need
to use these drugs or vitamins regularly, and other people
who need to use them occasionally. Nevertheless, there is
no good reason for the excessive use of medicine found in

4

today's society. People have mistakenly concluded that
if a drug can make one "better" when he is sick, then by
the same principle, that drug will improve his condition

| P ?

when he is not sick. ∧ What could possibly be "better"

"But" for
clearer
coh and
emph.

than good health? Overdosing oneself with medicine is
not the way to find out. In fact, excessive ~~drug use~~   "use of drugs"
will surely cause more harm than good. Drug companies
have had ample time to warn the public about the need to
take care when using their products. More stringent
methods are obviously required.

*A   Good, clear, sharp presentation throughout.
a few weak or awkward spots will bear
attention. The overall argumentative structure
is good, with pros and cons appropriately
balanced, but in a couple of spots it's
a little stiff; the machinery clanks a
bit. When you revise this for resubmission,
see if you can smooth the jumps a
little.
        You might have saved a stronger
point to use as your final one, and
you might have offered a more specific
recommendation. Nevertheless, the conclusion
is effective.*

Sample Essay No. 11

Guaranteed Satisfaction

In the past two years, violence in hockey has become a major concern of thousands of sports fans in North America. Myself being a sports fan, I too have witnessed the disgusting changes which have taken place in the professional and junior hockey ranks. I have spent hours deliberating over this problem and am happy to announce a sure-fire solution.

This solution will benefit all parties involved. It will definitely pick up the attendance at every game. We all know how quickly it has been falling lately, and surprisingly in a few cities which, until two years ago, always had sell out crowds. *[sp (hyphen)]* This increase in attendance will certainly put more money into the owners' bank accounts and consequently more money into the players' *[Consider the less awkward order: "the wallets of our favourite players..." because of the following appositive.]* *[frag ✗]* wallets. Especially in our favourite players' wallets, the "goons," who are grossly underpaid while providing the fans with most of the entertainment. Sales in the concessions and the souvenir booths at the rink are bound to go up. The possibilities are endless. I cannot see any *[P + awk ref. try: "my proposal, a proposal which..."]* *[MS]* loopholes in my proposal which could, if properly carried out, turn hockey into the booming business it once was, but this time on a scale at least three times as large.

First off, we must rid ourselves of some unnamed *[sp (passim)]* polititians across the nation, who have spoiled the game *[P?]*

sp by charging some of the league's best players with such
<u>attrocities</u> as creating a public disturbance, brutality,
assault with a lethal weapon (hockey sticks), and even
manslaughter. After being pressed with such charges, these
players, and the teams they play for, have to think twice
before they touch, let alone slug, punch, <u>kick and beat up</u>
a player on the opposite side. Thus the quality of the
game is destroyed. Who wants to watch a team <u>which</u> is
afraid to fight? I'm sure that with a bit of pushing and
kicking in the right places we could easily rid ourselves
of these cruel <u>polititians</u> who are out to destroy our fun.

P — *that would be better*

Secondly, after the <u>polititians</u> are out of the way, we
must solve the problem of the players who will not fight.
Many players, whom I cannot blame, are still <u>leary</u> of fight- *sp?*
ing after two years of government suppression. It is hard
to get back in the swing of things (arms, sticks, legs, etc.)
after two years of idleness. But I'm sure the owners will
id not put up much of a fight to the second part of my proposal.

The players would surely start fighting again if there
was a little cash up for grabs. If a cash bonus <u>was</u> awarded *subjunctive?*
sp to players who were <u>profficient</u> in acts of violence or even
slang works well here. for the <u>guys</u> who tried hard to be, we would see plenty of
action at every game. The owners need not worry about losing
P money <u>since</u> the increased attendance would make up for it
three times over. We could easily urge the Hockey Night in
Canada crew to include a weekly series of fights for <u>between</u> *hyphen*
period entertainment. It would be something like hockey

Shouldn't this be "Hockey Showdown"?

P

mm?

showdown but with the toughest guys in the league. A
trophy could be included in the year end hockey awards, *sp (hyphen)*
for toughest player in the league. We could call it the
Goon Trophy or the Entertainer Award. They both amount ✓
to the same thing.

I am sure that everyone will agree that this proposal *hyphen*
can do nothing but improve our present-day hockey. Our own
ww little hockey players will finally have idols which deserve

Good! The "which" works nicely. respect. It will also open up many new jobs. There will
be a need for many new doctors and dentists (and they will
do good business), since there will always be a few players
on any team who are not quite tough enough. Our labourers
will get their chance by building many new hospitals. We
could call them Hockey Hospitals. Bookies could make a
killing, taking thousands of bets on some bloody good fights. ✓
Of course sponsors for the televised games could get a big

✓ *gr*
nice touch chunk of extra business. Like I said before, the list
goes on and on.

id I do not wish any credit endowed upon me for this
modest proposal. A few of my friends forced me to write
it. I am in the toothpaste business anyway and I don't
stand to make any money from this. My friends guarantee
your satisfaction, though.

B+ These friends are other sports fans who are only
satisfied by brutality.

Good details, good intentional stylistic error to help characterize the speaker; the slang and other "defects" work well too. But your misspellings and other errors betray you, I fear. It's too bad so many careless little errors mar this otherwise nice piece. The final sentence strikes me as anti-climactic, and might better have been omitted. Watch your spelling much more carefully. Learn about hyphens.

Sample Essay No. 12

Sonnet LXV, by William Shakespeare

Since brass, nor stone, nor earth, nor boundless sea,
But sad mortality o'ersways their power,
How with this rage shall beauty hold a plea,
Whose action is no stronger than a flower?
O! how shall summer's honey breath hold out
Against the wrackful siege of battering days,
When rocks impregnable are not so stout,
Nor gates of steel so strong, but Time decays?
O fearful meditation! where, alack,
Shall Time's best jewel from Time's chest be hid?
Or what strong hand can hold his swift foot back?
Or who his spoil of beauty can forbid?
  O! none, unless this miracle have might,
  That in black ink my love may still shine bright.

An Appreciation of Shakespeares' Sonnet 65.

Throughout this sonnet Shakespeare has the villain
as time; active enemy of youth, beauty and love. The
numerous metaphors telling us this are all conveyed by
the desperate voice of one speaker, and it is the
structure of the poem that helps to convey his despair.
He asks many rhetorical questions that get progressively
shorter as the sonnet continues, interjected with exclamations of his despair. The speaker begins three
of his questions with "O" or "Or" which stops us when
we are reading. We read it as an excited cry, which
it is. These crys, and the progressively shorter
sentences, make us more aware of what he is talking
about--time. We see his haste and get a sense of time

being continually over his shoulder--he must hurry to
his conclusion. This helps convey to us the despair
he feels about time's effects upon his love and youth.

The speaker uses mixed metaphors, but all of them
convey the idea that time is an active villain. Time
is the enemy that rages, decays and spoils. We see
time as strong and violent in the form of a battering
ram, and as a powerful rage that can even overpower
the earth and seas. And since Time wins all its battles
it is inevitable that it will eventually capture youth
and love.

Love is depicted as a passive flower whose only
defence against destruction is to stop us in our assault,
still with appreciation of its beauty. The action of
the flower and the action of beauty are one and the
same, they have no defence but to awe us.

Youth is depicted in the speaker's second lament
as being "summer's honey breath." As the critics René
Wellek and Austin Warren explain, this is again an image
of flowers in the summer, their scent being the breath
of their body--the earth. This is a somewhat different
idea but the fragile, transient and beautiful image of
youth is retained, they live as the inhabitant of a
fortress that is being specifically attacked by time.
Again the battle between the two is contrasted to that
between time and stones and steel--which are decayed
by time in spite of being strong and stout.

The speaker's next cry has time as the owner of a precious gem that has gone missing--and the gem is one that time wants back. Here the sense of battle is somewhat changed; youth is no longer seen as the enemy of time, but as the possession of time. Youth is the "spoils" in the battle, the possession over which the battle is waged, not the participant battling over something else. Youth is truly time's "best jewel" and although the speaker despairs at it being taken back he sees it as impossible to stop. This is as it should be, as youth without time is meaningless, and time without youth would be too ugly--and savage, as it is in this sonnet. The speaker's despair at being able to do nothing is given by the image of time striding on even though its foot is being clutched at by the strongest hands.

The couplet at the end begins with the cry of "O" again but immediately becomes quieter, slower and more deliberate. The last line is somewhat paradoxical; we know that the only thing of the bright shiny beauty of youth and love that will endure will be the black print of the poem praising it. Although they can shine brightly by themselves they will be gone, and the only way left for them to shine is through the words of the poem, which of course can not shine brightly, but only convey a small sense of their brilliance.

Sample Essay No. 13

Reflections on a Tourist Poster

Hey, lady! Yes, you--the one smiling up from the smokeless campfire on that poster advertising Canada's great outdoors. Did anyone ever tell you your eyes exactly match the lake water behind you? I guess everybody must, the colour is so remarkable. I never have seen a lake that colour; it's exactly the same aquamarine green that bath salts turn the water in my tub. Still, the fish must like it--I see you have four nice ones lined up in the pan beside your shiny aluminum coffee pot. Who caught those fish, anyway? Certainly not those two immaculate children playing games over on the lake shore; surely not your perfect husband, poised with his foot up on a convenient tree stump. He's too shiny-new! All polished teeth and polished boots, he looks like he just walked out of Eaton's catalogue. I wonder why I always look like I went swimming after the fish I try to catch. Well, it doesn't matter, really. I'll let you get back to your breakfast preparations and your plans for a perfectly marvelous day. I only stopped to ask you: Doesn't it ever rain where you are? Don't the campsites get overcrowded sometimes? Who are you really supposed to be?

Sample Essay No. 14

Wishing for a Dog

I don't own a dog but wish everytime I see one that
I did. My parents have a dog, so you could say, I suppose,
that I do part time. This occasional enjoyment is tanta-
lizing. You have to have owned and been close to a pet
of your own in order to understand.

A pet, especially a dog, has so much to offer by
just being itself. That is, if you are the kind of person
who is able to realize and appreciate this presence of
personality in an animal. Some cannot.

It is the most fabulous feeling to have your pet
greet you at the door and not quite know what to do with
himself because he's happy. A dog never holds back feeling
because of some silly hangup. Neither is he too busy nor
too tired to let you know he's glad your home.

Have you ever had a pet try to comfort you in sorrow?
Somehow they know what is going on, something is wrong.
Again their are no hangups stopping him from licking away
the tears or just staying by you when you need comforting.
These are afew of the reasons why I wish I could have a
fulltime dog of my own.

Sample Essay No. 15

A House But Not a Home

The house where I long ago spent three years of my life seems today, shrouded in a mist of greyness. This structure is not living as it once was; instead its life has gone and only its physical body remains. Spacious yards and wide, tree lined boulevards complement the beauty of its hilltop setting. The underlying beauty has remained until today, yet many subtle changes have occurred. Trees' limbs have grown rounder and the shade of the house's paint has become dull; perhaps caused by the exposure to thousands of hours of rain and fog. Eleven years ago children made a fort in a Mountain Ash tree. On the roof of the backyard garage they had a ship. Today only a stump remains of the tree and the garage silently serves the purpose that it was intended to do.

When the house was young an elderly man came through the community. He neatly painted the address numbers of the street's houses on the curb. When he came to our house he painted in brilliant white the numerals one nine seven five. He accepted only twenty-five cents for the job that he had done so carefully. Recently the numbers were repainted; the old man's work had become barely recognizable.

The house is now a stranger and not a home as it once was. The expanses of cold grey granite foundations and pale green walls are omens of the blank faces of strangers behind its closed doors. The numerous people who through the years have dwelled in the house must never have experienced the attraction to it that I did, eleven years ago.

Chapter XI The Correction Symbols Explained

This chapter provides an alphabetical list of the abbreviations commonly used to mark students' essays, and a short list of proofreader's marks and symbols that are also useful in such marking. Each correction symbol is followed by a brief explanation of its meaning and of the steps necessary to correct the error or weakness it indicates; usually one or more examples of the error are included, along with revisions. Probably no one instructor will use all the correction symbols listed here, and some instructors will use one or more that are not included. We have tried to include all the most common symbols and to provide cross-references for those that have more than one form. Some instructors, for example, will use *fs* (fused sentence) to indicate that egregious error; but since we believe the majority will refer to it as a *run-on* sentence, we have made the latter form the main entry and included *fs* only as a cross-reference. Inside the back cover you will find a complete list of all the symbols with space for the addition of any others you may be informed of.

When you approach a marked paper for the purpose of revision, you will probably consult this chapter first. If the brief explanation you find here does not enable you to correct a specific error, then follow the cross-references provided to the fuller discussions elsewhere in the book. Only a few of the items listed below, such as *awk, nsw,* and *ss,* are not discussed specifically elsewhere in the book.

ab   Undesirable or Incorrect Abbreviation

Generally, you should avoid abbreviations in formal writing. Avoid abbreviations like *e.g., viz., etc.*; use the more formal expressions *for example, namely, and so forth.* Sometimes an abbreviation has become so common that it is almost a substitute for the full words. *B.C.* and *U.S.A.* are obvious examples. We often speak or write of British Columbia as *B.C.* and of Prince Edward Island as *P.E.I.*, but never of Alberta as *Alta.* or of Ontario as *Ont.* Abbreviations like *B.C.* in writing are acceptable (but the name should be spelled in full the first time it appears), whereas *Alta.* and *Ont.* are not. If you are ever in doubt about a particular instance, it is wiser to use the full words rather than the abbreviation; the full word or words will never be inappropriate.

See #46 for more information about abbreviations.

ack   Acknowledgment of Sources

Whenever you include in an essay *information, ideas,* or *wording* that you obtained from any other written source, you must acknowledge your indebtedness to that source in accordance with the conventions of documentation. Even information from lectures and conversations should be acknowledged.

Failure to indicate indebtedness is PLAGIARISM, or literary theft. Students guilty of plagiarism will be subject to severe penalties.

See #71e; see also *doc* (Documentation: Notes and Bibliography).

ad   Adjectives and Adverbs Confused or Misused

The most likely kind of error in this category is the use of either an adjective or an adverb where the other one should appear. For example:

ad: He doesn't present his argument very *good.*

Here the adjective *good* should be replaced by the adverb *well.*

See #9, #10, and good, bad, badly, well in #60.

agr Agreement

1. Agreement between subject and verb:

A finite verb must agree with its subject in number and person.

> agr: The falseness of the paper daffodils *were* to Vera like his words; they were "almost too sweet to bear."

The singular *falseness,* not the plural *daffodils,* is the subject; to agree in number, therefore, the first verb should be *was,* not *were.*

See #7.

2. Agreement between pronouns and their antecedents:

A pronoun must agree in person and number with its antecedent, the word—usually preceding it—to which it refers.

> agr: When the teacher asked for volunteers, nobody in the class raised *their* hand.

The indefinite pronoun *nobody* is singular; to agree with it in number, the pronoun that refers to it must be changed from *their* to *his* (not *his or her* or *his/her*; if necessary, rephrase the sentence: "When the teacher asked for volunteers, not a single hand went up." See *he or she, his or her* in #60).

> agr: If one is to write a good report, *you* must take careful notes.

The subject pronoun *one* is third person; to agree with it in person, the second-person *you* must be changed to the third-person pronoun *he* or *one.*

See #4; see also #26.

al Illogical or Incongruous Alignment of Elements

Revise to remove the illogicality. It may be a matter of faulty predication, predicating something illogical about a subject:

> al: His *job* as a schoolteacher *was* one *way* he could earn the community's respect.

A *job* is not a *way.* The error can be corrected by revising the sentence:

> revised: His job as a schoolteacher helped earn him the community's respect.

revised: One way he could earn the community's respect was by being a schoolteacher.

Other alignment errors also result from trying to make words behave in ways that their meanings do not permit:

al: The general believed that acts such as cowardice and insubordination should be severely punished.

But cowardice and insubordination are not *acts*.

revised: The general believed that acts of cowardice and insubordination should be severely punished.

See #30; see also *log* (Logic), *comp* (Incomplete Comparison).

ambig **Ambiguous**
 amb Ambiguity is a particular kind of lack of clarity, namely that which lets a reader understand something in two different ways. Although ambiguity is sometimes intentional, for example in poetry where it can enrich the meaning, it has no place in expository prose, where it only confuses the reader and thus obscures the meaning.

ambig: The Prime Minister was in favour of elimination of oil price controls and tax reductions.

Here co-ordination appears to link *price controls* and *tax reductions*; the meaning then would be that the Prime Minister wanted to eliminate tax reductions—a most unpopular and therefore unlikely political stand. The ambiguity can easily be removed by rearrangement or by changing the syntax:

clear: The Prime Minister was in favour of tax reductions and the elimination of oil price controls.
clear: The Prime Minister was in favour of reducing taxes and eliminating price controls.

In this second version, the parallel gerunds *reducing* and *eliminating* help enforce the intended meaning.

ambig: George Delgarno, a teacher, wrote an essay on the educational system in England in 1680.

Was the essay written in 1680? Or was its subject "education in 1680''? It is impossible to tell, though the first is more likely. Simply putting *in 1680* before *wrote* or after *essay* would then make it clear.

See also *cl* (Clarity), *dm* (Dangling Modifier) and #24, *mm* (Misplaced Modifier) and #23, *fp* (Faulty Parallelism) and #27, *p* (Punctuation) and Chapter IV, *ref* (Faulty Reference) and #5.

apos Apostrophe Missing or Misused

1. The apostrophe is used to indicate the possessive inflection of nouns.

> apos: She mended the girls dresses.

Here *girls* is obviously possessive, but in the absence of an apostrophe it is impossible to tell whether it is singular or plural: either *girl's* or *girls'* is necessary to make it clear.

2. The apostrophe is NOT used for the possessive case of personal pronouns.

> *Wrong:*   her's, your's, their's

3. The apostrophe is used to indicate the omission of letters in contractions.

it's (it is)	we're (we are)
isn't (is not)	you're (you are)
hasn't (has not)	who's (who is)
haven't (have not)	we've (we have)
aren't (are not)	he'll (he will)
she's (she is, she has)	you'll (you will)
he's (he is, he has)	shouldn't (should not)
they're (they are)	wouldn't (would not)
won't (will not: an irregular contraction)	

To omit such an apostrophe is to misspell the word.

4. Do not confuse a contraction with a possessive form.

> *Wrong:*   *Who's* book is this? (Whose)
> *Wrong:*   Is this where *your* going to sleep? (you're)

Note: Contractions are not usually desirable in formal

writing. If you want a relatively informal tone, however, contractions are not only permissible but desirable.

See #51v and #51w for complete information on the apostrophe.

art Article Missing or Misused

> art: At end of the story everyone is happy again.

Supply the missing *the* before *end.*

> art: It was *an* humiliating experience.

Change *an* to *a.*

> art: It was at this point in *the* life that he decided to reform.

Remove *the,* or change it to *his.*

See #9a; see also *id* (Idiom) and #58.

awk Awkwardness
k *Awk* (or *k*) is the symbol most teachers use when they know that there is something wrong with a sentence but are unable to put a finger on any particular error, or when the combination of several faults is unusually complicated. *Awk* could be translated as something like "Take this sentence into the shop for diagnosis and repairs." Awkwardness can stem from several causes. It can result from laziness or haste, from indiscriminately writing down the first thing that pops into one's head. It can occur because an unsophisticated writer uses as many words as possible—and the bigger the better—and thereby contorts the normal arrangements of English sentences, mistakenly thinking that such things will impress a reader; the truth is that the simple expression is frequently the most effective and even the most elegant expression. Awkwardness often results from clumsy use of the passive voice (see #6h), or from poor punctuation, or from confused thinking. Here are some examples of awkward sentences from student essays, each followed by our attempt (and in some instances a student's own attempt) to straighten it out:

awk: Caught up in this new way of life, I felt a closer existence to every thoughts of today.

revised: Caught up in this new way of life, I felt myself to be more intimately involved in contemporary thought.

awk: Now, as I began to get some feeling of confidence restored in me, I thought how silly my previous experience had been.

revised: Now, as I regained confidence, I realized how foolish had been my response to the earlier experience.

awk: I looked for a familiar face among that great sea of faces, but this was done in vain.

Here faulty idiom (*among* instead of *in*), the passive voice (*was done*), wordiness, and unnecessary co-ordination combined to produce a slovenly sentence.

revised: I looked in vain for a friend in that great sea of faces.

awk: Since Canada nowadays comprises many people of different origins, television provides an excellent means for different ethnic groups to communicate with ones of the same origin who do not reside closely or even to introduce their customs to others of different origins.

revised: In Canada, whose far-flung population includes people of many different origins, television enables ethnic groups to communicate with their fellows elsewhere in the country and also to introduce their customs to others.

awk: The essay is written in a way that he relates his beliefs to the reader, but does not force the reader to digest his beliefs.

revised: He explains his beliefs although he does not expect the reader to share them.

awk: The poem also gives a sense of lightness in the way it rhymes and in its metre.

revised: The poem's rhymes and metre contribute to the light tone.

awk: During the eighteenth century, chemistry became a real science instead of the previous alchemy.

revised: In the eighteenth century chemistry became a real science, evolving out of and replacing the pseudo-science of alchemy.

awk: In the poem, "To an Athlete Dying Young," by A.E. Housman, the speaker poses an argument of why the athlete benefited from dying young.

revised: In A.E. Housman's poem "To an Athlete Dying Young," the speaker argues that it was preferable for the athlete to die so young.

ca Case

The case of a pronoun depends on its function in its own clause or phrase. A pronoun that is a subject or a complement must be in the subjective case:

ca: Hans and *me* dug the ditch ourselves. (I)

ca: He's the one *whom* I predicted would win the race. (who)

ca: That is *her*. (she)

A pronoun that is an object of a verb or preposition must be in the objective case:

ca: They told Albert and *I* to leave. (me)

ca: It was up to Peggy and *I* to finish the job. (me)

ca: It doesn't matter *who* you take with you. (whom)

See #3d. For information about the possessive case of nouns and pronouns see #3a, #3b, #3c, and #51w.

cap Capitalization Needed or Faulty Capitalization

cap: Near Hudson bay in the Northwest Territories is the region known as the barrens.

corrected: Near Hudson Bay in the Northwest Territories is the region known as the Barrens.

See #47; see also *lc* (Lower Case).

cl Lack of Clarity

Like awkwardness, a lack of clarity can result from many causes. The parts of a sentence may fail to go together in a meaningful way, or the words chosen to express an idea may not do so adequately, or the writer may have had only a vague idea in the first place.

cl: There is also a general sense of irony in the plot or story behind the play.

What is a *general sense* as opposed to a *sense*? What is *a sense of irony* as opposed to *irony*? Why the choice of *plot or story*? And how is it that the plot (or story) is *behind* the play? It is impossible to know what the writer meant, but here is a clear sentence that uses the major features of the original: "There are ironic elements in the plot of the play."

cl: This blessing is intended to restore faith in God when things happen such as death which you don't understand and want to blame God for letting them happen.

This sentence could perhaps have been marked *awk* as well, but the muddiness of the thought and its expression seems to be its principal fault. Sorting it out and adding some logic as well as some careful syntax produce a clearer and more succinct version:

This blessing is intended to restore faith in God, which may be lost when incomprehensible events like death make one question God's justice.

But here is an example of an unclear sentence that remains impenetrable; not even the context offered any help to understanding it:

cl: Absurdist plays work on the situation in much greater detail than the dramatic level.

Here is another sentence that goes astray; one can only wonder what the intended meaning was:

cl: He compares the athlete's achievements and victories to that of death.

Sometimes even punctuation is part of the trouble:

p: Before I really had time to think they wanted me to report for work in the morning.

A comma after *think* makes it more likely that the sentence will be understood on the first reading rather than the second or third.

See also *ambig* (Ambiguous), *awk* (Awkward), #5, and #23–#31.

cliché Cliché
See *trite* (Trite, Worn-out, Hackneyed Expression).

coh Not Coherent; Continuity Weak
Coherence is weak or faulty when there is insufficient transition between two sentences or two paragraphs. The first sentence of a paragraph, whether it is the topic sentence or not, should in some way provide a connection with the preceding paragraph. Similarly, sentences within paragraphs should flow smoothly from one to another. Here for example are two sentences which are not smoothly connected:

> Rachel is invited both to dine at Willard's and to go out with Calla. Despite her desire to accept one of the invitations she declines both of them because it is her mother's card night.

Granted that the idea of the invitations is present in both, the sentences nevertheless need something more by way of transition. Either a *But* to begin the second sentence or a *however* (between commas) after the word *invitations* would provide the necessary coherence.

See #62; see also *tr* (Transition Weak or Lacking), and Sentence Coherence, #31.

colloq Colloquialism
See *inf* (Informal, Colloquial).

comb Combine Sentences
An instructor may write *coord* (Co-ordinate) or *sub* (Subordinate), or even *coord or sub* together, to indicate that some kind of improvement (economy, coherence, logic) could be gained by putting two (or more) sentences together. Sometimes, however, rather than specify which (*sub* or *coord*), or in instances where neither subordination nor co-ordination would be desirable, an instructor may write *comb,* meaning simply "Combine these two (or more) sentences in the way you think best." In the following, for example, which could have been marked *w* (Wordiness) as well, the improvement is great—and obvious:

> w-comb: The whiteness of the snow piled on their out-
> stretched branches gave their green colour an extra

richness. This added attractiveness seemed to enhance their beauty.

revised: The whiteness of the snow piled on their outstretched branches gave their green colour an extra richness, enhancing their beauty.

See *coord* (Co-ordinate), *sub* (Subordinate), and #28.

comp Incomplete Comparison
inc Revise to correct imcomplete or illogical comparisons.

comp: She is a better skater than any girl on the team.
revised: She is a better skater than any *other* girl on the team.

comp: Life in a small town is better than a big city.
revised: Life in a small town is better than (*life*) *in* a big city.

comp: I think tomato juice is as good, if not better, than orange juice.
revised: I think tomato juice is as good *as,* if not better than, orange juice.
revised: I think tomato juice is as good as orange juice, if not better.

comp: Fresh vegetables have more vitamins.
revised: Fresh vegetables have more vitamins than canned or frozen ones.

comp: I like skiing more than David.
revised: I like skiing more than David does.
revised: I like skiing more than I like David.

Note that *ambig* (Ambiguous), *cl* (Lack of Clarity), or *log* (Logic) would be an appropriate mark for some of these sentences.

See #29 and #30.

conc Insufficient Concreteness
Revise by increasing the concreteness of your diction. Replace abstract words and phrases with concrete ones, or expand upon abstract statements with specific and concrete details.

conc: Seymour was a very *deep* person, known only to those who really loved him—his family.

The word *deep* here is suggestive, but too abstract to be very meaningful. *Deep* can mean several different things here (consult your dictionary); more information, especially in the form of concrete examples, would enable the reader to understand precisely what the writer meant to convey.

See #54.

coord Co-ordination Needed; Combine Sentences

When two sentences are closely related, for example in expressing a contrast, it is usually preferable to combine them, using either punctuation or a co-ordinating conjunction or both.

> coord: Life in the North can be very challenging. Life in a large city offers more variety.
>
> revised: Life in the North can be very challenging, but life in a large city offers more variety.

Depending on context and desired emphasis, such sentences could also be joined with a semicolon, or one or the other could be subordinated with a beginning *though* or *whereas*.

See also *sub* (Subordination), *comb* (Combine), *cs* (Comma Splice), *fc* (Faulty Co-ordination), *coh* (Coherence), and Faulty Co-ordination, #28.

cs Comma Splice

A comma splice results from putting a comma between independent clauses that are not joined with a co-ordinating conjunction; "splicing" the clauses together with only a comma is not enough. More than one independent clause can of course exist in one sentence, but the clauses must be either properly joined with co-ordinating conjunctions or separated by the correct punctuation.

> cs: The flight from Vancouver to Toronto takes only about four hours, it seems to last forever.

The comma between the two clauses is not enough. A semicolon (or period) would be "correct," but a poor solution because the two clauses obviously are closely related. Here the desired contrast would best be emphasized either by using an appropriate co-ordinating conjunction:

> The flight from Vancouver to Toronto takes about four hours, but it seems to last forever.

or by using a subordinating conjunction to turn the first clause into a subordinate rather than an independent clause:

> Although the flight from Vancouver to Toronto takes only about four hours, it seems to last forever.

Here is another example:

> cs: Contemporary Canadian poetry is, if nothing else, at least plentiful, it pours daily from a number of influential presses.

Here, since the second clause illustrates the notion expressed in the first, a co-ordinating conjunction would not be appropriate. One could argue that *for* would do the connecting well enough, but a better way to handle this sentence would be to emphasize the syntactic integrity of the second clause by changing the comma to a semicolon (or, in this instance, even a colon).

> Contemporary Canadian poetry is, if nothing else, at least plentiful; it pours daily from a number of influential presses.

Comma splices, then, can be corrected by replacing the comma with an appropriate mark—usually a semicolon (or a period if you decide to turn the clauses into two separate sentences)—or by showing the actual relation between the clauses by using the precise co-ordinating or subordinating conjunction.

See #33e; see also *comb* (Combine), *coord* (Co-ordination), *fc* (Faulty Co-ordination), *sub* (Subordination), and #28.

d Faulty Diction

Errors in diction are often marked with one or another specific symbol, such as *ww* (wrong word), *nsw* (no such word), *inf* (informal or colloquial), or *id* (idiom). But sometimes a teacher will simply use *d,* implying either that the error does not fall into one of those particular categories or that the student is expected to find out just what specific kind of error it is. In either event, the first thing the writer should do is consult a dictionary; *d* could be said to stand for *dictionary.*

> If we regard the poem in this way, the recurring images of the "unwatered," aimless, barren mind of modern man would be one of the musical themes, and the imagery of
>
> d: water *plus* its symbolism of replenishment would be another.

In this otherwise well-wrought sentence, the word *plus* creates a stylistic disturbance. *Plus* is normally a mathematical term; it is not a conjunction, nor appropriate to this context. The meaning of *plus* in expository rather than mathematical terms is conveyed by the conjunction *and*; the preposition *with* would also serve the meaning here.

Diction can also be poor by being weak or imprecise. In the following sentence, for example, the word *outlined* is inadequate for the job it is being asked to do:

> d: The program should be *outlined* in such a way that learning can take place in the field as well as in the classroom.

A word like *designed, planned,* or *organized* would be better.

See Chapter VII. See also *inf* (Informal, Colloquial), *conc* (Concreteness), *id* (Idiom), *jarg* (Jargon), *nsw* (No Such Word), and *ww* (Wrong Word).

dev Development Needed
This mark indicates that an idea, point, or subject needs to be further developed, expanded upon, whether by supplying details, examples, or illustrations, by defining or explaining, or by some other method. It most often applies to an inadequately developed paragraph.

See #64e and #54.

div Word Division
See *syl* (Syllabication).

dm Dangling Modifier
Correct a dangling modifier either by changing it so that it no longer dangles or by providing a logical noun or pronoun for it to modify.

> dm: Running too hurriedly around the corner of the building, a newsstand suddenly loomed in front of me.

corrected:

corrected:	When I too hurriedly ran around the corner of the building, a newsstand suddenly loomed in front of me.
corrected:	Running too hurriedly around the corner of the building, I was suddenly confronted by a newsstand looming before me.

See #24.

doc Documentation: Notes and Bibliography

Observe the correct forms for your notes (whether footnotes or collected at the end as "Notes") and your bibliography. In Chapter IX, "The Research Paper," you will find model footnotes and bibliographical entries. Beyond this, your best source of information on these conventions is the latest edition of *The MLA Style Sheet* or the more easily understood *MLA Handbook for Writers of Research Papers, Theses, and Dissertations* (1977), which is based on the earlier pamphlet; both are published by The Modern Language Association of America, and should be available in university libraries and bookstores.

Even if you are not writing a full-fledged research paper, when you consult books or periodicals for information or for ideas or quotations which you use in writing an essay, you must provide full and accurate documentation in the form of notes. You should also include a bibliography at the end of the essay in the form of an alphabetical list of all your sources.

See *ack* (Acknowledgment of Sources) and Chapter IX.

emph Emphasis Weak or Unclear

Make the sentence or paragraph properly emphatic by re-arranging or by clarifying the relationship of its parts.

emph:	The older generation of our society, like the younger, is also continually confronted with both beneficial and harmful advertisements which are effective on our society *in some way or other*.

This is a flabby sentence in general, but what little strength it has is almost entirely dissipated by the limp final prepositional phrase; simply removing it would somewhat sharpen the end of the sentence, which is its most emphatic part. But further improvement can be gained by sorting out and re-arranging the sentence's content and cutting out the repetition and deadwood:

> revised: All of society—not just the young but the older generation as well—is bombarded with advertising that can be beneficial as well as harmful.

This may not be the best version possible, but at least it has clear emphasis.

See also Faulty Co-ordination, #28.

euph Euphemism

Avoid unnecessary euphemism ("good sounding," though not necessarily good in fact). Often directness and precision are preferable to even well-intended delicacy and vagueness. Is someone lacking money to buy enough food really made to feel better by being described as "disadvantaged" rather than "poor"? During a war the destruction and evacuation of whole communities are made to seem perfectly right and proper when the process is called "pacification." When you are tempted to use a euphemism to avoid an unpleasant reality (for example describing a person as "inebriated" or "in a state of intoxication" rather than "drunk"), consider the possible virtues of being direct and succinct instead.

See #56.

fc Faulty Co-ordination

Faulty co-ordination occurs when unrelated clauses are linked by means of co-ordinating conjunctions, or when related clauses are linked by co-ordinating conjunctions which fail to indicate the correct relation.

> fc: Chaucer was born in 1340 and he was the greatest poet of medieval England.

The date of Chaucer's birth and the extent of his reputation are not related or equal in value as the co-ordinating conjunction *and* implies. The significant comment is contained in the second clause; the opening clause contains a minor fact which should be subordinate to the main statement.

revised: Chaucer, who was born in 1340, was the greatest poet of medieval England.

revised: Chaucer (1340–1400) was the greatest poet of medieval England.

fc: He had worked all summer at handsome wages *and* had earned enough to see him through the next year at university.

The two clauses are not separate statements, but related statements of which the latter is the more significant one. The opening clause should either be subordinated with the conjunction which precisely indicates the relationship between the ideas in the sentence:

revised: Since he had worked all summer at handsome wages, he had earned enough to see him through the next year at university.

or even be changed to a participial phrase:

revised: Having worked all summer at handsome wages, he had earned enough to see him through the next year at university.

See #28; see also *comb* (Combine), *coord* (Co-ordination), and *sub* (Subordination).

fig Inappropriate or Confusing Figurative Language

Revise to change or remove figurative language (similes, metaphors) that is inappropriate or mixed.

fig: Physical Education provides a stepping stone on which students can learn what to do with their leisure time.

The image of a stepping stone adds nothing but oddity to this sentence. Some more appropriate figure may have been in the writer's mind, but the statement is probably better without the metaphor:

revised: Physical Education offers students an opportunity to learn how to use their spare time.

Here is an example of a mixed metaphor:

fig: Like a bolt from the blue the idea grabbed him, and it

soon grew into one of his most prized pieces of mental furniture.

One of the troubles with clichés that are dead metaphors is that we often fail to visualize them; result: absurdity. The *bolt from the blue,* even if allowed, could scarcely *grab* anyone, nor could it grow (like a plant?) into a piece of furniture. The urge to be metaphorical backfired on the writer.

See #53.

fp Faulty Parallelism

// Revise by making co-ordinated elements grammatically parallel.

> fp: For me England brings back memories of pleasant walks in Cornwall on some windblown lea, looking out to sea dressed in warm woollen jerseys, and feeling a warmth brought about by being with my family in that place.

The preposition *of* here has three objects: *walks* is a normal noun whereas *looking* and *feeling* are verbal nouns (gerunds). Although they are all nouns, they are not strictly parallel. Repeating *of* before *looking* and *feeling* would improve the sentence, but it would be better to make the elements strictly parallel:

> revised: For me England brings back pleasant memories of *walking* dressed in warm woollen jerseys in Cornwall on some windblown lea, *looking* out to sea, and *feeling* a warmth brought about by being with my family in that place.

(The phrase *dressed in warm woollen jerseys* seems more appropriate to the windblown lea than to looking out to sea.)

There is also the kind of error in which a parallel structure breaks down—or rather is not sufficiently built up. Consider the following sentence:

> fp: During my visit I had the chance to get involved with the children, help with the shopping and cooking—all of which helped make the experience enjoyable.

The implication of the sentence structure here is that we are going to be given more than two things (and the phrase *all of which* makes it sound as though we had been told more than we have been). That is, the implied parallel series after *to* is not fulfilled.

revised: During my visit I had the chance to get involved with the children and to help with the shopping and the cooking; these activities helped make the experience enjoyable.

Alternatively, at least a third element could be added to the abortive series.

See #27.

frag Unacceptable Fragment

Word groups punctuated as sentences but which do not fulfill the requirements of sentences are usually unacceptable. You should avoid them. The fragmentary pattern is one of the most common and disrupting of these patterns. Fragmentary patterns either lack one or more of the essential sentence elements or are grammatically dependent upon a word or words in a preceding sentence.

frag: Corbett was chosen to be the next attorney general. *He being clever and remarkably well versed in all aspects of the law.*

The italicized group of words lacks a finite verb (*being* is a participle) and is therefore not a major sentence; yet it does not fit into any of the classifications of a minor sentence. It is therefore a fragment.

frag: The convention was held at the Cornish Hotel. *Because it has a large banquet room which would accommodate us all.*

The italicized group of words is grammatically dependent upon the verb *was held* in the preceding sentence; it answers the question "why?" and is therefore an adverbial clause, and cannot be written independently as a sentence.

In some fragmentary patterns both faults may occur:

frag: I stayed home last weekend. *Having no money.*

The italicized group lacks both a subject and a finite verb and is grammatically dependent upon the pronoun "I." Therefore it must not be written as a sentence.

frag: Toll-roads would result in a general saving for everyone. *Lower sales taxes on automobiles and parts, and decreased levy on gasoline.*

The italicized fragment lacks a finite verb and is also in apposition to *general saving* in the preceding sentence.

Any word group which cannot stand by itself and communicate effectively is suspect. Avoid this serious error.

Note: Fragmentary patterns can sometimes be used effectively as a stylistic device by skilled writers. Unless you belong in that category, write complete sentences. If you deliberately use fragmentary patterns in essays, indicate in a marginal note that their presence is intentional. Your instructor can then tell you whether they succeed or fail, and why.

See #16.

fs Fused Sentence
See *run-on.*

gen Inadequately Supported Generalization
See #54b.

gr Error in Grammar
Although several errors, such as *agr, dm, ref,* and *t,* fall into the category of grammatical error, instructors will sometimes simply mark an error *gr* either because it includes more than one kind of mistake or because they want a student to discover for himself what the particular error is. An instructor may want to emphasize that an error like *The reason . . . is because* is not merely a matter of careless wording but an error in grammar: Since *is* is a linking verb, it can correctly be followed only by a complement that is either an adjective or a noun (see #8d); but *because* introduces an adverbial modifier: the construction is therefore ungrammatical. There are, then, errors in grammar that are not in any of the specifically identified categories.

id Faulty Idiom, Unidiomatic Usage
Idiom refers to the forms of expression and the structures peculiar to a particular language. Idioms are not necessarily

logical or explicable in grammatical terms. Correct marked errors by changing the unidiomatic usage to an idiomatic one. Errors in idiom most often occur with prepositions, as in the following examples:

> id: The extent of Creighton's influence *towards* our view of Canadian history is not fully appreciated.

Change *towards* to the idiomatic *on*.

> id: Iago has a reputation *of* honesty.

Change *of* to *for*.

See #58; see also Articles, #9a.

inc Incomplete Comparison
See *comp*.

inf Inappropriate Informal or Colloquial Diction
Replace the inappropriate word or words with something more formal.

> inf: He is the most *stuck-up* boy in the class. (*conceited, vain, egotistical, snobbish*)

See #52b.

ital Italics Needed or Incorrect
Correct by italicizing or by removing unwanted italics. (In typed or handwritten material, italics are represented by underlining.)

> ital: "A Night to Remember" is about the sinking of the Titanic.
>
> corrected: *A Night to Remember* is about the sinking of the *Titanic*.

See #49; see also Titles, #48.

jarg Jargon
Revise to avoid unnecessary jargon.

> jarg: A truly professional-type player, he seemed able to judge every move from the standpoint of its bottom-line effect.

> revised: A true professional, he seemed able to judge the ultimate effect of every move he made.

See #59h.

k Awkward
See *awk* (Awkward).

lc Lower Case
Change incorrect capital letter(s) to lower case.

> lc: You can now find Champagne made elsewhere than in France.
>
> corrected: You can now find champagne made elsewhere than in France.

> lc: I had always planned to get a University education.
>
> corrected: I had always planned to get a university education.

See #47.

leg Legibility, Illegible
Messy or poor handwriting or struck-over typing that cannot be read clearly needs re-doing.

lev Inappropriate Level of Diction
See #52.

log Logic: Illogical as Phrased; Logicality of Reasoning Questioned
Illogic underlies many different kinds of error and much weak writing and thinking. For fuller information, consult the section on logic, #29. Nevertheless, *log* is frequently the mark used to indicate an error of logic arising out of the way something has been phrased. For example:

> log: Insecurity *is* a characteristic basic to Davies's nature and it *becomes* a *consistent* weakness of his *throughout* the play.

If insecurity *is* a basic characteristic, it can scarcely *become* consistent in the course of the play. Similarly, it can scarcely *become* consistent *throughout* the play, since *throughout* logically contradicts the meaning of *become*. Here is another example:

log: In giving a precise definition of what this mental science
       is, Asimov is very vague.

The illogicality is obvious. At least three meanings are possible:

clear: Asimov fails to provide a precise definition of this mental science.

clear: Asimov's definition of this mental science is very vague.

clear: Asimov deals only vaguely with this mental science and makes no attempt to define it.

See also #29, *al* (Alignment), and #30.

mix Mixed Construction

A shift from one pattern of syntax to another within a single sentence.

See #25.

mm Misplaced Modifier

Revise by moving the modifying word or phrase to the logical place in the sentence.

mm: The solution is to make Demetrius view Helena as the object of his love *rather than Hermia.*

revised: The solution is to make Demetrius view Helena rather than Hermia as the object of his love.

mm: Sauron wished to be the Dark Lord of Middle-earth, and *almost* had enough power to succeed *twice.*

revised: Sauron wished to be Dark Lord of Middle-earth, and twice had almost enough power to succeed.

See #23; see also *wo* (Word Order).

ms Improper Manuscript Form or Conventions

A conscientious writer is careful to follow certain conventions pertaining to the form and presentation of a manuscript. These include such things as indenting paragraphs clearly, leaving two spaces after a period, not underlining one's own title, being consistent with punctuation marks, and leaving spaces between the dots of an ellipsis.

See Chapter V.

nsw No Such Word

Inventiveness and originality are commendable virtues in most instances, but they are inadequate substitutes for knowledge. When you need a particular word to do a special job, it is usually unnecessary to invent it; the English language is rich in vocabulary and is unlikely to let you down if you will take the trouble to look for the word you need. If you have any doubt about a word you've used, if it seems somewhat unusual or if it does not quite ring true, your dictionary can in a moment settle the question. A little extra care will enable you to avoid using such concoctions as these, all of which occurred in students' essays:

> ableness (ability)
> afraidness (fear)
> artistism (artistry)
> condensated (condensed)
> cowardism, cowardness (cowardice)
> deteriorized (deteriorated)
> enrichen (enrich)
> eternalty (eternity)
> freedomship (freedom)
> fruitition (fruition)
> infidelous (unfaithful)
> irregardless (regardless, irrespective)
> nonchalantness (nonchalance)
> prophesize (prophesy)
> scepticalism (scepticism)
> superfluosity (superfluity, superfluousness)

num Incorrect Use of Numerals

See #50 for the conventions governing the use of numerals.

org Weak or Faulty Organization

Repetition, choppiness, lack of proportion or emphasis, haphazard order—all these and more can be signs of poor organization. It may be necessary to rethink your outline.

See #65.

p Error in Punctuation

Punctuation marks are symbols that should be just as meaningful to readers as the symbols of speech (words) with which they are associated in writing. In speech, "punctuation" takes the form of inflections of voice, pauses, changes in pitch or intensity of utterance. In order to communicate meaningfully and clearly on paper, one must pay as much attention to finding the precise punctuation as one pays to the selection of one's words and structures. When you find *p* in the margin of your paper, refer to Chapter IV to find out not only *what* is wrong or weak, but also *why* it is so. Learning the nuances of punctuation is not easy. Although some of its conventions are arbitrary, good punctuation is to a considerable extent an expression of good taste and rhetorical understanding. Try to develop these qualities by learning the language of punctuation.

See Chapter IV, #32–#44.

para Paragraphing
See ¶, no ¶, below; see #64.

pas Weak Passive Voice
This mark means that in the reader's opinion the sentence in question would be better served by a verb in the active voice than by one in the passive voice. (A verb in the passive voice consists of some form of the verb *be* followed by a past participle; it converts the subject of a clause into the receiver of the action.)

> pas: In these lines the comparison of himself and his lover to flies *is made.*
> active: In these lines the speaker *compares* himself and his lover to flies.
>
> pas: Davies always finds his fears *being played upon* by Mick.
> active: Davies always finds that Mick *plays upon* his fears.
> active: Mick always *plays upon* Davies's fears.

See #6h.

passim Latin for *throughout*; used to indicate that an error, such as the misspelling of a name, needs to be corrected throughout an essay.

pred Faulty Predication
    See *al* (Alignment) and #30.

pv Point of View Inconsistent or Unclear; Shift in Perspective
Revise to remove the awkward or illogical shift in tense, mood, or voice of verbs, or person or number of pronouns.

      pv: One should never forget *your* snowshoes. (*one's* or *his*)
      pv: It was four in the afternoon, beginning to get dark, and we *are* still only half-way down the mountain. (*were*)

See #26.

Perspective can also seem to shift because of a lack of parallelism:

      pv, fp: Ralph said that it was raining and he preferred to stay home.

If "he preferred to stay home" is meant as a part of what he said, then a second *that* is required after *and*; otherwise, *he preferred* could be taken as parallel to *Ralph said*. That is, without the second *that, he preferred* would be from the writer's point of view rather than Ralph's.

See #27a.

q, Q Error in Handling of Quoted Material or Quotation Marks
Sometimes this will refer to nothing more than the careless omission of quotation marks—usually at the end of a quotation. But it could also refer to incorrect punctuation with quoted material, awkwardly introduced quoted material, and the like. If the error so marked is not an obvious one, you may have to consult the section on quotation to find out what is wrong.

See #43.

red Redundancy
Redundancy can mean simply wordiness, but it is often used to refer specifically to the awkward and unnecessary repetition of the meaning of one word in another word. In the sentence "But he was not unfriendly though," the *But* and

the *though* do the same job; one of them must go (obviously the *though,* since it badly weakens the end of the sentence). Here are two more examples:

> red: Throughout the entire story the tone is one of unrelieved gloom.

Since *throughout* means *all through, from beginning to end,* the word *entire* merely repeats what has already been said.

> revised: Throughout the story the tone is one of unrelieved gloom.

But this is still redundant, for if the tone is *unrelieved,* then it must be constant throughout the story. Hence further tightening is possible:

> re-revised: The story's tone is one of unrelieved gloom.

Again:

> red: Puck's playful pranks include tricks on housewives and village maids.

Here the writer's choice of the word *pranks* is accurate and effective, but since *pranks* are *frolicsome tricks,* the addition of the word *playful* is redundant and destroys the effectiveness.

> revised: Puck's pranks include tricks on housewives and village maids.

One might even want to try to get rid of the word *tricks:*

> Puck plays pranks on housewives and village maids.

See #59c; see also *w* (Wordiness).

ref Weak or Faulty Pronoun Reference

Pronouns must clearly refer to their antecedents. The following sentence, for example, is muddled because it is not clear whom the pronouns refer to:

> ref: Because of all the attention which Seymour and Buddy gave to Franny and Zooey when *they* were young children, *they* never allowed *them* to develop *their* own ideas of life.

One can, by careful rereading, extract the sense of this

sentence, but it is the writer's job to make clear sense, not the reader's to puzzle it out.

> revised: When Franny and Zooey were young, Seymour and
> Buddy gave *them* so much attention that the children
> were never able to develop their own ideas of life.

One clear pronoun instead of four confusing ones (and the redundant *young children* has been broken up, as well). Here is another example:

> ref: Merlin's power, quite naturally, is partially a result of his
> "Sight" and what are thought to be his magical powers.
> An example of *this* is given during the battle between
> King Ambrosius and the Saxons.

Clearly one must also be careful with demonstrative pronouns: here the reference of *this* is obscure. Probably in the writer's mind *this* somehow referred to the entire idea expressed in the first sentence. In other words, *this* has no precise antecedent, and the reference is therefore loose at best. A clearer and more precise version (clearing up the awkward parallelism and the passive voice as well) is possible:

> revised: Merlin's power derives from a combination of his
> Sight and his reputed magic. The battle between King
> Ambrosius and the Saxons provides an illustration of
> this fact.

Changing the demonstrative pronoun to a demonstrative adjective usually makes things clearer. But the passage is still clumsy and wordy. Try again, combining the sentences:

> revised: As the battle between King Ambrosius and the Saxons illustrates, Merlin's power derives from a combination of his Sight and his reputed magic.

Much tighter.

See #5; see also #4.

rep Weak, Awkward, or Unnecessary Repetition
This is another kind of wordiness that requires pruning. Although repetition is often useful for achieving emphasis and coherence, unnecessary repetition only encumbers.

rep: The snow was falling heavily, but I didn't mind the snow, for I have always enjoyed the things one can do in the snow.

The repetition of *snow* at the end is all right, but the middle one must go; replace *the snow* with *it,* or with nothing at all.

See #59b.

run-on   Run-on or Fused Sentence
fs   Failure to put any punctuation between two independent clauses not joined by a co-ordinating conjunction results in a run-on sentence. Along with *comma splices* and *fragments, run-ons* are considered extremely serious errors. Since the run-on is often merely a careless slip, caused by writing too fast and not proofreading carefully, it should be easy to prevent.

run-on: Vancouver is the most beautifully situated city in Canada it also has some ugly slums.

Like the comma splice, a run-on can be corrected by inserting a semicolon, by inserting a comma and a co-ordinating conjunction, or by subordinating one of the clauses and inserting a comma. One could also insert a period, making two sentences; this would be the best correction if indeed the error was merely careless omission of the period. In the present instance, however, one of the other methods would be better. For example:

Vancouver is the most beautifully situated city in Canada; it also has some ugly slums.

This is correct, but weak in the same way that a period would be; a conjunctive adverb, however, will make the point of the contrast clear:

Vancouver is the most beautifully situated city in Canada; however, it also has some ugly slums.

The other two ways of correcting a run-on work well here:

Vancouver is the most beautifully situated city in Canada, but it also has some ugly slums.
Although Vancouver is the most beautifully situated city in Canada, it also has some ugly slums.

See #33j; see also *cs* (Comma Splice).

shift Shift in Perspective
See *pv* (Point of View).

sp Spelling
When you make an error in spelling, do not simply try to guess how it should be corrected, for you are likely to get it wrong again. Instead, check the word in your dictionary, and take the opportunity to find out all that the dictionary tells you about the word, not only for the sake of learning something, but also because it will help fix the word in your mind and thus help you avoid misspelling it again. Then check Chapter VI to see if your error fits any of the categories discussed there; if so, study the principles involved. It is also important that you keep a personal list of all the words you misspell; review it often so that you will become thoroughly familiar with the correct spelling of those words.

See Chapter VI, #51.

split Unnecessary Split Infinitive
See #11b.

ss Sentence Structure or Sentence Sense
Sometimes an instructor will put *ss* (or only *s*) in the margin opposite a sentence to indicate that something is wrong with its sense or its structure, leaving it to the writer to discover what particular error—if any—is present; it may for example be a grammatical error, or a faulty arrangement, or a lack of clarity. Or the sentence may be faulty in some way not covered by any of the more specific categories. If this mark appears often, you may need to review Chapter III, on sentences.

stet Let it Stand (Latin)
This mark indicates that you were right the first time, that when you changed something, such as a punctuation mark or the spelling of a word, you should have left it the way it was. To correct, therefore, merely restore it to its original form. (Note that an instructor will be able to advise you of this only if you cancel a word or mark with a single line through it; if you blot out the original entirely, you may never find out that your first instinct was correct.)

sub Subordination Needed; Combine Sentences.

> sub: Forster has also done a superb job in his use of examples. His examples are clear and precise.
>
> revised: Forster has also done a superb job in his use of examples, which are clear and precise.

As two sentences this example was very wordy. Even the revised version could be made tighter.

> better: Forster has also provided clear and precise examples.

See also *coord* (Co-ordination), *comb* (Combine), *fc* (Faulty Co-ordination), *coh* (Coherence), and #28.

syl Syllabication

This mark (or sometimes *div,* for *word division*) indicates that you have incorrectly or inappropriately broken a word at the end of a line. Consult your dictionary to find out where the syllable breaks occur in the word. If that is not the problem, then check Syllabication and Word Division to find out what you have done wrong.

See #45b.

t Error in Tense

> t: I often think back to the day, five years ago, when I bought my first horse. To many people this wouldn't be very exciting, but I *have wanted* a horse for as long as I *can* remember.

Change the present perfect *have wanted* to the correct *had wanted,* which is past perfect, and *can* to *could,* which is past.

See #6d.

title Manuscript Conventions for Titles
See #48.

tr Transition Weak or Lacking
Provide some kind of transitional word or phrase, or improve upon an existing one, or otherwise improve the transition at

the place indicated—which will be either between two paragraphs or between two sentences.

See *coh* (Coherence) and #62.

trite Trite, Worn-out, Hackneyed Expression
Remove unnecessary or weak clichés; if necessary replace them with fresh diction or reword the sentence. Some clichés will simply be wordy and therefore wholly or partly expendable; others will have to be replaced with something fresher. The following example contains both kinds:

> trite: *It goes without saying* that *over the years many and diverse* opinions have been held regarding the origin of the universe.
>
> revised: Ever since men began thinking about it, astronomers and others have held many different opinions about the origin of the universe.

The passive voice of *have been held* was also contributing to the sluggishness of the sentence.

See #59e.

u Unity of Sentence, Paragraph, or Essay Weak
See #61 and #28.

us Usage
A subcategory of *diction,* this refers specifically to the kind of advice given in the Checklist of Troublesome Words and Phrases.

See #60.

w Wordiness
If your desire to reach a required word-count has been greater than your desire to achieve crisp, clear, effective communication, you may find this mark haunting the margins of an essay. Try to think of the words in each sentence as costing money, say a dollar apiece; perhaps that will make it easier to be economical. Mere economy, of course, is not a virtue; never sacrifice what is necessary only to reduce the number of words. But do not use several words when one will not only

do the same job but even do it better, and do not use words that do no real work at all. Here are some examples of squandered words:

> w: In today's society, England has earned herself a name of respect with everyone in the world.
> revised: England has earned universal respect. ($11.00 saved)

Again:

> w: His words have a romantic quality to them.

The phrase *to them* does no work. In fact, its effect is negative because it destroys the emphatic crispness of the meaningful part of the sentence.

> w: Hardy regarded poetry as his serious work, and wrote novels only in order to make enough money to live on.
> revised: Hardy regarded poetry as his serious work, and wrote novels only to make a living. ($5.00 saved)

> w: Othello's trust in Iago becomes evident during the first encounter that the reader observes between the two characters.
> revised: Othello's trust in Iago becomes evident during their first encounter. ($8.00 saved)

> w: The flash of lightning is representative of God's power.
> revised: The flash of lightning represents God's power.

Only $2.00 saved, but the sentence is much more direct and vigorous.

See #59; see also *red* (Redundant) and *rep* (Repetition).

wo Word Order

This mark means that you should examine the word order of a sentence to see how it can be improved. A misplaced modifier is one kind of faulty word order, but there are other kinds not so easily classified.

> wo: She was naturally hurt by his indifference.
> revised: Naturally she was hurt by his indifference.

The potential ambiguity could also have been removed by putting commas around *naturally,* but that would slow the sentence down unnecessarily.

> wo: I will never forget the day July 17, 1975, when I began my first job.
>
> revised: I will never forget July 17, 1975, the day I began my first job.

> wo: The image created in the advertisement is what really makes us buy the product and not the product itself.
>
> revised: The image created in the advertisement, not the product itself, is what makes us buy it.

This is not the only possible revision, of course, but it is the simplest, and the sentence is now clearer and less awkward.

> wo: Only at the end was clearly revealed the broad scope of the poem and the intensity of the emotions involved.

There seems no justification for such awkward distortion of normal sentence order.

> revised: Only at the end were the poem's broad scope and the intensity of its emotions revealed.

Note: In a stated comparison using *similar to*, a noun modified by the adjective *similar* should precede, not follow it:

> wo: The film has a similar plot to that of Shakespeare's *The Tempest*.
>
> revised: The film has a plot similar to that of Shakespeare's *The Tempest*.

See #20, #21, and *mm* (Misplaced Modifier).

ww Wrong Word

This category of diction error covers those mistakes which result from confusion about meaning or usage. For example:

> ww: England is a nation *who* has brought the past and the present together.

Who refers to persons, not things; usage demands *which* in this context. (See #3c.)

> ww: He came to the meeting at the special *bequest* of the chairman.

A glance at the dictionary confirms that *bequest* cannot be the right word here; the writer probably confused it with *request* and *behest*.

See #57; see also #51l and #51m.

Here are a few other symbols often used in marking essays:

⅄	Delete, omit
¶; no ¶	Paragraph; no paragraph (sometimes abbreviated *para*); see #64.
//	Parallelism; see *fp*
✗	Obvious error (e.g., typographical)
∧	Something omitted? Insert
?	Something questionable or unclear: Is this what you mean?
∼	Transpose
◡	Close up
#	Space
✓	Something especially good

ChapterXII: Omnibus Checklist for Planning, Writing, and Revising

Here is a list of questions to ask yourself about any piece of writing before you consider it finished. If you can conscientiously answer all of these questions in the affirmative, your essay should be not just adequate, but good.

1. After completing the sentence outline, ask yourself these questions:

Subject Have I chosen an interesting *subject*?

Thesis Have I sufficiently *limited* my subject?

Outline Does my *T.S.* state a proposition about that

Organization subject?

Is each heading and subheading, including the T.S., a *single complex or simple sentence*?

Have I *at least three* and *no more than about seven* main headings?

Is the content of my T.S. *equal to* that of the main headings combined?

Is the content of each main heading and each subheading *equal to* that of any subheadings under it?

Are my main headings reasonably *parallel* to each other?

Are the items in each set of subheadings reasonably *parallel* to each other?

Does each set of parallel subheadings consist of *at least two* and *not more than about seven* parts?

Have I chosen a good *order* for the main parts?

Have I chosen a good *order* for each set of subparts?

See Chapter VIII for discussion of these matters.

2. After completing the essay, ask yourself these questions:

Title	Does the *title* of my essay clearly indicate the subject?
	Does the *title* have something to catch a reader's interest?
Structure	Does my *beginning* (introduction) in some way try to engage a reader's curiosity or interest?
	Have I kept the *introductory part* of my essay from becoming disproportionately long?
	Have I clearly stated my *subject* (and perhaps my *thesis* as well) somewhere near the beginning of the essay?
	Is my *ending* (conclusion) such as to convey a sense of completion?
	Have I kept my *ending* (conclusion) short enough, not overdone it with unnecessary repetition and summary?
Unity *Development* *Emphasis*	Is my essay *unified?* Do all its parts contribute, and have I avoided digression? (#61)
	Have I been sufficiently *particular,* and not left any generalizations unsupported? (#54)
	Have I devoted an appropriate amount of space (*emphasis*) to each part? (#63)
Paragraphs	Does the first sentence of each paragraph (except perhaps the first, and last, and any patently transitional ones) *mention* the overall subject of the essay in some way? (#64d)

Does the first sentence of each paragraph (except the first) provide a clear *transition* from the preceding paragraph? (#64d)

Does the first sentence of each substantive paragraph clearly state the *topic* of that paragraph—or, if it is not the first sentence, is the *topic sentence* effective where it is placed? (#64d)

Is each substantive paragraph *long* enough to *develop* its topic adequately? (#64e)

Does each paragraph *conclude* adequately, but not too self-consciously? (#64f)

Coherence Do the sentences in each paragraph have sufficient *coherence* with each other? (#62)

Is the *coherence* between sentences and between paragraphs *smooth,* or have I inserted unnecessary transitional devices? (#62)

Sentences Is each sentence (especially compound, complex, or longer ones) *coherent* within itself? (#31)

Is each sentence clear and *emphatic* in making its point? (#28)

Have I avoided monotony by using a variety of *kinds* and *lengths* of sentences?

Have I avoided the *passive voice* except where it is clearly necessary or desirable? (#6h)

Diction Have I used *words* whose meaning I am sure of, or checked the *dictionary* for any whose meanings I am not sure of? (Chapter VII)

Is my diction as *concrete* and *specific* as possible? (#54a)

Have I avoided *unidiomatic* usages? (#58)

Have I weeded out any unnecessary repetitions and other *wordiness*? (#59)

Have I excluded *jargon* and unnecessary *clichés* and *euphemisms* from my diction? (#59d–h, #56)

Have I avoided *slang* and *informal* diction—unless intentional—and also any *over-formal* diction, or "fine writing"? (#52)

Have I avoided inappropriate or confusing *figurative language*? (#53)

Grammar Are all my sentences *grammatically sound*—free of dangling modifiers, agreement errors, incorrect tenses and cases, and the like? (Chapters II and III)

Have I avoided *run-ons* and unacceptable *fragments* and *comma splices?* (#33j, #16, #33e)

Punctuation Is the *punctuation* of each sentence correct
Spelling and effective? (Reading aloud, with special at-
Mechanics tention to punctuation, can be helpful.) (Chapter IV)

Have I checked all my words—reading backwards if necessary—for possible *spelling* errors? (Chapter VI)

Have I carefully *proofread,* and corrected all careless and typographical errors? (#65j)

Is my manuscript neat and legible, and does it conform to all the *manuscript conventions*? (Chapter V)

Have I introduced and handled all *quotations* properly? (#43; Chapter IX)

Have I checked all *quotations* for accuracy? (#71)

Acknow- Have I *acknowledged* everything that requires
ledgment acknowldegement? (#70, #71)

Have I checked my *documentation,* my notes and bibliography, for accuracy and correct form? (#73)

The Last Step Have I read my essay aloud as a final check on how it sounds?

INDEX

INDEX

(Correction symbols are in parentheses)

A

a, an, 57–62
Abbreviations (ab), 186–89
  of academic degrees, 187
  with dates and numbers, 187
  at end of sentence, 160
  in footnotes and bibliography,
    385
  in formal writing, 187, 463
  Latin, 187–88, 378
  period with, 160
  of titles of persons, 186–87
-able, -ible, spelling, 211
above, below, 283
Absolute constructions, 71, 86–87
  introductory, punctuation of, 144
  verbals with, 71
Abstract, concrete, 255–60
Abstract diction, in jargon, 280–83
Abstract nouns, 13, 59–60
Academic degrees, abbreviations of,
  187
Accents, in spelling, 207, 212, 214–15
Accusative case. *See* Objective case.
Acknowledgment of sources (ack),
  358–63, 463
  "common knowledge," 358–59
  purposes of, 358
  See also Research paper, sample.
Acronyms, 160
act, as linking verb, 52
Active voice, 41–44
A.D., B.C., 187
Addresses:
  numerals, in, 198
  punctuation of, 158–59
Adjectival modifiers, 85–86
  position of, 99
Adjective clauses, 88–89
  See also Relative clauses; Restrictive,
    nonrestrictive; Subordinate
    clauses.
Adjectives (ad), 56–57
  comparison of, 56–57
  compound, hyphens with, 222–23
  co-ordinate, punctuation of, 152–54

  degree of, 56–57
  demonstrative, 21, 25–26, 29, 489
  grammatical function of, 57
  indefinite pronouns as, 22
  infinitives as, 66
  inflection of, 56–57
  not comparable, 307
  participles as, 68–69
  position of, 99
  predicate, 52–53, 56
  prepositional phrases as, 73
Adjectives and adverbs, 65, 463
Adverbial clauses, 88
  diagrammed, 96
  punctuation of, 141–42, 148–49
Adverbial modifiers, 85
  position of, 64, 100
Adverbs (ad), 63–65, 73
  comparison of, 64
  conjunctive, 138–39
  degree of, 64
  formation of, 63
  grammatical function of, 64–65
  infinitives as, 66
  inflection of, 64
  position of, 64, 100
  as sentence modifiers, 64
Adverbs and adjectives, 65, 463
affect, effect, 284
afterward, afterwards, 306
agenda, 228
aggravate, 284
Agreement (agr):
  with *data, media,* etc., 228
  of demonstrative adjectives, 25–26
Agreement: pronoun-antecedent,
  24–26, 464
  with *anybody, everybody,* etc., 25
Agreement: subject-verb, 45–49, 464
  with collective nouns, 47–48
  with compound subjects, 46
  with *either* and *neither,* 46, 292
  in expletive constructions, 98
  with indefinite pronouns, 47
  with predicate nouns, 47
  when subject follows verb, 47
  when words intervene, 45–46

G

H

I

S